D0502142

HANK

HANK

THE SHORT LIFE AND LONG COUNTRY ROAD OF HANK WILLIAMS

MARK RIBOWSKY

LIVERIGHT PUBLISHING CORPORATION

A Division of W. W. Norton & Company

Independent Publishers since 1923

New York ✳ London

For information about permission to reproduce selections from this book,
write to Permissions, Liveright Publishing Corporation, a division of
W. W. Norton & Company, Inc., 500 Fifth Avenue, New York, NY 10110

For information about special discounts for bulk purchases,
please contact W. W. Norton Special Sales at
specialsales@wwnorton.com or 800-233-4830

Manufacturing by RR Donnelley, Harrisonburg
Book design by Dana Sloan
Production manager: Anna Oler

Library of Congress Cataloging-in-Publication Data

Names: Ribowsky, Mark, author.
Title: Hank: the short life and long country road of Hank Williams /
Mark Ribowsky
Description: First edition. | New York: Liveright Publishing Corporation,
2016. | Includes bibliographical references and index.
Identifiers: LCCN 2016026928 | ISBN 9781631491573 (hardcover)
Subjects: LCSH: Willliams, Hank, 1923–1953. | Country musicians—
United States—Biography.
Classification: LCC ML420.W55 R53 2016 | DDC 782.421642092 [B] —
dc23 LC record available at https://lccn.loc.gov/2016026928

Liveright Publishing Corporation
500 Fifth Avenue, New York, N.Y. 10110
www.wwnorton.com

W. W. Norton & Company Ltd.
15 Carlisle Street, London W1D 3BS

1 2 3 4 5 6 7 8 9 10

✦ CONTENTS ✦

INTRODUCTION

✳ ✳ ✳ ✳ ✳ ✳ ✳

JUST PLAIN HANK

Of the thirty-three records that Hank Williams placed on *Billboard* country and western Top 10 charts during his short lifetime, only two made the mainstream pop chart, and even those had much to do with pop artists like Tony Bennett having their own hits with them first. Yet, more than sixty years after his premature death at age twenty-nine, no country artist living or dead can approach the familiarity the general public has with Hank Williams, whose sad, lonely songs are playing right this minute on some roadhouse juke-box. Few musical legends live on as an almost touchable, feelable presence in the anatomy of modern popular music as does the enigmatic, goofy-looking guy who carried a nascent country music formula to its full potential, then exited stage right in total and abject loneliness.

Consider textural lyrics about robins weeping and leaves dying, the will to live lost, punctuated by the lament *I'm so lonesome I could cry*. Those are among the saddest words ever written and sung in music—Elvis once said so—and arguably the greatest. But the truth is, writing about music is never as effective as the act of simply *listening* to it. And when Hank Williams is listened to, something revelatory seems to happen. To make the point, a good prelude to reading these pages would be to find and listen to his first successful song, the 1947 twelve-bar blues rag "Move It On Over," which spins a melody instantly recognizable as Bill Haley and His Comets' "(We're Gonna) Rock Around the Clock," which birthed rock and roll to the masses a year after Williams died. (Haley had also ripped off "Cold, Cold Heart," retitling his record "Icy Heart.") Hank's honky-tonk classic "I'm a Long Gone Daddy" is the derivation of Bruce Springsteen's line about being "a long gone daddy in the U.S.A." His guttural blues lament "Ramblin' Man" ("I love you baby but you gotta understand, when the Lord made me he made a ramblin' man") foretold Dickey Betts's tune that "swaggers along in the grand tradition of Hank Williams."[1] Hank even sang about purple skies long before Prince was born. Keith Richards says "Honky Tonk Women" was written as a "Hank–Jimmie Rodgers sort of number."[2] The first popular reference to a "rolling stone" was heard in Hank's 1949 cover of Leon Payne's "Lost Highway." And, obscure as it is, on an early demo record, covering Lonnie Glossom's "Rockin' Chair Money," he sang, "And now I'll rock, yeah, rock, oh baby, rock, rock on down the line." That was in 1948.

Among the country set, there have always been similar assumptions about the broad lines of his work. For example, Wesley Rose, the son of Hank's publisher and producer Fred Rose, the hidden hand behind the magic of those songs, once said that had Hank lived, "I don't think we could have had a rock era," his point being that rock and roll was a cheap replacement for Hank's music rather than a logical extension of roots that included it. But then, the same people used to say Elvis wasn't welcome in Nashville unless he stopped with that wriggling, jiggling rock and roll stuff.

Even so, it was hard to deify him during his lifetime, so proudly unrefined was he. His songs, culled at times from the pages of comic books, celebrated simple human concepts—God, beer, a good woman, and a blessed break from loneliness. Yet to some, even then, he was the voice of not only a more liberal South but also "the common people," another way of saying white trash.[3] That quality still resonates in his music, explaining why in a cultural maw he never could have foreseen, there have been two Pepsi Super Bowl commercials built around "Your Cheatin' Heart," and that his music bleeds far beyond its strictest borders, the reason why Williams owns a posthumous Pulitzer Prize for lifetime achievement. The only other posthumous Pulitzers for music have been awarded to Thelonious Monk, John Coltrane, Duke Ellington, George Gershwin, and Scott Joplin. Yet none of the others ever sold a record as far and wide as "Your Cheatin' Heart," which has been played over three million times on the radio and jukeboxes, or 17.1 years if continuously played, the same level as "My Way" and "Love Me Tender."[4]

· · ·

As with Patsy Cline, Jim Reeves, Cowboy Copas, and the legendary rock and roll victims of lousy planes or their own vices, Williams's premature death, in the back seat of his baby blue Cadillac on New Year's Day 1953, romances his flaws and elevates his mythology, the loneliness of it lending believability to his litany of sad, sad songs. Dying as he did, he set the trend for the later rock and roll shooting stars who never made thirty, a sort of post-teen angel with never-re-solved issues but a beyond-cool epitaph. As the country singer Jason Aldean, whose 2010 album *My Kinda Party* was a massive crossover success, warbles on its title track:

> *You can find me in the back of a jacked up tailgate*
> *Chillin' with some Skynyrd and some old Hank.*

He has been sung and written about like this, as "Old Hank" without pause, a wraith for southern men old enough to remember him stamping their own youth. One of those was the Alabama-born journalist Paul Hemphill, who wrote the superb 1970 book *The Nashville Sound: Bright Lights and Country Music.* He authored a book late in his life called *Lovesick Blues: The Life of Hank Williams,* prefiguring his own times on the lonely byways of the South, a bond created when as a teenager he sat in his daddy's truck in 1949, hearing Williams's "nasal wail," which sounded "like a hurt animal."

> They were the loneliest sounds we had ever heard . . . cries from the darkness; made to be heard, it seemed to us, while running through the lonely night, racing with the moon, the wind whistling through the cab, gliding past See Rock City barns and Burma Shave signs and spooky pastures milling with dumbstruck cows. With the whining of the tires keeping time, we laughed at each other's attempts to emulate Hank's yodel.[5]

That is really the thematic outline of Williams's near-subconscious grip on culture: his music—centrally, what Loretta Lynn calls the "throb" in it[6]—and his persona are markers of a time long gone, and so stripped of modern glamour and convenience that his own failings, like his successes, cut right to the bone. At times, we wish we could crawl inside those songs and ride them like an old truck through time, and that is essentially what this book does, race with the moon through history, and tell not just the story but the backstory of uniquely American circumstances and influences bred by other pioneers of country. Williams's tortured soul and his drug and booze addictions were the result of weakness and recklessness, but on a grander scale wrote the script for the "live fast, die young, leave a pretty corpse" ethos of the modern rock and roll movement. Not that some haven't drawn a line at such a seduction. In "Hank Williams Syndrome," a broken-down Waylon Jennings, one of the primal country "outlaws," sings of Hank as his inspiration, less a singing model than an "obsession."

> *But to tell you the truth, it's no thanks to you that I'm still living today.*

In truth, to be sure, Hank himself was a poor excuse for a rebel. What separated him from moral reproof was that he carried on his ruinous lifestyle in pain, not pride; cautionary tales lurked beneath the grooves of his music. True enough, as Hank himself pointed out, was that his songs explained who he was. The best ones are a catalog of unrelenting agony and the hopelessness he sold—"I'm So Lonesome I Could Cry," "Cold Cold Heart," "I'll Never Get Out of This World Alive," "Lost Highway," "Your Cheatin' Heart," "Take These Chains from My Heart," "Alone and Forsaken," "I'm Blue Inside," "Moanin' the Blues." (Often forgotten is that "Lovesick Blues" and "Lost Highway" were not written by Williams.) But he also wrote of finding a way through the dark clouds and landing, if even for a few minutes, in a glen of relieved burdens, like the toe-tapping reverie of "Jambalaya," "Hey, Good Lookin'," "I Saw the Light," "Baby, We're Really in Love," "I Can't Help It (If I'm Still in Love with You)."

It's telling that, because these songs hit home so squarely, no one knew him as Mr. Williams; he was just plain Hank. Sometimes, Williams recorded under the pseudonym Luke the Drifter, an alter ego with which to preach morality tales and semi-rapped "talking blues" records like "Ramblin' Man." But by any other name, he was just plain Hank. For a guy who was such a good time, though, Hank was, let's face it, seriously disturbed. He was a dysfunction junction. When sober, he could be kind and humble; when drunk, "a mean, moody, raving egomaniac."[7] He humiliated his two-time wife and hinge-voiced singing partner, the tempestuous temptress "Miss Audrey" Williams, and shot either at her or over her head while in a haze once—and according to lore later remarked that because he missed, "Well, I'll just have to go back and kill her."[8] He didn't, but their marriage was still a battle zone during which she nearly died from a coat-hanger abortion; after his death she took control of his estate, managed the career of their son, Hank Jr., formed a singing group called the Cold Cold Hearts, was a raging alcoholic and pill-popper herself, attempted suicide, was arrested for drunk driving, and lived with the guilt of feeling that she had caused Hank's drinking and early demise. A day before the IRS was to raid her home in 1975, she died young and addicted herself, at fifty-three.

• • •

Williams was indeed the aboriginal ramblin' man, tryin' to make a livin', doin' the best he could. Which only happened when he wrote a song. Today, his catalog attests to the raw power of a good country song, of a good song, period. The connection between his "folk" and rock is clear, given that in what the British music writer Nik Cohn calls "the twisted roots of rock and roll" both idioms sprang from the same blues root—which was why it was so absurd that country became synonymous with white power. For his part, Hank made a point to credit blues man Rufus "Tee Tot" Payne for teaching him blues guitar as a kid. Bob Dylan, who became transfixed by him as a prepubescent in Hibbing, Minnesota, says Hank's songs carved "the archetype rules of poetic songwriting."[9] This was a key element common to the country "rebels" spawned by Williams, like Willie Nelson and Johnny Cash, who brought country firmly into the rock family.

Remember that there was no such creature called "country music" for around two decades of its existence, and certainly in no way anything like the "mass cult" it became, to borrow a phrase from Christopher Lehman-Haupt.[10] It was by default called "hillbilly" music. Even the more charitable terms applied to Hank—"the Hillbilly Shakespeare," "the Hillbilly Hammerstein," "Irving Berlin of the straw sack,"[11] "Sinatra of the hillbilly set,"[12] "Sinatra of the Western ballad"[13]—were hollow. As rock's most sage critic, Greil Marcus, notes, Elvis, too, was pegged as "the Hillbilly Cat."[14] This was probably why Hank himself called his idiom "folk music,"[15] though it must have occurred to him that he was, as Garrison Keillor once said, "the first really sexy hillbilly."[16] By any other name, he created what one music scholar calls a "unique vocal vocabulary," even if by accident.[17]

He could neither read nor write music. He once said he knew two melodies—fast and slow. His voice was technically all wrong. Another musical academic wrote that, "measured against any conventional criteria either of songwriting or of singing, Hank's appeal makes no sense."[18] Except when he was actually singing. Then he transcended his small, mortal self. Nor was he much of a guitar player, playing only one solo in his career, and some songs were inscrutable.

Music, Greil Marcus writes, was the South's great shelter and unifier, bringing under its collective roof even society's rejects—"tramps, whores, rounders, idiots, criminals." The singers who rose highest "could take the community beyond itself because they had the chops and the nerve to transcend it," though often they were "doomed . . . too ambitious, too ornery, or simply different to fit in."[19]

For Hank, there would be a price to pay for that: his life. His children and grandchildren would carry that same gene. All of them sing country, most notably Randall Hank Williams, who's been doing business as "Hank Williams Jr." since he was in puberty in the 1950s, later finding immense popularity as a beer-bellied, bearded doppelganger of the father he barely knew. Randall earned a fortune and a brace of awards from his rowdy drinking songs, like his best-known rag, his "Are You Ready for Some Football" that opened *Monday Night Football* for years. However, he was possessed of the same tendencies to screw up; his fulminations in 2012 about Barack Obama being a "Hitler" and a "Muslim President who hates farming, hates the military, hates the U.S." cost him the football gig and reduced him to an aging warhorse in his late sixties, covered in a ten-gallon hat and goggle glasses.[20]

Hank Jr. symbolized an anti-intellectual country genre his daddy never did, one that is happily crumbling these days. Where country once grinned smugly as Merle Haggard crooned, "We don't smoke marijuana in Muskogee," it must have felt swept by a raging tide when, in 2014, twenty-five-year-old Kacey Musgraves won the Grammy for Best Country Song with "Follow Your Arrow," a sly metaphor of gay acceptance that urged, "When the straight and narrow gets a little too straight, roll up a joint" and follow that arrow "wherever it points," whether it be to "kiss lots of boys or kiss lots of girls." This so unnerved some country allies that a Colorado pastor who advocates death for gay people lamented, wistfully, "If she had sang that thing in a country bar in the 1920s . . . somebody would've called for a rope."[21] But even during those bygone days, Hank Williams *pere* had more common sense than the country establishment and its lunatic right-wing retainers had, never allowing himself to be the stereotype of a doltish redneck buffoon; his notion of rebelliousness was to unburden what he felt within about *himself*, not to give ignorance and bigotry a free ride.

. . .

Although he recorded only two studio albums, both going to No. 1 on the country charts in the early '50s when the long-form disk came into vogue, at last count forty-five posthumous studio, live, and compilation albums have been issued. Of these, sixteen have made the country charts, some with layers of strings overdubbed, as on the 1966 MGM *The Legend Lives Anew—Hank Williams with Strings*, fairly ruining their intent. Thirty singles have as well, only one fewer than when he was alive. In all, twenty-six singles of his have made the Top 10 of the country chart; the year that he died, four straight went to No. 1.

As a result, he is in the Country Music and the Rock and Roll Halls of Fame, the latter as an "early influence" and an "American Master." He has won two Grammys—an award born seven years after he died—and his songs have been and continue to be covered by, well, *everyone*, with tribute albums by Roy Acuff, Ernest Tubb, Don Gibson, George Jones, Charlie Rich, Johnny Cash, Ronnie Hawkins, Del Shannon, Roy Orbison—and, of course, Hank Williams Jr. *The Lost Notebooks of Hank Williams*, an all-star tribute album that included Bob Dylan—whose vanity Egyptian label teamed with Columbia to issue it—Sheryl Crow, Merle Haggard, Levon Helm, Vince Gill, and Norah Jones, went to No. 11 on the country chart, Top 50 on the Billboard 200 in 2011. Four movies have been made about him. There was also one Drama Desk–nominated Off-Broadway musical called *Hank Williams: Lost High-*

way in 2002, produced by the Manhattan Ensemble Theater, which still plays around the country.

As another redoubtably wise acolyte, Willie Nelson, once said he learned from Hank, "If a song is true for you, it will be true for others."[22] That category now numbers in the millions. And if only Ol' Hank knew what he was feeling, what a song meant, where it came from, the clues can be found sprinkled all over the South, the most trenchant ones in sweet home Alabama. That is where this story can only begin, and never stray much from, in the sun-baked soil of hopelessness.

PROLOGUE

✳ ✳ ✳ ✳ ✳ ✳ ✳

A WHEEL IN THE DITCH AND A WHEEL ON THE TRACK

At the Georgiana Gas and Garage station off Interstate 65, exit 114, somewhere in southern Alabama, May 2015

The Alabama sky isn't, as Hank Williams sang in "I'm So Lonesome I Could Cry," a sad purple today. It's bright blue, and the burning sun tears through it with no mercy as two men in their sixties stand at a pump, squeezing unleaded gas into their tanks. One, a cherubic, red-faced fellow with a dinged-up maroon Pontiac, wearing rumpled jeans and a T-shirt reading GENUINE FORD PARTS, is asked if he's from around here. He nods.

"Do you know where the old Hank Williams house might be?" is the next question. "He lived around here as a boy, didn't he?"

"From what I've been told," the man says in a thick drawl, a cigarette dangling from his mouth, "he had to move 'cause the law was after his daddy. They also say his momma ran some whorehouses, too, so you get the picture."

"Didn't she run boardinghouses?"

"Well, they couldn't call 'em that. You still can't. But down here, you know, people gotta eat. Gotta make a living. You do what you gotta do on Saturday night, then go to church on Sunday morning and make it all right with God."

A belly laugh. Having heard the questioner's New York accent, he knew he was enlightening an out-of-state guy about Alabama, and there had to be a little clarification.

"These are *stories*, you understand? A big star like Hank Williams was treated like God here, because there aren't many stars who ever came from Alabama. God don't put us here to make a lot of money. We're all in the same situation. So everyone knows everything about everybody else. And then someone makes it big, goes to the top and kills hisself with booze and whatever other shit he's doing, and those little secrets about him get out."

Another laugh. "Sometimes it pays to stay a nobody in Alabama." Then, getting into the Pontiac, "But I'll say this, Hank was good folks. He sang what the folks around here were thinkin,' what they would sing about if they could sing a lick. And no matter what anyone would say about him or his daddy and momma, nobody's gonna ever think bad about him. When you talk about a legend, that's what you're talkin' about."

. . .

GO TO CHURCH OR THE DEVIL WILL GET YOU
—Billboard sign on I-65, north of Prattville near mile marker 191

Interstate 65 snakes 360 miles from Gary, Indiana, all the way down to the Gulf of Mexico, ending in Mobile, Alabama. It runs down through Birmingham and Montgomery, before veering southwest. Although it didn't exist when Hank Williams was alive, and was called Route 31 until 1959, following it can take one on a tour of Hank Williams's life. Indeed, in 1997, the Department of Tourism designated the several hundred-mile stretch of it "the Hank Williams Trail," though people also call it "the Lonesome Highway" and "the Lost Highway," the latter being engraved on bright green signs at spots along the road. Some will even tell you the highway is haunted, not just by Hank but because it was paved over Creek Indian burial grounds. Then, too, they say Hank was part Creek.

Only one of his boyhood homes still stands, in Georgiana, its white wood frame and wraparound porch now the exterior for a Hank Williams museum, which contains items like his old bed, records, straight razor, first guitar, the Victrola he listened to when country music was in its infancy, and the church bench he sat on with his mother and sang hymns to the glory of God—which couldn't keep the devil from getting him. An old boxcar painted red, white, and blue, sits on nearby abandoned tracks, adorned with a red, white, and blue sign that says: HANK WILLIAMS BOYHOOD HOME AND MUSEUM . . . DRINK COCA-COLA. Every summer for the last thirty-seven years they've played honky-tonk blues here at a festival in his memory.

In Montgomery, where Hank Williams went on this road to become *Hank Williams*, his grave—beneath a twenty-by-twenty family plot out at Oakwood Cemetery Annex—dwarfs most of the other stones, including those of three Confederate generals and four Alabama governors. Unlike in Nashville, where Hank molded country music as we know it, Hank seems to be in the loam and woodwork of Montgomery. You don't have to find Hank's past; it finds you, in the life-size bronze and pewter statue of him decked out in his cowboy hat and natty suit, strumming his guitar, at Dexter and Perry, where he first lived here, a block north of the City. There is the whore—er, *boarding*house once run by Lillie Williams on Catoma Street, and the stately brick building now a home for the elderly but once the Jefferson Davis Hotel, where Hank sang on the radio. The baby blue Caddy, long as a city block, its gigantic chrome grille kept shiny, is in the Hank Williams Museum on Commerce Street. The car's back seat is still indented by the backside of the man who didn't see that New Year's Day in '53, the walls around it displaying items of his wardrobe such as a brown leather fringed three-quarter length sport jacket and brown cowboy boots with green, red, and white trimming.

Montgomery is a cosmopolitan city anchored by a good ol' boy ethos and some ugly history of its own. It was here, of course, that Rosa Parks refused to sit in the back of the bus in 1955. In 1957, Martin Luther King was roughed up by cops during a sit-in at a lunch counter during the Montgomery Bus Boycott sparked by Parks's arrest. The city, nonetheless, is sometimes called "the Birthplace of the Civil Rights Movement," a birth that somehow occurred as George Wallace sat in the State House here, dragged out of the dark ages by marches such as the one after the 1965 "Bloody Sunday" massacre in Selma, capped off by King's "How Long, Not Long" speech.[1] Yet for years after, it was where ancient laws banning interracial marriage stood until 2000;[2] where the Stars and Bars flew until 2015.

But things like that never mattered much, or so it seemed, when Hank was around. Go south on the Lonesome Highway and you'll see why. Here, largely forgotten by time, country churches are preserved for once having been the Williams family's Sunday morning sanctuary, where he prayed and sang gospel songs while his mother played the organ like a good church lady. There are barbershops where he might have once gotten a haircut and shot the breeze, gas stations where he might have pulled the Cadillac in for a fill-up, chicken shacks where he ordered a bucket of wings, heavy BBQ sauce. Here, you know why Hank Williams could never have come from, say, Texas, could never have pulled off feigning humility where none exists.

Many songwriters have been inspired by what they saw in Alabama, good and bad. Long past the time when people sang about coming from Alabama with a banjo on their knee, a black blues song like "Alabama Bound," covered by Lead Belly in 1940, reflected temptations of the flesh Hank could relate to:

Why doncha be like me? Why doncha be like me?
Drink yo' high-tension whisky, babe, an' let yo' cocaine be

Decades later, modern songwriters were more focused on deconstruction, the most indelible Neil Young's "Alabama":

> *Alabama, you got the weight on your shoulders that's breaking your*
> *back*
> *Your Cadillac has got a wheel in the ditch and a wheel on the track*

Young didn't stop there; in "Southern Man" there were imprecations that "Your crosses are burning fast." That sparked Lynyrd Skynyrd's "Sweet Home Alabama," defending Southern men from Northern meddling. Yet Hank Williams himself wrote exactly one song about his home turf, "Alabama Waltz," which he rendered as a mournful ballad, not a hootenanny. But Williams still carried Alabama with him, and was an amalgam of everything written or sung about it. All the despair and hopelessness, all the evil and the good about it, informed his sensibilities. It winks at a listener, or spits in his eye.

Although almost no one is left who knew him or heard his music in real time, Alabama still claims him, still owns him. Proudly, the folks along the Hank Williams Trail inform a visitor from the North that it was *they* who gave Hank to the world, *personally*. And then they make very clear to the Northern visitor, *Don't you ever forget it, son*.

PART ONE

1923–1937

1

✳ ✳ ✳ ✳ ✳ ✳ ✳

KING HIRAM

Hank Williams's granddaddy was in the Union Army during the Civil War. You read that right. To be fair, there is a catch, and a long story to it, proving how resourceful Williams men could be, at least sometimes, in keeping themselves alive. Irvin Polk Williams, a South Alabama farmer—who, like the rest of the Williams clan, could only imagine owning a plantation and slaves—joined the Confederate 18th Infantry, Company F in 1861 and fought in the Battle of Shiloh. Not long after, however, he was captured by the Union Army during the Battle of Richmond. Because he knew a great deal about Confederate troop movements around Mobile Bay, Alabama, he was not your common prisoner and thus was offered a deal—he could avoid imprisonment, or worse, if he revealed some of those movements. In a bind, he did just that, and was promptly inducted into the Army of Abe Lincoln.

After Robert E. Lee surrendered at Appomattox, Irvin was given an honorable discharge and allowed to return home, keeping his turncoat activities quiet.[1] Irvin, who had some Indian blood on his father's side, that of Muskogee Creek and Tsalagi Cherokee, gave up farming and worked a more in-demand job, chopping down trees used for building railroad tracks. He married a woman named Martha Ann Autry, and in time they settled in McWilliams, Alabama, and had a son, Elonzo Huble Williams, known as "Lon," in 1891. His life was stamped by tragedy and misery early on. Martha Ann committed suicide when he was six, and Irvin died in a virus outbreak when he was seventeen, sending him off on his own. He found work, like his father, cutting down trees, as well as driving railroad trains full of logs to lumberyards around the Southeast. This work took him to Georgiana, Alabama, and in 1914, he met a sixteen-year-old girl there named Jessie Lillybelle Skipper, called "Lillie."

To their friends, Lon was considered to be from the wrong side of those tracks; his family history was in Lowndes County, which was regarded as where the white trash came from, and folks, never mind their own dirty laundry, tended to look down on him, shaking their heads about his mother and all. Lillie was from the right side of the tracks, hailing from Butler, just below Lowndes, where the betters were said to live. (The irony is that today, Butler ranks just ahead of Lowndes in per capita income).[2] She was a pistol and, though seven years younger than he, seemed to be the one in charge. Neither was a prize, to be sure; he was the shorter, already going bald, and she was a plain-looking, hatchet-faced woman, around two hundred pounds and getting bigger.

No one would have confused Lon with one of those handsome young men in the military schools, or Lillie with the belle of the ball. But they had each other, and in 1916, after he sneaked Lillie out of her parents' house in Georgiana, they eloped and were married in a church in the now-ghost town of Starlington. Lon then moved in with her and her presumably shocked parents. Before they could start a family however, the United States was called into World War I, and his orders stationed him with the 113th Regiment of Engineers in France, where he sustained a non-war-related head injury of some sort and was discharged in 1919. The country doughboy came home and resumed work on the railroad, for the Ray Lumber and W. T. Smith Lumber companies, which kept him moving from one job to another on the nexus of railroads around the Southeast. He found one promising job in Mount Olive, which today is one of Alabama's most affluent towns but back then was a dirt-poor logging community. Here, streets like theirs, called Kendrick Place, were mainly unpaved muddy clearings in the underbrush.

Sadly, their first child, a son named Ernest Huble Williams, died two days after being born in July 1921 and was buried behind the Mount Olive West Baptist Church, where Hank would sing in the choir as a boy. Lillie soon became pregnant again and gave birth in August 1922 to a daughter named Irene.

Soon after starting work in the town, on September 17, 1923, their next child, an undersized boy, was delivered by a doctor Lon paid thirty-five dollars to come and make a house call, assisted by either a black housekeeper, according to Lon's later recollection, or a neighbor named Ada Grace, according to Lillie's. By one account, both mother and child were sick for the next few days, and Ada Grace stayed at the Williams place tending to Irene and Lon.[3]

At the time, most of America was enjoying the Roaring Twenties, though in Alabama the economy and quality of life never seemed to roar. Still, the second child of Lon and Lillie Williams arrived with high hopes. They named him after the Hebrew King Hiram I, who reigned in the Phoenician city of Tyre from 980 to 947 BC and built the first Temple of the Israelites. They picked the name because they were members of the secretive Masonic fraternal/pseudo-religious society—or cult—tracing back to the 1800s, steeped in ancient freemasonry guilds and castes, in which King Hiram's stone-masonry feats were legend. As Lon Williams helpfully recalled many years later, "I chose [Hiram's] name from the Scripture, I Kings, 7th Chapter, 13th verse."[4]

However, Hiram was, in effect, a nonperson. In the poorer quarters of the South, the births of most children not born in hospitals were recorded only if parents registered a birth certificate with the local Bureau of Vital Statistics office, and Lillie and Lon wouldn't get around to the paperwork until 1934, when Hiram was already eleven and they were living in Garland. His name was misspelled on the birth certificate as "Hiriam." This anomaly would be almost eerily repeated when Elvis Presley's middle name was spelled "Aron" instead of "Aaron" on his tombstone. Not that it mattered a whit to Hiram King; he had by then already discarded that for something more chummy. He was, unofficially but eternally, "Hank." "King" would also be dropped, high irony indeed when people took to calling him the king of country music.

. . .

The house where Hank was born looked rickety, built as it was with logs not unlike those Lon cut down and transported, sitting four blocks from the Louisville and Nashville Railroad tracks—which, ironically, Lon did not traverse, W. T. Smith running its own trains on other lines. The house was fairly typical, a South Alabama town of farmers, cotton-pickers, migrant workers, and fellow loggers, the kind of town Harper Lee—born and raised in nearby Monroeville, smack on that ramblin' man's Highway 41—wrote in *To Kill a Mockingbird* were distinguished for their "grubbiness."[5] Called a "double-pen," the place looked like two homes slapped together, which in fact they were, connected by a walkway. Lon agreed to pay the rent, eighty bucks for the year; as he once said with pride, "I was makin' one hundred fifty, one hundred sixty dollars a month, which was good pay." Indeed, he was offended to no end when, he said, "somebody once put out a book showing a picture of a house I wouldn't keep hogs in and saying the boy was born in it."[6] Even so, Lillie hardly considered herself livin' high. "A two-mule nigger farmer," she supposedly once said, "is better off than this family."[7]

They were well-mannered, good churchgoing Christians, taking pride and solace in that in equal measure. Their Masonic temple activities did not conflict with their devout Baptist exercises, in which Lillie played piano for the congregation at the Mount Olive church and sang songs of God's love and mercy with her baby boy usually crying in the first pew, held by Lon. Lon Williams was the kind of man who took fatherhood in stride, sometimes too much so, turning cold and distant—in speaking of Hiram to neighbors he would simply call him "the boy," not by his name. Lillie, on the other hand, doted on the little fellow. One previous Williams biographer, Chet Flippo, applying undocumented, scripted history using the literary device called "extrapolation," wrote that "although she was big and full-bosomed, [Lillie] did not breast-feed Hiram as she had Irene. She fed him on Eagle brand canned milk, warmed up a little bit on the stove." Meanwhile, Little Hiram, who was usually called "Harm"—"Hiram" in a Southern drawl—"Herky," or "Poots" by family and friends, was said to sleep with a Bible under his pillow.[8]

In a male-dominated society in which women were generally relegated to childbearers and drudges serving husbands who spent more time down at the barroom than with their families, it was noteworthy that the pants in this family were worn by the wife. Her resolve and air of knowing it all matched her physical size, and she came to almost completely disregard Lon as the head of the household. Lillie made the decisions on practical matters such as the kids' schooling and churchgoing. She also grew vegetables and strawberries in her backyard garden and sold what she could to neighbors and passersby. Lon was away from home anyway for long periods, doing seasonal work in the lumberyards, his regular absences and tales of railroad adventure carving both a sense of isolation and picaresque idealism in his son, who would one day fashion a song from those feelings. He'd call it "The Old Log Train," and the lyrics, transposed from his youth, went:

Every morning at the break of day
He'd grab his lunch bucket and be on his way
In winter or summer, sunshine or rain
Every mornin' he'd run that old log train

But even when Lon was home, he was a cipher. A hard-staring, lantern-jawed man of middling stature who wore glasses and a hunted sort of look, he was regularly so weak that he couldn't get

out of his bed. This was in part from his work and in part a carryover from that mysterious head injury he sustained during World
War I. Lon would explain it many different ways, the one constant
being that he took a tumble off a truck, his head slamming into the
ground; he did like to go on, though, and sometimes said it was the
result of a fight with another soldier over a French mademoiselle. He
seemed to recover and was sent back into combat, but was left feeling occasionally disoriented, something he also liked to claim was
the result of being gassed on the battlefield, to which he attributed
his bouts of facial paralysis that crept up, rendering him unable to
speak, then just as suddenly disappeared.

Whatever the cause of Lon's woes, by 1930, Lillie thought of him
as a millstone, and neighbors would stare at their feet when she would
insult him to his face, in front of his own children at times, telling him
what a good-for-nothin' tramp he was. She was a demanding, volatile
woman prone to gaining weight and arguing about the smallest things,
and may have taken some pride in cutting her husband down to size.
However Lillie dissed him, Lon was usually was too weary to defend
his honor, or too busy worrying if he could keep the paychecks coming in. He would rise from his bed to take many jobs, quitting W. T.
Smith, then returning, then quitting again for a short stay with another
lumber company, bouncing around on the railroad—they didn't own
one of those new-fangled automobiles—to other encampments, in
Chapman, Atwater, Garland, Bolling, Ruthven Mills, McWilliams.
Sometimes Lon went on his own, for days or weeks, which to Lillie
was a kind of relief, as she detested being a migrant instead of setting
down roots somewhere, though it all seemed as if he were a running
like hamster on a treadmill. He had also taken to the bottle to get him
through the grind of life. And if Hiram emulated few of Lon's traits,
in this case the moonshine didn't fall far from the tree. Of him, a
magazine writer began an article in the '50s:

"I'm nothing but a drunkard," Hank Williams once cried out to an
old, respected friend. "Why do people expect me to be anything

else?" And then he laughed his dry, bitter laugh and said: "You think I'm a drunkard? Hell, you should of seen my old man!"[9]

. . .

The notion of mobility, of going places on tracks or paved roads, was a welcome relief to many in the South who once felt trapped, mired in a backwoods log cabin with an outhouse. Now, there was the promise of worldliness, of breathing free. The talking motion picture offered a worldly look at which tastes the public was finding to its liking—and simple men of the earth with good hearts and pleasant singing voices were the most popular of Hollywood stars, led by singing cowboys who had replaced the nonsinging cowboys of the silents such as Tom Mix and Hoot Gibson.

Although rowdiness was a staple of the hillbilly side of the emerging idiom (as it still is of today's version), once Hollywood found that such music was a new, profitable angle for movies in the late '30s a trend began that still exists—"country" and "Southern" music and movies made not in the South but in Southern California. The first such cowboy multimedia star was an actual Southern boy, a mellow, guitar-strumming Texan named Orvon Grover "Gene" Autry. Gene was among the disciples of Bob Wills's Texas swing band music and had followed Wills to KVOO in Tulsa, where he had his own show as "Oklahoma's Yodeling Cowboy."

Autry had his first hit in '35, "That Silver-Haired Daddy of Mine" for the bargain-bin Vocalion label. He also recorded his Christmas songs that still are the biggest-selling records of all time. Also in the early '30s, a lanky, baby-faced Ohio native, Leonard Slye, formed the Pioneers Trio, who became the Sons of the Pioneers. After signing with the recently established Decca Records as its first "country" act, Slye and his band recorded "Tumbling Tumbleweeds" in 1935, and got a big break the next year when Autry sang the song into a hit in a movie of the same name. Slye even appeared as "Roy Rogers" in an Autry movie, then was given his own movie deal, the first *Under*

Western Stars. Rogers, an immediate success, would vie with Autry for the top rung in the singing cowboy market. His records with the Pioneers all but eclipsed Bob Wills and his Texas Playboys.

Still, the dim-witted redneck caricature was the overarching image non-Southerners had of Dixie. Even as Dizzy Dean was striking out bunches of big-league hitters, he clung to his own hillbilly lexicon, with stories of players who "slud" into third and "swang" a bat. Criticized for saying "ain't" so much, he replied, "A lotta folks who ain't sayin' 'ain't,' ain't eatin'." That certainly applied to the new country singers, who wrote the lyrics to their songs in their native vernacular. As Diz put his breeding as a Southern man, "The Good Lord was good to me. He gave me a strong right arm, a good body, and a weak mind." For several generations of Americans, the last trait in particular would be synonymous with country singing.

• • •

Lon did the best he could, trying his damnedest to make his boy look up to him, but life was just too hard. He even sent Hank to earn a few dollars for the family kitty, once recalling that his son was out on the street of a logging camp selling peanuts at age *three*, no doubt another of Lon's little fibs. As he told it, "I bought the peanuts from a farmer, and the boy sold 'em. He even knew how much he was owed him, and on payday he'd collect." But Lon's pride stung when years later he'd read about his then-famous son growing up poor as dirt, a reflection of having a ne'er-do-well old man. "'Course he didn't *have* to sell peanuts for a living. Anybody who tells you that is crazy," he'd append.[10] Lon would have given his right arm to make his son proud of him. And it was he, not Lillie, who was concerned when he began to notice his son had a small raised brown spot on his lower back. Lillie said it was nothing, and a doctor was never consulted about it. However, the little twinges of pain Hiram started to feel, and the more stooped posture he began to walk with, were proof that Lon was right to worry about it.[11]

As life dragged on in South 'Bama, it became evident that both men of the family were living in discomfort, not that real men ever complained about it. To be sure, hard work in the face of pain earned men like Lon Williams very little. To those outside the South, these hapless laborers, many levels down from the nineteenth-century image of Southern gentlemen who ran their plantations and hosted cotillion parties in their mansions at night, were looked down upon with scorn and little pity. For the first half of the twentieth century, in fact, the Southern culture was taken by Northern men of letters as no more than refuse. H. L. Mencken, in 1917, railed at the "white trash" that had "dislodged the better elements" and clung to bigotry as a way of personal elevation from the gutter, where the slave descendants were relegated.[12]

Hiram Williams, like his old man, was brought up believing he was white trash—and this sensibility was his means of finding success, not by pushing it away but by turning it into engaging commercial appeal. As he once said, "To sing like a hillbilly, you had to have lived like a hillbilly. You had to have smelt a lot of mule manure."[13] He also said, "You got to know a lot about hard work"—which only proved that the man was a good huckster, inasmuch as he actually never lived on a farm, never slopped hogs or plowed a lower forty, never did work with his hands and his back, the latter being a congenital problem, and was pretty much a pampered mama's boy, even when his persona changed into a drinkin', spittin' drugstore cowboy. Hiram was plainly not anyone's idea of manly. A photo, perhaps the earliest of him taken, when he was around ten, shows him to be a geek with thick specs and Dumbo ears, though, no doubt at Lillie's command, wearing a natty dark suit and tie, his brown wavy hair slicked with goose grease. Not quite able to muster a smile, his expression is one of utter embarrassment. While he was a well-adjusted child whose troublesome moments were usually something like setting off firecrackers or hanging down by the tracks with his buddies until past dark, meaning Lon would have his belt in his hand when he got home, no one thought of him as impressive.

His sister Irene, a swarthy, pretty girl more popular than he, called him "pretty frail" and said that "he was no athlete. Every time he tried sports, it seemed he broke something."[14] Worse, some of those injuries, such as a ruptured disk, were to his already weak back, worsening his spinal structure, which did not bode well and kept him isolated from other kids, who more often than not mocked him in the yard for his awkwardness. And yet the thing about the Williams boy was that he'd suck up the mocking and the pain and the puniness of his frame and get right back into the huddle or batter's box. He was game, that's for sure. Lillie and Lon worried about him to no end, but they were more than a little impressed that he usually did what he was told. Doing so was what introduced him to the call of music. While he was hardly a progeny, it helped that Lillie had a musical ear. Her father, John Skipper, had written church hymns, and she could always rouse the congregation with her organ playing. And Lon could do a mean turn on the Jew's harp when at home or at a wing-ding in town. It was Lillie, though, who put rhythm in her son's head, usually along with the fear of God. She was the voice of God for him.

As he recalled toward the end of his life to music writer Ralph J. Gleason: "My mother was an organist at Mt. Olive, Alabama, and my earliest memory is sittin' on that organ stool by her and hollerin.' I must have been five, six years old, and louder than anybody else."[15] He meant the Mount Olive West Baptist Church, where his grandfather was buried. The church, built in 1894 adjacent to the one-room Grace Schoolhouse used for Sunday school lessons, still stands today, that very organ bench having been preserved there as part of a Hank Williams shrine before it was moved to the Hank Williams Museum in Georgiana. Back then, services were usually conducted by two rabid reverends, I. T. Taylor and J. H. Higdon. When Lillie had Hiram sing hymns, she expected conviction, emotion, so that God would hear him. And he would wail at the top of his lungs when the choir revved up. If he developed an inordinate fear that the good Lord would punish him plenty if—when—he became a sinner, the idea must have had some sort of seductive outlaw scent, because he would have no hesitation looking for and finding the sinner's road.

Singing in the congregation wasn't bad, but he wanted to be more like the singing cowboys in the early talkies. For that he needed a means of playing music, the first of which was a harmonica, which he found under the Christmas tree when he was six. His enthusiasm for making noise come out of it was such that Lon would recall years later, "He like to run me nuts with that thing, runnin' it back and forth in his mouth."[16] This not being sufficient to Hiram's image of a singing cowboy, he soon got it in his head that he needed one of those sleek-looking guitars. But for now, the choice would have been a three-dollar guitar or a three-dollar meal on the table. The guitar would have to wait.

Whatever the instruments of his choice, the message he heard from gospel was a strong one, for him and for most everyone in South, and was pivotal to his generation's transition. Here, as young people of every generation will do, they sought music they could call their own, not merely take their cues from their parents' notions and godly hymns. And their notion of the Lord's music was tuned into a broader, more liberal beat, with a greater appreciation for its black roots. Indeed, though racial restraints remained mostly unbroken, the '20s were a time when secular pursuits challenged the rock-ribbed social restraints of the church. Stories in the paper and newsreels in the theater showing loose women in revealing flapper outfits dancing the night away in speakeasys, of Babe Ruth painting New York City red, of men deliriously pouring bathtub gin, may have shocked the good Christians of the rural South, but their children were, well, *curious*.

2

✴ ✴ ✴ ✴ ✴ ✴

AN AMERICAN TWANG

By 1920, the spread of cowboy and backwoods music was so pro-found that it caused a spike in the sale of various musical com-modities. The two major mail order companies, especially Sears, Roebuck and Montgomery Ward, had made room in their catalogs beside sewing machines and washboards for musical instruments and accessories—mainly pianos, piano rolls, sheet music, and pho-nographs for early records, but also nicely crafted six-string guitars. Indeed, this growth was seismic; forgotten was Tom Edison's 1877 archaic phonograph/recorder with its tinfoil-wrapped cylinder and wax-paper tapes. The real breakthrough came at the turn of the century with Emile Berliner's Gramophone, later the Victor Talking Machine, which played 10-inch, 4-minute, 78 RPM vinyl disks. Now, America could listen to its native music, the most popular being folk songs sung by working cowboys in the West and Southwest.

These tunes from the hills carved a new vernacular, phonetic English language, mostly the doing of black singers and musicians in those same hills who composed what some whites called "sinful" songs—with "darky" language—telling realistic stories of splitting rails for the railroads that linked Southern towns. It was what they sang about having, and praying to be released from. As John Lomax transcribed one such song sung by a poor black man in a New Orleans barrel house:

> ... th'own' ten pounds fum my hips on down,
> Jes' lissen to de cole steel ring,
> Lawd, Lawd, jes' lissen to de cole steel ring.
> Cap'n say to John Henry,
> "I b'leeve dis mountain's sinkin in."

The scratchy recordings of unknown black blues men by Lomax's son Alan spoke of moonshine, hunting, and the sins of a cheatin' heart (acceptable for men, sinful for women, a creed bridging the races), and the same technology captured white mountain singers performing similar tunes with bouncier tempos on the banjo, fiddle, and stand-up string bass, which themselves derived from early African instruments.

The early "race records" were not only a joy to hear but also tutorials for those who cared to learn. Papa Charlie Jackson, Big Bill Broonzy, Georgia Tom Dorsey, Ma Rainey, and Tampa Red, and songs like "Papa's Lawdy Lawdy Blues" and "Salty Dog Blues" on the Paramount label's "race record" division led rival Columbia to sign black talent for its subsidiary label Okeh Records, an acronym for its founder, Otto K. E. Heinemann. Its own "race record" scout, a canny white man named Ralph Peer, began making field recordings on treks through the Deep South and in landmark 1924 studio sessions in New Orleans. But the white backwoods singers and pickers beat them all into a studio.

The first recording of what could be loosely called "country" music happened on June 30, 1922, in New York, when Arkansas-born, Texas-raised singer/fiddler Eck Robertson, along with seventy-four-year-old fiddler Henry Gilliland, laid down two tracks in RCA Victor's studio—the eighteenth-century folk tunes "Arkansaw Traveler" and "Turkey in the Straw."The first country—country folk, to be accurate—record to sell a million copies was "The Prisoner's Song," backed with "The Wreck of the Old 97," by Texas-born Vernon Dalhart in 1924.

Peer jumped into the country pool as well and, in 1927, agreed to audition a small, wafer-thin singer who had a radio show in Asheville, North Carolina. His name was Jimmie Rodgers.

Rodgers was born in Mississippi in 1897. His father was a foreman on the Mobile and Ohio Railroad, and he was taught the guitar by rail workers and bums at the railroad yards. Despite his thirst for performing, he became a brakeman until tuberculosis, which he contracted in 1924, forced him to quit and return to singing. Rodgers became gripped by horrible coughing fits but sang of the affliction in his repertoire, which deviated from Southern folk to more personal songs of family, life riding the rails, and travail. The first songs he cut for Peer, "The Soldier's Sweetheart" and the 1860s lullaby "Sleep, Baby, Sleep," sold well. Peer then brought him to a studio in Camden, New Jersey, for subsequent recordings, the breakout "T for Texas," the first of Rodgers's ingenious "Blue Yodel" series, in the W. C. Handy, blues-derived, twelve-bar blues progression. "T for Texas" was an epiphany, for sure, linking Southern pride with a woman's fickle love—*T* being not only for Texas but also for Thelma, the gal that "made a wreck out of me."

• • •

Sweeping the new market, it became country's first million-selling record. Rodgers's relaxed, confident, swaggering tone, with its undercurrent of pathetic inevitability, made it seem as if a listener were in a boxcar with him rolling over lonely country tracks. In "Waiting for a Train," he wailed, "I haven't got a nickel, not a penny can I show / He said get off you railroad bum and slammed the boxcar door," followed by yodeling sounding like a mournful coyote off in the distance. This became his signature, a lonesome trill in between syllables or to draw a one-syllable word out to its peak extension, a whole new yodeling style very different from that of Alpine sheepherders. It had a strange appeal, surfacing not only into early cowboy and folk songs but the music of nascent blues and country singers like Riley Puckett, a blind singer from Georgia who wrote a lovelorn song recorded in 1924 by Emmett Miller, a minstrel show performer also from Georgia. Its title: "Lovesick Blues."

Rodgers, who had picked up yodeling from the black vaudeville circuit, was given faint praise for it, one music critic calling him a "white man gone black."[9] But he made a huge impact on young singers with his sense of conviction and authenticity, and lonely despair. And through that door came other country troubadours almost as momentous. By then, Hank Williams had a template in which to frame his own songs of despair.

• • •

By 1930, when his son was seven, Elonzo Williams's facial paralysis grew more consistent, again making him unable to speak, and relatives and neighbors began to think he was dying of some horrible condition. Lillie's explanation for his malaise was that he had "shell shock" from the war. She could be rough on Lon but seemed genuinely concerned for his health. Her cousin Taft Skipper recalled on his visits seeing her nursing her husband, bringing him coffee—"that black, thick Luzianne brand"—in bed "to keep us kids quiet for his sake."[3] But she was no less assiduous in turning to a more serious treatment for him when she could no longer see him suffer. Either out of pity or frustration that he had become an anchor, she had already taken to telling people she was a widow rather than have to explain about the useless husband she had at home. And, as though it were a way to get him out, she began looking into confining him in a hospital.

Given his status as a wounded war veteran—no matter if the wound came in a fight over a mademoiselle—such a stay would be paid for by the government. And so, with Lon having no real say in the matter, and her assurances that he'd get the help he needed and be back real soon, he packed his bags and Lillie took him by train to the nearest Veterans Administration hospital, in Pensacola, Florida. There, he was evaluated and diagnosed with either—depending on which account one reads in the literature—a brain aneurysm or dementia, or both, and transferred to another VA facility in Alexandria, Louisiana. The difference between these two diagnoses is, of course, wide, dementia being a broad catchall term for brain dysfunction that could have physical or psychological causes. As Lon would tell it, he was sitting under a tree when he felt his head was bursting. The problem, however, was always treated as mental in nature,[4] and he was kept under observation for nearly a decade, rendering him all but a rumor to a family that would apparently visit him exactly once.

Neither Hiram nor Irene was ever told where Lon was, nor why he left. Lillie's only explanation was that he was sick and went to a place where he could get well, her "shell shock" diagnosis all that was necessary to anyone who inquired. It's likely he and Irene both were scarred by their dad's sudden departure, especially Hiram, who now had no adult male authority figure. He would grow closer to his mother as a result, which deepened his love for her but also may well have constructed an ambiguous sense of female dominion and dependency, and made him unable to put any separation between them as he got older. Neither could he develop any sort of bond with his dad, since Lillie would for years not take the kids to visit Lon, her belief being that it was best to sever that bond, as she had no intention of ever allowing Lon to return.

Lillie was too busy taking charge, flexing her new role as mother and father, to think much about her husband. Shortly after Lon was committed, her brother-in-law Walter McNeil, who lived with his wife, son, and three daughters in a Garland farmhouse with Lillie's widowed mother, suggested Lillie come and stay with them. She took him up on the offer, and once again the Williams brood—now a threesome—was on the move, in an old second- or thirdhand flatbed truck.

They stayed with the McNeils, picking cotton and strawberries to help out. Then Lillie, not wanting to live on charity, decided to

move once more, down Mobile Road, now Highway 31, to Georgiana, a town of around 1,480 people, a good 20 percent black. Why
she settled there isn't clear, but it was regarded as a "big town," as
opposed to the hick towns they had been in. Businessmen streamed
through because of the bustling cotton trade there—its cotton gin
one of only eight in Butler County.

This was as big as a small town in southern Alabama could get,
and Lillie saw opportunities. As bold as a Southern woman could be,
she arrived with her children, not knowing what she would be doing
or where the family would live, but prepared to work, hard. Reading
signs posted at the train station, she quickly rented a place steps from
the tracks. Known as the Metcalfe residence, it was an old wooden
subdivided shack on Jane Avenue. It was hardly a slum, though; one
next-door neighbor was Herman Pride, a former mayor of the town,
whose family ran the local *Butler County News* and were elders of
the Georgiana Methodist Church. But for whatever reason—be
it carelessness or bad wiring—the house caught fire soon after, on
October 23, 1930. Awakened by the smoke, Lillie got Hiram and
Irene up and running, all in their pajamas, out to the street, where
they watched helplessly as the house crumbled in embers. The blaze
spread to the house next door owned by one W. H. Knox but spared
Herman Pride's. The next day, Pride's *Butler County News* reported
under the headline FIRE DESTROYS TWO RESIDENCES that "when discovered by the occupants, Mrs. Williams and children, it had made
such headway they were only able to save a few things" before the
Greenville Fire Department arrived to put it out.[5]

Undaunted, and with almost nothing salvaged, Lillie moved
ahead. In the wake of the fire, when she became known around
town, a local man, whose wife was Hank's second-grade teacher,
helped arrange for the family to stay the night at a house a few hundred yards from the burned-out place, called the Edgar Ansel Black
residence. Soon she and the children were on the move back up the
highway to Garland to stay again with the McNeils while she made
trips to Georgiana looking for another house. On one such excur-

sion, according to Irene Williams, Lillie stopped into a post office to mail a letter, and a well-dressed man walked up to her, it having been pointed out to him that she had been victimized by the fire. After they spoke for a few minutes, he had a startling offer. "I am Thaddeus B. Rose," he told her. "I have a house you are welcome to rent free until you get on your feet."[6]

As it turned out, Thaddeus Rose was perhaps the most respected man about town. According to the folks at the Hank Williams Boyhood Home and Museum, Rose and his brother Luther had worked in some capacity for the railroad, then became well-off landlords in Georgiana, having bought empty lots and developed a few homes that they rented out mainly to businessmen. Luther Rose had built the house Thaddeus referred to, on a street the brothers named for themselves, at what is now 127 Rose Avenue. Unmarried and in his thirties, Rose was perhaps no more than a kindhearted soul. Moreover, the house he offered her to live in was like nothing she had ever seen. It was enormous, replete with two stories, four bedrooms, and a white-shingled exterior, with the foundation raised off the ground by six-foot-high stilts as protection from floods. There was no bathroom, just an outhouse in back, but the kitchen had running water and a wood-burning stove.

Although the train whistles and clanking steel wheels on the L&N tracks could be heard, the house seemed like a Southern manor. But when the neighbors saw that there was no lord of the manor, only a strong-willed woman and her kids, it set tongues to wagging. As Paul Hemphill put it, "People could talk all they wanted to about Lillie's abrasive personality—and talk they did, about just what kind of 'deal' she may have made with the rich bachelor."[7] Not that everyone was so cynical. Some neighbors, taking pity on the lessers, came by with picnic baskets filled with food for the family. But Lillie, who was likely skittish of the gossip, was embarrassed by such charity and soon was earning money in a variety of ways. She sold strawberries, beans, anything edible, from her garden and took a job as a night nurse at a hospital in town operated by a doctor who has been identified as either J. Crawford[8] or H. K. Tippins.[9]

Lillie wanted no excuses from her children for not pitching in on the expenses, nor any more alms from the neighbors. Irene recalled years later that Lillie "made our clothes from whatever was available," such as feed sacks, adding, "but we were always clean." Some mornings, she said, Lillie "would hunt rabbits and squirrels for our lunch."[10] Lillie also worked in a nearby cannery—"a saurkraut [sic] canning plant," as Walt McNeil once recalled, curling his nose. "They used to call it the smell of success around there."[11] This was of help to Hank, since if the house didn't stink of pickled cabbage, he knew he would be free to go knock around without having to sell his peanuts, which would only draw a rebuke from her when she got home and ordered him to go sell until he made up for a lost day. That wasn't easy with the going rate of a nickel a bag, but Hank would be out on the street, either out by the cotton gin or on the platform of the train yard. He and Irene freshly roasted the nuts every day to get the edge on the other snack sellers. When he made a sale, he would offer to shine the buyer's shoes for another few-cent tip. Other times he did odd jobs, made deliveries for grocery stores, whatever came up.

Skinny and weak as Hiram looked, he was a precocious kid, for sure, every day growing taller, and less shy and geeky. He was no problem child, often seen playing cowboy in his front yard. Herman Pride would recall him as a "nice-lookin' little boy, right lively but not smart alecky . . . crazy about cowboy things. We used to call him 'two-gun Pete,' all decked out in his hat, belt and boots. He used to run along the brick wall of my place till I thought sure he'd break his neck."[12] Lillie later told the story that with his peanut earnings one day, Hiram bought ingredients for beef stew at the grocery store, and when he came home he dropped them on the kitchen table and said, "Momma, fix us some gumbo stew. We're gonna eat tonight!" She went on: "The next day, he made another thirty cents.

But Hank, never a business manager, used his money for firecrackers, a cap pistol and some caps."[13]

But the young Hank was already scheming to fool her, skimming from some bags after he left the house in order to fill a few more, the money from which he'd hide from her along with his tips. This was an early sign that the kid from rural Alabama knew he would need to save whatever he could, lest his mother take every nickel he had.

3

✳ ✳ ✳ ✳ ✳ ✳ ✳

"COUNTRY MUSIC AIN'T NOTHIN' BUT WHITE PEOPLE'S BLUES, ANYWAY"

As months lengthened into years, Lillie Skipper Williams had gotten to know a lot of people, doing what would be called in future generations "networking." Herman Pride was always a help, and when another pol, Lister Hill, was running for the US Senate and campaigned in the town, Irene Williams approached him. "My ma wants to see you very badly," she said, later recalling, "He went home with me and sat on our front porch talking to her. Then he got her a pension."[1] Lister also was able to pull strings to have Lon's VA disability checks sent directly to Lillie; she'd run into miles of red tape trying to arrange that herself. But what really turned the corner for her was when she had an idea about making money from that wonderful house. Instead of going to Thaddeus Rose with it, however, she had Lister impress upon Rose the good sense of allowing Lillie Williams to rent out rooms there, as the proprietor of a boardinghouse for the business set that came through Georgiana.

Rose had no objections, as long as he was given a cut of the money, and Lillie was in business. Soon after, there were even more loose lips around the town about what might have been going on inside some of the rooms, and with whom. In Paul Hemphill's suggestive take, Lillie "found her calling as a boardinghouse operator—some would say, unkindly, a madam—in a town throbbing with people just passing through."[2]

Whatever was going on, if anything, it turned into the most profitable of Lillie's professions, one that would become her only profession for many years. She didn't fool herself that she was getting to be rich, but at least the family had one thing they could boast of. "We were poor people," Irene Williams once clarified, as proud as her father; despite hardship, she said, "we weren't in poverty. No matter what anyone says, we never begged." Even more prideful to the family, she said, was that despite their hand-me-down existence and time spent on streets paved or otherwise in town, Lillie had a rule: as soon as they walked in the door, they were to bathe, change their clothes, and comb their hair. In fact, Irene pointed out, "the welfare department refused to give us aid because [we] were *too clean.*"[3]

· · ·

The man of the family was getting more and more confident as he reached puberty in the pit of the Depression. It didn't hurt that he had cowboy clothes that Lillie—it was said she would have done anything to make her boy happy— sometimes spent her last dollars on. She did the same when she finally acceded to Hiram's clattering about getting a guitar. With Lon gone, it seemed the least she could do for him. He was eleven when she went to a music store and bought a used Silvertone model for $3.50, to be paid off at fifty cents a month. However, in keeping with Hank lore, others would claim to be the benefactor of that guitar. One of them was the proprietor of a Ford dealership, Fred Thigpen, in whose store the radio was tuned to stations playing hillbilly. When he gave the teenager his first guitar, he said, he also taught him the words to cowboy songs that came over the radio. Another was Jim Warren, who also had been a musician and owned a jewelry and musical instrument store. Of course, none of these narratives could approach the one Lillie, a born storyteller, would want to stick. Hers came with a possibly apocryphal extension. While "the little fellow was overcome with joy when I brought the guitar home from the music store," she would write years later, he subsequently "ran into the yard and swung the gate. He leaped on a young calf that was lying just outside the yard and twisted the calf's tail. The yearling bawled with fright. He leaped into the air and before Hank knew what was happening the calf had thrown him to the ground, breaking his arm. It almost broke his heart too, for he couldn't play the guitar with a broken arm. Three days later, though, when he could wiggle his fingers, Hank was trying to chord the guitar."[4]

As industrious as he was, Hiram had a way of ingratiating himself to people he met. He also would not be deterred from sidling up to someone who might have had a reputation among the town folk. Jim Warren, for example, had gotten himself into trouble on the suspicion that he had befriended a black family. The local Ku Klux Klan chapter believed in the fever swamps of their minds that he was sleeping with a female member of that family—the worst crime a white man could commit, according to the canons of bigotry. Though Warren took a beating, he refused to be intimidated, denied the charge, and said that a lot of white preachers he knew were having sex with black women.[5] This was clearly a brave man, and listening to him broadened the young man's purview, breaking down the conditioned reflex so common in his world to stereotype and reduce the dignity of people of color.

When Hiram would sit around with Warren, he would hear the black musicians the music store owner knew. One was a guitar-playing blues man known as "Tee Tot," who lived several miles down the road in Greenville, the seat of Butler County, but came over to Georgiana a few times a week on the L&N to play and sing on the street for spare change; sometimes he'd get a gig at a church supper or black dance and make the joint jump. Hank apparently witnessed this Tee Tot fellow; as Herman Pride would later recall to author Roger Williams, "there was always a crew of little boys around him, followin' him from store to store," a group that included Hiram.

With his guitar in tow, and not really knowing how to play it, Hiram began strumming and singing cowboy songs on street corners and at the train depot, hat at his feet, which some passersby may have dropped coins into just to get him to *stop* playing.

· · ·

Lillie again took Hiram to a doctor to have his back checked out, but this time, too, there was no diagnosis of anything major amiss. It would only become known later that Hank Williams had something called hemangioma, a clumping of blood vessels, which would lead to fully blown spina bifida occulta, a spinal deformity that is present in 10 to 20 percent of people. The condition can be benign unless the spinal cord is tethered, or not attached properly to bones, causing chronic, at times severe, neurological problems and debilitating pain.[6] Though the condition is now preventable with prenatal supplements like folic acid, it was far too exotic at the time for many country doctors to even know about. Instead, the boy was told he was fine and the pain would one day be gone. But along with loneliness, the pain knotting his lower back would be constant.

At age five, Hiram would begin to write rudimentary songs. Those tunes were not about cowboys on a distant range but rather the emotional attachment to his dad and the void not having him around created. In fact, Hiram filled up entire notebooks of pages with feelings of emptiness and abandonment, the lines structured like a song. The beginning of one such passage, which was titled "I Wish I Had a Dad," went:

> *I guess I'm awful lucky, my mother says I am*
> *She says why son you have a lot*

And I reply yes mom, I've got a knife
I've got a bike, I've got a dog named Tad
I've got a lot of comic books, I've got a drawing pad
I've got a Roy Rogers gun and I ain't doing bad
But if I really had my wish I'd rather have a dad[7]

Sometimes on cold days he would slide into the crawlspace under the house and sidle up next to the draft of the fireplace to keep warm, sit in the dark, and sing hymns while picking at the guitar. Hiram lugged his old Silvertone wherever the day would take him, trying somehow to get his guitar to sound like the beat-up guitar of Tee Tot. However, before he had any real idea of where he was headed along a musical locus, he had some more growing up to do. As it happened, he would do some of that courtesy of an unwitting Lillie, who, too tired from work to keep tabs on a son becoming more restless with each day, paved the way for him to get more enlightened than she would have wanted.

Not that he was trouble or anything, even if it was a chore just worrying about him. But she made it her business to lay down the law when she had to, such as when he used some of his secret earnings to buy firecrackers, which in another of those Hank tales reputedly were in his back pocket when he was just a shaver and she gave him a whipping one day, and they began to explode, burning his butt worse than the switch did. Seeing how restless he was, Lillie thought it would be good for the young ramblin' man—who had already lived in more places than most do in a lifetime—to go live with the McNeils. They had recently relocated to the "country," in Fountain, smack on that ramblin' Highway 41, in Monroe County, about a hundred miles to the west. To make room for him, Walter McNeil sent his teenage daughter, Opal, to live with Lillie and Irene. The McNeils were settled in a logging camp, in two converted boxcars, and while it was hardly the Ritz, these prototypical "mobile homes" could be quite roomy. Hiram would also be around his cousin J.C., who was always up for a good time and a bit of trouble.

Walter and Alice McNeil took a hands-off approach to the kids, as long as they went to school and didn't stay out late. But Alice McNeil did have one rule, identical to her sister Lillie's: the boys' attendance at church on Sunday was nonnegotiable. Hank had no problem with the mandate, especially considering it was on those mornings that he always could connect with the Lord and pray for deliverance.

Being separated from Lillie also opened new doors. By 1934, he was eleven and a *man*, by the ethos of the hills and backwoods. He and J.C., who was a little older and manly, became inseparable. They'd hunt and fish in the daylight, and when darkness set in, J.C. seemed to know where to go to meet up with young girls in the moonlight, and where to be able to tickle the tongue with some moonshine. Hell, sometimes he could do that right at home. Walter McNeil was no choirboy himself; he was said to have stashed bottles of liquor under his mattress. And out there in the woods, there was no dearth of mountaineers willing to spill some of their hootch into the kids' cups—to help "make a man of you." Saturday night barn dances at the camp were eagerly awaited, as that was when booze flowed like water, and like a river in '33 after Prohibition was lifted.

Those parties were of value for other reasons, too. When the amateur hillbilly bands began to play, Hiram could jump up onstage and play with them, the booze in his belly making his voice seem splendid to him, if not to everyone. His confidence at those moments felt so good that he saw no reason why he should avoid getting tanked on firewater whenever he sang. The only downside was that he and J.C. would have to stumble back into the camp car, where Walter was already passed out drunk, and know that their heads would be in a vise when Alice got them up to get dressed for church. The only solution, it seemed to Hank, was pouring so much hootch into himself that his body would surely learn to obey its commands to feel good. It was like medication without a doctor writing one of those prescription things. It seemed a hell of a plan, a minor exception to the rules of his Good Book.

When he returned to Georgiana after a year's sabbatical, Hiram was a head taller, a year bolder, and not in need of a dictionary to know what "vices" meant.

. . .

Hiram "Hank" Williams wasn't particularly taken with the emerging caste of country singers. He was more lost in his own prism of feelings and music as it applied to his life; yet what was happening in the evolution of country would have everything to do with his own emergence. He would grow in tandem with the not entirely admirable phenomenon of the *Grand Ole Opry*, which began on the radio when he was a toddler and lurched into something that was both advantageous and damaging for the country brand. The first murmurs of the *Opry* arose on November 28, 1925, when a radio program called *Barn Dance* began on a small Nashville station, WSM. The studio was housed in an office building owned by the National Life & Accident Insurance Company, and the show copied the format of a show on WLS in Chicago, *National Barn Dance*. The Nashville station hired away the Chicago station's program director, George "Judge" Hay, and his first show featured a seventy-seven-year-old fiddler, "Uncle" Jimmy Thompson. Each Saturday night new, mostly unknown acts in the "barn dance" idiom appeared, the names including a then-obscure Bill Monroe, the Fruit Jar Drinkers, the Crook Brothers, and so on. The show followed an NBC network feed of a classical music show, and two years later, Hay announced:

> For the next three hours, we will present nothing but realism. We will be down to earth for the earthy. . . . We have heard grand opera from New York, but now we will be listening to the Grand Ole Opry.[8]

The show became progressively more popular, necessitating that National Life & Accident Insurance build a larger studio for it. In 1934, the *Opry* took up residence in the Hillsboro Theatre, then two years later moved to the Dixie Tabernacle theater in East Nashville.

Hank, of course, grew up aware of the *Opry* but usually had better things to do on a Saturday night than sit in front of a radio, and Lillie didn't even own one until 1934 or so. As for his own music, that pretty much came out of expressing what he saw around him. He did seem to appreciate the yodeling thing, because his throat was supple enough for him to do it naturally. Mainly, he just trilled in the manner of the singing cowboys, regarding it as "folk."

Though there wasn't a cowboy within a thousand miles of South Alabama, the cowboy culture was the beau ideal for a generation of maturing boys all across the country. In the South, however, all that blues music could find a neat context when a guitar was thrown into the mix. So while he may have sounded like a white-gloved, sharply pressed, campfire-singing Gene Autry and Roy Rogers model, Hiram wanted to be a dirty-fingernailed, dusty-booted, sweat-and-soot-faced southern Alabaman, animated by black blues and mixed with a reminder that God was the big cowboy. And for this ambitious and seemingly unreachable objective, his timing was perfect.

Perhaps not having his father around helped, too. While Lon never believed his boy's obsession with music would amount to a tinker's damn, Lillie had the makings of a stage mother from the start, and far more sense than her husband. She knew her son had singing ability; from what she heard on the radio, he was just as good as anyone playing hillbilly music for profit. If he could, through her work on his behalf, get himself on the radio and make records, the family might even break the yoke of dead-end Alabama living. Lillie had scraped together enough money to send him to a voice teacher for a while, but he refused to change what he felt when he sang to what he was *supposed* to be doing with his voice and diaphragm. There was just something about singing from the heart that wasn't meant to be tamed, he believed, and he would ride a long way down the road on that impulse.

. . .

Looking at times like a geek with his wire-rimmed glasses over his nose, he was not the worldly fellow he saw himself as. But when he would cut school and hang at the barbershop by the tracks, he mingled with the grown men as if he were one of them. The owner of the shop, Austin Reid, later recalled him even further back in time, in the early '30s, as "a little bitty feller, with legs no bigger'n a buggy whip. He hung around here a lot, looking for food and cigarettes. . . . If I tossed a cigarette butt away, he'd dive for it 'fore it hit the floor." Reid remembered Hank then as "a happy boy," exactly the *opposite* of the way Hank's cousin J.C. once described him, as "a real loner. He never was a happy boy. . . . He didn't laugh or carry on like other children. It seemed like somethin' was always on his mind."[9]

Even then, barely a teenager, he seemed to be a split personality, his real feelings known only to himself. A schoolteacher who taught both Hank and Irene during their days in Georgiana once said that it was Irene whom she remembered as "much more forward, with a good bit of braggadocio." Hiram, she said, was "so ordinary he merges with the crowd in my memory."[10] Something always seemed to keep him distant from the world he lived in. It was probably a factor that the world changed so *much*, never really giving him a breather before he was on the move. That happened again in September 1934 when Thaddeus Rose suddenly up and died. Rose's family let it be known that the house he had so nobly (or not) allowed her brood to live in would be sold. Lillie, aware that her income from the boarders would dry up, reckoned the time was right to make a go of that business in a bigger town.

By chance, the McNeils had also moved again, from Fountain to Greenville, and did some scouting for Lillie of possible houses where she could live and turn a profit in the town where old tattered signs at the rail station called it "the Camellia City." In May 1935, she loaded up her pickup truck again and headed for Greenville, with enough money to settle into an even bigger house with a lot of sunny rooms; the street name is lost in the dustbin of history. This was quite propitious for Hank, who was now an able and ready man of twelve and bent to take his street singing to a higher level. And good Lord almighty, sometimes things happened for a reason, he must have believed, because beating his feet up to Greenville would bring him into closer proximity with the man who may have influenced him the most. It was neither Lon Williams nor Jimmie Rodgers but the stooped, gray-haired old black man he had trailed on the streets in Georgiana, the one they called Tee Tot.

Tee Tot's real name was Rufus Payne, and he was a classic example of the black Alabama underclass, a bluesman with talents deserving of great attention who only became known in death by the testimonial graces of a white man. He went through life with no status as a living human. By his own rendering to those he knew, he was born in Greenville, but a birth certificate was never found for him, and one created ex post facto for him after his death had blank lines for the names of his mother, father, and date of birth.

According to latter-day research by the Alabama historian Alice Harp, he was born in Sandy Ridge in Lowndes County circa 1884, the son of freed slaves who moved to New Orleans around 1890. Only later, after his parents died and he had become a minstrel, did he arrive in Greenville.[11] He never made a record, never made it into the Lomaxes' research, never recorded, never seen in a photograph. His real identity was not known until he was long in his unmarked grave, and the only time Tee Tot was on a record, he was not heard but rather mentioned, when Hank Williams Jr. recorded a tribute song called "The Tee Tot Song" on his 2002 album *The Almeria Club Recordings*. Apparently the name was given him because he usually had beside him a bottle of something that he liked to say with a wink was tea. While his street playing earned him notice, he never had more than a few pennies in his pocket. Hank later told one of his band members that Payne had a job as a janitor in a Greenville high school—actually only one of his jobs, another being as a delivery man for a drugstore called Peagler's—but when he went out with his guitar to the street corners, white people would reach in their pockets and throw some change into his hat or cigar box.

Contrary to oft-stated lore, Hank's praise of him was never full-throated but measured, limited by the conditioned native tongue of the racist South; by example, in 1952 he told the then-young Ralph J. Gleason:

> I learned to play the git-tar from an old colored man in the streets of Montgomery. He was named Tetot and he played in a colored street band. They had a washtub bass. You ever seen one of them? Well, it had a hole in the middle with a broom handle stuck in it and a rope for the strings. I was shinin' shoes and sellin' newspapers and followin' this ole Nigrah around to get him to teach me to play the git-tar. I'd give him 15 cents or whatever I could get a hold of for a lesson.[12]

It hardly helped elevate Payne, who had died in 1939, that he was consigned to history as "this ole Nigrah," or even years later by J. C. McNeil as a man with a "hunched back with long arms that extended almost to his knees," much the way one might describe a simian. Neither did Hank apparently ever learn, or care, what Tee Tot's name was, his paean not nearly as heartfelt as narratives told by other white musicians in the South taking inspiration from black performers. Neither was Hank much interested in becoming skilled as a professional musician. In later years he would have no trouble admitting that "I never have read a note or written one" and "I don't know one note from another." What he *did* want was to vicariously live the life of an itinerant street performer, who knew how to make the guitar set a tone, a beat, become an extension of the feeling in his gut. Hank had always been introverted with strangers, not warming up to anyone until he knew them. But that wasn't going to cut it singing for strangers he had to make like him enough to put a dime into a hat. "Keep the crowd's attention," Payne was said to have told him. "When they start to slip, you're in trouble." The secret in doing that lay in the music he would sing, and by listening to Payne at close range he absorbed the "personality" of music; how to stress certain notes, how to make them sound *hurtin'*, how to turn up the corner of his mouth in a wary smile or yodel as a sign of relief. And perhaps it's not so ironic that decades later Payne's son revealed the delicious tidbit that "Hank wanted to learn how to play blues. My dad knew how to play blues, but he didn't like to play blues. He wanted to make money playing hillbilly music. [Laugh] They go together regardless of black and white."[13]

That the two forms indeed went together was proven by the fact that in '49 Hank would record "My Bucket's Got a Hole in It," a classic drinking song from the Prohibition days. And even with revamped lyrics replacing the song's warning "Better look around, police firin' squad is on their beat an' you'll be jailhouse bound," and a steel guitar, it was pure blues, closely tracking the 1933 Clarence Williams composition, later redone in 1937 as "The Bucket's Got a Hole in It" by several blues acts, the best known being Washboard Sam. The languid, slow-motion cadences of many of Hank's records certainly gave them a bluesy feel; so did the yodel, which, like Jimmie Rodgers's, was more in the black wailing tradition than the upbeat, goofy hillbilly style. "It's sooo obvious," Hank Williams Jr. has said. "Man, that E chord and that blues. If Daddy wasn't a blues singer, just tell me who was. Lightnin' Hopkins, he said that country music ain't nothin' but white people's blues anyway."[14] Added Henderson Payne, "Anything my daddy played, Hank could play it, too. Very few people know how to play blues. Hank knew how to play blues. That's why he sings so good."

However, so much would be embellished about the Tee Tot connection that it is impossible to separate fact from fiction. While several biographers have repeated Irene Williams's 1993 recollection that Payne had called Hank "Little White Boss,"[15] there is something scripted about the notion that Payne was the wry, wise old sensei and Hiram Williams was his "karate kid." Irene also gave Lillie the props for Tee Tot becoming a mentor to her son; "Mother was afraid that Hank would get lost or hurt" somehow in Greenville, she said, and "she asked Tee Tot to give Hank music lessons in exchange for food." If so, Lillie deserved props, since this sort of racial comingling by an Alabama boy would have raised a lot of eyebrows. Not that Lillie ever bowed to many people's rules of behavior—Irene once said that "if you made her angry, you had a wildcat on your hands," and that for her children "she would turn the world upside down."[16] Still, Payne gave many white kids tips about playing guitar, and when he died he might not have known any of *their* names.

After Rufus Payne died a pauper in a Montgomery charity hospital on March 17, 1939, his age thought to be around fifty-five, no one really knew where he was buried. His death certificate read "unknown" for his age and profession. He probably was taken to the mainly black Lincoln Cemetery, a few miles from Oakwood—the "white" cemetery—and put in the ground, without a marker, resting in a kind of potter's field for African Americans.

To this day, Lincoln Cemetery is a neglected, outrageously unkempt place, where headstones are often displaced, left in disrepair, or vandalized. Some 6,700 people have been laid to rest in this graveyard designed for 700 graves. "When somebody would be buried here," says Phyllis Armstrong, a volunteer who has been trying to trace and identify them, "they were burying people on top of people." Says another volunteer, "What people don't understand is that [racism] also applied in death. Not just at bus stations or restaurants or bathrooms, but in death also."[17]

The best that can be said of Hank's brief intersection with Rufus Payne was that it happened at all. Obscure blues men like Rufus Payne spread their influence in small doses, putting the blues in the whitest of singers and musicians with only a word or two of tribute in exchange. Hank would never actually sing or play with a black man onstage or in a studio. But at least he would remember the stooped-over old black man, even if he didn't know his real name. For the times he rambled through, that was called progress.

4

✴ ✴ ✴ ✴ ✴ ✴ ✴

I GOT A HOME IN
MONTGOMERY

The rigors of the Depression only seemed to produce more themes of angst and hard-toiling, hard-working men that defined most of the songs being sung in the honky-tonks—the blues, albeit by another name. The irony is that while sales of records dropped off precipitously, country music found its audience in the burgeoning of radio. At the start of the 1930s, only three decades after the medium was patented, around twelve million Americans already owned a tabletop or console radio. By the end of the decade that number would grow to twenty-eight million.[1] The demand, and the Depression, made them more affordable—the price dropping from $139 to $47 in four years for popular models marketed by Philco, RCA, Zenith, Emerson, Galvin, and many more. By 1933, America had nearly half the radios that existed in the world, sparking an explosion of stations, 599 in all, most under 1,000 watts, generating revenues of $60 million.[2] Some higher-powered stations, such as WHO in Des Moines, Iowa, WBAP in Fort Worth, Texas, KFRU in Columbia, Missouri, and KVOO in Tulsa, Oklahoma, featured western bands like Otto Gray and his Oklahoma Cowboys, though the biggest star was Bob Wills, who in 1934 left Waco with his Texas Playboys to do a show on KVOO.

Wills, a big, handsome man and a former barber who once had worn blackface in minstrels and medicine shows, had cut his teeth with Texas bands like Gid Tanner and his Skillet Lickers before forming the Wills Fiddle Band. He took a giant step in the early '30s by unabashedly applying what he called the "rowdy city blues" to country swing. Wills's noon show, from the bandstand at Cain's Ballroom, highlighted his Playboys' reach and daring. They had a sax, a trumpet, a steel guitar, lead and rhythm electric guitars, fiddles, a lead singer, and most crucially in the lens of history, a drummer to keep the beat. The Playboys were half a fiddlin' country band, half a big band playing dance music. But Wills wasn't the only Oklahoma voice making a name for himself on the radio.

Woodrow Wilson Guthrie, born in Okemah in 1912, was among the scores of Okies who hit the road dreaming of a new life in sunny California. Woody Guthrie's folk songs about working-class grit would soon get him hired by Los Angeles station KFVD, where he'd host a left-wing show on which he performed protest songs along with hillbilly tunes.

By the early '30s, the medium of recording had matured. The inevitability of constant change in the industry hit home in the country sector when the first "king" of country, Jimmie Rodgers, who had made the kind of money the other hillbilly singers could only dream of, neared his end. In May 1933, he recorded "Mississippi Delta Blues" and the dewy-eyed "Years Ago" in Victor's New York studio, so weak that he had to lie on a cot between songs to save his ebbing strength. Two days later, the Singing Brakeman died in his Taft Hotel room from a pulmonary hemorrhage at thirty-five, the first sad denouement of the biggest country star.

Rodgers's sad, keening voice and soaring yodel had influenced a coterie of singers, and the one positioned to take his place was Roy Acuff. A tall, frail, curly-haired man—it seemed all the semi-

nal country crooners were cut from the same cloth—he had a widow's peak jabbing at his low forehead, and his flashy white teeth and
high cheekbones made him look almost pretty. Acuff had a highly
manicured style, his doe-eyed, emotional balladry clashing with the
flannel lumberjack shirts and work boots he and his band wore. Born
and raised in Tennessee, he taught himself to play the fiddle in his
late twenties, around 1930. Soon after, he joined a medicine show
band, then formed the Tennessee Crackerjacks. He won a fervent
following, which had a lot to do with his own devotion, which would
sometimes grow so intense that tears would roll down his face as he
sang about God. In 1934, Acuff signed a deal with the American
Record Corporation, the leader of the "three records for a dollar"
bargain market.

In 1938, ARC would be purchased by the Columbia Broadcasting System, its price inflated in no small measure by the booming
sales of Roy Acuff records, including "The Great Speckled Bird" and
"The Wabash Cannonball," two of country music's most important
recordings of all time. The former, written by a Carolinas singing
preacher who billed himself as Reverend Guy Smith, was a deep
gospel allegory about the moral imperative of adhering to funda-
mentalist Christianity. Its melody was later conscripted by Hank
Thompson's 1953 "The Wild Side of Life" and Kitty Wells's "It
Wasn't God Who Made Honky-Tonk Angels," then by David Allen
Coe in his 1985 "If That Ain't Country," which ends: "I didn't know
God made honky-tonk angels and went back to the wild side of life."

. . .

The song brought Acuff to the *Grand Ole Opry*, where, it was
reported, "In the din, Acuff's brief and impassioned solo spots stood
out like gunshots at midnight."[3] Until then, the *Opry*'s biggest star
was Uncle Dave Macon, with his cohorts Sam and Kirk McGee. But
Acuff and his Smoky Mountain Boys quickly gained what would be
the most listened-to program on WSM, his audience so large that he
took his band out on the road with Macon and other *Opry* perform-

ers. By the late '30s the radio show was reaching around a million listeners every Saturday night, and in the early '40s, Acuff and the band were traveling in a cream-colored limousine, WSM GRAND OLE OPRY painted on its windows. His private DC-3 airplane was emblazoned ROY ACUFF'S—THE GREAT SPECKLED BIRD.

That level of achievement would beckon many young singers. For Hank, it still seemed a million miles off in the distance. But in 1937, he moved a few hundred miles closer.

• • •

By the age of thirteen, Hiram had been playing on corners in downtown Greenville for a good three years. Even though that city was four times the size of Georgiana, with a district of honky-tonks and businessmen with cash for his hat, his sights were already beyond that horizon. Not by coincidence, Lillie's brother-in-law Walter McNeil, who was as itchy-footed as his nephew, had once again prefaced movement by the Williams clan, relocating his family up to the state capital in 1936. Hank, who missed the company of his cousin J.C., began to bug Lillie to migrate again, to a real city where the dirt roads and whining whistles of the L&N would be replaced by buzzing streets and downtown honky-tonks. Always the doting mother, she didn't shoot him down. For Lillie, the possibilities for renting out rooms in a big town were enticing, so she and Walter went up to Montgomery to scout places for her to live and found one at 114 South Perry Street.

Lillie enrolled Hank and Irene in school, and Walter came down to Greenville to help her load the family's belongings—including a new stove she had bought—into a trailer hitched to a logging truck. Before long, she had rented rooms in the house and planted seeds in another of her vegetable gardens. Hank, too, was again back at it, selling peanuts in the street and working as a house painter.

When he wasn't hawking nuts or painting, however, he was playing music, and in Montgomery there was no shortage of places to do it. His aim was to go where the moneyed people were, making his

way to the sidewalks outside the Pizitz department store and singing for quarters. Or he'd take up a position along the docks on the
Alabama river where the speakeasies, brothels, and dive bars were.

The town already had a pedigree in music; Erskine Hawkins, the
composer of "Tuxedo Junction," helmed an orchestra that played at
the Casa Loma, the Cavalier Club, Club 31, Clyde's, the Colonial,
the Hi-Hat, and Lake Haven. The Elite Cafe, open around the clock
serving split tenderloin, oysters on the half shell, and Maine lob-
ster, was a wee-hours destination for young folks after masked balls
at the City Auditorium or mezzanine makeouts at the Paramount,
Empire, and Strand theaters, all "separate but equal" facilities. This
bustling scene had a strong appeal for a country boy looking for a
portal into showbiz, and it felt good being a loner where humanity
shuffled through these streets to escape a wife, boss, or some other
responsibility.

If Hank was less than attentive in school before, he was there in
body only now, and often not even that. He got through Baldwin and
began at Sidney Lanier High, but everyone seemed to know that he
would never see a cap and gown or diploma. His mates would more
often than not be guys his age who'd long dropped out of school,
who habituated at the honky-tonks. As he moved into higher gear
with his singing, even Lillie began to care less, the thought of which
excited her for the money he might make if she called the shots
for him. He had also begun to assimilate into the bar scene, his
road-weary "Kerouac" look masking his tender age. The hard-bitten
musicians he began to meet had no idea he was only fourteen. Neither was he the rube some might have taken him for. He had street
smarts. Indeed, it was no coincidence that when he began doing the
street minstrel thing in Montgomery, his beat was the sidewalk outside the Jefferson Davis Hotel.

There, up on the twelfth floor, was the studio of WSFA, the
call letters meant to promote the recently opened Montgomery
airport—the "South's Finest Airport." It was the town's first radio
station and one of four 1,000-watt stations in Alabama, and the only

one in Montgomery. The station had gone on the air in 1930 when Seth Gordon Persons, a man with big ambitions himself, partnered with a local businessman to lease the rights to the frequency. But it would soon become known as the place where Hank Williams became bankable.

Hank, however, was only now becoming aware of the emerging idiom, and cultural framework, he was stepping into. He'd never had much to listen to back where he'd been before, but now radios at home and around town made him aware of people like Jimmie Rodgers and Roy Acuff. And in that vein, he was writing fragments of songs that reflected the marketability of those two. For a teenager not particularly interested in learning in school what Franklin D. Roosevelt's New Deal was, it was impressive that the first tune he ever sang for a formal audience was not anything about goats and Fords but one with a very topical theme—"WPA Blues." That song likely reminded little Hank of his mother trying to find a job through the enormous federal agency that would put eight million lower-income Americans to work constructing buildings, roads, and bridges.

It was the kind of stuff that inspired blues metaphors, given the long hours and skimpy pay. In 1936, country blues slide guitarist Casey Bill Weldon had a decent hit with the first "WPA Blues." Billie McKenzie recorded "That Man on the W.P.A." And Big Bill Broonzy did a jazz stomp called "WPA Rag." Hank, who could assimilate what he heard on the radio, used as his melody Riley Puckett's "Dissatisfied" and employed some quite grown-up lyrics, apparently, though the only fragment that is known was recited by Lillie years later:

> I got a home in Montgomery, a place I like to stay
> But I have to work for the WPA, and I'm dissatisfied, I'm
>   dissatisfied

Sadly, Hank would never record the song, nor was it ever copyrighted. He began playing it in the street, as a sort-of Woody Guthrie workingman's blues. Using a trace of Puckett's yodel breaks, Hank soon had people coming back regularly at lunchtime just to hear it, requesting it over and over as the coins clanged into his hat. Stoked by the reaction, he hitched up his britches and when he was fourteen entered a talent show at the Empire Theatre, playing "WPA Blues." Lillie, who chaperoned him, would recall that he sang it as "a cry of despair" and that "most of the audience worked for the WPA at the time [and] they laughed and stormed. Hank got the $15 prize." She added that Hank "took the money and set up all his school friends," meaning spending it like a big shot, something she clearly bridled about, though she would not be able to hoard enough of his money to suit her. "He never stopped doing that," she said, her irritation palpable. "When Hank was in the chips, so were his friends, as long as the money held out."[4]

What Lillie was owed would become an ongoing bone of contention between mother and son, but in those early days, Hank was focused laserlike on conquest. After winning the Empire show, he boldly marched into the lobby of the Jefferson Davis Hotel and then upstairs to the WSFA office, where he said he'd won a contest and should have an audition. Liking his moxie, program director Caldwell Stewart told him to sing right there on the spot, and was impressed enough by what he heard to gave him a slot on a program hosted by local bandleader Dad Crysell. The first time he sang "WPA Blues" on the air, letters and calls came in asking for more of the kid. Stewart sometimes ran a microphone hookup from the street so he could catch the vibe of Hank's homey act, the strength of which was connecting at close range with people.

As with so many other aspects of the story, there are other claims about how Hank got on the air. Guitarist/singer Gordon Braxton Schuffert, seven years his senior and the host of WSFA's very popular 6–6:30 a.m. morning program, as well as a truck driver around town, told of making a stop at Lillie Williams' boardinghouse in Montgomery, where he spotted a "boy-sized" guitar. He picked it up and played a couple of songs, whereupon, he said, "I heard Miss Williams holler, 'Hiram, Brack's got you beat.'" He added: "And I did." Then, when he was on his way out the door, "I heard this voice that was just as strong and clear. It was a man's voice in a boy's body. Hank was only 14 at the time, but he could sure sing. Even then I knew he had a one-of-a-kind voice."[5]

Brack Schuffert invited the aspiring singer to accompany him on his truck route the next morning. "I told him we'd sing all day. That's all he needed to hear. He was for anything to do with music." He also had to listen, he said, to Hank not so subtly asking him if he could get his own show at the station. Not long after, Hank was a guest on Schuffert's show, which the latter insists was Hank's first time on the air. It would have been early in '38, but this was before stations preserved programs on tape and is impossible to corroborate. Similarly, it can only be assumed, given fleeting references in the literature, that, weeks later, the management gave him a fifteen-minute show of his own, twice weekly in late afternoon after school. If so, this was not as startling as it seems; the paucity of employment records went along with the fact that the station doled out these shows like candy to all manner of performers, probably with no contracts signed, hoping to fill airtime, usually for a week or two before the next singer or band took their place. There indeed was no contract signed, no hard terms of payment, no promise of long-term employment. Hank would be on one week, off the next, not anything close to a regular for another three years.

Still, it *was* startling that he had landed an actual gig at a big-city station at his age, which no one at the station realized was fourteen but with his baby face made for a marketable novelty. Stewart took to introducing him on air as "the Singing Kid." This was in part a goof, but Hank took it seriously. He was paid fifteen dollars per show, more than he'd ever seen at one time for singing, and every penny of it must have seemed like it was dropped from heaven.

• • •

Lillie Skipper Williams had developed a hard crust that helped her cope with the more hectic pace and competition for opportunities.

And, just as in Georgiana, people did talk about her boarding of men who came through town for one night, or perhaps shorter stays. By the Montgomery phase, the subject of just what she was running in her home seemed less of a secret. When the BBC produced a documentary about Hank fifty years later, it found a photo of Lillie in the middle of a group of very young and very winsome girls, with a sheepish but hardly uncomfortable Hank at around thirteen seated beneath her, his arms around the shoulders of two of the girls. It also found a jovial fellow named Lewis Fitzgerald, a cousin of Hank's, who had no compunction riffing, "Do you know what kinda house Lillie run? You only *think* you do. Yeah—call girls, prostitutes. All kinda girls were comin' in and out of the house all the time, some good looking, some not so good looking. Now, where she was getting all these girls I have no earthly idea." The same documentary gave equal time to a family friend who denied this was ever the case, saying, "I know this for a fact."[6]

There was, however, more to Lewis Fitzgerald than the BBC knew. Born in 1943, he was the son of Walter McNeil's daughter Marie, and Fitzgerald liked to tell people he just might have been Hank Williams's illegitimate son, meaning that Hank would have knocked up his own cousin. This kind of gossip seems to breed around Hank like fruit flies, and as if transfixed by the subject of Madam Lillie, the BBC put *another* source in its film, country singer Billy Walker, who claimed that Hank told him when he was thirteen that "he'd sing down at the end of the stairway in [the house], and these men would gather around and she'd come down and take 'em upstairs. He said it was just a come-on for the guys at the place where [Lillie] was doing her trade." Chet Flippo salaciously wrote that the goings-on at 114 South entailed "strange noises in the night, moans and groans and bed springs creaking [and] the sucking sound of wet, hot flesh sticking to and popping loose from . . . wet, hot flesh."[7]

If Hank was a teenage accomplice in the flesh trade, no one knew if he was a willing accomplice or instructed by Lillie. But even if he was so sickened by what he heard in the other rooms that he jammed his fingers into his ears during those hot, sticky nights, he had no choice but to obey her. And when Christmas came around in '37, Lillie, seeming to cater to her boy's musical whims, bought him a *real* guitar, a Gibson Sunburst, the body of which seemed to indeed burst in a gush of red, brown, and yellow. Of course, it's possible that Lillie changed her tune once she had come to see that Hank was proving his mettle as a performer and that her own upward climbing would be aided if she tied herself to her son's advancement. If so, she was prepared to move mountains for him.

WSFA promoted itself by sending out its on-air talent to perform in clubs and at barn and high school dances around town. When Hank began to make his first appearances, going out with Brack Schuffert, Lillie started calling around to see if she could get other bookings for him, and he soon had a pretty fair fan base. Wisely, Lillie didn't shoot for the moon; she booked him first back on his old turf, in the gym at Georgiana High School, then in Greenville at the Ritz Theatre, with Schuffert, who recalled it as "the first show Hank ever booked. After that we played in pretty much every theatre in Alabama and Florida. I'd like to say I helped him out, but I didn't give him that voice and I didn't teach him to write those songs. That's something you get from God."[8]

✶ PART TWO ✶

1938–1948

5

✷ ✷ ✷ ✷ ✷ ✷ ✷

"DON'T TELL MAMA"

Brack Schuffert not only played guitar for Hank; he played nanny, drinking mate, and tour guide on those gigs around Alabama. They also wrote some songs together, notably one Hank would copyright, called "Rockin' Chair Daddy." On many of these excursions, Irene Williams would accompany her brother as a sort of road manager, in charge of collecting whatever alms the promoters would turn over by way of compensation, and Irene would bring the loot home for Lillie to decide what cut to give Hank, the rest going into her bank account. Of course, in the big picture it was small change, but Hank's timing was perfect. As he was moving upward, so was the nature of the music he was singing.

The hillbilly, Texas swing, and bluegrass genres—geared around an acoustic guitar, a stand-up bass, a fiddle, and maybe a banjo or mandolin—were collecting new fans by the day. There was a new instrument, too: a modified guitar played while held on the lap had evolved from the Hawaiian technique to lend an "electric" feel to a song before the invention of the electric guitar. It would be further refined in the electric era, as a four-legged console table with foot pedals and a metal tone bar, and would become known by the '50s as the pedal steel guitar.

These were influences that shaped Hank's world far more than the father he thought of only now and then. Lon Williams had been holed up in the VA hospital in Alexandria, Louisiana, until January 1937, when he was sent to another facility in Gulfport, Mississippi. During his confinement there, little was heard from him, or of him. It was as if he had been wiped from the earth, a proposition Lillie didn't exactly discourage. Although Lon would recall that she brought Hank and Irene to visit him over Christmas in '37— apparently the only time she did so—she was still telling people around Montgomery, and especially men who had romantic ideas, that she was a widow; it would get back to Lon, who would say that "it was reported in some parts that I was dead."[1] Even his brother and sister seemed not to want to find out if he was dead or alive. During this time, Lon came to see Lillie as his nemesis, not his wife.

He later claimed that she had him permanently committed; in response, J. C. McNeil maintained that Lon "didn't particularly want to get out" and "would pull all kinds of tricks" to keep doctors from releasing him, like hiding under his bed so he wouldn't be found.[2] Lon also came to some conclusions about the disability money that Lillie had sent directly to her, thanks to Lister Hill; his understanding was that she had gotten a lump sum of "several thousand dollars," which belied what he said were claims made later on, after Hank died, that Lon was a deadbeat dad who hadn't provided for his children. "They talk about 'no support' from me," he said. "Where in hell was my money goin' to then?"[3] It did seem as though whatever it was that ailed him had by '38 healed or receded sufficiently for him to blow the joint, and soon enough he would, putting him and his wife, at least by law, on a collision course.

Meanwhile, the son Lon knew as Hiram was on the prowl in Montgomery, soaking up the clues and directives. Turning fifteen in 1938, he was rough around the edges and his voice not yet tamed. He still had his on-again, off-again radio show, mostly playing old folk

and cowboy tunes, not being bold enough to play any original compositions—which he had none of, anyway—but displaying a studied aw-shucks persona that always poured out of radios like syrup.
"Friends," he would purr, lowering his pubescent voice to sound like
Roy Acuff, "here's a song ah'd like to do for ya now." The station
let him read commercials between songs, too, and he seemed to be
able to play the pitchman for whatever store, barbershop, or bakery
bought time. With such a cachet, he was able to put together a band
as if *he* were the boss, which he believed he was, in all matters—
except when Lillie was around.

By the middle of the year, he had prevailed upon Brack Schuffert
to not only help form the band but be in it—though it was made
clear only Hank would sing lead vocals. Brack brought in his bass
player, Smith "Hezzy" Adair, a homeless eighteen-year-old orphan
whom Schuffert and his wife put up in their home. He had established a modest reputation as an adjunct comic foil on the country
circuit, with a tag line that went "Ready, Hezzy?" His shtick was
basically his rubbery face and Coke-bottle eyeglasses, with his hat
pushed back on his forehead, the sort of thing many country bands
liked to utilize as comic relief à la Gabby Hayes and Smiley Burnette
in the movies. Soon, another habitué of the town's country scene
joined up, fiddler Freddy Beach, who had played in swing bands and
also traveled as an evangelist in medicine shows for spare change.

It was a motley crew, to be sure, led by a kid barely old enough
to shave but a pro at drinking. Late in '38, the original foursome
of what would be a revolving-door lineup assembled in the parking
lot of the Jeff Davis for their first publicity picture, dressed not in
cowboy duds but more like boxcar hobos. Their collective name had
already been determined by Hank and Hank alone—the Driftin'
Cowboys, with a dropped *g*—but both Hank and Brack were able to
pitch the act on their radio shows. They went out to play wherever
they could, piling themselves and their instruments into Brack's old
Ford wagon. The only limit was that the gig had to be close enough
to get back to Montgomery, since a hotel stay would have eaten up

the profits. Hank also made sure to enter talent shows run by Dad Crysell in a hall on Commerce Street, which he usually won, pocketing a quick fifteen bucks. Along the way, Irene Williams, who continued as Lillie's proxy manager and money collector, was taken into the band as a female backing vocalist, which Hank thought would sweeten the repertoire of cowboy rags and love songs.

Hezzy soon moved in with Hank at the boardinghouse, and the two would usually spend their days knocking around. Hank, of course, was supposed to be in school, but, Schuffert said that "he skipped school a lot" and, telling the usual kind of apocryphal Hank Williams tale, that once he heard of Hank falling asleep in class. When another kid asked the teacher if he should wake him up, she said, "Naw, don't wake him up, he ain't gonna learn anything anyway."[4] Fable or not, for Hank school was a dreary, irrelevant chore. Sidney Lanier High School, named after the Civil War–era poet, was and still is a stately-looking place. The irony is that Hank is by far its most famous student—not to be confused with most famous *graduates*, a list that includes Zelda Fitzgerald and Packers quarterback Bart Starr, given that in the fall of '40, after starting tenth grade, he ended the charade and dropped out. If Lillie was aghast at such a turn, she didn't show it. But it wasn't as if he were just some nobody, after all. He was being heard on the radio, he had a band, he was bringing home the bacon.

Indeed, his real schooling was happening on the stage, and while he was still maintaining notebooks of his inner thoughts, from which he would begin writing songs, he was cautious about the band getting outside of its comfort zone to indulge his personal feelings. Mostly they played stock tunes, folk songs, and Roy Acuff ditties that Hank belatedly took to because of Acuff's highly emotive style, saying years later the Smoky Mountain Boy was "the biggest singer music ever knew."[5] Hank would throw in a song or two about a great and forgiving God, and there was some bantering between songs, Hank bouncing some well-worn comic put-downs off Hezzy.

The two of them were capable of getting gigs on their own,

billed as Hezzy and Hank, which was quickly flipped to Hank and Hezzy, as Hank's name sold most of the tickets, especially when they'd head to Hank's old breeding ground and play the Ga-Ana Theatre in Georgiana on Sunday nights. The Driftin' Cowboys were like any other band scratching and clawing for attention; they were always en route to or back from somewhere. Most of the venues were roadhouse dives reminiscent of the joint in the *Blues Brothers* movie, where if the people onstage were lucky there would indeed be chicken wire erected in front of the stage to protect performers from the audiences that paid to see them.

South Alabama was "dry" at the time, meaning that no alcohol could be served, at least by law, but this hardly put a dent in the wholesale smuggling of beer through the door, sometimes in bottles labeled as Coke. When those bottles began to fly, hurled by sloshed patrons, often the only defense for a singer or musician was one's own quick reflexes—or preferably, a song the crowd could get with.

On sawdust-, tobacco-juice-, and bottle-strewn hardwood floors, couples attempted to do early versions of line dancing that wound up more like sleepwalking and groping. Ralph J. Gleason, seeing these native tribal rites of the South years later, would write that the outside world called them "shit-kicker dances." Of the women, Gleason noted, "There were lots of those blondes you see at C&W affairs, the kind of hair that mother never had and nature never grew and the tight skirts that won't quit and the guys looking barbershop neat but still with a touch of dust on them."[6]

Hank at fifteen was no stranger to the dangers of life on the road. This was why he preferred to take a ride down to Georgiana and Greenville to play a nice, safe high school dance or a club where the folks knew him—his favorite venue being Thigpen's Log Cabin. The bandstand was in a converted skating pavilion walled off from the dining room. Here, where signs offered steak and chicken dinners, sandwiches of all kinds, gasoline and oil—the last two not on the menu but outside at a Sinclair gas station—Hank felt like family, but that was not enough to prevent fistfights from breaking out when besotted patrons heckled him and he heckled them back. After too many skirmishes for comfort, both inside and outside the honky-tonks, Hank obtained blackjacks (leather-wrapped billy clubs) and gave one to each band member, though when fights erupted during shows, his defense would first be his fists.

In one incident at a dance hall in Fort Deposit, when the band left the stage and was packing up, a guy for whatever reason came at him with a knife. Seeing the assailant, Hank brandished his Gibson Sunburst like a Louisville Slugger and smashed it on the guy's head, sending blood spurting and knocking him cold. For Hank, the hardest part of the incident was having to ask his mom for money to buy a new guitar. "I'm sorry, Mama," he later said he told her, "but it was either get the guitar broke or my head broke."

Because these almost vaudevillian scenes of crazed violence, which weren't funny at all when they happened, became so routine, a kind of seriocomic undercurrent would form around him as his career lengthened, with Hank helping to stoke the vibe with lines like "Durn it, I ruin't a perfectly good twenty-five-dollar instrument on that fella's head." Other tales had him using whatever else he could find as makeshift cudgels, such as a tire iron, the wooden stanchions of a pedal steel guitar, the steel bar with which it was played, and of course beer bottles broken over assorted heads.[7]

One more thread common to his escalating lifestyle of violence and mayhem was that Lillie Williams herself, right from the start, took to acting as her son's bodyguard, getting involved in physical confrontations when she came on the road with him that left grown men tasting their own blood and pleading for mercy. Again, much of this aromatic scent of hillbilly justice and mayhem may be just so much country corn pone stoked into legend. Yet to many who soldiered with Hank on the chitlin' circuit there seemed to be an assumption, for friend and foe alike: you might come after Hank for some real or perceived grudge, but you would never, ever, cross his mama. Because she'd make you pay, in blood and tears. The shadow Lillie cast over Hank clearly was getting longer every day, with the accompanying effect that both mother and son were growing more contemptuous of anyone outside their tight knot, even the band members Hank joined with. Like Hezzy, the other unmarried Cowboy, Freddy Beach, stayed at the boardinghouse, with Lillie, to their surprise, charging them rent—a minimal one, she assured them, and just perhaps with some fringe benefits available from the female "guests."

With Lillie having decided to accompany the band on their travels, she relieved Irene of the chore of collecting receipts, and she bought a Ford station wagon for their transport that she herself drove most of the time. When she was around, and soon that was almost always, the money for all of them was practically invisible. Hank could skim a few bucks for himself, but everyone else was paid at Lillie's whim. Her rationale was that she was spending money for their sake, buying clothes, feeding them at the house, and deducting from their pay what she swore was a nominal rent—twenty-one dollars a month, though she herself was paying only forty a month for the whole place—as well as paying for gas and car upkeep.

• • •

It's no wonder the first coterie of Driftin' Cowboys would soon begin to splinter, the limited rewards for driftin' with Hank not enough to make life with Lillie tolerable. By '39, Brack Schuffert and Freddy left, and Hezzy moved out of the boardinghouse, a breach of protocol that put him on Lillie's bad side. New members came through. An accordion player, Pee Wee Moultrie, was offered the job after appearing on a new country station in Montgomery, WCOV, where he would soon host a show five nights a week. Moultrie recalled that Hank and Hezzy, who were seeking talent wherever they could, happened to be in the studio of the rival station when Pee Wee was performing and made the offer to him and his fiddler "Mexican" Charlie Mays. As Mays recalled: "We moved our stuff into his mother's boardinghouse . . . on South Perry Street. It was just an old white frame, two-story house, one or two blocks off the main drag. Mizz

Williams gave us a room on the second floor. Hezzy lived someplace else. I doubt if Mizz Williams had over three or four people, regular boarders. She had some young girls going to college. Hank took an interest on one of 'em."[8]

Hezzy soon would go his own way, though the last straw for him may not have been Lillie's hectoring as much as Hank's unabated guzzling. Moultrie told of a tour the band did late in '39 through Alabama, Georgia, and northern Florida. At one gig with Hezzy Adair at the Ga-Ana Theatre, the manager handed Hank a bottle of peach brandy before the show, and he and Hezzy drained it. Onstage, both were a mess, unable to play the right notes; Hank lost his pick and tried to play, in vain, with his fingers while incoherently babbling to the audience in a slurred voice, leading many to walk out. Hezzy, looking blue, ran off the stage and puked his guts out in the wings. Disaster that it was, Moultrie was shocked that the owner of the joint "was laughing his head off." Evidently believing it was all part of the act, "he said it was the funniest thing he'd ever seen."[9]

· · ·

By the 1940s, gigs cropped up for Hank in some strange ways. When the rodeo came to Montgomery, its star attraction, a cowboy performer named Jack Wolf, who went by the stage name Juan Lobo, heard Hank at a club and invited him, quite literally, to join the rodeo, singing between bull roping and bullwhip slinging (Lobo's specialty was knocking a cigarette from a man's mouth from fifty feet away). It went so well and the pay was so good that Hank—without telling the band—stayed with the rodeo, going with it through Texas and into Mexico. Stories would be told, emanating from Hank, that "Hank Williams the Singing Cowboy" actually did some bronco ridin'. Some of the stories mentioned that he didn't come out of the chute until he had knocked back enough corn whiskey that he didn't know what he was about to do. Given his frailty and bad back, this seems risible. Indeed, when Hank sent letters from the road to his mother, they dealt not with rodeo exploits but with money, or lack thereof, a subject Lillie always complained about in her own letters to him. In one, sent on the rodeo's stationery from Handley, Texas, on November 18, 1940, he wrote:

> Mother, the reason that Jack has not sent you any money is because he just bought $600 worth of cowboy suits and boots for all of us. . . . I just signed a contract to advertise the Rodeo over the air for them [that] will mean $50 a week for me, and I will send you money. . . . I all so sent you a letter with a $5 bill in it, did you get this orc not. . . . I will be back in 7 months with a real band and pleanty of money. . . . Love, Hank.[10]

Some of his remarks in the letter were pointed. He said he was so happy to be in Texas—or, one can construe, away from Lillie, Alabama, or both—and declared, "This is the greates [sic] country in the world, Texas." Only reluctantly did he return to Alabama, Lillie later saying he did so after being thrown from a horse in the rodeo, exacerbating his back woes. But he was always uneasy having to stay put, often talking of going back to the rodeo in Mexico; he'd even set out on the road, only to run out of money before crossing the border, and either hitchhike to Montgomery or call Lillie and beg her to wire some cash for a train ride home. In some of the literature it is said that Lillie persuaded him—after he came home from touring—to go back to school and take bookkeeping courses at Draughons Junior College in Montgomery. If she did, the idea of Hank as a bookkeeper even then must have been preposterous, and he was done with it soon after.

Sometimes he would go on the road only with Irene. Another time, in 1939, he took Moultrie and Mays for a short run he did on the radio in Huntsville, keeping it from the powers that be at WSFA, something he also did when he was given an early morning show of his own on WALA in Mobile, meaning that for a brief time this sixteen-year-old kid had two radio shows. Thinking he might stay there a while, he wrote to Lillie asking her to send a "big picture of myself" and a book of popular songs from which he broadened his repertoire, only to be sacked from the station when he came in drunk. Yet another time that year he went alone to perform on a show hosted by Pappy Neal McCormick and his band the Hawaiian Troubadours on WCOA, a high-powered station located in the San Carlos Hotel in Pensacola, Florida. Joining up with this band for outside gigs as well, Hank, who had never sung with steel guitars and loved the effect, seemed contented in Florida; in a photo of him from that interim, he posed for a snuggly picture with Pappy's pretty teenage daughter, Juanealya, her forehead pressed against his cheek. He was able to camp out in Mobile; luckily, his uncle Bob Skipper had a flat there, and he slept on his couch. But this gig also ended, sending him reluctantly back to Montgomery, and back on the air at WSFA.

Despite a rolling-stone existence, he was making strides. When the *Grand Ole Opry*'s own road show rolled through town, he and the ever-changing Driftin' Cowboys were on the same bill as Roy Acuff, which is probably when Hank met the *Opry*'s biggest star, though Acuff would say that he had met Hank in '39 while he was with Pappy McCormick's unit. Seeing Hank sloshed onstage, Acuff told him after the show that night, "You got a million-dollar voice and a ten-cent brain."[11] As Pee Wee Moultrie told it, however, Roy may have been pissed off because Hank made him look bad, given that "We usually got a better response than his *Opry* folks." As for those early meetings, Acuff said:

I guess in a way he idolized me as a country artist. He'd usually come by my dressing room, sit around, sing songs and play the guitar. He was just a little fellow, and he just hunkered around in the corner, waiting for a chance to sing. He'd sing some of my songs and sometimes one of his.[12]

He noted that Hank "didn't try to copy anybody much," adding, "I guess he copied me more than anybody, but he was developing a style of his own."[13] As Boots Harris recalled, while Hank had the ability to hold an audience's attention drunk or sober, by 1940 and at only the age of seventeen, "Hank's drinking problem was getting worse." That boded ill for everyone, most of all the musicians, since as Harris, a steel guitar player who arrived in 1940, said, "All we were getting was three meals a day and most of the money was going to Hank's mother."

By 1941, the original Cowboys had scattered to the Alabama wind. In addition to Moultrie and Mays, a new edition now also included a thirteen-year-old steel guitar player, James Porter, and bass man and comic foil Shorty Seals, who came from Pappy McCormick's band and would willingly play the village idiot role, complete with blackened teeth. Lillie, of course, couldn't have cared less who the supporting players were, and often didn't know their names, nor one from the other; to her, and more and more so to her son, they were disposable parts. Anything but the unseen force behind Hank, she sucked up every ounce of oxygen in any room she was in, not a nanny as much as a drill sergeant, never letting the band drift far from the objective that she had in mind for them, and the enrichment it would bring her. Through her son, wrote Paul Hemphill, Lillie had "found her destiny."[14] It certainly had to bring her a feeling of exhilaration that *everyone* was scared to death of her. She would have done something she rarely did—smile—if she knew that whenever Hank could sneak a drink behind her back or even pocket a few dollars and keep it from her clutches, he would tell whoever he was with the same thing, to the point of it being a mantra:

"Don't tell Mama."

• • •

While Lillie may have wished, or even taken steps, to keep him confined and forgotten, the husband and father no one ever spoke of turned the tables when, over the Christmas holiday back in 1938, Lon Williams was able to check out of the VA hospital in Gulfport. Lillie had pressed to keep him there; she had even said everyone in

Lon's natural family was dead, forcing him to have his brother Mack come to the hospital with affidavits that he was indeed his brother as a requirement for release.[15] Lon then headed home—at least to what he *thought* was home, in Georgiana, where he believed Lillie and the kids still lived. When he got there and found that they had moved, he asked around and was dumbfounded when people began doing double takes, having been told by Lillie that her husband had died years ago.

With nowhere to go, he checked back into the hospital, but when he was able to locate the brood he again split and showed up at the boardinghouse in Montgomery during the holidays. In spite of Lillie spreading the lie that he was dead, he never had even thought about divorcing. And so he dropped by her home unannounced, seeking to resume the marriage and fatherhood. However, he was disabused of *that* plan straightaway. Tales were told that he found her in bed with a man and trailed away, not saying a word, his plans crushed. However, Lon did spend some time with Hank, and later said that, to his dismay, he found his son "in a drinkin' place," stewed on beer, and that "I done my best to talk to him." It seems that Hank had no use for a father that day, other than putting the screws on him to buy him more drinks. As Lon recalled, with pride, "I never did buy him whiskey."[16]

Those old notebooks full of deep feelings about being abandoned were forgotten now. Lon, it seemed, was a closed book to his own family, and so he returned to Gulfport, then checked out for good, going back to McWilliams to live, not needing to find work after he convinced the VA to send him his full disability checks, ending Lillie's gravy train. Their marriage was over, but officially in a state of limbo; on the 1940 census, Lillie is listed as being "single," while Lon said he was "separated."

With Hank's money augmenting her rent collections, Lillie moved her family and her boarding business to a larger house at 236 Catoma Street in '41, advantageously for Hank closer to the downtown clubs clustered near the Alabama River. Still the optimist, Lon would periodically drop by there for brief visits with his children and then be gone, though as Hank would bridle ever more about Lillie, he would be in the mind to seek out his father, if only to remind himself of those songs stored up in his head from childhood memories.

In that 1940 census, as well, Lillie told the taker her son's name was Hiram, a name that would never *legally* be changed. But if "Hank Williams" was making a name for himself, his future was not going to thrive unless he could move beyond the radio signal and honky-tonks of Montgomery, the blood buckets of Georgiana, and the cow manure of the rodeo in Texas and Mexico. The problem was, as good as he was, the gathering clouds of war in Europe and a mood of impending uncertainty about America's role in global war stopped him in his tracks.

6

✶ ✶ ✶ ✶ ✶ ✶ ✶

DRYDOCK

Hank Williams, never again to be called Hiram, at age eighteen was six feet tall, still skinny as a swizzle stick in 1941 but able to buy department store clothes that didn't hang off him like ripped burlap. His face had filled in, too, and even when he wore his specs he had a mature, square-jawed look. In a modern looking glass, he resembled a cross between the squinty-eyed George W. Bush and the unworried Alfred E. Neuman. He had not only the vague look of a boozehound, his jaw grinding and his face puffy, but also the temperament. Offstage especially, he was short-tempered and sometimes incoherent. However, he oozed charm and sensitivity when singing, cultivating a seemingly carefree macho preening and pelvic-thrusting, hip-swiveling moves that were only tempered by the vulnerability in his voice, and it was no shock that he was so endearing to the ladies. Knowing the seductive power he had, he had no compunction pushing it to the limit. One reason he got into so many fights in the honky-tonks was that when a sweet thing came waltzing through the door, Hank disregarded the man whose arm she was on.

He would amble up to her and begin his sweet-talkin' while the man next to her, in many cases her husband, began to boil, with chairs and tables soon being overturned and people running for cover, though not Hank, who would be prepared by having one of those steel guitar bars on him. Apparently, when the dust cleared, he notched more than one bedpost having stolen away a woman from another man, causing who knows how many marriages or other relationships to crumble. That was a consequence he could not have cared less about. If Hank Williams was a gambler, he was not one to fold his cards or run from the table. Indeed, he was delighted when his bandmates began to describe him in light of this sort of encounters as a "go-getter," as in he would go after anybody's gal.

Stories about him and painted-up city women got back to Lillie, to her horror. She dreaded the thought of any woman taking him away from her. "I must admit I was a little jealous at times," she once said, hastening to add, unconvincingly, "Not really, I'm joking," before reiterating, "Hank's mother was always his first girl, and he never forgot it. He was always as sweet and kind to me as anybody could be. He wrote many 'mother songs' to me. One was 'Last Night I Heard You Crying In Your Sleep.' "[1] This might have been wishful thinking on her part, given that the song seems alternately needy and snarky, with the kiss-off to a lover, "You know that you are free to go dear. I know that I can never make you happy."

Still, he would indeed find room for "mother songs," and was probably writing personal tunes of that kind in his late teens that were far more polished and personal than "WPA Blues." These include some that were never published or recorded, such as "Back Ache Blues" (apparently a different song than blues pioneer Bo Carter's identically titled 1920s classic, though no lyrics have survived and it was never recorded) and "My Mommy"—and others that were, such as amazingly foreboding numbers for a teenager like "I Don't Care (If Tomorrow Never Comes)," "Never Again (Will I Knock on Your Door)," and "Six More Miles." Clearly, he had no trouble following the trend set by Jimmie Rodgers that painted highly depressing themes—another genetic trait of the blues—to simple, catchy melodies; indeed, "Miles" was a flagrant cop of the Carter Family's "Will the Circle Be Unbroken," a fugue about a man witnessing his mother's casket being carted away by the undertaker, singing, "Lord how I hate to see her go" even though "there's a better home a-waitin'."

By the early 1940s, Hank would run the songs he would sing on his radio show by the bosses at WSFA. But when he would sing them a few bars of his own tunes, he invariably was told, "Not good enough, boy."[2] Perhaps that held him back from believing too much in his own writing ability. So he sat on them, frustrated that all the work he'd put into his career was never going to pay more than pocket money. Lillie, who could always earn him a few bucks booking him into some honky-tonk or another, could sense his frustration that he had no bites from a legitimate record company. But the thing Lillie should have indeed cried about was her son's escalating alcohol dependency, which success, or lack of it, seemed to have little to do with. Whether in a good or foul mood, he had to drink. Any time of the day.

Boots Harris, who was seventeen when he migrated in 1940 from Opp, Alabama, where he'd been in a hillbilly act with his brothers, first heard Hank on the radio. He tracked him down to the boardinghouse and found him sprawled out on a couch in the parlor. Introducing himself, he began to strum his guitar, and the two broke into song. Liking what he heard, Hank took him down the street to a restaurant where whiskey was always served. It seemed Hank only wanted one thing from Harris. "Have you got enough for a half-pint?" he asked. Recalled Harris: "I didn't drink at all then . . . but thirty minutes [after meeting him] I bought him a half-pint of whiskey."[3]

But in so doing he passed Hank's version of a Driftin' Cowboys audition, which entailed demonstrating obeisance and an open pocket as much as musical ability. Which also meant he received the privilege of being ripped off by Lillie. He was paid like everyone else in the group, $21.50 a week—or as Hank used to say, "twenty-one hamburgers and fifty cents," which left them all of fifty cents when the rent was paid. What is remarkable is that this was not much more than Hank himself was pocketing once Lillie counted up all the receipts and made her deductions. Usually they had enough in their pockets to drink it away in one shot and wonder if putting up with a drunk and a harpy was worth it.

. . .

Like the pop stars, country music stars kept moving ahead during World War II. The awful singing-cowboys movies were still money-makers. In 1940, Roy Acuff, sniffing that movie money, went with his band to Hollywood, where they appeared in the motion picture *Grand Ole Opry*. Acuff's success led to an inevitable falling-out with the penurious lords at the *Grand Ole Opry* who refused to pay him like a star and terminated his contract. But it hardly slowed his roll. In 1942, Acuff and an Indiana-born, Tin Pan Alley–bred country music songwriter named Fred Rose, who hit the jackpot with "Back in the Saddle Again," would join in Nashville to create Acuff-Rose Music, a publishing company for fellow niche songwriters who they believed had been ripped off for years by the cartel of New York publishers.

It would take a while for Acuff-Rose to lift the boot Tin Pan Alley had on country's neck, but both men had considerable weight in the industry, and a widening pool of young talent to cast their net over. One of the most promising was the sharecropper's son and former beer truck driver from Crisp, Texas, whose songs Hank was already singing. This was Ernest Dale Tubb, who so revered Jimmie Rodgers that when the latter died the teenager wrote to Rodgers's widow for an autographed photo of the Brakeman. Continuing the correspondence, she grew fond of the young man and arranged with RCA to sign him to a contract. His first offerings did little, but Ernest Tubb would be around for a very long run.

Country's future boy king, meanwhile, mired in Montgomery, seemed primed for anything but a long run. Hank, his back as wretched as it was, gained a 4-F deferment. He would not have to fight for his country but was able to sing in the war zone known as the country-western circuit. He continued going out on the road with the latest edition of the Driftin' Cowboys as the ranks of civilian men thinned out in the honky-tonks, not that the ones still at

home were much better behaved. Driftin' Cowboy Sammy Pruett recalled of one altercation that Hank was "beatin' the guy on
the temple with the bar when another local guy, coming to Hank's
assistance, almost cut the first guy in two. He had to hold his guts
in. They took Hank into court the next day, but the judge let him
off." Hank himself may have been referring to this episode when he
told of "poundin'" a guy "on the head with the steel bar, and he was
"about to go under. One more good blow woulda done it. But he
reached out and bit a plug outta my eyebrow, hair and all."[4]

Other anecdotes had him in possession of a tire iron in the parking lot outside a dive bar, leaving a man, according to Roger Williams, that "wound up in critical condition," whereupon the local
authorities "were determined to try Hank for murder if he died. Fortunately, the man lived, and Hank was able to wheedle his way out
of a sticky situation."[5] But if his life never became manicured, his
work did. While he could sneak one of his tearjerkers into his usual
lineup of cowboy rags and blues covers, he knew a depressed cowboy with antiheroic angst was not what an America at war needed
to hear. And so on the air he sang upbeat, schmaltzy Roy Acuff
ditties and don't-leave-me-dear ballads. By this time, Hank's voice
was wrapped in unnaturally high keys, the only backup instruments
a steel guitar and bass played respectively by new Driftin' Cowboys
Boots Harris and bass man Herbert "Lum" York.

Only one song in his radio and stage repertoire was written by
Hank, and it would be the only one of them he would record: "I'm
Not Coming Home Anymore," a song of mixed messages. Sung
in a mournful wail, it begins with a letter explaining why he isn't
coming home, seeming to decry a straying wife in the third verse
for ruining "a happy home" by going "astray." However, he ends the
verse as if *he's* the one who split, taking the blame by saying he'd
"much rather be dead" and lamenting that "the baby I will miss him
so." Perhaps this schizoid nature was his way of blaming *both* his
parents for his alienation, though whom he blamed more for going
astray was his secret.

. . .

A storied career never seemed as far away for him as it did in the early war years, during which Hank, apparently feeling guilt that healthier men were taking his place in combat, decided he had to serve his country, on the home front. In August 1942, WSFA fired him for showing up for his show drunk once too often. Having been courted by the other country station in town, WCOV, which had hit the air in 1938, he signed on there in the same early morning slot. However, after only a couple of months, Hank soured. Many of his favored backing musicians were drafted or enlisted, leaving him in limbo, and he felt he was stagnating and making only chump change. Dispirited, he said to Lillie, "You can't eat fan letters, Mama, not even with ketchup on 'em."[6] So in November he packed a grip and, barely stopping to say goodbye to Lillie, set out for Mobile and the shipyards. As Lillie wrote in her memoirs, Hank "gave up all hopes of ever making the big-time as a singer and went down to Mobile."[7] Once there, he roomed with his uncle Bob Skipper, who had relocated to work in the yards himself.

Hank was hired as a welder by the Alabama Dry Dock and Shipbuilding Company, working close by the naval base where his granddaddy had been sent by the Union Army during the Civil War. He tried to grit it out, the pain in his back nearly doubling him over, and lived for when the five o'clock whistle blew and he could go to the bars where sailors and fleetworkers congregated and get up and sing a few songs for enough spare cash to numb himself with more liquor. He also apparently tried to restart his radio career at WALA, but the bosses pointed him to the door.

In the summer of 1944, he saw an ad by the Kaiser Shipbuilding Corporation in Portland, Oregon offering drydock jobs, free training and lodging, and a free railroad ticket to get there. And so he hopped the train for the long, long journey westward.[8] According to a steel guitarist buddy of Hank's named Millard "M. C." Jarrett, he and Hank, along with two other guys from the shipyards he had played music with, bassist Bill Brown and sax man Leo Hudson, caught that train to Portland together. Jarrett recalled that "it was a good deal there. They paid you, and you had a place to stay and a dining hall where you could eat three meals a day and drink beer. We'd play and sing for loose change from the shipyard workers sitting out on the grass."[9] He, Jarrett, Brown, and Hudson jammed at a company bar, singing one song—"Over the Waves"—because it was the only song that the bartender, who played fiddle, knew.

However, manual labor was hell on his back, and after just two weeks of self-medicating with booze he either left of his own volition or was canned, leaving him without a penny to get back home. Jarrett remembered Hank, homeless and sleeping on the floors of honky-tonk bars, bumming cigarettes and feeding on table scraps. "Then he called his mama and said, 'I need some money; I'm coming home.' Hank just wasn't born to do work like that." Lillie wired him enough for the five-day return trip to Montgomery.

Lillie's own version omitted any mention of Portland and said she had gone to Mobile and brought him back. Either way, when he arrived at the boardinghouse, his cousin Marie said she was stunned by how he looked. "He was near dead, starving," she would recall. "I sat down at the kitchen table and I fed him myself. He was shaking so he couldn't get a fork in his mouth."[10] Lillie then took charge of rekindling his career. "I believed in Hank . . . ," she wrote later, "so I rented a car and went to every schoolhouse in the Montgomery area. I booked Hank solid for sixty days. . . . When Hank saw the datebook for those shows, he gave me the sweetest smile I've ever seen [and said,] "Thank God, Mother, you've made me the happiest boy in the world."[11]

• • •

Lillie wanted him nowhere else but Montgomery, where she could continue booking appearances for him and taking a cut of the profits. She had also taken something else, another husband, a guitar player and sometime Driftin' Cowboy named "Indian Joe" Hatcher, whose real name was much better—Homer C. Hatchett. How and why they decided to get hitched is a mystery, but to be able to do it she agreed to divorce Lon, the decree signed on July 1, 1942. Lon, too, had found a new mate, a young woman named Ola Till, whom he married on September 12, becoming a father again when she gave birth to a daughter, Leila, shortly after, a half sister that Hank would barely know. Lillie wasted no time herself, marrying Indian Joe a week after the divorce, with Hank away in Mobile.

However, tragedy struck when Hatcher's appendix ruptured. Not seeing the need to get him to a hospital, Lillie tended to him herself, feeding him homemade preparations to flush out his system, but the rupture worsened, and he developed a terrible fever and died within a few days. Lillie didn't mourn, or stay a widow for long, though. She took a liking to another young man she was boarding, a well-built, blond-haired army soldier named James C. Bozard, who evidently comforted her well in his room. In September, the same month Lon remarried, so did Lillie, again. Bozard, who may have been on leave when he married and then gone back on active duty, was a fleeting presence. He can be seen in uniform in a photo taken around 1944 with Lillie on a Montgomery street beneath a sign reading MCDONOUGH CHEVROLET CO, TRUCK SERVICE, ENTRANCE AROUND CORNER, perhaps helping Lillie buy an automobile,[12] but the marriage ended on May 1, 1946, by which time she had found yet *another* new man to marry.

Lillie may also have had a hand in getting Hank his job back at WSFA, in the accustomed early morning slot. Hank had to promise to keep his drinking under control, a promise he had no desire to keep, and in return the station bosses let him broadcast from the Fort Dixie Graves Armory, where the Alabama National Guard bivouacked and where his voice would reverberate off the walls. The Driftin' Cowboys were, during and right after the war, mainly whoever he could rustle up. One of those, Boots Harris, an on-and-off member of the band, usually wound up quitting. Harris would recall, "I told him, 'If you keep drinkin' ain't nobody in the business gonna pay us no attention.'"[13]

The band would eventually be culled from among a cast that included Lum York, guitarists Paul Compton, Sammy Pruett, Jimmy Porter, and Indian Joe Hatcher (before his unfortunate demise while Lillie's patient); steel guitarist M. C. Jarrett; rhythm guitarists Paul Dennis, Daniel Jack "Beanpole" Boling, and Zeke Crittenden; guitarist/fiddler/mandolin player Allen Dunkin; guitarist/dobro player Charlie Hill; pianist/drummer/guitarist/banjo player "Wimpy" Jones; and bassists Rufus "Puddin" Taylor and Jimmy Wilkinson. Steel guitarist Don "Shag" Helms, who would join in '44, as a seventeen-year-old, and become the most consistently identifiable element of Hank's records besides the voice itself, remembered the mandatory ritual all new Driftin' Cowboys went through. "He took us to a hock shop and he'd say, 'Hey, Jake, you got any more of those blackjacks back there?' 'Yeah.' And he'd say, 'Gimme five of 'em.' He'd tell us, 'Boys, if you're gonna play with me by God, you're gonna need these.'"[14]

Hank was taking no chances. He would travel with a Colt .35 inside his guitar case. Fortunately, at least from what is known, he never had to use it, not that he never took it out of the case for effect when a jealous swain came at him. Sometimes, said York, he'd keep the case onstage during a set, the lid open to block the audience from seeing the piece, which was locked and loaded if needed. Again, only through the grace of God, it seems, did he not pull the trigger in anger.

Unlike most stage mothers, Lillie did not advise her son to turn the other cheek. If anything, she was even more primed for battle. She never failed to aggravate and even frighten the men of the band as much as she did promoters who thought they could hold back on the receipts until they had to do some explaining to her. Irene now served as the booking agent for the outfit, but Lillie trusted no one but herself with collecting ticket receipts, personally. Things were still rough out there, in places where, Don Helms said, "they swept up the eyeballs every morning."[15] Charlie Mays was said to have been taken to a hospital for stitches after someone broke a bottle over his head in another melee in Fort Deposit. And the story is told that Lillie herself, wading into a fight to save Hank's hide, was flattened by a punch, then got up and performed some surgery of her own with a broken bottle on the man who sent her down. That was one time when Hank could be happy she was around, but there were others, too, explaining why he once said, "There ain't nobody in this here world that I'd rather have standin' next to me in a beer joint brawl than my maw with a broken bottle in her hand."[16]

"She was somethin' else," Driftin' Cowboy Joe Pennington said years later, "but she thought a heap o' Hank. Yeah, she really thought a heap o' Hank."[17] For all her sense of backwoods smarts, however, Lillie's maternal instinct and inherent trust that he would follow her orders led to her conning herself into believing that she could prevent Hank from drinking. She would later tell an interviewer that "we were going down to Georgiana and some of the boys kept asking him to drink and he would never drink when I was along. But he said, 'Mother, I think I'll take a drink.' I said 'No, you wait til the show is over and then get you a bottle and then carry it home with you.' He said, 'No, I'm not going home anymore. If I can't have it now I'm not going home anymore.'"[18]

Lillie knew an empty threat when she heard one. She would parry an ultimatum like that with a hard stare and a clenching of the fist and a punch to the shoulder, or a crisp slap to the face. Stories are told about how Lillie would hear Hank on the radio slurring his words—something he trained himself not to do, with remarkable success—march down to the Jeff Davis Hotel, wait until the show was over, then pull him by the ear or the hair out of the building and not let go until they were back home on Catoma Street. It became a running joke what Lillie would do next—and how Hank would devise ways to hide his drinking from her. The Driftin' Cowboys would be sworn to silence, lest they be fired. And so they would grit their teeth and watch him drink himself silly in the shadows. Some of them would drop hints that he was walking a perilous line, the most direct being Don Helms, who would warn him he'd be nothing if he didn't stop. It was wasted breath.

7

* * * * * * *

"AUDREY, GET ME A BOTTLE"

Despite the gradual changes in the landscape and culture of the South, Hank Williams seemed stuck in Alabama mud during the long, cold years of the war. His auditions and acetates had gotten him nowhere close to Nashville, and with gigs at clubs running dry—club owners not able to keep the lights on during blackouts—Hank had to stop dreaming about Nashville and instead lower his sights. In 1943, he took a job playing in a medicine show, requiring him to sing from the back of an old house trailer, then wade into the crowd to sell snake-oil miracle cures. This was a laughable waste of his talent. Yet it would be during this phase that he found the best—and worst—thing that ever happened to him, both in the same person.

Her name was Audrey Mae Sheppard Guy, a tall, striking, and married woman and mom, with curly blond hair, high cheekbones, and an aquiline nose, who if not knockout beautiful had a sort of distant, smoky, heavy-lidded Marlene Dietrich sultriness, though some would have just called her cold. When they met on a late summer day in '43, it began a chemical process not unlike the one scientists were working on in the secret Manhattan Project. Indeed, the atomic bombs that ended the war were only slightly more powerful and toxic than the relationship that began when the medicine show rolled into Banks, a rural speck on the map in Pike County, in south-eastern Alabama—its population of around 250 able to be fit into a midsized Montgomery nightclub.

Seven months older than Hank, she had grown up and still lived there, brought up on a farm owned by her parents, Shelton and Artie Mae Sheppard. Like Hank, she sang as a child, to guitar played by her granddaddy, but unlike him, she was uncommonly strong and athletic, once the star of her high school basketball team, and could dance up a storm. She may also have been psychic, at least so she thought, claiming she'd had a premonition of her brother's death, which came true when he was ten, she thirteen, and he caught pneumonia, unable to be saved.[1]

Audrey seemed to like letting her hair down once in a while. In 1940, when she was eighteen and still in high school, she eloped with a man named James Erskine Guy. They moved to Gadsden, up near Birmingham, but only until he got her pregnant, whereupon he up and disappeared, never to speak again with Audrey, or at all with the daughter he sired, Lycrecia Guy, born on August 13, 1941. Audrey moved with the child back to Banks, and while legally married hardly acted it, again hitting the honky-tonks seeking company and a man with some money to take care of her. She was no floozy; her father had bought her a new Oldsmobile to get around town in, and she had a good job as a clerk in a drugstore in Brundige.

That hot summer day in Banks, she and her aunt Ethel had driven to the medicine show and parked the Oldsmobile near the stage. Hank was singing at the time, and when he climbed down from the trailer to sell some snake oil, he came upon them in the car. As Audrey recalled, Hank went into his sales pitch. "He had a bottle of herbs and said, 'Ma'am, don't you think you need . . .' He just kind of glanced and looked back, did a doubletake, and said, 'No, ma'am, I don't believe you do.'"[2] It was corn, but tasty corn, doused in butter. Audrey, who liked to present herself as a lady, might normally have dismissed a seeming backwoods huckster as too crude, but she was taken with him, sensing that his aw-shucks humility was part of a front of clever charm by a man slicker than he let on. Indeed, he had more than a few notches on his cowboy belt. But the way he looked at the magnetic blonde, he didn't just have a roll in the hay on his mind. He wondered if this was what love at first sight meant.

Both seemed to know it would not end there. Aunt Ethel, seeing the chemistry ignite, helpfully asked the skinny young man if he wanted to go clubbing with them that night in Troy. Now, *that* was an offer he couldn't refuse. Wrote Audrey: "We had fun that night." Hank then asked her if she could pick him up the following day. She did, though when she saw him she was shocked that he was unshaven, barefooted, rumpled, and stinking of booze. Still, she waited while he cleaned up, then drove him around, getting him coffee and tomato juice from the general stores. During the ride he told her his life story, about his music, about how he'd been fired from the radio because "I drank too much." He also, mysteriously, wanted to tell her something else, "But I can't now." She had to admit to herself that she was intrigued by this troubadour tramp, but not half as much as when he blurted out, "I know you're gonna think I'm crazy, but will you meet me in Troy tomorrow and marry me?"

He was right; she *did* think he was crazy.

It didn't happen quite that soon, but neither did Audrey run for the hills before he could ask again. They would spend almost every minute he was offstage together, during which Audrey tried to get one thing straight: he would have to stop drinking if he wanted her to be his wife someday. It was an easy promise for him to make, as opposed to fulfill, which he had no intention of doing. All he needed to do was stay sober for a few days, wear down her resistance, then do what he always did when Lillie was around, sneak a shot here and there out of sight. There were times when he even went a week staying dry, and even when he had the inevitable backslide, another promise would keep her mollified.

He would sing to her, melting her, making the oddball qualities vanish. Hank was a complicated man, surely trouble, but the way he looked at her with those brown basset-hound eyes, she could tell he needed someone to keep him straight or he'd never get far. Musing to her aunt, she already saw some kind of partnership, telling her, "This guy will be number one of the *Grand Ole Opry* one of these days." She recalled: "I had that feeling very strongly. . . . That's how strongly I believed in Hank. He was lucky with a God-given talent, and I was lucky with a few brains."[3] It seems not coincidental at all that Audrey was as steely as his mother, which is to say he was a little afraid of her but believed he needed her for all those reasons. Perhaps there was some sort of carryover Oedipal mechanism at work. And, of course, she had some undeniable attributes. As Chet Flippo put it, she was "built like a brick shithouse and fucked like a snake." Just thinking about her one day on a bus, Flippo extrapolated, "he got a hard-on right there . . . and took off his hat and put it on his lap [knowing that] he'd be dipping into Audrey's soft flesh in another two hours [and then] stroked himself under his hat and thought of Audrey."[4] Hank, indeed, may have gotten himself *prepared* for her. They surely burned up a lot of beds, and for Hank, it was more than sex; it was proof that he could feel loved by a woman he desperately *wanted* to be loved by.

For Audrey, there may well have been a rush of a different kind. She knew how to use her sexuality to get what she wanted, which, against all logic and opinion besides her own, was to be a singing star herself. He knew better; hers was a voice with neither melody nor range, flat notes spilling from her mouth like an excess of rainwater. Yet that desire to be Hank's Dale Evans, and the control it represented, was her goal, and for that there was precedent.

Women were making inroads in country. There were the two Carter Family women but also the Girls of the Golden West, whose songs reflected one theme: to be the mate of a handsome cowboy. Indeed, the million-selling record that made a star of Patsy Montana, née Ruby Rose Blevin, an Arkansas-born thrush who took her name from a famous rodeo roper, Monte Montana, was "I Want to Be a Cowboy's Sweetheart" in 1935. Another was Ellen Muriel

Deason, a perky, dark-haired Nashville singer. In 1937, at age eighteen, she married aspiring country singer Johnnie Wright and began
touring with Wright's Tennessee Mountain Boys, with Muriel—now
renamed Kitty Wells—the headliner, en route to inordinate fame as
the "Queen of Country Music."

Sheppard seemed to be just that ambitious. But if she was to
become the wife of a singer, of anybody, there was business to do.
Just days after the medicine show she initiated a divorce from James
Erskine Guy, but the rub was that he had enlisted in the army. Under
the law, a divorce could not be granted a woman whose husband was
overseas during the war. And so she waited for Guy to return home,
as did Hank, who with her encouragement now took whatever gig he
could. In fact, he lived constantly on the road, Audrey by his side,
renting a trailer for them to live in. He was able to line up a steady
appearance on Monday, Wednesday, and Saturday nights at the Riverside Club, a dance hall in Andalusia, and filled in the week with
gigs in a honky-tonk in Opp. Seeing him perform up close, not to
mention the reaction he would get from the crowd, convinced her
that Hank was on a path to the stars, and she told him so.

She was right, too. When the fiddler and bandleader Pee Wee
King made an appearance in Dothan, Alabama, in '44 he crossed
paths with Hank, who had been told by a member of King's troupe
that Pee Wee was looking for a patriotic number. And so Hank
wrote one, proving he was no ordinary songwriter. With the drums
of war beating in Europe and the South Pacific, he came up with a
seminal folk song about war, "(I'm Prayin' for the Day That) Peace
Will Come," pining for the day "when the black clouds roll away and
the skies are bright and gay / And the guns are silent once more, /
And the bombs no longer fly from the planes up in the sky." It closely
channeled "We'll Meet Again" and "(There'll Be Bluebirds Over)
The White Cliffs of Dover," the sentimental wartime songs sung
by British thrush Vera Lynn that helped England through the Nazi
blitzkrieg, but it had a harder, even somewhat protest-like bite at a
time when American wartime songs normally didn't make mention

of the sorrows of war, only the shared resilience and faith of seeing it through. When he sang "Prayin'" for Pee Wee, he was cool to it but agreed to try it onstage. And when he did, the crowd ate it up, convincing him to buy it. Hank would tell folks he pulled in seventy-five dollars for it, a kingly sum.

Also in King's troupe was a rubber-faced comedienne from Tennessee born as Sarah Ophelia Colley Cannon, aka Minnie Pearl, in the role of a "mountain woman." In her bit, wearing a hat with a dangling price tag, she squealed "Howwwdyyyy!" and told stories about stereotypical hillbillies named Uncle Nabob, Aunt Ambrosia, and Lucifer Hucklehead, a shtick that won her a place in the *Opry* in 1940. She also would become close with Hank, whom she remembered years later meeting by sheer coincidence, though Hank had a way of making such "coincidences" happen by being in the right place at the right time, as if he had antennae. Often, that would be in the office of some radio station God knows where, hoping to get an offer for more money than WSFA was paying him. On the day they met, Pearl said,

> we went to the country radio station [in Dothan]—it was a dreary day—and there was a man sitting there in an old beat-up cowboy hat, old boots, and a beat-up brown suit. . . . He was sort of crumpled up, like a stick man, on the sofa. . . . It was Hank Williams. He wanted to sell a song. . . . He was obviously down on his luck, and Pee Wee bought it from him for ten dollars.[5]

Whatever amount the transaction was for—other references say it was twenty-five—King did nothing with the song, even as war made such songs much in demand. But there was a side benefit for Hank, who, while his name was listed on the song when it was registered, had willingly signed away any claim of publishing ownership. Those rights were shared by King and the publishing house he sold it to—Acuff-Rose Publications, the first time the Nashville company became connected with a Hank Williams property, even if indirectly. Minnie Pearl remembered little of the song in future years, but everything about Hank. "Especially his eyes," she said. "He had the most haunting and haunted eyes I'd ever looked into. They were deep-set, very brown, and very tragic."[6] She also remembered that with him that day was "a very, very pretty" woman he introduced as his "wife." That was Audrey Sheppard, who in every respect except taking the vows was married to him. They were continually interlocked, arm in arm, gazing at each other between arguments. And for Audrey, the fringe benefit she wanted began to accrue when, acceding to her not-very-subtle hints, he allowed her onstage to sing some of his songs as duets. This wasn't much of an intrusion for him, as he'd used female singers periodically to spice up the act. The difference was that, now, while Audrey could project personality and sex appeal, and banter with him with an innate sense of playful, coy innuendo, he was doing it as an obligation, a favor to her as the price of keeping her. And while few in the audience would show any disfavor when she did her turns, the fact became clearer all the time that Audrey Sheppard simply couldn't hold a tune, and that every time she sang she was undercutting his talent and personal connection to those audiences.

He may have also let her have some of his spotlight as a way of mollifying her father, who from the start was dead set against their relationship, not so much because she had fallen for another man while still legally married but because of *whom* she had fallen for. To the tall, stone-faced Shelton, Hank was no more than a bum and a drunk who made his living performing for other drunks. It was no kind of life for his daughter, who had quit her job in the drugstore to tag along with the skinny drifter on the road to nowhere.

Fortunately, Banks was far enough from Montgomery not to hear some of the choicer rumors already afoot about Hank, such as that he had fathered a bastard child after knocking up Marie McNeil, his *cousin*. That one got started after Marie married a serviceman named Conrad Fitzgerald and then in June 1943 gave birth to the aforementioned Lewis Fitzgerald. Conrad was either away at war or otherwise absent, and Hank took a most effusive liking to the boy, nicknaming him "Butch" and saying things like "That's my Butch," thus giving rise to the tawdry claim advanced years later by Butch that Hank was his real daddy. By 2000, he was embroidering the tale, saying that Lillie, in whose home Marie lived in a room next to Hank's on the second floor, had more than once walked in on Hank and Marie having sex.[7]

Clearly, there was much inherent craziness in his life. In courting Audrey he would assume a veneer of normalcy. He tried to win points with Shelton Sheppard by going hunting and fishing with him, but the old farmer never took a liking to Hank. Not that this deterred him, or her. Audrey, as the wife of an active serviceman, was receiving an eighty-dollar allotment check from the government every month, which she now was using to help feed and clothe not only Lycrecia but her new boyfriend, who obviously had no objection to accepting such alms in exchange for his attention and allowing her on stage with him.

• • •

As their romance intensified, so did Shelton Sheppard's disgust. He was so horrified that he would tell people only half in jest that if his daughter didn't come to her senses he'd take that hunting rifle and use it on the driftin' cowboy. As it was, her little girl, Lycrecia, hardly saw her mother, out as she was with her "husband" on the road in a trailer. Lycrecia lived with Shelton and Artie Mae Sheppard on the farm, Shelton adamantly refusing to allow them to take her with them when they traveled. At the same time, in equal measure, Lillie was just as aghast that her son was running around with the painted-up married woman.

Hank was so sure his future lay with Audrey that only days after they met, he took her home to Montgomery to meet his "maw." On the way, he told her what it was that he had wanted to tell her but couldn't right away. "It's my mother," he said. She was going to complicate matters, he told her; any woman who wanted to be with him would have to accept that "mother" came with the deal. She had her good qualities, he told Audrey; she was loyal and would move mountains for him. But she was also volatile and insanely protective of him, and no woman would likely be acceptable to her. Indeed, he knew what she was in for. As she recalled in 1973, "He said, 'I want to take you home and introduce you to her,' then he said, 'You know what she's gonna say when she meets you? She's gonna say, 'Where'd you get this whore?' "

"Hank," she said, laughing, "your mother couldn't possibly say that. I know she couldn't."

Then they got to Catoma Street and went inside. Hank asked Lillie to say hello to the woman he said he loved.

"Where'd you get this whore?" Lillie said, right on cue.[8]

The crack initiated yet another yelling match between mother and son that turned into a fist-throwing affair. Audrey must have looked on like a spectator at a prizefight, mouth agape, realizing that nothing Hank had said about Lillie was an exaggeration; she *was* a complication, about six feet and two hundred pounds of horned-toad complication. Audrey's own recollection was that, thrown back on her heels, "I ran back to the car. Hank and [Lillie] fought like men would fight. I tell you, *she* was his trouble. . . . When I met him, he didn't want to live, and he was like eighteen or nineteen,"[9] apparently unaware at the time that he was in fact twenty.

While Hank and Lillie went at it, Audrey may have cried in the car, but she had no intention of letting the "complication" crimp the fable she'd created in her mind. She recognized that it was Lillie's way of setting ground rules, but Lillie would have to recede, if grudgingly, and never fully. What else could she do? They were hellbent on getting hitched, just waiting for Audrey's divorce to finalize. Hank was willing to take a bloody nose to make the point. And that night, Audrey moved into Hank's room. Soon, both women had committed to an understanding. Lillie would remain in charge of Hank's career and would still go along on some gigs to collect the receipts. But when she didn't, Audrey would fill that role. What's more, Lillie was pleased that Audrey was already letting Hank have it about his drinking. She would tell him, "If you're going to go with me, you're going to have to leave whiskey alone." Yet even on the way to Montgomery, Hank had stopped several times, ordering her, "Audrey, get me a bottle." She would hem and haw, but sometimes he'd be so tortured, and plead like a child, that she'd go get him one just to keep him pacified. Once she and Lillie got to talking the problem over, they began to practice a ritual whenever he went out for a gig. As M. C. Jarrett recalled it, "Audrey and Mrs. Williams kept him dry till intermission time, then they let him have a pint. By midnight, the show was over and they had all the money. He'd be drunk . . . and they were in charge."[10] It was hardly a curative, but the women believed they were at least doing *something* about it.

In the opinion of many who knew them, when Audrey said "I do," what she meant was "You do what I want." Still, she bent to his will when just after New Year's 1944 he got all patriotic again and wanted to go back to Mobile, where he could reclaim his shipyard job and make some money while continuing to play the bars around the bustling navy base. Audrey could at least appreciate that this would create separation from Lillie.

Down in Mobile, Hank and Audrey had few of the comforts of the boardinghouse. Both found work as welders at the shipyard, working shoulder to shoulder, blowtorches in hand. Audrey would write later that after work "we'd go back to this terrible little old hotel room and I'd wash out our clothes for the next day." This being nothing like the life she believed she was meant for, after a few weeks she laid down the law.

"This is just not it, Hank," she told him. "I want to go back to Montgomery. I want to get a band together for you and get you back on a radio station and start working shows."[11]

She didn't need to add that these plans also included her getting onstage with him. Lillie, who for once didn't have to pay the freight to get him home, was pleased to have him—as opposed to *them*—back, always keeping his room undisturbed, unrented, and cleaning it every day. But no longer did he exist as a single entity; he was soldered to Audrey as one. That she would be part of his musical pursuits was obvious when he called her his "secretary." Marie McNeil, notwithstanding her own rumored visits to Hank's room, recalled that the place became "the craziest house you ever lived in in your life," what with the rigors of trying to sleep in a room next door to equally loud arguments and lovemaking, rehearsals with musicians, Lillie's constant turmoil, and her own arguments with Hank and Audrey.

It was clearly a relief when they could flee the tension and get on the road again. Sometimes, they repaired to a farmhouse out in the country where Hank could breathe a little and go hunting and fishing with bandmates. Audrey would dutifully fry up the fish for everyone to eat. Even though they were still living by the seat of their pants, Audrey became enamored of the on-the-road lifestyle and being part of a musical unit. Hank, relieved she was there and able to dodge her efforts at keeping him off the booze, not only entrusted her to collect the proceeds at the clubs but more and more included her in rehearsals and in the shows. The other Driftin' Cowboys would try hard not to wince when the notes came out of her mouth, and per Hank's instructions to them in private the guitar players turned up their amps when she sang, the objective to drown her out. If she noticed, she was having too much of good time playing a bargain-basement Kitty Wells. Someday soon, she would tell Hank, they wouldn't have to be doing the act in the sticks. They'd be doing it in Nashville. The way she said it, he believed her.

· · ·

In the winter of 1944, James Erskine Guy was still nowhere to be found. Audrey's lawyer had gotten the papers to a Pike Country circuit court judge who on December 5 granted her a divorce on grounds of "voluntary abandonment" and ordered Guy to pay her the same amount in alimony and child support that he had when his government checks were sent to her, around eighty dollars monthly.[12] (She later said he never paid her a cent.) But Hank and Audrey were still not in the clear. By Alabama law any divorce had to be followed by a sixty-day waiting period before either party could remarry. Not willing to wait that long, Hank and Audrey decided to marry anyway, damn the law. Said Audrey later: "Pretty soon [after they met] he said, 'I love you' so often that I got to believing it. I had wanted to believe it a long time." Then, "all of a sudden one afternoon, he asked me, and I said 'Yes.' He'd been doing real good, not drinking."[13]

They were in Andalusia at the time, playing the Riverside gigs, and the only justice of the peace they could find willing to perform the ceremony under the tricky circumstances was a man named M. A. Boyett. So on December 15, 1944, Hank spent the morning finding a doctor in town to give him a required certificate that he was venereal-disease free, then a notary public to endorse a marriage license, which he did, ignorant of, or perhaps given a little something extra to ignore, the sixty-day restriction. On the marriage certificate, Hank wrote in his profession as "Band Leader." As it happened, Boyett owned a filling station in town, and because he was there when the license was signed, Hank and Audrey, wasting no time, strode to an empty spot under the Texaco sign with Boyett, a couple of Driftin' Cowboys coming along as witnesses, and recited their vows as cars drove up over cables on the ground setting off that familiar *ding*. It was just impetuous enough to fit the lifestyle they were living.

It could even be called romantic in a rustic, manic way, with carefree young lovers too much in love to know what the hell they were doing. Audrey, who had told her aunt that she hated the sound of "Audrey Williams," took it as part of the toll for snaring him. It happened so suddenly that, perhaps as a tangential factor, the *other* Mrs. Williams could not be there, nor would she have made the long trip to a *gas station* to see her son marry; and indeed Lillie would hold it against her son that he had done it this way. When Hank called her after the pumpside ceremony, Lillie expressed her disgust and anger, though Hank expected nothing less of her. There would be no wedding gift from Lillie; merely allowing them to stay at the boardinghouse was grudging acceptance enough.

Ironically, their marriage was in name only, never to be declared legal by the state of Alabama and officially falling under common law. Yet they seemed to live by their own common law. When the sixty days were up, they considered the union to be legal. Who needed the law when their love was so strong?

· · ·

The marriage came six months after the D-day invasion of France, and the bitterly won victory in the Battle of the Bulge a month later presaged the impending fall of Berlin and defeat of Hitler in the spring, though too many more marines would have to die in the Pacific, and a monstrous new weapon would incinerate two Japanese cities before the end of all hostilities in late summer. The sudden arrival of a terrifying and uncertain nuclear age—and revelations of Nazi death camps where civilized men actually went about nonchalant genocide—would change all calculations of war and notions of morality and immorality, and just as in the aftermath of American slavery, lessons about right and wrong would not be learned easily as the Cold War dawned and black men who fought in segregated units came home to face Jim Crow and the hanging tree.

If Hank was seemingly ill suited for stardom before and during the war, the world was moving in a direction in which living on the edge, and on the edge of disaster, and comfortably in amorality would be a perfect context for his songs, which would feel something like dancing on a grave. His problem was having to deal with the Audrey issue. To her, being made a member of the Driftin' Cowboys may have been her reward for putting up with the primitive conditions of the early years of their marriage and trying to keep his nose clean. But as Hank and the boys seemed to know, her pushing him to a higher level was being undercut every time she warbled. Don Helms told of Hank's dilemma. "He came off the stage one time shakin' his head. He said, 'Man, it's hell to have a wife who thinks she can sing, and she can't.'"[14]

Worse yet, while Hank knew the kind of fight that would ensue if he told her as much, and thus bit his lip and held his tongue, Audrey seemed to live in an ether of delusion, not just about her singing but *his*. Guitarist Clent Holmes, who came along a few years later, recalled that Audrey, as she had been almost right from the start, was Hank's biggest critic. "When he would write a song and sing it on the radio," he said, "she'd tell him he wasn't singing right. And that'd upset him. He said, 'I wrote that song and I know how it's supposed to go.' And that would cause a big argument. But she never would back down. They'd have a real row."[15] It was the classic example of not being able to live with a woman or without her.

There were so many psychological and pathological undercurrents about them, individually and together, ranging over love, need, control, ambition, cultural gender roles, egos, and, at worst, boiling hatred. As volatile and able to unfurl so many turn-on-a-dime emotions in the blink of an eye as they were, when their fighting peaked and then was replaced by making up, their lovemaking must have been like the Fourth of July. No one ever knew if one of them would wind up killing the other, yet when they weren't fighting they wandered about with their eyes fixed on each other like school kids. It was no small wonder that Hank's songwriting in the mid-'40s took off, in direction and depth. They would come from a place he hated but which gave him creative sustenance.

He didn't know whether, at any given moment, he loved or hated Audrey Sheppard, but that mix of bravado and fear would be at the crux of almost every song he would write and sing from now on.

8

✱ ✱ ✱ ✱ ✱ ✱ ✱

"IT AIN'T A FUNNY SONG"

No one knew better than Hank how much creative juice Audrey set flowing and burning inside him. If Lillie had been vital to keeping him in the music game, Audrey was surely the pathway to the top. The trade-off was that one of them might indeed kill the other before they got there. They were absolutely brutal to watch when they fought. Cat and dog. Oil and water. Fire and rain. Any of these metaphors seemed to apply to them. The only question was how far they'd take it. One night in Andalusia, when Hank came back to the trailer stewed to the gills, the usual fireworks began. Fed up with her, he gathered up her clothes and threw them outside, into a puddle of mud. As Don Helms remembered, "She called the police and had him put in jail. I had to go get him out." When Helms got there, Hank was sitting forlornly in a cell, half sober and still steaming as he explained what set him off.

"What do you want me to do? Stand on my darn head?" he said, meaning that a man had to do *something* in the face of such abuse by a woman.

The cops apparently enjoyed having him, it being something of a red-letter day with a guy they liked to go hear themselves in their jail. Helms paid the thirty dollars to get him out, and as they were leaving one of the cops called out brightly, "Come back 'n' see us, Hank." He took it as sarcasm, not flattery.

"All of you can go to hell," he growled.[1]

When he got back to the trailer, he and Audrey did what they always did after a spat: they hit the sack and burned up a few more bedsheets. For Helms and the other musicians, this sort of episode was part of an ongoing soap opera—"Life with Hank and Audrey," something like the quarreling radio couple on *The Bickersons*. Hank and Audrey were wacky, but few ever thought their warfare was funny. Indeed, for Audrey it was serious business. She was willing to brave hell and high water to see that business through all the obstacles of Hank's crazed life. Sadly, he had been right; Lillie Williams came with the package, and that was another drama in itself.

As often as Audrey and Hank went at it, Audrey was also at loggerheads with "Mother," especially after Lillie felt stabbed in the heart when Hank and Audrey married and Audrey apparently had legal rights on his earnings. As Marie McNeil once said with prodigious understatement, "Aunt Lillie and Audrey didn't get along." She even told of hearing an "awful noise" coming from Lillie's room one day. Peering in, she saw "Lillie and Irene had Audrey down on the bed and they were fighting," hair being pulled and fists thrown. "I went to pull them off her," she said, "but my hand got tangled in Audrey's long hair." According to Marie, mother and daughter "ganged up" on Audrey "quite often," but Audrey "wasn't afraid of nobody."[2] In fact, Hank was impressed by his wife's grit, even *depended* on it, as it would become the source of many of his song lyrics, even if they cast her in the role of the heavy, to Audrey's dismay.

• • •

The irony of Hank's tussles with Lillie was that he had inherited his combative nature and his arrogance from her. Unlike her, though, he had little sense of right and wrong. While he never got a driver's license, and refused to put on his glasses when he did get behind the wheel, he bought a 1935 Ford sedan and tooled around in it, putting everyone in his path, including himself, in immediate peril. Indeed, if Hank got a hankerin' to do something, no law and no woman was gonna stop him. A car was often the place where he and Audrey would find something to argue about. Once, said M. C. Jarrett, en route to a club called Mose's, Hank ended an argument by telling the driver, a guy nicknamed Cannonball, "Stop the car." Said Jarrett: "I swear he just opened the door, snatched Audrey out by the hair of her head, got back in and said, 'Take off,' and left her there in the ditch. Then we stopped at Mose's and Hank got four or five Falstaffs. And we stopped a couple more times for beer. When we got to Andalusia, Audrey was already sittin' there waiting for us . . . and they got back together and everything was all right again."[3]

They seemed to know they were joined in a tinderbox. Not that either could stand the other for any extended period. Unable to stomach Lillie, or Hank, or both, Audrey several times fled to her parents, to spend time with Lycrecia. Hank would come after her, and Shelton Sheppard would stand in his way, until Audrey inevitably had a change of heart. Still, Hank made no effort to pull his punches or hold his tongue when it came to his wife. M. C. Jarrett recalled that he "heard Hank say things that ought not to be repeated about Audrey," while adding, "but there's no doubt in my mind that he loved that woman better than he loved life."[4] And that was the rub. No matter how bad the circumstances, Audrey believed they had a love only the poets could write about, and that would keep her going back. She had committed herself to sticking it out, getting him a record contract, and she intended not to stop until she did. With the fervor of a missionary, she convinced the bosses at WSFA in '45 to rehire Hank and give him back his morning show.

And Hank himself was seemingly under her spell. Not a secondary consideration was that he was writing so many good songs now. The kind of music he wanted to sing and the flavor of the act he wanted were being refined almost daily. Some of the country genre he himself had no use for, including Texas swing; he called the popular

Bob Wills idiom "longhair crap,"[5] presumably meaning too hoity-to-ity for the common-man country crowd—which Audrey wanted him to look beyond, another bone of contention between them.

Audrey was, however, adamant about cleaning him up, washing his face, elevating him from the junkyard dog life he knew so well. As he indulged his drinking habits, he had grown slothful, sometimes wearing the same clothes for days and avoiding the shower stall. Audrey would have none of that. She dragged him to men's shops to buy double-breasted gabardine and linen suits, which he usually ignored in favor of cowboy chic but for more than a few photos slipped into one of those city-slicker suits to prove he wasn't merely a hillbilly. She kept on him to go more pop, something classy and not suggestive of flea-bitten overalls and manure-caked boots. And Hank himself often turned back to the blues for creative comfort, highly admiring black performers who not only sounded but looked cool and sophisticated. When alone with a Victrola, he would pull out records like Blind Lemon Jefferson's "Matchbox Blues," prefiguring in his head when, a decade later, that song and other blues rags would be the vehicles of rockabilly music. Blues gave him his marching orders, it seems, keeping pop firmly off his stage.

In fact, before performing, hearing the band tune up by playing Tin Pan Alley standards, he'd tell them, "Awright boys, get them pop licks outta ya before we get out onstage 'cause we're gonna keep it vanilla."[6] This sounds odd now, since in modern parlance "vanilla" means without soul or fiber—in other words, too *white*; but for Hank, it was the opposite. Another song he listened to for cues was Delta blues man Tommy McClennan's "Bottle Up and Go," which was also recorded by Sonny Boy Williamson (and later John Lee Hooker) and was filled with racially charged lingo—"Now the nigger and the white man playin' seven-up, nigger beat the white man [but he's] scared to pick it [the winnings] up"—and sexual innuendo that he toned down. To some of the musicians, it was *too* simple. Sammy Pruett once said, "I always thought Hank was too corny," a common reaction upon first listen. Pruett spoke in musician language about

Hank doing no more on his guitar than playing an open "A or D or G, just as plain as you can get."

But such palaver was Greek to Hank, who barely knew what an A or C was, only what he wanted to play and sing, explaining why he *didn't* get too carried away with what was technically possible. If he screwed up, got too drunk to remember the lyrics or chords, the band would nod at each other and play the correct song—or, as they had agreed was the best all-purpose song to cover for him, "Blue Steel Blues," playing so loud it drowned him out.[7] If they were lucky, he'd never even realize it; if he did, he'd give *them* hell for it, never admitting he'd screwed up.

They could put up with Lillie and Audrey, but Hank would wear their tolerance down to a nub. And because they ran in their own circles, other musicians would hear the horror tales. Once, so the story goes, Hank was hanging at WCOV and got into an argument with Dad Crysell. It was on the latter's program at WSFA that Hank had made his debut, but Crysell left, his feelings hurt that he'd been shunted into the background by the bosses in favor of Hank—a not uncommon reaction at the station. What the argument was about is not known, but by one account Crysell's band took "great pleasure in beating [Hank] senseless and tossing him out onto the street."[8]

. . .

Hank had written a large number of songs, still reluctant to play most of them. Believing he needed to collect and present his emerging oeuvre, Audrey suggested he bundle them up and put them into a songbook, a popular means of presenting songs either for sing-along purposes or as hymnals. Not having any recorded or even copyrighted songs, he could at least semi-copyright them and protect them from pilferers by paying to bind a collection of just the lyrics, as he had no idea how to pair them with sheet music.

In June 1945 he took seven songs—"Grandad's Musket," the perhaps wishful "Mother Is Gone," "Won't You Please Come Back," "Six More Miles (to the Graveyard)," another perhaps wishful "I'm Not

Coming Home Anymore," "You'll Love Me Again," and "Honkey Tonkey"—to Leon Johnson, a Montgomery print shop owner, and came away with a few hundred copies of *Songs of Hank Williams, the Drifting Cowboy*, with a cloying introduction written by Audrey calling him "a lean, lanky fellow [with] a lazy good-natured air about him which endears him to his radio audience and to all who see him and his gang on their personal appearances throughout the South."[9] Audrey talked Johnson into doing the job on credit, with a promise to pay later when they sold.

And they did. Selling them from the stage, Hank, the great pitchman, sold every book. In March 1946, he then paid his bill to Johnson—in a pile of nickels and quarters—and had him print up an expanded second volume, the *Deluxe Hank Williams Song Book*, adding to the first songs around two dozen more. For the preface, Audrey took a few, well, liberties with the truth, going from his appearances in the South to the claim that he had now "traveled through thirty-eight states [and had] appeared on dozens of radio stations and also in several rodeos out west," which would have been a whole lot of traveling in nine months. Wishful herself, she added: "He is happily married and he and 'Miss Audrey' are already famous as a team."[10]

This remarkable, prodigious collection ranged over the themes of unrequited love, personal confession and lamentation, and religious purging that would be his signature—"Am I Too Late to Say I'm Sorry," "The Days Are So Long," "I Bid You Free to Go," "A Helpless Broken Heart," "I Just Wish I Could Forget," "Some Day You'll Be Lonesome Too," "I Loved No One Like You," "I Don't Care If (Tomorrow Never Comes)," "Won't You Sometimes Think of Me," "Take Away Those Lonely Memories," "I Watched My Dream World Crumble Like Clay," "Why Did You Lie to Me," "I Never Will Forget," "I Just Wish I Could Forget," "Me and My Broken Heart," "Never Again (Will I Knock on Your Door)," "In My Dreams You Still Belong to Me," "Let's Turn Back the Years." There was the self-explanatory "Back Ache Blues," mandatory gospel numbers like

"Calling You" and "The Heavens Are Lonely Too," and one written with Audrey, "My Darling Baby Girl," one of two songs about his stepdaughter, Lycrecia, the other being "There's a New Light Shining in Our Home."

These songs prove he was quite adept channeling loneliness, heartache, fatalism, faith, regret, and vindictiveness into commercial fodder. The songbooks became underground "gets" for his growing cadre of fans, and a fair revenue stream. WSFA, seeing a promotional hook, released an edition of it, altering the title to *Hank Williams and His Drifting Cowboys, Stars of WSFA, Deluxe Songbook*. However, in typical fashion, just when things were running smoothly for him again, he was once more taken off the air in early 1945 for continually showing up drunk, at 6 *a.m.*, yet. This so upset Audrey that she henpecked him to do *something* beyond making idle promises to stay off the booze. It was getting grotesque now, the incidents that made people shake their heads about him escalating. En route to one gig around this time, he passed out in the car, and when he couldn't be awakened the band went on alone, leaving him snoring in the back seat. Halfway through the set, Hank opened his eyes and stumbled onto the stage, making an idiot of himself. That was one of those nights they had to play "Blue Steel Blues" a *lot*. Then, afterward, Hank got into an argument with a cop and was thrown in jail for the night, again, like the town drunk sleeping it off, before Lillie and Audrey could get there to take him out.[11]

The solution was to check him into a sanitarium over in Prattsville early in 1945. All he really would need to do there was sleep most of the day. As M. C. Jarrett once said, "He'd done that before. He'd get the d.t.'s and all. It'd get so bad that his mother'd put him in the hospital. The reason that he had to go to Prattville that time in '45 was because they wouldn't take him anymore at the hospital in Montgomery."[12]

And still he kept gaining fans and gigs. After a yearlong absence from the air, WSFA reinstated him a second time in January 1946. It seemed that whatever he did by impulse to strike back at the ills life had dealt him, none of it was going to stop him from climbing beyond himself.

• • •

Even with his songbooks and demos, Audrey believed he was still playing in the bush leagues. He needed to make a bold move, she concluded, and he would take her up on her continual directives that he had to go to Nashville. He got the name of the station manager at WSM, home of the *Grand Ole Opry*, from WSFA's program director and, early in the spring of '46, drove up Route 31 to Nashville. WSM—the call letters for "We Shield Millions," the slogan of its owners, the National Life and Accident Insurance Company— was situated in an office building downtown on Seventh Avenue and Union Street, but its famous diamond-shaped 878-foot tower was located out in the country. There it pumped out a 50,000-watt signal so strong that during the war it was used as a backup transmission source for American submarines and during the Cold War was part of the CONELRAD national defense network.[13]

In May of 1946, Hank, expecting to be received as a star, sat himself down outside station manager Jud Collins's office. Collins recalled that when he came out, "this guy with blue jeans and a white hat" leaped to his feet.

"I'm Hank Williams," he said. "Charlie Holt from WSFA told me to come up here and see you. He said you'd tell me what I have to do to get on the *Opry*."

Collins had never heard of him, and sized him up as just another shambling singer, the likes of which he saw dozens of times every day. He gave the latest pretender the same line he did the others: he'd need to audition for Jack Stapp, the *Opry*'s talent coordinator and soon to be co-composer of "Chattannoogie Shoe Shine Boy," which Red Foley had a No. 1 country hit with in 1950. However, Hank would not budge.

"You tell Jack Stapp I'm here," he said, as brazen as a twenty-three-year old could be.[14]

Collins did no such thing, shooing him out of the building, and when Hank got back in his car, he drove back to Montgomery, personally insulted by the frigid reception he'd gotten. It had been a long shot anyway, but he didn't help himself with his arrogance, as Audrey kept reminding him. She too was arrogant, however, enough to believe he'd make Nashville come beggin', if he made the masses sit up and take notice. It was to his advantage that the lay of the land in country was ripe for guys like him. Its many branches—singing cowboys, bluegrass, hillbilly, rockabilly, western swing, jug band, backwater boogie, banjo boogie, etc.—were becoming more and more fused, waiting for someone to unite them. And Ralph Peer yet again was the protagonist. Peer in the late '30s had established his own publishing company, Southern Music, from which came classic tunes by Louis Armstrong, Count Basie, and Fats Waller, and country classics like "Deep in the Heart of Texas" and "You Are My Sunshine." In 1940, when ASCAP stubbornly refused to license country songs, the new, rival BMI stepped in, and Peer, supported by radio stations, funneled country as well as blues and gospel songs to it, making life easier for song publishers to commit to country artists.

The *Opry* itself seemed not to have any bounds. Unable to accommodate the demand for 25-cent tickets, in June 1943 the show moved to the Ryman Auditorium, a block-long, brown-brick fortress of a building with a high, sloping A-shaped roof and elliptical stained-glass windows—an ideal setting for what would be called the "Mother Church of Country Music." On Saturday nights, its crowds spilling onto the street outside, mobs came seeking to be purged of sin and jump for joy, served a steady supply of top acts, the most popular being Roy Acuff. A possibly apocryphal story had it that when Japanese soldiers mounted *banzai* attacks at Okinawa they would scream "To hell with Roosevelt! To hell with Babe Ruth! To hell with Roy Acuff!"[15] Also enormously popular were Bob Wills and Ernest Tubb. In every way, it was the white version of Harlem's Apollo Theater, a homegrown communal mass.

One hour of the *Opry* was nationally broadcast by the NBC Red Network starting in 1939, and would go on uninterrupted until 1956, for much of its run airing after the program that had inspired it, *National Barn Dance*. As the war neared its end, one could barely have recognized the town now being billed as the capital of country music as the one where the *Grand Ole Opry* had begun in 1923. Nashville's population, around 118,000 then, had grown by 30 percent in the '20s and after the war sat at around 170,000. The *Opry* was a vivid advertisement for the still-growing music it presented in its most cleaned-up form but also uncomfortably synchronous with the Old Confederacy, a whites-only affair of flashy rhinestones, rigid rules of behavior, and worship of a tightwad ruling elite that thought of this society as "high class," even as it perpetuated the self-mockery of hillbilly singers.

With his radio work, Hank was tracing the path of Bob Wills, who had cultivated a large fan base through the '30s, helping root jazz, pop, and the blues into his country swing. After leaving the army in 1943, Wills had moved to Hollywood and reorganized the Texas Playboys, becoming an enormous draw where many of his Texas, Oklahoma, and regional fans had relocated during the Depression. He was of such import that his appearance at the *Opry* in December 1944 became a historic coup, temporarily breaking the taboo against drums and horns.

As for Hank, he was still seemingly trying to catch up with the trends that occurred in country music during the war. Other than "(I'm Prayin' for the Day That) Peace Will Come," his lone wartime song was "Grandad's Musket," a country-fried marching song that told of "the boys in the mountains" closing down their stills and moving to the city to make "leaded pills" and using the old musket to "join up with MacArthur and even up the score." It took another six years before he did a patriotic turn, warning Joe Stalin in one of his Luke the Drifter "talking blues" songs, "No, No, Joe"—written not by him but Fred Rose—that "The Kaiser tried it and Hitler tried it,

Mussolini tried it too / Now they're all sittin' around a fire and did you know something? They're saving a place for you."

But it wasn't hot and cold wars that fueled Hank's writing. It was the war with his sometime wife/sometime enemy, who between fights had convinced him—or else—to try, try again in Nashville, and do what Joe Stalin wanted to do: conquer the world. Not one country but one song at a time.

9

✶ ✶ ✶ ✶ ✶ ✶ ✶

BOTTLE UP AND GO

In the summer of 1946, Mr. and Mrs. Hank Williams moved into a house of their own, clear of Lillie and the chaos that was built into the woodwork at the boardinghouse. It was a small, rented house at 409 Washington Avenue, and for Hank it was a chance to show he could be a family man. Audrey had felt it was the right time to have him be a father to her daughter, Lycrecia Guy, though Hank would not adopt her, or legally change her surname to his, something she would do informally. Still, he made it clear that she should address him as a daughter would her father. As she recalled: "I had always called him 'Hank' because that's what everybody called him. [Mother] told me later that he had asked her, 'Do you think she'll ever call me Daddy?' After I started, he never let me call him Hank again. I really don't think he ever looked at me and said, 'She's not mine; she belongs to someone else.' Daddy even told people that I was the spitting image of him."[1]

With Audrey an active mom, she had to stay off the road more, giving Hank a pass to carouse. Lillie couldn't possibly keep up with his schedule, so he was often on his own, though when he got home he was still required to kick back money to his mother, who by informal agreement with him expected to get 80 percent of any show and never thought he wasn't holding out on her. But Audrey expected money, too, for the family. Sometimes she would be waiting at the boardinghouse when he came back, ready to rassle with Lillie like dogs going after table scraps. Lycrecia, whom she'd take along, remembered that this competition also applied when Hank was smashed. "Daddy especially didn't like the way his mother and his wife tried to beat each other to his pocketbook when he got drunk. The truth of it was, though, that if they hadn't, he wouldn't have had a dime of it left."[2]

Such was his propensity to screw up, get smashed, and miss a show that Audrey and Lillie would have to go out searching for him. This became so routine that they could only shrug when he blew a gig at a small club. Bernice Turner, the wife of Drifting Cowboys (the g was now made mandatory, for higher-brow purposes) steel guitar player Doyle Turner, would sometimes be in the search party. "Audrey would be crying as we went to all the places we thought he might be," she said.

Audrey was still actively steering his career, and would revel in taking credit for the rest of her life, with a dash or two of exaggeration but not without cause to brag. As Don Helms said of her, "She went door to door tryin' to get that boy started. If it hadn't been for her, he might not've made it, I believe that."[3] Audrey had a battle plan in her head. She had resolved that getting Hank back to Nashville would rest on his ability not as a singer but as a songwriter. That could best be effected through the biggest Southern-based song publishing house, Acuff-Rose, and as time went by, Helms got the feeling that, rather than a singer, "the main thing Hank wanted to be was a songwriter, a successful songwriter."[4]

The strategy was a sound one. Acuff-Rose's near-exclusive hold on new country songs was such that when a big record label in the North chose to record one, it came to the Nashville firm. This was, to be clear, a still-rare occurrence, since those labels generally paid little attention to the hillbilly genre, most not having a division or even an A&R man who knew a thing about it. Some, like Mitch Miller, who came to Mercury Records in that role after the war, openly avowed his hostility to country, as he did later at Columbia with the idiom that sprung from country, rock and roll. Acuff-Rose, because of its ability to penetrate hoary bastions of the industry, was closely intertwined with the *Grand Ole Opry*, its president Fred Rose wielding as much power as anyone at the *Opry*, or more. "I knew about Fred Rose," Audrey would recall in 1973, "and I felt he could maybe help Hank. So we called and set up an appointment."[5]

Rose, a wily old bird, didn't take the haughty approach that so many did at the *Opry*. He was eager to mine the fields of the South for new songwriting talent. With the antennae he had to scour the land for such talent, he had to know who Hank was. Not only had Rose copyrighted for Pee Wee King "(I'm Praying for the Day That) Peace Will Come" after Hank sold him the tune, those songbooks had gotten around, and Rose said later he met Hank down in Alabama in '45. But then Rose was not averse to auditioning just about anyone. The appointment was made for the same locale where Hank had been shot down, the WSM studios, a place where Rose could acquisition studio time with the snap of a finger. He made it for September 14, 1946.

That morning, according to Audrey's chronology, she and Hank packed; apparently to make sure Hank wouldn't feel the need to stop along the way and get a drink, they rode the rails. Audrey liked to point out that she "made the call" that set the process in motion, and that she had to go with him or he might not have gotten to Nashville on his own, adding: "I had an appointment with Fred Rose and Hank and I came from Montgomery on the train up to Nashville. [But] the nearer the time came, the more Hank backed out of goin'. And I said, you're going. If I have to push you every step of the way, you're going."[6]

If Hank was a tad skittish, it may be because he knew he had a dodgy reputation in country music circles, and especially among the ruling elite at the *Grand Ole Opry*, who had heard stories about the enigmatic Alabama boy from Ernest Tubb, who'd encountered Hank

on his trips through Alabama. Tubb had made it his business to put
Hank on his *Opry*-sponsored shows And M. C. Jarrett recalled that
before one of those shows, "Hank was given 500 tickets to sell. But
when he got the tickets, he went on a drunk, traded them all off
for whiskey or gave them away to friends. By the night of the show,
most of Hank's tickets were unaccounted for."[7] The promoters had
to put him on anyway, his name having attracted much of the audience. Still, Tubb was supportive of him. Hearing Hank sing "Me and
My Broken Heart," Tubb told his manager he wanted to sign Hank
for the rest of the tour. The manager convinced him not to—"too
undependable," he said.[8] Even so, when Ernie got back to Nashville,
he floated the idea of bringing Hank to the *Opry*, only to get the
same cool response. A story would even get around that, on Tubb's
urging, Hank *did* go to Nashville and audition for the *Opry*, unsuccessfully, though this seems fanciful.

In fact, among the divergent stories that crop up all through the
passage of Hank's life, how he got to see Rose is the most streaked
with varying claims made by people swearing that they, not Audrey,
had arranged it all. Another was by country bandleader Paul Howard, who also ran across Hank in Alabama. As he would say, "I told
Fred Rose about him and Fred told me to have him come up and
talk to him," adding that Hank did just that, making an appointment while staying in Howard's Nashville hotel room.[9] Then there
was Molly O'Day. She had known Hank fleetingly back in Alabama
and was signed to Acuff-Rose. O'Day, along with her husband and
bandleader, Lynn Davis, heard Hank in a Montgomery honky-tonk
turning himself inside out singing a countrified rendition of Grady
Cole's gospel parable "The Tramp on the Street," which likened
Jesus Christ to a homeless tramp. That led O'Day—whom the *New
York Times* music writer Robert Shelton in 1987 called "one of the
greatest, if not the greatest, women singers in country music"[10]—to
record the song in 1944; two years later she and Davis again ran
across Hank, who was drunk and offered to sell an entire folder of
his songs to her for twenty-five dollars. Leaping at the chance, Davis

paid him, then felt guilty about taking advantage of the kid. The next day, he took the songs back to Hank, telling him they'd one day make him a fortune. Hank too regretted the deal but told Davis he'd drunk away the twenty-five bucks. Davis said forget about it and handed him the songs. When O'Day recorded "Tramp," she said, she told Fred Rose about the guy who turned her on to the song, and, like others, suggested Rose contact him.[11]

Still another version came from Fred Rose's then-twenty-eight-year-old son, Wesley, an accountant who was working for his father at Acuff-Rose. He remembered that they were playing Ping-Pong in the WSM recreation room when, unannounced, Hank and Audrey strode in and Hank asked for an audition. "They looked like average country folks," Wesley Rose once said. "The woman said, 'My husband would like to sing you some songs.' It isn't normally done that way. I mean, you don't just walk in cold and say [that]. My father turned to me and said, 'Have we got time?' I said, 'Sure, why not?' It's lucky we had nothing more important to do than go to lunch."[12] However the fateful connection was made, the songs Hank came to Nashville to present to Rose were, as Lynn Davis knew, golden. Most had a familiar ring, as well they should have, emanating from the same place in his life. As Lillie put it years later:

> Never in the history of "country music" were so many songs to pour out of the love of one boy for one girl. . . . They loved each other like lovers in old ballads love and out of their joys, troubles, spats and trials came dozens and scores of love ballads. . . . They say the course of true love never runs smoothly. Certainly it didn't in this case. One day they'd leave each other—"forever"— and the next day they'd be back in each other's arms, having a big cry—both of them—and collaborating on the latest sad song Hank had written about their "parting."[13]

The audition took place in the station's Studio B, next door to Studio C, where what is regarded as the first modern country recordings, that is, ones with technical proficiency, were made by Eddy Arnold in 1944. Rose put Hank in front of a microphone, and accompanied only by himself on guitar, he worked his way through his original songs. They were indeed all too biographical—e.g., "My Love for You (Has Turned to Hate)" and "When God Comes and Gathers His Jewels." The latter was metaphoric, his way of putting death in its best possible light, and a sage warning of the false prophecy of "earthly wealth" that "won't save your wicked soul." Another, "Six More Miles (to the Graveyard)," was his allegory about the death of one's true love; her body would arrive on a train, whereupon he would bury her and then "leave my darlin', the best friend I ever had."

These were not happy songs; they dealt with dying, dreams, and tainted love. There was also the now-standard country sexism. Hank was so good at expressing *that* as a fact of life that a music writer in 1985 thought that the chain of country was "emotional music [which] often had sexist elements in it, from the blues and Hank Williams to punk rock."[14] They were what B. J. Thomas defined in the 1970s as "somebody done somebody wrong songs," and the first somebodies were almost always women, who arose as necessary evils, turning good men into scoundrels and drunkards, the good women cursed by early death. Obviously, this was not a great reach for Hank. As sometime Drifting Cowboy bassist Lum York would recall, "Once we went to a picture show, just me and Hank, and this cowboy in this movie had turned this girl over his lap and was spanking her. Hank turned to me and said, 'That's what you got to do to these women,' and later on that's what he done to Audrey."[15]

But it was his deft touch and twinkle of the eye when singing a condemnatory song, his accepting of his own guilt, his optimism in the face of dread, that seemed so refreshing, even daring in the backwoods culture. Rose knew this was a different kind of country music, by a different breed of cat, who knew how to make those sad and jarring words seem ticklish. Unlike so many of the ambitious songwriters he auditioned, Hank did not seem captive to "hillbilly" stereotypes. His mien was not limited to themes of Tobacco Road, moonshine, Saturday nights at the honky-tonk, hunting 'coons, and tired love attestations. They were backwoods in a generic way, with bite and clever punning. What's more, Rose had a grudge about the degrading of country not only in the industry but in the country as a whole. In a typically pedantic "open letter" addressed to "Mr. Advertiser, Radio Agency and Program Director" in *Billboard* on August 3, 1946, he wrote that Americans "read all kinds of books that will give us an understanding of foreign 'folklore,' but what do we say and do about our own good ol' American 'folklore?' We call it 'hillbilly' music and sometimes we're ashamed to call it music."

• • •

Hank and Audrey were let down that Rose had not offered to buy anything that day, much less give him a recording contract. And it's possible, too, that Rose had to think about whether it was worth it to invest in a man whose drinking was a known fact. Pale, bespectacled, and balding at forty-eight, Rose himself was an alcoholic who had once stood on the edge of a river about to drown himself before seeing the light. He'd been to Alcoholics Anonymous and had become a Christian Scientist, living on the edge of relapse. He could hardly expect anyone from the Alabama backwoods not to be on familiar terms with the bottle. However, if Audrey was again to be believed, it only got done because of her. Rose, she said, issued a challenge to the young man. He had on his desk a song title he intended to turn into a song, "Mansion on the Hill," which he gave to Hank to work on after the couple returned home. Audrey's take on the writing of the song was that

> Hank worked with this song and worked with it, but he never could do much with it. I think the reason was because it wasn't his idea . . . and one night J had just finished with the dinner dishes and I had sat down in the little kitchen area and I started . . . "Tonight, down here in the valley . . ." I just was coming along

with it. After I got through with it, I walked into the room there and said, "Hank, what do you think of this?" Well, he really liked it. So between my lyrics and Hank's lyrics and some of Fred's. That's how "Mansion on the Hill" came about. For a long time I wouldn't let nobody know I had anything to do with it because I wanted it to be all Hank.[16]

The finished product furnished elements that would become a familiar Hank template. Part croon, part hoedown, it was a metaphoric lament of loneliness (down in the valley) and the promise of a reward too far (up on a hill). If Audrey had unlocked it for him, the rest was pure Hank corn, syrup, and vinegar, the last verse a still life of light shining from his paramour's window and him assuming that she is "alone with your pride dear, in your loveless mansion on the hill."

But was this poetry the result of Audrey's henpecking? Wesley Rose on his part insisted that Hank was actually signed, sealed, and delivered within thirty minutes of that first visit. His story was that a contract *was* immediately proffered, no strings or writing tests attached, although Fred Rose didn't issue a contract for "Mansion" until Hank recorded it in November 1947 and it wasn't copyrighted until a year later. At the time, all Fred Rose wanted, said his son, was to keep Hank writing songs for Rose's other acts. As well, it is certain that he sent Hank a contract dated November 8, 1946, for two other songs, "When God Comes and Gathers His Jewels" and "Six More Miles (to the Graveyard)," giving him a standard writer/ artist arrangement: two cents for every record he made, three cents for each sale of sheet music, a half-cent writing royalty per record side, and five cents for every song sold that was recorded by another artist, such as Molly O'Day. Rose took his bounty—a 20 percent cut of all Hank's future royalties, and ownership of 100 percent of the publishing rights on the songs. He could also attach his name to the writing credits of any song, no matter the contribution, adding another source of royalty revenue, sometimes under the pseudonym Floyd Jenkins.

If one is to follow Audrey's version, Hank mailed Rose the lyrics to "Mansion" and he was knocked out by it, immediately setting his mind to how he could tailor it into a country-flavored pop tune. When he produced the song with Hank in 1948 as "A Mansion on the Hill"—published with the writer's credit "Fred Rose/Hank Williams" (Audrey was left out)—it would be fitted with familiar country ingredients and a finger-snapping 4/4 blues beat, tickled by solo lines on fiddle and pedal steel as bridges between verses. And Hank's yearning full-throated vocal would jump from the grooves. Even just seeing the words on paper, Rose was, she said, sold on the odd young man. Probably contrary to how his son remembered it, Rose had his secretary type up the contract and mail it to Montgomery, as Audrey said. Lycrecia Williams, years later, produced a letter Hank wrote back that clearly proves he had done just that. It read:

> Dear Mr. Rose:
>
> I have received my contract. Thanks very much. Here's hoping you can send me some good news.
>
> I have 3 or 4 more numbers I'd like to send you. I think maybe you can use them. And I have several of which I'd like to get copyrighted.
> Sincerely,
> Hank Williams[17]

Rose eagerly awaited them. He was already scouring Hank's songbooks for material to copyright and shuttle over to Molly O'Day, as he did with the two songs he'd already signed for. Rose seemed to refrain from the dance-happy, chuggin'-down-the-road pieces in favor of simple, heartfelt, ethereal songs, something that might be called "gospel pop." He would select "Singing Waterfall" from the songbooks for the deeply religious O'Day, though he waited two years to have her record it. She also recorded three of Hank's other songs—"When God Comes and Gathers His Jewels," "I Don't Care (If Tomorrow Never Comes)," and "Six More Miles (to the Graveyard)," without much success, and then another in 1949, "On the Evening Train"—the only song ever recorded that had Hank and Audrey credited as co-writers. But O'Day would become less and less a priority for Rose, and would quit the business in 1952 at thirty-two after she contracted tuberculosis, she and her husband then becoming ministers in the Church of God.

In the meantime, down in Montgomery, Hank was convinced he not only had a foot in the door, but both feet. He told a friend, "You and I are both poor boys trying to get a start, but someday I expect to have some real money rolling in." Asked what he meant, he went on, "I've just signed a contract to make records in Nashville. It won't amount to much at first, but after a year or so I will really be in the money."[18]

• • •

In early December of 1946, Hank sent demos of two more songs, writing to Rose, "If you can use more at any time, let me know and what types."[19] But Rose, having seen the backwoods manner of Hank's lyrics, knew he had to make something clear to him. He replied that he had begun working on the songs he already had in hand, and "I must change the lyrics around in order to make them consistent. These will be minor changes, and will not interfere with what you have already written." What did this mean? When Fred got through with them, would there be anything left of *Hank* in Hank's songs? Hank wouldn't know until he heard what Rose had in mind, but was wary. Not only did he believe it to be impossible for Rose or any other record honcho to know what was in his gut, but his language and delivery were what made them *his*. As it was, Hank had heard on the radio how the pop side of the music divide cleaned up blues songs, turning them antiseptic—whiter—to make them "consistent" with mainstream buyers. And Hank was always trying to make his own songs "blues-ier."

Drifting Cowboy Don Helms once recalled that "a lot of the things we did on dance dates were like nothing you'd ever expect Hank Williams to have done. He'd do some of the dirtiest, low-down blues numbers you can imagine—old Blind Roy Fuller songs, 'Matchbox Blues,' that type of thing—real old blues numbers he'd picked up."[20] But would that pass muster with Rose? Hank hadn't yet recorded anything for him, but when he sang a song his authenticity would come from a bluesman's mindset, such as "Matchbox Blues." This was a decade before Carl Perkins renamed the tune "Matchbox," drawling, as would Ringo Starr still decades later, "I'm sittin' here wonderin', will a matchbox hold my clothes / I ain't got no matches but I still got a long way to go." The letter from Rose worried him that he'd be straightened up and toned down, but as Hank told Helms, he was going to "get my own style"—somewhere between Roy Acuff and Ernest Tubb, with a touch of "real old blues" to keep it real. And it worked, too, which baffled Helms.

"I didn't know what it was about Hank," Helms once said. "He wasn't all that great a singer and he wasn't that good lookin'. He just knew what to say to the people and how to say it."[21]

· · ·

If Rose intended originally to simply have Hank on retainer as a writer, he evidently became convinced Hank's way with a song on his demos deserved studio time, too. The timing—always the best ally for an epochal and cultural mover—was right for it. Days before, Rose had gotten a call from one of the many industry people on his Rolodex, Al Middleman, the owner of a fledgling New York label, Sterling Records, which had begun in 1945 and had been almost unnoticed. Middleman, needing to keep his head above water, wanted to record a country group and a "hillbilly" band, so Rose was a logical conduit. Checking his roster, he recommended a western swing band, the Oklahoma Wranglers, who sometimes were billed as the Willis Brothers, which is what they were, three brothers from rural Oklahoma. Unsigned to a record contract, they had performed on a Shawnee, Oklahoma, radio station and after serving in the war reunited, recently coming to Nashville to do a regular Saturday night gig at the

Princess Theater, as well as appearing on the *Grand Ole Opry*. They agreed to sign with Sterling and record four Acuff-Rose songs.

But then Hank entered the picture. Rose meanwhile had rethought what he wanted from Hank. Again, the versions of who prompted Rose to record Hank vary. Wesley Rose again took his bows for it, and he may well have talked his father into the idea. However, when Hank had come to Nashville in mid-November with his Drifting Cowboy bass player Lum York and laid down some demos at WSM, York said, Rose told Hank he deserved to be signed by a record label. Then, in early December, Rose broached the Sterling offer to Hank, assuring him the big play was on him: Fred would be able to record four of Hank's songs and knock the socks off Al Middleman.

The Wranglers, it turned out, would record four songs in a session arranged for them, but also be Hank's backup band on his session, with bass player Charles Wright also stepping in. The dual sessions were booked for December 11, but the pay would be for one combined session. Hank would be paid $82.50, per union scale as "leader" of an act, though he would only sing on his songs, while the Willises would each get $42.50 as "sidemen," even while singing their own songs. He had no option other than to trust Rose; it wasn't like anyone else was willing to sign him. Above all, he'd gotten his other foot in the door in Nashville. That seemed worth its weight in nickels.

Hank rolled back to Nashville on December 10, this time on a bus, alone, without any of his favored musicians. Fred Rose had made it clear that the Drifting Cowboys were not needed, something they would need to get used to hearing. Hank got off the bus and came straight to WSM, as Vic Willis, the brother who played piano and accordion, would recall, in an "old beat-up-looking coat and a big dirty cowboy hat . . . a skinny, scrawny guy."[22] Willis realized he had seen him before, when Hank had, on a previous visit, dropped by the Princess Theater to catch Ernest Tubb singing there. They proceeded to rehearse the eight songs they'd be recording. Willis had been told by Rose that the new guy was a little strange, that he sang to his own meter, not necessarily what was called for.

He found Hank off-putting, "a quiet guy and kinda negative," but with a "hell of a dry sense of humor." After spending the night at the Clarkson Hotel, they all came in the next morning and gathered in the studio—this time Studio D, the big one, at the time the only semi-advanced studio in Nashville. The brothers laid down their tracks while Hank, said Willis, "hung around in the control room." During a break for lunch they all went to the Clarkson, where a waiter asked Hank if he wanted a beer.

"You don't know ol' Hank," he said. "Hank don't have just *one* beer."[23]

Willis recalled that when they returned to WSM, Rose, again playing Ping-Pong with Wesley, asked an odd question: "Was Hank drinking?" Vic, sensing the wrong answer could queer the deal for Hank, said no. That was the right answer.

"Good," Rose replied.

The Wranglers were given sheets with the lyrics to Hank's four Acuff-Rose songs—"Calling You," "Wealth Won't Save Your Soul," "Never Again (Will I Knock on Your Door)," "When God Comes and Gathers His Jewels"; their backing parts were underlined. When it came time for Hank to sing, however, what was written on paper didn't quite match up with how it sounded in his colloquial—or bumpkin, to the Wranglers—accent. Willis gave as an example Hank's pronunciation of "poor" as "purr," as in "wealth won't save your *purr* soul." According to the Colin Escott take, Fred Rose, the de facto producer of the session, with Aaron Shelton and Carl Jenkins his engineers, yelled from behind the glass, "Dammit, Wranglers, sing it the way Hank does!" If so, then Hank wasn't as much a bumpkin as an infighter; he had to suck up the grammatical and other stylistic changes Rose made to his songs, but when he felt a word or a phrase was right, he pretended he couldn't do it another way. Thus when he later covered Roy Acuff's hymn "The Battle of Armageddon," it came out something like "Armegodden."

Sterling did release the songs recorded that day as separate acts, the first Hank Williams record ever to see daylight being "Calling

You" as the nominal A-side, backed with "Never Again." It took only a month for records to be pressed and labeled "Hank Williams and the Country Boys," with catalog numbers 201-A and 201-B. The first Oklahoma Wranglers record, pressed as 202-A, "I Can't Go On This Way" with "You Don't Have to Worry" on the B-side, also was scheduled for release. When a mid-January date was set, Middleman was pumped enough to play the side game music companies played to get noticed, buying a pricey ad in *Billboard*.

Fred did his part, too, playing a game *he* too knew well: sending advance pressings of the record and sheet music to radio stations and music store owners, and perhaps some Christmas "favors" under the table, a pay-for-play practice that wouldn't be labeled as "payola" for another decade. As it was, he may already have had a dramatic influence on *Billboard*. By coincidence, or not—and if not, it may well have led Middleman to rush out Hank's record—the cover story of that issue, on January 18, 1947, a red and pink eye-catcher, featured a photo of Rose client Pee Wee King ("Chanter in Chaps") in cowboy garb and hat, and a cover line read: HEP HILLBILLIES MAKE MUSIC BIZ TALK TURKEY. The article inside, titled in part HILLBILLIES ARE HEPPING TO DOLLAR SIGN, DOTTED LINE AND BIZ, began with some irony, given Middleman and Rose's moves and the magazine's use of the slur that was used as the article's opening word:

Hillbillies! Once they were complete suckers for the less-ethical money boys in the music biz. Organizations sluffed 'em; disk companies paid them off in the coal mines; pubs ruined their eyesight with small-print contracts. There was gold in them thar hillbillies, but the folksters—artists or writers—always wound up at the end of the pay line. But things are looking up! Slowly but surely the h.b.'s are getting on to all angles of the biz. [This] prompted one major disk exec to remark painfully that "I expect in a short time to give The Billboard a story on how the country bumpkins are putting things over on us."

That, however, was positively enlightened beside Middleman's ad, which had a crudely drawn, stick-thin "country" musician, barefoot, unshaven, in torn jeans and a T-shirt, a jug of moonshine at his feet, playing a fiddle with a baffled look on his face. About Hank, it read: "For singing real country songs Hank Williams is a big favorite wherever he is heard." As if to remind readers that Sterling did other things as well, a blurb was tacked on saying, "Rhythm Spirituals Still Going Strong," and pitching two songs by the Sunshine Quartet, including "Rocka My Soul." This was a tip-off that Middleman was not overly enthused about Hank, whom in promotional material he called, almost dismissively, "an Acuff-type of hillbilly who sings a real country song," while saying the Oklahoma Wranglers "do a higher class song and can sell anywhere."

Rose couldn't do anything about the "hillbilly" label dispensed so freely and often patronizingly—and may have gagged at the ad and promos. But the heavy-breathing prose about country was most welcome. If Rose took stock of country, it wasn't so far removed from the pop mainstream. The song most played on the radio was Sammy Kaye's version of "Lamplighter." This was hardly incompatible with country, and while a country chart was still a year away, the "Most Played Juke Box Folk Records" chart was tantamount to it, with two of the first three top spots held by Ernest Tubb with "Rainbow at Midnight" and "Filipino Baby"; others included Bob Wills, Merle Travis, Bill Monroe, and Tex Ritter. There was also a section called "American Folk Tunes: Cowboy and Hillbilly Tunes and Tunesters," a roundup of chatter about country artists.

Neither Hank nor the Wranglers made it to those pages, but they were on the "Advance Information" list of upcoming records in all categories. As well, the ad campaign for Hank's record, and the airplay it got, combined with the novelty of Hank's voice, at least what could be heard of it, sold a fair amount of records. As "Calling" was selling, *Billboard*, possibly fulfilling its quid pro quo, ran a review on February 1 of Hank's two-sided record in an eclectic roundup of "Additional Reviews." Sitting next to a huge ad for Gene Autry's "Here's to the Ladies," it read, in typical *Billboard* fashion:

> With real spiritual qualities in his pipes, singing with the spirit of a camp town meeting, Hank Williams makes his bow . . . an auspicious one. . . . [He] scores with his own spiritual song, Calling You. And in true backwoods fashion, with a tear in his voice, sings it effectively for the waltz melody, Never Again Will I Knock At Your Door, a song supplication to his girl to be true to him.

One needed a translator to decipher this shorthand, pidgin English, but to Rose it was crucial exposure. Then, only three weeks after "Calling" came out, Sterling released Hank's other two songs, "Wealth Won't Save Your Soul" and "When God Comes and Gathers His Jewels"—mislabeling it "When God Comes and *Fathers* His Jewels." Another session was made for February 13, 1947, to record new songs of his that Rose had or would copyright, and when Hank came back to Nashville, Rose was ready to up the ante. Now, he was prepared to become more than a publisher for Hank. He offered to manage him and make him a staff writer at Acuff-Rose. Their relationship would be open-ended; it could run forever or be terminated by Rose on a whim at any time. But for Hank, it was something like a baptism.

He had come to trust Rose so much that, hearing Wesley call his father "Pappy," Hank began to call him that, too, a term of endearment that Hank's own pa, Lon Williams, had never heard from his son. When Fred produced a contract to make Hank's broader role legal, Hank told him it wasn't necessary. There would never be an official agreement between them. "You really didn't need a piece of paper with Hank," said Wesley. "He stayed loyal to Acuff-Rose even later on, when people tried to tempt him to leave," and when friction arose between them. For this session, his pay was bumped up to $250 and he would be backed by some real studio cats booked by Rose. The songs were "I Don't Care (If Tomorrow Never Comes),"

"My Love for You (Has Turned to Hate)," "Pan American," and the older "Honkey Tonker," changed by Rose to "Honky Tonkin'."

That wasn't the only alteration Rose made to "Honkey Tonker." He winced at Hank's too-accurate portrait of a backwoods road-house and its denizens, editing the line "We'll get a quart of whiskey and get up in the air" to a Sinatra-esque "If you go to the city, baby, you will find me there." Rose also came upon a unique way to keep the boogie beat; Zeke Turner would play the bass notes of his electric guitar in 2/4 time, with the alternate two beats filled in as echo notes by Louis Innis on his stand-up bass. This unique sound, described as a "crack backbeat" by Paul Hemphill, was "the pulse of the song, *boom-chuck, boom-chuck*, the basis for Johnny Cash's signature sound a generation later."[24] But Rose wouldn't crimp Hank much. Though yodeling had fallen from favor, Hank seemed to know just when it would work, as an emotional stimulus. On "Honky Tonkin'," his voice broke from midrange to a smoothly trilled "Honk*eeeee*," then just as smoothly returned to the midrange. Wesley Rose, like his father, knew they were on to something. "Honky Tonkin'" "established a style," he said. "It was like magic. He sang out of the groove."[25]

If it seemed like a throwback, and a bit anachronistic for the times, it was Hank's heartfelt nature that made it work as settled country music law. "Pan American," too, went against the grain. It was a train song harking back to Jimmie Rodgers, referencing the Louisville & Nashville line that rumbled through his childhood Alabama towns, cherry-picking the stops on the line as he sang of the urge to "stick your head out the window and feel that southern breeze / You're on that Pan American on the way to New Orleans." It sounded suspiciously like Roy Acuff's rendering of "The Wabash Cannonball," but nothing was stale about it. It opened with clever fiddling to sound like that ol' train whistle whining, and the funky, high-pitched electric guitar riffs were, as listening to it now would reveal, a clear forebear of rockabilly.

Country singers of his generation were getting more pop oriented, more mainstream and secular in approach, their songs soothing and uncomplicated. Eddy Arnold, for example, five years older than Hank, was light-years more mature, the beau ideal of the *Opry*. The "Tennessee Plowboy," son of a fiddle-playing sharecropper, Arnold had racked up nineteen No. 1 country singles, nine Top 10 songs in '48 alone. The differences between Eddy and Hank, as singers, as men, were infinite. As Arnold biographer Michael Streissguth wrote:

> Eddy never had the soul of Hank Williams. . . . Eddy generally sang love songs while Hank coughed up gritty, hurting songs. Hank's life, at least as it's interpreted, resembled a gothic tragedy; no such mystery or desolation pervaded Eddy's. Hank and his equally legendary wife, Audrey, feuded in public, while the Arnolds lived quietly. . . . While other "Opry" stars drank too much, Eddy drank prune juice for breakfast and sipped an occasional Scotch. Hank Williams died young; Eddie endured.[26]

Hank would have readily admitted his serrated life was mirrored in his music; he once came up with the metaphorically accurate observation that his songs came "from a mean bottle."[27] And for all his deviations from the norm, he was pure country; if anything, Hank's accent seemed to be getting *more* twangy with age, as if sending a message that no one was gonna take the country out of the boy. Another example: the closing number of each show was one of his cathartic religious songs, a tradition in country that went back to Rodgers and the Carter Family. To Hank, that was more than tradition, it was the soldering of God to men like him with great flaws who weren't rebellious enough not to beg for redemption. And in keeping with this bond, he had started early in '47 to write a song that would be his most personal pastoral vow. He called it, only hoping it was true, "I Saw the Light."

10

* * * * * *

FROM A MEAN BOTTLE

Hank's loyalty to Fred Rose was already set in stone, and Rose needed that loyalty, since his assumption that Hank could be the new thing in country and pop was put to a stern test. The diffidence that most record company honchos paid to the still-congealing idiom was palpable when Rose began making the rounds on Broadway. A cockeyed optimist, Rose went straight to the top of the list, delivering six demos Hank had made in Nashville to Art Satherley, the president of Columbia Records—"Won't You Sometimes Think of Me," "I Watched My Dream World Crumble Like Clay," "I'm Going Home," "Mother Is Gone," "A Home in Heaven," and "In My Dreams You Still Belong to Me."

The British-born Satherley, an avuncular bloke people liked to call "Uncle Art," was the logical choice to hit up first. He had come to America in 1913, he once said, "to see the cowboys and Indians,"[1] and while he had pioneered in many directions—recording Bessie Smith and Ma Rainey—he made Columbia *the* country label in the '30s and '40s, albeit high-tone country. A hands-on executive, he recorded Gene Autry's first hit, "That Silver-Haired Daddy of Mine," in 1930 and persuaded the head of Republic Studios to star

Autry in movies. Satherley also provided the title for Bob Wills's most popular song, "San Antonio Rose." Satherly passed on Hank, and Rose next gave it a go with Steve Shoals at RCA, who had only a few country artists and wasn't eager to sign more.

Rose pushed on, trying Paul Cohen at Decca, where Bing Crosby ruled the roost of a very versatile roster that included not just pop but Billie Holiday and the Ink Spots. Cohen had gotten on the country bandwagon, such as it was, back in the early '30s with the Sons of the Pioneers and later Roy Rogers, Ernest Tubb, Red Foley, and Kitty Wells. Cohen said he'd think about it and get back to Rose, who wouldn't wait. There was apparently someone else he tried, described as "an executive of another major record company," who after turning Rose down called Information in Montgomery and dialed up Hank directly, offering him a contract. Hank gave him the back of his hand.

"Get hold of Fred Rose," he told the guy.

"I'm not interested in Rose," came the reply. "He's just out for himself. Besides, he can't do anything for you."

"He got you to call me, didn't he?" Hank said.[2]

Rose, again pushing on, next rang up Frank Walker, president of the fledgling MGM Records, created only a year before as the music division of the Metro-Goldwyn-Mayer movie studio to issue "soundtrack" 78 RPM records from the films, a term coined by MGM. Walker, a short, stocky, bespectacled fellow with an austere, tough-guy demeanor, had quite a résumé. He had been president of Columbia and RCA Victor, and before that the former's "race music" division head, signing Bessie Smith. He was hired by MGM with the proviso that he build a deep bench of big-band acts and turn a profit, regardless. He paid his staff little, and cut the price of MGM's records from seventy-five to sixty cents, yet he had MGM's money to throw at talent and the security of knowing that the parent company had its own pressing plants in New Jersey and controlled its own record distribution.

Walker, working from the MGM office at 901 Seventh Avenue,

had signed only a few country artists so far, obscure ones like the Korn Kobblers and Carson Robison, but like Rose he projected a bigger swath for the even more obscure Hank Williams, at least if he could sell some records right off the bat. Starting out with caution, Walker would not commit beyond two albums. Like Rose, Walker's take was entirely his share of the publishing income, following the blueprint written by Ralph Peer, who worked solely on that basis, with no salary or claim on sales royalties, which were divided up equally between the record company and the artist. However, as with so much else, the amount Hank would get per record sale is in dispute. One account claimed that Rose, making it easier for Walker to accept, unilaterally shaved the royalty rate to a puny 1.25 cents per record sold, from what Colin Escott called "the standard rate of 2 cents per song."[3] However, when Walker met up with Hank on March 6 in Nashville with the paperwork, Hank was a mite confused.

"I don't understand per cents," he said, misunderstanding the "percentage" clause.

"Well," the record chieftain replied, simplifying it with a sweeter pot, "let's make it three cents a record then."

"That I understand."

Although it was hardly a bonanza for Hank—it never is for any artist until he proves he can sell records—he avidly signed the contract on April Fool's Day 1947. Walker would split what would be incredibly lucrative publishing rights with Rose, who would consult and brainstorm with him on songs and marketing, while Rose and Hank would have the final say in what records would be recorded and released.

In the years to come, Walker would often travel to Nashville for sessions and sit beside Rose in the control booth. Until he began to sing, Hank would be basically a bystander. Audrey, of course, had her own, fanciful spin on this. "Decca, Columbia, all the big ones. They heard about Hank and was [*sic*] trying to sign him up. He almost went with Decca, but the way I felt about it, Decca had

Ernest Tubb and Red Foley, and MGM was just starting. I said to Hank, 'Why don't we go with MGM and build with them?'"[4] The emphasis was definitely on *we*.

. . .

Sifting through songs, Rose signed off on a new one, "Move It On Over," the very sort of swingy country pop tune Walker wanted. The first session for MGM was on April 21, 1947, in Studio D, again with Red Foley's band, a fuller one now. The four songs on tap were "Move It On Over," "I Saw the Light," "Last Night I Heard You Crying in Your Sleep," and "Six More Miles," the second of the two songs that Rose had originally bought from Hank and that since had been covered by Molly O'Day.

It was one of the most momentous sessions in country music's evolution, famous for the first two of that most trenchant of Hank's songs. "I Saw the Light," one of the best homilies of spiritual healing ever written, took gospel more deeply into the pop sphere than perhaps any other song of its time, clearing the underbrush for country singers to personalize matters of faith, burnishing the idiom with a whole different twang than the Delta blues kings had in their evolution from the Negro spiritual singers.

Hank had been working on it for months, the genesis according to lore being when Hank and the Drifting Cowboys were returning from an out-of-town gig in the dead of night and Lillie, accompanying them, peered through the windshield at the corona illuminating the Montgomery skyline and remarked, "My God, I saw the lights!" If that gave him the germ of an idea, he attacked it. Discarding draft after draft until he was satisfied, Hank tried to catch the vibe of the highly influential Oklahoma gospel writer and evangelical song publisher Albert E. Brumley, who wrote "sentimental secular" bluegrass standards like "He Set Me Free," "I'll Fly Away," and "I Found a Hiding Place"; one of his early verses went "Just like a blind man that has regained his site [*sic*] / Now I know my saviour / (Praise the lord) I saw the light."[5] The song he would record in Nashville, clearly chipped off "He Set Me Free," moaned of an aimless life of sin being salvaged by Jesus, in the guise of "a stranger in the night." Hank ended, as had Brumley,

Praise the Lord I saw the light

It was more effusive, more rollicking, than the occasional gospel numbers sung by country performers. Hank *sang* it as pop, with a wry Southern-fried glibness and a touch of moonshine. The hook of the title, repeated over and over, was jubilant, church-choir release, by a sinner who had enjoyed every minute of his descent into perdition but knew he had to make amends somehow. What made the song resonate was the way he sang the hook, each syllable seeming to weep, drawn out like a wet piece of wash, to wring maximum emotion—"Purr-raise," he began, the word forming in a yodel, then "the Lorrrrd. Ahh sawwww the laaaaattt."

One could quibble if he ever really saw that light. Indeed, future musicologists and even theologians would find it an odd sort of gospel clang. Yet if Hank wasn't a true believer that the kingdom above was any better than the sinners' pit below, he sure *sounded* like he was, or at least was open to the idea. It was redemption with foot-stomping credibility.

Rose was floored by Hank's studio performance, but his best bet for release was the spunky, seemingly more commercial "Move It On Over." The song was the best evidence yet that Hank considered his stormy life with Audrey juicy, fertile turf for material. In it, he went through his "day in the life" litany of static—being in the doghouse, the locks being changed on his house, straggling home in the wee hours. Every line was coated in mirthful sexism and defiance to any woman's directives, joyfully amplified and repeated by the band. Sounding a lot like the Sons of the Pioneers, they echoed his refrains telling the "little dog" to not only move but slide, tote, scratch, sneak, pack, shove, sweep, drag, and show it on over, "'cause a big dog's moving in." Clarifying further, "big dog" in some verses was replaced by "hot dog" and "bad dog."

The sexual euphemisms were obvious, but tempered by the perfect, self-deprecatory wink in his voice, a tip of the cowboy hat to the blues men. It was clever stuff, creating instant cultural slang, coming from a man who could cut through pretension right to the bone.

As with so much else, however, the genesis of "Move It On Over" is in dispute. Hank for his part claimed, "I was just talkin' to the dog. There ain't a man livin' who hasn't talked to his dog."[6] Lillie's take was, "Hank once said that if Audrey locked him out he would 'go out and tell that little dog to move it on over in the doghouse,'" which would be his new sleeping quarters. While that seems the most logical explanation, he didn't mind if the "dog" moving over was assumed to be, well, the bitch in the bedroom.

Either way, it was highly clever. However, much later on, it became clear that on a good many songs Hank had not found his lyrical elixir in any personal travail but by doing what came naturally to him—spending many apparently wasted days and nights reading comic books. The *Louisiana Hayride* singer Claude King told the BBC decades hence, "I asked him one time, I said, 'Where do you get your ideas for your songs?' He says, 'Well, I don't think anybody knows this but you, but I get my ideas from these right here'—and he had this stack of funny books, ten-cent funny books they used to have." King's songwriting partner Merle Kilgore (their 1962 smash "Wolverton Mountain" was King's biggest record)—who would later manage Hank Williams Jr.—remembered, "I said, 'Hank, why you readin' those sissy magazines? My sister reads those books.' And he said, 'Sissy? Hell, boy, where you think I get ideas for my songs?'"[8]

Lines written in semi-jest by comic book writers, especially dime-store romance grist with pictures, indeed offered him a trove of material about love and battles between the sexes to bolster his own, whose basic themes, of course, came from the landmines of his marriage. In Hank's hands, a line here and there from a comic book could turn unfocused thoughts into commercial candy corn. Even so, the image of Hank as a hick whose intellect reached no higher than drugstore comic books is a little misleading; it seems the man loved to read, anything he could get his hands on. Audrey's sister Lynette Sheppard once said, "Hank was a very smart man. I've come across many people that thought he was illiterate. Well, he was not. He read poetry." But there was no doubt where his most commercial instincts derived from. As Lynette noticed, "the floorboard of [his] car was always full of comic books."[9]

. . .

Fred Rose was given to songs written with a strong moral code and happy endings, but more important was structural order. In musician-speak, his template was the AABA format, featuring two or three very simple chord changes over twelve bars divided into a verse, another verse, and a refrain. This was a classic blues composition, often expanded by pop and country writers to include a bridge and thirty-two bars, roughly four verses of eight bars. While Hank himself wrote and sang only on instinct, not structure, there was much fertile territory for Rose to plow. On "Move It On Over," there was a key element added, a crucial kick to the beat. Because of his and Rose's continued use of the ingenious "crack backbeat" double-bass technique, there is the distinct feeling on most of Hank's records that one is hearing brush sticks on a snare drum, forming that resonant *chik-a-chik-a* backbeat, even though Hank used a drummer on only two recordings, adhering to the common law handed down by the *Grand Ole Opry* that drums did not belong on a country record, and certainly not on its grand stage.

MGM released the tune as the A-side of Hank's first song for the company on June 19, 1947, on a bright-yellow-and-black inner groove label as catalog number 1033—as a sop to Hank, it was credited as "Hank Williams Sings 'Move It On Over,' With His Drifting Cowboys," though none of the latter had a thing to do with it. The flip side was "I Heard You Crying in Your Sleep." And while "I

Saw the Light" would endure more cosmically when *it* saw the light, "Move It On Over" established the imprimatur of a new star setting himself down in the country pop mainstream. As the fiddler Jerry Rivers, who wouldn't join the Drifting Cowboys until Hank was ensconced in Nashville, noted, "'Move It on Over' hits right home, 'cause half of the people he was singing to were in the doghouse with the ol' lady."[10] Given full-on promotion by MGM, a *Billboard* review promptly ran in the June 21 issue, reading:

> A lusty lyric singer, Hank Williams has an attractive rhythm novelty in Move It On Over, telling the little dog that the big dog is moving in. His Drifting Cowboys add toe-teasing vocal and instrumental support with Williams as potent on the electric guitar pickings as he is on the singing. For Crying In Your Sleep, also an original, Williams sings the torch ballad with sincerity, adding a stanza of his plectrum sparkle.

On August 9, the song hit the trade paper's "Most-Played Juke Box Folk Records" list, at No. 4. The next week, it was replaced at No. 4 by Johnny Bond's "The Daughter of Jole Blon." Then it fell off, but was well en route to selling an estimated 108,000 records. Al Middleman, unable to pay what it would take to keep Hank after his breakout, got a delayed reward, too, when residual sales of "My Love for You (Has Turned to Hate)" / "I Don't Care (If Tomorrow Never Comes)," and "Pan American/Honky Tonkin'" got a boost. Now, as well, cover versions of "Move It On Over" began to pop up, among them those by Cowboy Copas, Grandpa Jones, and Fairley Holden, and the *really* blues version, by the wonderful, gravel-throated Monroe Moe Jackson.

"Move It On Over," a song that may well have initiated the concept of rockabilly, would put a few bucks in Hank's bank account. But it didn't move him on over to the *Opry* stage. His affiliation with Fred Rose notwithstanding, the Nashville panjandrums still held off. Thus, Hank's time in Nashville was limited to the session work that brought him there. Then, with his $250 in his pocket, he was back in Montgomery right after the April session and on the dead-end circuit of honky-tonks.

Nevertheless, he was feeling the first pangs of pressure and living hard. Approaching fame, and his twenty-fifth birthday, he looked and felt worn out, his aches and pains making his walk stiff and painful. A photo of him and Audrey outside their home during this time shows a man skinny as a lamppost, swimming in his clothes. Almost comically, Audrey holds her hands in front of her eyes, as if she can't bear to look at him.[11] He had been not only a boozer but a chain-smoker for years, and his hands bore nicotine stains, his complexion was sallow, and he reeked of tobacco. Sometimes he'd go without a shower or a shave for days. His stomach burned from the aspirin he shoved down his throat with his booze, which was eating away at his liver. Still, he could seem young and impish when he cleaned up, wrapped his guitar around his neck, grinned that crooked grin, and sang his songs. He could also feel a sense of getting somewhere when early in the new year he and Audrey cashed some of his first royalty checks to put a $2,200 down payment on his first home, a small brick house with a $10,000 price tag at 10 Stuart Avenue, about a mile south of the boardinghouse.

But the change in address didn't keep him home much. He was damn near always out on the hustings, and it was as if he wanted that separation from the sort of places where people would give him grief about his boozing, even if, as during a show at a bucket of blood club in Fort Deposit, some redneck fired off a gun, putting a slug in the wall behind Hank.[12] He didn't mind that sort of thing, happy as he was that he was in charge, his mother and wife ceding him at least some of that privilege as their responsibilities at home kept them off the road.

Lillie, to his relief, had remarried yet again, on March 1, 1947, to William Wallace "W. W." Stone, another of her young male boarders. A widower who was working as an antique furniture restorer, he had hired her brother-in-law Walter McNeil to work with him. Hank's life, meanwhile, was a haze of drinking and screwing around on the road, leading his Drifting Cowboys through the usual gauntlet of his booze-fueled brawls and blown gigs when he didn't show up, all while insisting he had the whole alcohol thing under control.

"I done learned how to drink," he told Lum York one day.

"Hank, I been learnin' that for years,' Lum said.

"No, I'm not talking about that. I can drink and I can quit when I want to."

"Hank, that's fine, I'm glad to hear that."

Knowing that Lum didn't believe him, he waved his arm. "Come on," he said. York had an immediate reaction.

"I said, 'Uh oh,'" he would recall, going on: "So we got into the car and drove around the corner, and after we'd stopped in the first beer joint I said 'uh oh' again. That's where I left him. The next morning I found out he had gotten drunk and hit two cars. I walked in [his house] and Hank was layin' in bed, and I said, "Yeah, I see you done learned how to drink, uh huh."

Hank, everything hurting but his eyebrows, reacted to the sarcasm with a growl. "I don't want to hear nothin' about it," he said.[13]

That after smashing into two cars he was permitted to simply go home and sleep it off suggests that Hank was being treated on his home turf with kid gloves by the authorities, that whenever he smashed up a car he simply dispensed some cash to the other drivers and went his own way. Another time, Drifting Cowboy R. D. Norred saw a crowd of people standing over someone in the road. He elbowed through the crowd and there was Hank, flat on his ass, out cold. No one seemed to know how he got there, but he had no apparent injury, just seemed to have collapsed dead drunk in the road, with cars steering around him. When the cops got there, Norred said, they "hauled him home rather than to the drunk tank."[14] While the joke was that taking him home to face Audrey was worse than any jailhouse, the reality wasn't anything to snicker about. In his rise, Hank seemed to have determined he had a virtual license to do what everyone was trying to get him to stop.

. . .

Hank detested spending any time alone, and would flee the house whenever Audrey and Lycrecia left to go visit their relatives back in Banks. He would still spend time at Lillie's boardinghouse, where the Drifting Cowboys continued to room and be used by him as mules to go fetch him booze, keeping Lillie none the wiser. Lum York recalled that most anywhere Hank went in Montgomery there was someone who would give him a drink. "He was good at sneakin' a fast one. A couple of steps or so out of the boardinghouse, you'd come right in the door of a little cafe. I toted many a bottle of beer under my arm back to the house. He'd meet me in the bathroom and drink that beer down so quick you wouldn't hardly know it."[15]

The musicians came to resent being turned into smugglers for him, and soon only Lum was left of the wartime Cowboys. Newer members included guitarist Winston "Red" Todd and steel guitarist R. D. Norred, who replaced Don Helms; Helms had gone into the service, and when he came back, he couldn't put up any longer with Hank or his loony family and walked. Another entered the picture in November of '47 after Hank's guitar player Clyde Chriswell grew homesick for his home in Tampa, Florida, and recommended a guy from that area, Joe Pennington.

Hank, who liked to joke that he had already gone through all the guitar players in Alabama, rang up Pennington, who'd heard another spin to that joke—"Folks who knew about him said he'd hired all them guitar players and fired 'em all." Still, Pennington hurried to Montgomery and soon knew why so many previous Drifting Cowboys had left a trail of skid marks. He recalled:

He hired me for seven bucks a show and told me to go over to his mother's boarding house and drop my stuff in a room, then come right down to the radio station to rehearse before his show came on. First time I met him he and Audrey came in the studio and said hello. They seemed nice enough, it wasn't like he was drunk or nothin', 'cause, you know, you'd hear stories. Lillie was all business, I don't think she ever said a word to any of us. And Hank was all business, not buddy buddy. We did a run-through of a couple gospel songs, "Where the Soul Never Dies," "I'll Have a New Body," and some others. He wanted to hear me sing and I could, so it became me and Red Todd singing harmony vocals too. He liked to give nicknames to people so he told me I was "Little Joe" and then the mikes went live and we were playin', just like that.[16]

Life with Hank was rarely that smooth or easy. Little Joe learned that his pay was about all eaten up by rent at Lillie's place. He would need to scrounge up enough money to buy his own stage clothes: a cowboy shirt, houndstooth jacket, hat and a pair of trousers. However, at times he wondered if it was worth all the trouble. Indeed, Pennington, upon hearing Hank sing for the first time, was unimpressed. "To be honest, I didn't know who he was. I'd heard him on jukeboxes but I thought it was [country singer] Jack Guthrie, who sang kinda like him. After I went to Montgomery, I didn't think Hank was all that good. I wasn't a real big oldtime country fan, I played mostly western swing, and he seemed like just another hillbilly boy with a band though he had come pretty far. I thought he was middle of the road as a singer."

Neither was Pennington taken with Hank as a human being, what with the booze and the penury. "He just didn't let you get close to him. He kept you at a distance, as if friendship would get in the way of his plans for himself. He was a thorny guy, an insecure guy. For all his ego, he could be depressed. He was still struggling and he'd blame everyone but himself." But here, too, he could fool you. The Hank who had a million friends but not one he could trust could be generous with total strangers and screw his own band. Lum York recalled that "we'd be ridin' around and he'd see a black guy playin' a guitar and singin' and he'd always stop and pick him up and ride him around and let him play for us for a couple of hours and then give him some money when he let him out. Anybody playin' on the street like that he'd usually give them a little money."[17]

With the Cowboys, loyalty was a one-way street. Hank expected that they'd all drop whatever else they were doing and come running when he played a gig. He kept promising "the boys" they'd all get to Nashville if they stuck with him. In July 1947, when he was approached by a radio station in Washington, DC, to do a show, Hank, who was doing one-nighters in the Midwest at the time, had York wire the other Drifting Cowboys airfare to DC so they could back him up. But when they got the tickets, they were so skeptical that Hank would actually make the date that they cashed the tickets in; just as they thought, Hank didn't show up in DC.

As Pennington says with a smile, "We knew him better than he knew himself. If he'd been on the road for a while, we knew he'd be so drunk that he'd forget about some of them later gigs."

When Hank went to Nashville for another recording session on August 4, 1947, Rose did allow him to bring two of his bandmates, Sammy Pruett to play electric guitar and L. C. Crysel (apparently no relation to Dad Crysell) to play fiddle. They would join three Nashville sidemen, guitarist Tommy Jackson, steel guitarist Herman Herron, and rhythm guitarist Slim Thomas. Pennington didn't get the call, and says he wouldn't have gone even if he had, thinking it more secure to play local gigs around Montgomery instead while Hank was away.

The studio configuration in Nashville meant there were three guitars present, four with the pedal, a rarity for the times. Rose seemed to want a kind of "wall of sound" effect to make the rhythm kick harder on the four songs slated to be cut that day. These included Rose's own compositions "Fly Trouble," and "I'm Satisfied with You." The other two were Hank's songs, another version of "Honky Tonk Blues" and "On the Banks of the Old Ponchartrain." The latter he had written after getting a fan letter in the form of a poem from a disabled woman from Louisiana named Ramona Vincent, who was

given a co-writing credit for the narrative of an escaped prisoner falling in love on a trip to Louisiana before being recaptured; sitting in
his cell, he yearns for her to wait for him, knowing she won't. It was
bathetic even for Hank, but it was a better song than "Fly Trouble,"
a washboard-and-jug-style rag that reduced Hank to singing, "Buzz
buzz buzz goes that busy little fly / Buzz buzz buzz, he's takin' off
and high." His cheeky way with it nonetheless elevated the record to
a marketable commodity, and Rose released it and "Ponchartrain" as
the next single, leaving it to the disk jockeys to choose which side got
better response.The quirky songs, however, had trouble aplenty, neither selling well, leaving Hank to look back in mock horror. Pimping
far better songs in future interviews, he would say, "Sure am glad it
ain't another damn 'Ponchartrain.'"[18]

Rose ordered him back to Nashville on November 6 for what
would be two more days of intense sessions, necessitated by the fact
that recording nationwide was about to go dark for a while. The
American Federation of Musicians was threatening a strike at the
end of December, when its agreements with the record companies
expired. The AFM feared that as more disk jockeys were hired to
play records on the radio—a major reason why networks like NBC
and CBS also owned record labels—musicians who played live on
the air would lose their jobs. "Those records are destroying us,"
union boss James Petrillo barked. Of course, the truth was just the
opposite; records only whetted the public's appetite for seeing live
shows such as Hank's. But the union was adamant. Petrillo had led
similar strikes, and when the newest one would commence early in
1948, there would be a freeze on new commercial recordings until it
was settled late in the fall.[19]

Hank again wanted to bring one of his Drifting Cowboys, R. D.
Norred, in for the sessions, but Rose put his foot down. He told
Hank that the last session, when two of Hank's boys sat in, had been
a strain; Lum York, he said, had wasted valuable time fidgeting with
his bass parts, and the session ran all night. "This time," he said,
"you ain't gonna get to try it twice."[20] York would point out that he

had not played on that previous session, or any for Hank in Nash-ville. But Hank capitulated. On those two days, eight songs would go in the can. The only one written by Rose, "Rootie-Tootie," was for many a novelty, but Nik Tosches would note it historically as "proto-rockabilly."[21] The others would be a second stab at "Honky Tonkin'," the wishfully titled "I'll Be a Bachelor 'Til I Die," "I'm a Long Gone Daddy," "I Can't Get You off My Mind," "My Sweet Love Ain't Around," "The Blues Come Around," and at long last, "A Mansion on the Hill."

The first record to come out as a single, "My Sweet Love Ain't Around" (covered by George Jones in 1963) backed with "Rootie-Tootie," was on the market just after the new year of 1948, though a review in the December 27 *Billboard* did not qualify as a rave: "Band sets just fair blues scene behind Williams mournful vocal" and "Peppy ditty with okay novelty lyrics. Vocal by Williams and band fine." The disk caught a break in that *Billboard* had begun a new chart ranking records among disk jockeys, dealer and jukebox operators. Hank's pair of songs didn't rise high but made this chart, ranked 72 and 82, respectively. Rose now began to rethink his strategy for Hank. He had cast him as an amorphous creature in an attempt to make him too familiar, too fast, and didn't have faith in Hank's own songs, moving most of them over for his own middling fluff.

Rose was still holding "I Saw the Light," which on sheet music alone garnered attention; a cover version was already out in October, by Clyde Grubb on RCA Records, and again in December by no less than Roy Acuff—Rose obviously not wanting to crimp his partner's version of the song by having it compete with Hank's original. Possible, as well, was that Hank had become turned off to the song himself. Recently he had forwarded to Rose a demo of an alternate version of it, done as a duet with Audrey, who suggested it be done that way. Hank hated it, and why not? As R. D. Norred said, "Audrey couldn't carry a tune in a bucket, and the more she practiced, the worse she got."[22] And, adds Joe Pennington, "It really got to Hank. He'd try to tell her nicely she couldn't sing, but he was over a barrel."

It would take nearly another year before Hank's original version would get the call. Rose also held off on "I'm a Long Gone Daddy," another "ball-and-chain" song, with Hank in a midtempo lament, saying not move it on over but "I'm leavin' now" because "you never shut your mouth 'til I blow my top" and "I don't need you anyhow." This was false bravado, to be sure, since this was something he never could pull off for more than a few days whenever he split on Audrey. But now, Rose released "Honky Tonkin'," and was rewarded handsomely.

On April 3, backed by "I'll Be a Bachelor 'Til I Die," it landed on *Billboard*'s folk chart—although, bizarrely, the chart was arranged in *alphabetical order*, meaning there were no rankings.

When sales figures came in, they were heartening. Al Middleman benefited again, too; "Pan American," which Sterling had out at the same time, landed on the chart as well. Rose was pleased that he now had a resurgence with Hank. But down in 'Bama, his once-again meal ticket was making a damn fool of himself, and, by extension, of Fred Rose.

· · ·

Hank and Audrey had continued to careen toward madness. It was clear that each of them had cheated, Hank as if a matter of male privilege, and Audrey had no intention of being stepped on without stepping back. Hank had apparently seen her stepping out. In two of his unpublished songs from 1947, "The Broken Marriage" and "Prisoner of Memories," which seemed more like therapy, he held nothing back. "In the presence of our saviour," he wrote in the former, "we said that we'd be true. / But today I saw you darling with another by your side / It hurt me so darling that I went home and cried." He made no such confession about himself, and none was needed; saying "we lied" in breaking those vows was his mea culpa. The latter song was even more morose, with him wallowing in lines like "My heart has nothing but strife, no sunshine do I ever see," "No key can open the door, their [sic] is no freedom for me," and, most accurately, "For years I've tried to escape."[23]

By '48, the fights about adultery were the worst, but all of them were frightening. Lycrecia Williams remembered waiting in a car one night, sitting in Lum's lap, waiting for Hank and Audrey to come out of the house; Lum, hearing the shrieking from inside, refused to let the little girl go in. But Lycrecia broke free and, she said years later, "Daddy had Mother down across his lap, whipping her like a little kid. I guess he must have swatted her about one time, and as he came down the second time he looked up and saw me. He stopped right there and let her up. They didn't say anything, not a word. We all went out and got in the car and went to the show."[24]

The cycle of manic, crazed behavior followed by making up seemed endless. However, something had to give, and soon enough it would. Hank had already pissed away about all he had, though that may not have been as much as he deserved—he had been paid just over $2,000 in royalties on "Move It On Over," $439.55 on sales of about 22,000 and $1,709.11 in writer's royalties from Acuff-Rose. By one estimation, his royalties for 1947 should have been in the neighborhood of $15,000–$20,000,[25] yet he was basically living hand to mouth still, drawing advances from Rose he didn't fully realize were reimbursed from his royalties. To be able to buy the house, he persuaded the realty broker to kick back the commission. Meanwhile, he was still stiffing the Drifting Cowboys and giving Lillie whatever she demanded, and with his money she expanded again, renting another boardinghouse on 318 North McDonough Street, and soon after, another next door at 320 North McDonough, then a third, just up the block at 324 North McDonough.

Thus, the people who had claims on his earnings were doing better than he was. What he didn't give or drink away he spent, buying Audrey—but not the Cowboys—expensive clothing including a fur coat. Not that this tamed Audrey's discontent over his profligacy for long. She bridled that he bought a touring-size Packard even as the mortgage payments were overdue and the house in danger of foreclosure. It was good enough for Lycrecia to recall that "I always got what I asked for at Christmastime," but Audrey needed more than a falling-down drunk cheating on her and not paying the bills. Audrey believed in her heart she had earned a lot more, by toughing it out with him. She had done everything she could in service to his career, keeping him focused, writing letters, making calls. Not only did she sing when he let her, but she filled in when other Drifting Cowboys fell away, grabbing a fiddle or even a big bass guitar and playing them admirably well for a complete novice. Yet here she was, having to put up with an ingrate and a madman, who during one tussle tried to rip up her fur coat, as if it were a symbol of all that was wrong between them. But for Audrey, it was just one of many, none soluble.

PART THREE

1948–1950

11

✳ ✳ ✳ ✳ ✳ ✳ ✳

"SYRUP SOPPER" OR
"POPULIST POET"

J ust after New Year's 1948, Audrey had enough. She packed a bag and took Lycrecia in the dead of night to Banks, where they moved in with her parents. If she tried to tell Hank she was leaving, he may have been too drunk to hear. It wasn't until he came to the next morning that he figured it out. Calls to the Sheppard home in Banks were intercepted by Shelton Sheppard, who said his daughter didn't want to speak with him.

She spoke instead through her lawyer, who filed divorce papers in the Montgomery County Circuit Court, with Audrey alleging that Hank Williams had "a violent and ungovernable temper," that he "drinks a great deal," and that "my nervous system has been upset and I am afraid to live with him any longer. . . . Complainant avers that the respondent has committed actual violence on her person attended with danger to her life or health [and she] further avers [that] there is reasonable apprehension of such violence in the future."[1] Hank at first passed the filing off as just another of Audrey's

overreactions and trusted that she would withdraw the complaint
once she came to her senses.

Rather than be by himself in his own house, he went—where
else?—to Lillie's boardinghouse, his mother having made it clear
that if he ever tired of "that whore" he needed to come home to her.
Not that Lillie was eager for them to divorce, as that would entitle
Audrey to an immediate split of Hank's bank accounts, provided
the marriage was upheld as legal. Still, she felt like she had won
something here, the prize being the son who had strayed from her.
Fred Rose, meanwhile, was not happy that his meal ticket had drunk
and caroused himself into such a tenuous situation. Seeing the walls
closing in on Hank, he wrote him a treacly letter, by turns sounding like a shrink, a preacher, a pedagogue, and a daddy. "We have
nervous breakdowns," he wrote, "because we think drowning our
sorrows will make us forget our troubles. . . . You cannot hope to be
successful while neglecting the Principle of health."

That was pompous enough, but Rose knew he had to take sides
in the matter of the marriage, sucking up to Hank by unctuously
advising him to be the bigger person. He wrote:

> Don't let Audry [sic] pull the wool over your eyes making you
> jealous. . . . These women want to be scalp collectors. . . . If
> she doesn't love [a man], he is a chump to want her. . . . The
> three hardest words in the English language to say are "I Was
> WRONG" but when we muster enough courage to say it, we feel
> a sense of victory. . . . THE GREATEST VICTORY YOU WILL
> EVER GAIN IS OVER YOURSELF. . . . If Audry wants you to
> wreck your life because of this misunderstanding, fool her, show
> her you can be a success in spite of her not because of her.[2]

It went on like that for two full single-spaced pages, fusing religious zeal, drugstore philosophy, and rank sexism. Noting that "both
of you want to be the boss," because "both of you have pride [which]
is one of the most destructive lies on earth," keeping them from

"enjoying happiness and humility," he opined that only Hank had the right to be boss. "Live by the rules the Creator set down for you and you will be healthy, successful and happy. I know because I live as close to these rules as I know how and am healthy, successful and happy." He concluded: "I'm opening up my heart to you, because I love you like my own son, and you can call on me anytime when you are in a problem," although he seemed to preclude a call that might be requesting some cash:

> Wesley tells me you called this morning for more money after me wiring you four hundred dollars just the day before yesterday. . . . We have gone as far as we can go at this time and cannot send you any more.
>
> Hank I have tried to be a friend of yours but you refuse to let me be one. I feel that you are just using me for a good thing, and this is where I quit. You have been very unfair, calling the house in the middle of the night and I hope you will not let it happen again.
>
> When you get ready to straighten out let me know and maybe we can pick up where we left off, but for the present I am fed up with your foolishness.[3]

Yet by the time Hank would have read this, Rose apparently had thought better of it. Could he afford to lose a talent like Hank over a few hundred bucks and late-night calls? Besides, he had been working on getting Hank a nice gig as a stepping-stone to the *Opry*. A better tack, Rose quickly realized, was to lock Hank into a more formal arrangement with Acuff-Rose, which would keep him there, with conditions that would protect Rose. He had sent the contracts to Hank in February, a bit of bad timing that explained why there was no response. Hank, trying to clear his head after Audrey walked out on him, had also fled, to spend some time with Pappy McCormick down in Pensacola, writing songs and deciding what to do to. He apparently even went so far as to go see Lon Williams in McWilliams.

Meanwhile, Hank had no idea that there were any contracts wait-ing for him back home. Indeed, after days passed, Rose sent a set of the papers to the address he was given for Hank in Pensacola, which were returned to the post office there. Rose, in a bit of a panic, sent another set to Lillie, with some stern and insulting language about her son, writing to her that the contracts were "for his own protec-tion, so that he won't get too full of firewater and sign a bad contract with someone else. . . . I hope Hank has come to his senses by now and realizes that drinking never gets people out of trouble, it only gets them in deeper."[4]

When Hank did return to Montgomery in early April, just as "Honky Tonkin'" was being played on the radio, he saw the contracts and another condescending, alarmingly sexist letter from Rose, again aimed to appeal to Hank's parochial feelings about women. "I hear you have been doing a pretty good job of straightening your-self out and nobody is more glad to hear that than me," he began. "Hank, anything I've written you or said is for your own good as I know what a fool a man can make of himself with drinking. . . . In the future, forget the firewater and let me take care of your business and you'll be a big man in this business." He felt compelled to add: "Remember that women are revengeful and do all in their power to wreck a man when they are separate from him and the only way to win is for the man to become successful."[5]

This may have revealed more about Rose than it did of Hank, displaying the publisher's own hang-ups and need to put women in their place. Even Hank may have been repelled, since he made Rose wait a few more days, until on April 12 he signed the darned con-tracts. He did so, in part, to help win back Audrey, as a sign that big things were in store for him—for both of them. The contract put him on the Acuff-Rose payroll for three years to start—at the princely sum of fifty dollars a month, against royalties, and an obliga-tion to publish six songs of his per year. There were also protections for the company, mainly that it could "accept as liquidated assets all future royalties" due Hank, meaning that if Hank went legally broke, the royalties would be collateral against any loans Rose had made to him. And, not pulling back on his threats about Hank's drinking, there was a clause that ordered Hank to "conduct himself in a manner not detrimental to Acuff-Rose Publications." However, when it was signed, Rose had crossed that line out. Not that he didn't intend to hold him to it. He may simply have come to his own senses and realized Hank could only be pushed so much before he stopped listening altogether.

. . .

Hank would soon return to the business of making Rose money. But as 1948 lengthened, he had other things to do. Calling Audrey in Banks endlessly until Shelton put her on the line, he all but begged her to come back to him, even as they got word on May 26 that the divorce was official, ending a marriage that arguably was illegal in the first place. Judge Eugene W. Carter decreed that Audrey was "forever divorced" from Hank.[6] But "forever" in this case turned out to be a few weeks. By the time of the decree, they were vacationing in Norfolk, Virginia, and had just sent Fred Rose a postcard that they thought was hilarious; it had a cartoon of a woman riding a mule and read: "I'm not the first jackass to support a woman." On the back they wrote, in their own parlance for success, "Having Big Time, Hank and Audrey."[7]

They were still Mr. and Mrs., even if they were technically not, and the hell with anyone or any paper that said otherwise. Even though Hank had sold the house on Stuart, he and Audrey would live there until the sale closed, and the cold war and staredowns between Lillie and Audrey resumed. And now, so did his career. In the spring of '48, Rose turned from offering lovelorn advice to pulling some industry strings for a guy who at twenty-five still had only limited success. But the timing was right. The country was entering an era of unprecedented economic boom and materialism. It was paid for in blood—a half million US casualties in the war, more than 6,000 from Alabama, as were 469 Medal of Honor recipients[8]—but now the ball was teed up for men like Hank who were symbolic of change and fresh ideas

All around him, meanwhile, country music was broadening. And he was in demand. If his soul perhaps needed saving, his ego did not. The year before, in August of '47, he was interviewed by *Montgomery Examiner* writer William E. Cleghorn, and the article ran with a photo of a very cool-looking Hank not in cowboy gear but in a sophisticated snap-brim hat and casual shirt and jacket. Headlined HANK WILLIAMS RIDES ON DOWN TRAIL OF NATIONAL POPULARITY ON AIR RECORDS, the story called him "Montgomery's happy, roving cowboy" and "the spur-jangling Sinatra of the Western ballad." At the time, "Move It On Over" was sitting at No. 4 on the country chart. Cleghorn quoted a humble Hank explaining its genesis this way:

> "Where the inspiration for that song came from, I couldn't say," Hank admitted. It wasn't his own married life. Mr. and Mrs. Williams lead a model domestic life.
>
> "Miss Audrey," his wife, is the featured vocalist with the band. Hank taught her how to sing after their marriage.[9]

That, of course, was good for a few giggles among those who knew better. If the Williams marriage was a model for anything, it may have been domestic psychodramas like *Gaslight* or *The Postman Always Rings Twice*. And yet in a broad scope, he had almost missionary appeal. In fact, that same year, Reverend A. S. Turnipseed of the Dexter Avenue Methodist Church, who also wrote a column for the *Examiner*, saw him in concert at the Montgomery Municipal Auditorium and believed that Hank was stirring a "populist" fervor among an audience of "common people," ascribing much social portent to what was nominally hillbilly music, even calling him a "Populist Poet." Mixed in with "corny jokes and horse play," he wrote, Hank, with "real charm," brought the crowd to its feet with his up-tempo songs and religious hymns, "furnish[ing] a good means of escape from the hard reality of their lives [with themes like] love, sorrow, religion, work, etc." The white, unabashedly liberal Turnipseed wanted to believe he was standing on the cusp of a grand working-class remodeling of the South: "Hank Williamses are moving into all of the towns of Alabama . . . being organized into labor unions. . . . The South is changing. The Poll Tax . . . cannot hold back this rising tide. As Hank Williams plays, Rome is burning."[10]

Turnipseed was on to something about Hank's populist appeal, but sadly overoptimistic about the South, and Alabama in particular. The worst of Jim Crow had not yet been felt, nor had the rejection of temporary liberal politicians like governor "Big Jim" Folsom in favor of George Wallace. But if Hank had little idea of any social implications of his singing, he could recognize he was back in the game, and again with good timing. The AFM strike ended in December 1948, meaning he would soon be back to recording. Another local newspaper reporter, Allen Rankin of the *Advertiser*, caught up with him at WSFA, where he not only was rehired but was now doing *three* programs a day, morning, afternoon, and night. Hank had a mouthful for him.

"I got the popularist [*sic*] daytime program on this station," he crowed. "Fans? There's a mob of 'em up here every mornin' and every afternoon! Some come from 50 miles! A lady from Opelika wrote me just this mornin'—Here, read it. She says, 'Say, Hank. How much do it cost me to come up and hear you sing? If it don't cost too much, we may come up there.'"[11] "Love letters are nothing to Hank," Rankin commented, and duly noted that there were "four very pretty young ladies" around him in the studio, none of them his wife. The article, which carried the first mention of Rufus Payne ("the only music lessons Hank ever had [were] from an old negro named Tee Tot"), was a PR man's dream. The studio, wrote Rankin, "get[s] quiet and reverent when Hank looks like he might be even beginning to think of having another song idea. 'Shhh,' they say. 'That's Shakespeare. It used to be hillbilly. Now it's Shakespeare.'"

The notion of populism had clearly gone to Hank's head, even if he had no idea what the word meant. It was the public, he noted pointedly, that had built his success, not the men of the industry. "Just lately" he said, "somebody got the idea nobody didn't listen to my kind of music. I told everybody on the radio that this was my last program. 'If anybody's enjoyed it,' I said, 'I'd like to hear from 'em.' I got 400 cards and letters that afternoon and next mornin'. . . . They decided they wanted to keep my kind of music." And: "If anybody in my business knew as much about their business as the public did, they'd be all right!"

Rankin estimated that Hank would earn $20,000 for the year, prompting Hank to playfully chide him in a future story by the writer for making such estimations public knowledge. "Let's don't quote no money figures," he said. "Last time you wrote me up, a government man nailed me one week from the day. He had a copy of your story in his briefcase." "What did you tell him?" Rankin asked. "I told him these story writers is like these hillbillies. They stretch the truth sometimes."

But it was no stretch, and Fred Rose was working on making Hank as big as he saw himself. He still couldn't get Hank on the *Opry* stage. Neither could Rose get him on a radio station in Nashville. However, there were other alternatives. And the best, with providential timing, was just taking shape down on the bayou, in Shreveport. The question was how much Hank's head really was into upward climbing. If his ego seemed healthy, perhaps one new song he wrote that he dated June 1947 in his notebooks told of a weariness that already nagged at him. In the song "I'm So Tired of It All," he wrote forlornly that "all my dreams have died. And, now, I'm so tired of it all."

. . .

For all intents and purposes, Shreveport meant the *Louisiana Hay-ride*, a loosely affiliated branch of the *Grand Ole Opry*, much like the numerous other barn dance radio shows broadcast remotely from ballrooms and dance clubs. The *Hayride* booted up on April 3, 1948, carried on Shreveport radio station KWKH, broadcast live from the city's 3,400-seat Municipal Memorial Auditorium. The name of the show was cribbed from the 1939 "Louisiana Hayride Scandal," four years after the magnificently corrupt Huey Long was gunned down in the state capitol by a political foe and Long's successor as governor was busted for forgery, embezzlement, mail fraud, and tax evasion. (The phrase also dated back to a 1932 pop song and a 1941 book by Harnett Thomas Kane.) KWKH producer Horace "Hoss" Logan and station manager Dean Upson made a deal to broadcast the show on the CBS network on Saturday nights to thirteen Southern cities, but not directly competing with the *Opry* on NBC. Logan hosted the *Hayride* as well, and its charter was as a kind of minor-league *Opry*, giving exposure to lesser lights on the way up—such as, in 1954, Elvis Presley.

Upson, who had cut his teeth at WSM, taking the ball from Rose, vouched for Hank to KWKH's chief officer, Henry Clay. And, attesting to the reach of the *Grand Ole* Opry, the brass in Nashville, protecting any future investment in Hank, also pushed the *Hayride* to take him on, and even sent WSM executives Harry Stone and Jim Denny to Montgomery to pitch Hank on going to Shreveport. However, when they arrived no one could find him. While the honchos tarried at WSFA, they got an earful from staffers there. Stone later recalled the GM of the station warned him, "If I were in your place, I wouldn't consider hiring Hank Williams a minute. You're gonna be running after him all the time."[12] There were, too, the usual complications when it came to Hank. Lillie wanted him not to leave Montgomery at all, since she would have far less access to his money. Audrey, on the other hand, very much wanted him to, for the same reason. As Don Helms saw it, "They were both pushin' him, but in opposite directions, and that's when it started takin' its toll on Hank."[13]

But he sensed he had no choice but to head for Shreveport. And once there, he made a pest of himself. He called Logan several times insisting he was no problem. "It's Hank—I'm sober!" he told Logan, who was convinced but only to a point. He called Fred Rose and said he would hire Hank, *if* he could prove he could stay off the sauce for six months.

Hank, for his part, seemed to believe getting away from Montgomery was all the therapy he needed. He would make a fresh start, with a clean slate, without Lillie, even without the Drifting Cowboys, who were left on their own back in Alabama. Hank had soured on them anyway, making the decision to cut them adrift an easy one.

The falling-out occurred on the eve of a two-night run in Birmingham after Little Joe Pennington had wondered if the AFM rates were higher there and inquired of the union if the Cowboys would get higher scale. He was informed they wouldn't. "I thought that was the end of that," he says. "But someone from the union called Hank and told him one of his band went behind his back to find out if he was screwing them, which was completely false. I just wanted to know the rules." Later that afternoon Hank came into the boardinghouse, looking ornery. "I want to see all you boys out on the front porch," he said. When they gathered, he asked, "Which one of you bright boys called the union to find out how much we were supposed to make at the Birmingham Theater?" "Well, I guess that's going to be me," said Pennington, who recalls:

> Hank asked me what I was trying to make sure that we got. I told him, 'What was comin' to us.' Then he said, 'Listen, friend, you're gonna get what's comin' to you, all right!'" Then he turned and walked away. I didn't know what he meant, but I could guess. He never said much more after that, but Hank always thought everyone was ridin' on his back, looking to bleed him dry. That's why he didn't trust people and that was a shame 'cause we all looked up to him, we put up with a lot to play behind him. I wish I could've explained this to him, but I got the feeling he didn't want to hear it.[14]

The last time the Montgomery version of the Drifting Cowboys played with him was on April 8. Hank was slated to play two gigs that night in Montgomery, the first at the Charles Theater, hosting a show of touring *Opry* stars Cowboy Copas and Johnny Bond. From there he was to go to Club 31 and do a set with the Cowboys. However, he was drunk and wobbled onto the stage, uttering incoherently. He tried playing his guitar but couldn't. He began singing out of key, but was stopped by the audience hooting and booing and stumbled off the stage, collapsing in the Packard. Onstage, Bond scolded the crowd, telling them they didn't know what they had in Hank, who, he said prophetically, "won't be 'round here for very long."

At Club 31, Hank was nowhere to be found. The Drifting Cowboys asked around, and someone with Bond said, "Last we saw him, him and Copas was backstage with a couple of women and a bottle." According to Pennington, R. D. Norred concluded, "Well, you needn't look for him for a while." Indeed, Hank would miss the show he was to headline. Often when that happened, club owners had the Cowboys play and hope the audience wouldn't ask for a refund. It happened again this night, but they were offered a more permanent arrangement: to play all of Hank's remaining dates contracted for at the club.

This meant Hank had been fired from the club, which naturally created a sticky situation; worse, someone would have to tell Hank. It fell to Little Joe, who half in jest says it was because "I was the only guy not from Alabama," though it probably was because he was the only one not afraid of Hank.

Over the next two days, Joe couldn't find him. Then Hank floated into Lillie's boardinghouse as if nothing had happened, wearing the same clothes as two days before and a prickly beard. Livid, Audrey and Lillie packed his clothes and hustled him back to the sanitarium. A day later, Joe made his way there. Entering Hank's room, he saw him in bed, propped up by some pillows, and Audrey sitting in a chair next to him. Unaware of what had happened behind his back, Hank asked, "What's happening down at the club?"

Pennington swallowed hard. "Well, Hank, the owner's fixing to get another band." After another swallow, "He's offered us the job, and we took it."

Hank mulled it over a few moments, but while his pride was singed, he knew he was bound for Shreveport and would be leaving the band high and dry. Still, he told Joe nothing about that and started acting all offended. Soon he ignored Pennington altogether. Feeling the chill, Joe left. He and the other Cowboys moved out of the boardinghouse a few days later. "I was looking out the window and saw Hank sitting on the swing," Pennington says. "He was dressed in his usual suit and hat, looked like a million bucks. To him, we didn't even exist anymore." Soon after, Pennington would flee Montgomery himself, heading back to Tampa. He and the others found new gigs. None, save for Don Helms and Lum York, were ever to be in his orbit again.

. . .

In July 1948, Hank quit WSFA—of his own volition, for a change— and he and Audrey left Montgomery, while Lycrecia was sent back to the farm in Banks until they found a place to live. Lum York, fiddler George Brown, and Clyde Chriswell came with him to Shreveport; Hank rented a small garage apartment at 4802 Mansfield Road for him and Audrey, while the others lived in a trailer out back. The conditions were primitive, but Hank swore it was temporary, that far bigger things were awaiting him.

Unlike more cosmopolitan port cities such as New Orleans and Baton Rouge, Shreveport developed in the northwest corner of the state as a refuge for uprooted migrants of French, Spanish, English, and West African descent, a melting pot that included Cajun ancestors in Hank's own heritage. But these marsh lands and mountains developed a musical culture of its own, its vanguard being Lead Belly, who was born on an old slave plantation and played blues-rooted folk in the saloons, whorehouses, and dance halls—and jailhouses—along Fannin Street in the downtown red light district, St. Paul's Bottoms.[15] Firmly segregationist, Shreveport was in ascendance in the late '40s, its population around 100,000, its legacy of overt racism still felt today in the fact that Caddo Parish in recent history has had more black men on death row than any other single district in the country, per capita.[16]

Hank settled in for his first radio show on KWKH, the 5:15–5:30 a.m. shift on Wednesday, August 4, in a studio on the second floor of the ten-story Commercial National Bank Building. Shreveport was just waking up, but those who tuned in heard a live wire crackling. Sitting in the studio with his guitar, making breezy, homespun conversation and singing country tunes, was a man with a swagger. Three days later, he was on the stage at the Municipal Auditorium. The *Hayride* protocol was that performers generally did two songs, and if the audience reacted well they'd be brought back later for two more songs, which for nonstars meant there was a load of pressure. Logan put him in an even tougher spot, coming out fifth in the opening 8–8:30 segment when the audience was at its most demanding. He went on after the Bailes Brothers, a bunch of real stompers. Merle Kilgore, the future singer and songwriter of country standards like "Ring of Fire" and vice president of the Country Music Association, was eighteen then and among those backstage that night. Kilgore said he commiserated with Hank that he had to follow some tough acts. Hank just grinned that crooked grin.

"I'll eat 'em alive," he said as he moved toward the stage.[17]

Dressed in a sharp-creased cowboy-style jacket and slacks, Stetson on his head, he was cool as an ocean breeze, and needed only one song—"Move It On Over"—to percolate the building, most of the crowd of 2,000 people never having heard of him. Brought back during the second half of the show, he came on with Audrey, who was dressed to kill in her matching cowboy outfit, her skirt displaying a pair of fine legs above her white cowboy boots, as they sang, or she tried to, "I Want to Live and Love." Hank had been signed conditionally by a wary Logan, but that night Horace made him a regular on the *Hayride*, and Henry Clay proffered a one-year contract to permanently host the early-morning show at KWKH. His pay was twenty-five dollars a week plus another twenty-five for the *Hayride*, far more than the thirty dollars a week he'd earned at WSFA.

His second appearance on the *Hayride*, and first as a full-time act, came on September 20. The show's announcer, Red Bartlett, would station himself in the orchestra pit and punctuate Hank's yodeling by doing somersaults, then dancing a tango with the curtains at the side of the stage, inciting the crowd further, not that Hank seemed to need the help. He was beyond doubt the nucleus of the show, its firecracker, and a perfect pitchman given his megaphone he had at KWKH.

Not wanting to let the flame of "Move It" flicker, Fred Rose had MGM follow "Honky Tonkin'" with "I'm a Long Gone Daddy," backed with "The Blues Come Around," still under the name Hank Williams and His Drifting Cowboys. The song had already been recorded and put on the market in April by Decca. But Hank's original caught some real buzz, getting a shout-out in the June 19 *Billboard* as an "Advance Folk Record Release." The record made it onto the Most Played Jukebox chart on September 4, at No. 6. "I Saw the Light," released despite the overt gospel niche that both Rose and Frank Walker wanted to steer Hank clear of, not that they could have, didn't sell much. But the final release of '48, "A Mansion on the Hill," climbed to No. 12.

Placing two records high on the country charts provided some much-needed financial relief for Hank and Audrey. There was another dividend from "Honky Tonkin'." Rose had bought up the masters of the original version from Sterling Records to keep it off the market, and as compensation he shot $1,000 Hank's way.

Even so, Hank fretted because he knew little of the honky-tonk scene around Shreveport. Neither did the *Hayride* care much about promoting itself as the *Grand Ole Opry* did; it had no in-house booking agency, and its brass was entirely focused on the show and keeping costs low. So Hank asked Tillman Franks, a musician and booking agent in Louisiana and Texas, about setting up some outside work, which would include Franks in a reconstituted Drifting Cowboys. As usual, though, turnover in the band was high, and replacements came in, like guitarists Clent Holmes and Bob McNett, on loan from Patsy Montana's band, and pedal steel guitarist Felton Pruett. Hank took some of his cash and bought new wheels, a blue-black Packard limousine, to which was hitched the trailer carrying the instruments and outfits.

It was a rough go. Whatever money he made was spent on travel expenses and band outfits, and the dates were sporadic. A regular meal was a fond wish. Franks and his wife took the Williamses to dinner one night at the Bantam Grill across the street from the station, and Franks remembered that "we had a catfish supper and Hank and Audrey really put it away." After dinner, Hank and Audrey got up and sang two gospel tunes, "Will the Circle Be Unbroken" and "When the Roll Is Called up Yonder." Tillman's father, who was also there, wasn't much impressed. "Son," he said, "you ain't thinking of making any money with him, are you, 'cause he just cain't sing."[18]

• • •

This was a distinctly minority opinion. There was something about his voice, in song or not, that made ears want to hear more. In person, his Everyman face and dimples were part of the charm. On the radio, his aw-shucks affect and homespun homilies resonated from the first word out of his mouth each morning, reassuring hordes of working people waking up for another day of drudgery. To them, he was kin, as if there were no radio in the kitchen, only Hank, as real as rain. Signing on with "Hi, folks, I'm Hank Williams and I'm gonna sing a few songs for ya today," and signing off with "Well, friends, if the good Lord's willin' and the creek don't rise, we'll see y'all," he would rush off to some gig or another like the Jasper High School auditorium or a honky-tonk. During the show, he'd make sure to drop a mention of where he'd be, and always tease his appearances on the *Hayride*.

His image, in his cowboy hat in front of a KWKH/CBS microphone, was used on fliers and billboards for the *Hayride* show, his name twice as large as any others. Group photos of the performers always had him dead center, the hub of the wheel, his outfits impeccably tailored, inlaid with sequins or butterfly designs. *Hayride* advertisers would insist on having Hank perform in front of their ads for later use, explaining why there are photos of him framed by looming signs such as BLEVINS FAMOUS POPCORN VILLAGE, POPS BEST, TASTES BEST. While Hank would not record any new songs until December 1948, after the strike ended, he was being heard in an endless stream on the radio, on record, and in live performances.

And while his writing had slowed to a trickle, Fate was with him. He had begun singing a new song onstage, "Lovesick Blues," which he had sung once or twice back in Montgomery. But apparently he didn't know it dated back to 1922, popularized first by Elsie Clark in 1922 on the Okeh label, then recorded as "I've Got the Lovesick Blues" in 1923 by Tin Pan Alley tunesmiths Cliff Friend and Irving Mills for a Broadway musical called *Oh, Ernest*. Macon, Georgia, minstrel Emmitt Miller and his band the Georgia Crackers, which featured Jimmy and Tommy Dorsey, revived the tune in 1925, recording it for the country market under the aegis of Ralph Peer. However, it was also covered by country singer Rex Griffin in 1939, and that version was what had stayed in Hank's head, with its primal heartsickness about love lost and its tale of a fellow being dumped by the woman he loves—always Hank's biggest fear. The lyrics indeed were perfect: it segues from a dreamy past to a lonely, lonely present:

> *Such a beautiful dream,*
> *I hate to think it's all over, I've lost my heart it seems*

It also offered him a way to yodel his sadness with abandon. When he sang "I'm lonesome, I got the lovesick blues," he synchronized the yodeling with perfect undulation. It was the kind of stuff that made the women who were the bulk of his audiences openly weep and hold their men a little closer. When he hit that yodel, Merle Kilgore said, "everybody stood up and the women threw their babies in the air."[19] And it really *was* Hank's song. He liked that it wasn't a dirge but an up-tempo, *cheerful* melody against which the theme of despair would be contrasted—something he turned into a country staple. He'd do it differently each time, the yodels extending ridiculously long or his vocal changing keys within lines, making it hard for the band to keep up. The first time he sang it on the *Hayride*, it wasn't with his regular band save for Felton Pruett and Tillman Franks. The latter recalled that after rehearsing the song in F, Hank "went from F to B-minor or something."

"Hank," Franks shouted to him, "that one chord you got in there, I can't figure it out."

Hank shouted back, "Don't worry 'bout it, hoss, just stomp your foot and grin!"[20]

The reaction to the song was a lot of stompin' out in the audience. As Bob McNett recalled, "They simply would not let him off the stage. It impressed me that without any warning of any kind, suddenly Hank gets up and sings a song most of them hadn't heard before and gets a reaction that strong."[21] Hank would try to quell the hysteria by throwing his hat from the wings onto the stage, a hint that he'd had enough—and the damn hat would pull *another* ovation, forcing him out for yet another encore. Nobody had seen anything like it, and this sort of flat-out crazy adulation, which became typical for Hank on the *Hayride*, was real good for business.

Early in 1949, his quarter hour on KWKH picked up a sponsor, Johnnie Fair Syrup, the brand name of the Shreveport Syrup Company, which was persuaded to invest $5,000 in sponsoring the show. All Hank needed was one look at the ad script to launch right into an impromptu jingle, warbling in perfect pitch, "When I die, bury me deep, deep in a bucket of Johnnie Fair, from my head to my feet. Put a cold biscuit in each of my hands, and I'll sop my way to the promised land."[22] It also necessitated a new closing line: "Get the biscuits ready, I'm coming home and I need somethin' to put my Johnnie Fair syrup on." It was as if his voice were the syrup he was selling, and he sold it well; Shreveport Syrup was close to going under when they made their ad buy on Hank's show, but a year later they were thriving. People would tune in in massive numbers for the "Hank experience," which would include cornball repartee Hank was so good at. The dialogue between him and Frank Page was always a highlight.

"Say, Frank," he interjected during one show. "Did you know what Eve told Adam when he was kindly complaining to her a little about her cookin'?"

"No, Hank, sure don't."

"Well, sir, she up and said, 'At least you cain't compare my cookin' to your mother's!'"

Page only had glowing public remarks about Hank, once saying, "He used to tantalize me with new songs. He'd say, in that crazy drawl, 'Frank, come on in,' and there he'd be, sprawled out in a corner, his bony legs sticking out, his arms wrapped around a guitar. One of his favorite games was to play a song he'd already written, one I knew, and then weave in a new thought and new lyrics. My eyes would light up when I heard the new stuff, and he'd grin with delight."[23] Given his rare trait of connecting with unseen audiences, and that he so identified with Johnnie Fair, Hank was soon sticking around the station to read commercials for the syrup on other shows, something no one had ever done.

By early '49, Hank was hosting *three* shows, at 5:15, 6:30, and 8 a.m. He would spend idle hours at the Bantam Grill, playing pinball and picking at waffles covered with ketchup—which he'd pour on everything. The owner of the place, Murell Stansell, once said, "I wanted to stop selling him waffles. I was only gettin' twenty cents for 'em and he would use the whole bottle of ketchup that cost me eight or ten cents!"[24]

Smooth as syrup, and a savvy pitchman, he had created a marketing-friendly persona for himself—he was "the Ol' Syrup Sopper," which in parts of the Deep South was how he was known. He would routinely weave it into his stage act the way future rock and rollers would a beer sponsor, drumming up more sales. And with no shame—a trait he had in very short supply—he pitched himself on the air for any outside gigs that "you nice folks" in the audience might want to invite "Ol' Hank and his boys" to play. The resulting invitations would keep that Packard moving along the back roads leading to some roadhouse or dance hall. During these treks he would take short sabbaticals from the radio, and rather than have him off the air, the station bosses would rerun previous shows kept on rudimentary recording machines. He would always make it back for the *Hayride*, though.

Heretofore, the only radio personality who was given these concessions was Arthur Godfrey, the smarmily affable, hugely popular CBS network host, who in 1948 was being syndicated on KWKH. John D. Ewing, the powerful newspaper publisher who owned the station, wanted to have a stockpile of Godfrey shows to play at different times of the day and made a limited investment in acetate recorders that pressed "transcription disks" from live broadcasts.[25]

Hank's eclat was undeniable, and transferable. Audrey, for example, could take pride that Fred Rose had bought a song with the writing credited to Hank and her, "The Evening Train," which was recorded by Molly O'Day in 1949. However, in the euphoria of the *Hayride*, Hank had not felt the need to write much. He had enough originals, he believed, to fill out sets stuffed with old standbys like Jimmy Wakely's "Someday You'll Call My Name" and "I Wish I Had a Nickel," Sons of the Pioneers tunes like "Cool Water," and Bill Carlisle's 'Rocking Chair Money." It wasn't that he was lazy; he was . . . *comfortable*. He felt no need to unburden, rendering himself fairly useless to Fred Rose's plans for him, which was rooted in songs that told of his discontentments. What's more, he became less discontent still when just weeks after the move to Shreveport, Audrey, who'd been feeling out of sorts, came home from the doctor and announced she was pregnant.

Hank was thrilled by the news. People around him never saw him as happy. Without even trying, he would become a father just as his name was spreading. He and Audrey fetched Lycrecia from Banks to live with them as a growing family, and they would enjoy fish fries in the backyard with Kitty Wells and Johnnie Wright, Zeke and Helen Clements, Curley and Georgia Williams. Domestic life seemed to agree with him. But it was a difficult pregnancy for Audrey, and she came close to losing the baby several times. Hank bought her a comfortable rocking chair, a hassock, and a record player so she could play the acetates of his songs and feel she was still a part of the act, even if Hank was pleased she wasn't. Soon they moved to new digs, in Bossier City, a white-frame, two-story house on Lot 20 in the Modica Subdivision project at 912 Charles Street, Hank dropping a down payment of $2,000 on the overall price of $9,500.[26] (The house is now abandoned and ramshackle, and the city has refused to spend any money to preserve or restore it.)[27] With his fatter bankroll, he began paying his Drifting Cowboys sixty dollars—each—a week, a spike from the old seven-dollar-a-show scale in effect since the early days in Montgomery.

Feeling mighty good about himself, he figured it was time to put the Nashville people on notice. His way in was Oscar Davis, the *Opry*'s promoter in the sticks. The diminutive, loquacious Davis, who cut his teeth booking vaudeville acts, had already enlisted Hank on *Opry* road shows with Ernest Tubb, whom Davis personally managed. Hank had to listen to Davis tell him over and over that he wasn't yet ready for the Ryman stage. Now, with Davis aglow from his own breakthrough, booking country music's first major show in New York at Carnegie Hall in '47, Hank rang him up. He wanted Davis to know that when he played "Lovesick Blues" onstage, "Oscar, so help me God, I get fourteen, fifteen encores." He then played an acetate demo for him. Davis wasn't sure if it was a bad connection or a bad song, recalling years later that "in my mind I said, 'This is the most horrible goddamn song I heard in my life.'" Davis was still impressed with Hank's spunk, always had been, but as far as the *Opry* was concerned, his attitude was . . . well, maybe.

Hank had not the slightest doubt.

"Oscar," he said, "I'm ready for you."

12

✶ ✶ ✶ ✶ ✶ ✶ ✶

"THE SORRIEST THING I
EVER DID HEAR"

Staying dry for a few months was all the sobriety Hank could manage. By late autumn of 1948 he was renewing his latent addictions to booze and pills. Even Audrey's being pregnant and needing peace and calm could not alter his pathological thirst to wash down the painkillers with a shot of something hard. Don Helms would once say, "Everything he did was bad for his health."[1] No one knew that better than Hank himself. His guitar player, Bob McNett, saw him swigging from a bottle of bourbon before a show, which went fine, but afterward, surrounded by the usual mob of fans, Hank told him, "Bob, I wish I could get away from signing autographs because people are going to smell the liquor on my breath." McNett said years later, "I didn't have any sense of how severe his drinking could be—but obviously Audrey did."[2]

Not even the possible risk to their child could hold them back from sniping at each other during battles about his boozing. During one argument with Hank, Horace Logan recalled, Audrey reached for an expensive crystal set he'd bought her and began throwing pieces at him in the carport, leaving the whole set in shards. Another time, she took aim at him with teacups. Her aim was better this time, several cups smashing against his head. Bleeding, Hank had to go to the hospital to get stitched up, hiding the bandages onstage by wearing his hat slung low. Hank Snow, a young singer who had moved from Canada to Nashville, his deep, mellifluous voice rivaling Ernest Tubbs's, came to Shreveport late in '49 to do the *Hayride*, and Hank invited him back to his home after the show. On the way, Hank stopped downtown to pick up a pricey ring for Audrey, then gave it to her. Audrey gave it the once-over and threw it back at him, hissing, "If you can't do any better than that, forget it," whereupon Hank went out and got plastered. Johnny Wright remembered an Easter egg hunt at his home that year, when Hank bypassed the eggs to hunt for beer and was soon pickled. Audrey was so steamed that she took Lycrecia and drove home. Later, after Hank was dropped off, she was still seething. Looking around, she found an ice pick and slashed the tires of his car.[3] That same night, Audrey called Johnnie Wright and Kitty Wells to the house to stay with her. When they got there, Wright said, "Hank had got to arguin' with Audrey, and was wantin' to break up lamps and things. Audrey, since she was pregnant, was especially scared when he got violent."[4]

Audrey, in fact, went into a panic later that night when she went for a bottle of tranquilizers and found it empty. Hank had drained all the pills and was out cold in his bed. In a panic, she called Hank's doctor. When he got there he shook Hank until he came to and then asked him how many pills he'd taken.

"Too damn much," Hank mumbled, and collapsed back down.

Wright, who spent the night in a room with Hank, said that "the doctor went out and told Audrey, Hank was alright, not to worry about him."[5] That was malpractice, to say the least.

• • •

The band in Shreveport had never seen Hank drunk onstage, until a gig in Lake Charles when he wobbled on, picked up a fiddle, and

began seriously wrecking his rendition of "Sally Goodin." Felton Pruett recalled that the Drifting Cowboys kept calling to him, "That'll
do, Hank, that'll do," but he slurred, "Naw, them people jus' eatin'
it up."[6] He was right. To the audiences that paid good money to see
him, his condition was all part of the act, given that he could still
put on a good show regardless. "His time was right on," Pruett said,
meaning his timing. Damn, they would even say, he was good. So
were they, under much duress.

Hank's directive to Tillman Franks to just stomp and grin was
rare. He would ride the musicians and dock their pay if they couldn't
keep up. According to Bob McNett, he was a fanatic about having a
good, tight sound behind him. "Nothing complicated, just plain and
simple," McNett said. "He was a nut about his rhythm. It had to be
right and kept right. . . . If one of us got a little hot on the instrument he was quick to tell us to cut it out. He wanted the stuff played
straight."

McNett got the full Hank treatment one night, being put on the
spot when, before a show, Hank said that if McNett didn't make the
audience applaud with a solo Hank called "Fingers on Fire," *he'd* be
fired. "You haven't been doing as well as you should on that piece,"
Hank said. As the guitar man remembered, "He was serious. I played
the thing faster and more furiously than I'd ever done before. And I
did get applause in the middle of it."

Given such trials by fire, no one could ever really predict what his
mood would be. At least when he was sloshed, they knew he'd leap
out of that "mean bottle." Otherwise, it was a crap shoot. McNett
remembered a night ride to Monroe, Louisiana, for a gig when Hank,
drinking in the back of the car, suddenly "reached up over the back
and got me around the neck and hugged me. I remember the feel of
his unshaven face. He had never done anything like that before, and
I was dumbfounded. And he said, 'This is the best old so and so I
ever knew,' and then he laid back down."[7]

The soft-sided Hank could also be seen as Audrey grew more
uncomfortable in her pregnancy, chafing in the Louisiana heat and

away from her parents. She was "extremely nervous," Lycrecia said later. "She couldn't be on her feet for very long, and she could barely stand for her clothes to touch her."[8] Sometimes she would rip off what she was wearing in a fury. Knowing the one thing that would ease her jitters, Hank acceded to her wishes to still be onstage with him—at least until she wasn't able to fit into those hip-hugging cowboy outfits—even as his band and the *Hayride* people winced when she was.

Horace Logan minced few words about Audrey before his death in 2002 at eighty-six, describing her as "a pure, unmitigated, hardboiled, blue-eyed bitch" whose singing was "horrible, unbelievably horrible" and who "forced herself out onstage when Hank was out there. . . . I'd never let her out, but Hank would say, 'Logan, I've got to let her sing. I've got to live with the woman.' I said, 'OK, Hank, here's what we do. We put two mics out there. Don't let her sing on your mic. I'll bring down the volume on her mic, and keep yours up.'"[9] Hank also made an effort to keep from going back at Audrey when she blew her top at him over the slightest things. Once, when Hank fetched her a glass of water on a sweltering day, he began pacing the room, further irritating her. In an instant she grabbed the glass and let it fly. Like in the teacup incident, she once again hit him on the skull, drawing blood. As if used to it, he didn't go to a hospital this time; instead, he calmly picked up the glass, put it back on the table next to her, and cleaned the cut. Just another night at the Williams home.

Still, perhaps it was not a coincidence that Hank developed a real taste for travel beyond the regional borders, since Audrey could not make such long trips. He saw no downside in leaving her in the condition she was in. And he'd get away *fast*.

Cops around Shreveport came to know Hank's license plate by heart, pulling him over numerous times on those lonely back roads with 35 mph speed limit signs after seeing a blur go by at 80. Hank almost always sat in the back, hat pulled over his eyes, while the musician he picked to drive would floor the gas pedal. Reminded of the limit by one cop, he drawled, "Aw, we'll never get anywhere driving like that."[10]

In the summer of '48, Hank was feeling particularly relaxed on a long trip that took him to upstate New York, where he gave an interview to a teenager who was writing a story on him for the high school paper, blithely telling him, "Don't you start drinkin' now, just because your friends do," before going back to his car and breaking open a bottle. "A man has to know what he wants to do," he continued, "and then do it and keep your mind on it, and don't let nothing else get in the way to clutter up your life."[11] But all these sentiments were bromides, with no significance to his own life. Testifying to the Lord in song was the only way he could find any redemption. And now here he was, with the Lord's blessing, a man of distinction. Why did he even *need* to repent? Girls were coming after him the way an earlier generation had Frankie Sinatra. In Corpus Christi, a pack of frenzied young things in a very pre–*Hard Day's Night* scene came at him armed with razor blades, not to do him damage but to cut off pieces of his clothing, a tie, a lapel, anything, as keepsakes; sometimes his tires would be slashed, Audrey-style, by girls who didn't want him to leave town.[12] Said Clent Holmes: "Women would lay down and faint. I seen 'em lay down and faint right there on the floor watchin' him sing."

Their age didn't seem to faze him. If he had his druthers, it would be the younger the better, so long as they were old enough in the right places. According to an account

> Hank went in for the 14- and 15-year-olds who would follow him up to his hotel room . . . naively believing all they were going to get was his autograph. In one town, a peeping tom, who had a high-powered pair of binoculars trained on her idol's room, was so shocked at what she saw, that she called the police. When they broke into Williams' locked room, they found him playing a guitar accompaniment for a 15-year-old's strip tease. The girl had nothing left to take off but her skin.[13]

Few would have ever denied the man was a slave to instant gratification. The rub was that none of what he did to find it eased even a smidgen of his pain, which he had forever codified as if it were colors in an oil painting in "I'm So Lonesome I Could Cry." As Jay Caress, a country disk jockey who wrote sagely of Hank, said of the song, it was "straightforwardly-admitted pain, but it holds no self-pity. Hank does not draw our attention so much to himself, but to the . . . universe of the things he is feeling. The purple sky, the falling star, the dying leaves, the whippoorwill, all tell us . . . just exactly how it hurt for Hank Williams. What we really don't know, of course, is exactly why."[14]

·   ·   ·

Up in Nashville, Fred Rose was stewing. He had run out of Hank's songs, and his aim to release a new one each month was dashed. Expecting but not receiving any new material from him, in early '49 he sent Acuff-Rose singer and promotion man Mel Foree to Shreveport to lean on Hank and usher him into a studio so he could cut demos. The results were discouraging. Hank recorded a good two dozen songs, none of which he seemed to think much of, and lacked energy on the demos as he sang them, accompanied only by his guitar. Foree even had to sit him down and brainstorm a few songs with him, netting him a co-writer's credit on a couple. A cross-section of these artifacts would wind up on *The Complete Hank Williams*.

Many of the demos he did would be rerecorded later—he never seemed to put a song out to pasture—but Hank's batting average on these demos was not high. When Foree took them back to Rose, Fred was aghast. With the AFM strike having ended in the fall of '48, Hank would soon be back in the studio. Fred could only hope he'd come in with something good, or the *Hayride* might be as far as Hank Williams would ever go.

Now that the strike was over, with union musicians winning some nominal concessions—prompting Hank to finally join the union himself—Rose scheduled a session for Wednesday, December 22, in Cincinnati, at the E. T. Herzog studio on Race Street downtown. Since he was going to be in the Queen City at the time, recording and touring with Foley, he summoned Hank to come out.

Hank drove out with Audrey, who felt strong enough to go, especially given that she was going to record two duets with Hank, who arrived with four songs, only one of which Rose believed good enough to use as a single. That was most definitely *not* "Lovesick Blues," with which Fred had a multitude of problems. For one thing, Hank had not written it, and Acuff-Rose had no copyright on its publishing. It had been co-written back in the 1920s by Irving Mills and Cliff Friend. As well, Hank had transposed many of the lyrics, changing the first verse—"I'm in love, I'm in love, with a beautiful girl"—into the chorus, and the chorus—"I've got a feeling called the blues"—into the first verse. Rose had wanted him to change it back, but Hank refused. Neither would he budge an inch from insisting he had written the tune and that he had bought it from Rex Griffin. Rose, in a bind, went along with it, and in a fast one, claimed the song for Acuff-Rose.[15]

But the bigger problem was that Fred, like nearly everyone else who heard Hank sing it, except for his audiences, pretty much hated it. In Rose's opinion, it was "crap, pure crap. . . . It was out of meter, had no bridge, and was full of difficult chord changes."[16] When Hank began insisting on recording it, Rose sent his son to Shreveport to hammer it out. Then, just before Hank left Shreveport, Rose sent him an expense check for a hundred dollars with sheet music for the song he preferred Hank record, "There'll Be No Teardrops Tonight," which had copyright issues itself, Rose listing Cincinnati disk jockey Nelson King as co-writer with Hank. King later insisted that he and Hank had gotten together before the session and written it, but the truth was that the credit was pure payola, something Hank later admitted, saying he'd agreed to give King an unwarranted co-credit, having been assured by Rose that "Nelson King will go all out on a plug."[17]

This was, of course, a microcosm of the song-plugging game. Country's progress was such that there now were important disk

jockeys fronting the format. If these folks could be *persuaded* to play
a record, it was Rose's business to determine the means.

· · ·

Although Rose in his note to Hank strongly referred to "There'll Be
No Teardrops Tonight" as "the back of 'LOVESICK BLUES,'" his
intention may well have been to try to box "Lovesick" out of the session, urging Hank to "know the enclosed song good when you get to
the session. . . . Blue it up as much as you can and if you can better
the melody, go ahead and do it as I wrote it quick." Indeed, when the
three-hour session began at the Herzog studios, it seemed that Rose,
his shenanigans aside, hoped "Lovesick Blues" would just go away.

The room full, the musicians on one side, Hank and Audrey on
the other, next to the door, where the echoes were fatter, the session
began with the two duets—"Lost on the River," one of his demos,
and "I Heard My Mother Praying for Me," the former credited not to
Hank and the Drifting Cowboys but "Hank and Audrey," and with
Audrey's name as writer. Clearly, Hank wasn't kidding when he said
he had to keep her happy, though these were two more reasons why
Rose was so prickly, having to accede to Hank's choices that seemed
a waste of time. Audrey's song was never even pressed. And Rose
would have liked to do the same for "Lovesick Blues"—because he
had Hank cut "Teardrops" *before* "Lovesick," leaving Hank's priority
for last.

There was only about twenty minutes left when he got to it, and
as soon as he started it—there was no time to rehearse it—Rose
knew that Hank had ignored his advice about the chord changes and
the verse-chorus reordering. Rose was not keen on paying musicians
overtime—no matter that it wasn't him but Hank, as with all artists,
who was dunned for the costs for the sessions—so Hank knew he'd
have to nail it, pronto. But when he commenced singing, Rose had
nothing but objections.

First he harped on Hank's verse and chorus swap, but Hank
would still not reorder them. Then Rose turned to the problem with

the song's meter—the music term for the rhythmic "pulses" that keep the beat, familiarly seen in guitar players tapping their foot as they play. Hank's uneven beat-keeping in his singing, either holding a beat too long or cutting it too short, was an issue Vic Willis had brought up about Hank's first Nashville session. Now Rose, roaming the floor, stopped Hank.

"That song's out of meter! Got too many bars in it. And you hold that note too long!"

Hank, for whom such things were irrelevant, offered an explanation, half laughing, "Well, when I find a note I like, I wanna hold on to it as long as I can."

But when Rose kept pressing him, Hank's mood grew less blithe. "I'll tell you one damn thing," he said to Fred, "you might not like the song, but when I walk off the stage and throw my hat back on the stage and the *hat* encores, that's pretty hot. And you said that 'Pan American' was no good, and that sold pretty good."[18]

Rose had had enough. "Well, I'll tell you what I'm gonna do," he said. "That thing is so much out of meter, I'm gonna get me a cup of coffee and when I get back maybe ya'll have that thing cut." If not, he said he'd pay time and a half overtime. Glaring at him, Hank called to him as he was opening the door, "You're mighty damn free with my money!"[19]

Clearly, the successful but bumpy relationship with Rose was strained. And a cynic might wonder if Rose was messing with Hank's head when he walked out of the studio. If so, Hank held firm, and the band did its part, Turner and Byrd vamping a dual electric/steel guitar lick that they had played on a recent Ernest Tubb session for "Waiting for a Train." They ironed out the bumps that the song always seemed to have when Hank sang it live. It was still out of meter, and the musicians were not taking bows; Byrd even asked Hank afterward, "You ain't gonna release that are you, Hank?"[20] Rose knew that if he did release it, as the nominal producer, he'd take heat for the technical flaws. "Fred lived with that [out-of-meter song] the rest of his life," Don Helms said.[21]

But Rose kept his promise and paid, or Hank did, the musicians their time and a half. And now *Rose* was in a box. "There'll Be No Teardrops Tonight" was a good tune that he'd labored hard on, creating a very pop-friendly ballad of jealousy and regret on the eve of a former love's wedding. The meter was fine, and there was a saucy fiddle/electric guitar bridge. (On *The Complete Hank Williams* it would be ruined, overdubbed and clogged with strings and thick background choruses.) Rose thought hard about putting it out instead of "Lovesick Blues." In the end, though, he wanted something that would make more of a bang, something with that old "Move It On Over" groove, and so he decided he had to give the go-ahead to Frank Walker for MGM to put out the yodeling song he hated on January 9, 1949, saving "Teardrops" for a future release and backing "Lovesick" with an older song, "Never Again."

But the copyright issues of "Lovesick Blues" grew stickier, delaying its release. Rose submitted copyright papers to MGM that listed only Hank as the composer, a blatant falsehood—even though the musicians' session sheet filed with the union identified Mills and Friend. This matter even became public knowledge; an article about Hank in the *Shreveport Times*, titled "LOVESICK BLUES" ABOUT TO BE RELEASED, noted that "the authorship of [the song] is much disputed and under investigation."[22] Rose pulled back the release, dithered some more, and finally let it out on February 11, 1949. With so much flak around the song, and hearing so much negative about it from industry people—ones he respected—even Hank was having some doubts, saying for a time, "Maybe we'll put it on the flip side."

As soon as it was on the market, Irving Mills—who in the 1930s had bought out Cliff Friend and was legally the sole composer of record—filed a lawsuit for copyright infringement of his old song, which, as Rose had feared even while he forged ahead, was not in the public domain after all. To Rose, it hardly seemed that all this byplay was worth it, but as it turned out, even though it meant Friend was restored as its composer, Hank was right about the song, and Rose wrong—very wrong. It was "Lovesick Blues" that made Rose realize it wasn't technicalities but Hank's emotional quotient, his peerless ability to yank to the surface the sadness within nearly any song, even happy ones, that was his meat.

A winner out of the chute, in the February 26 *Billboard*—in which MGM had bought a large ad for its new releases, including Hank's, Billy Eckstine's "Bewildered," and Art Mooney's "Doo De Doo on an Old Kazoo"—"Lovesick Blues" was reviewed in the folk category with "Hank's razz-mah-tazz approach and ear-catching yodeling should keep this side spinning." And even though the song still sounded weird to Hank's band, it sold 48,000 copies in its first seventeen days. By the end of March 1949, it sat sixth on the folk chart, taking aim at Eddy Arnold, who again ruled the list, with "Don't Rob Another Man's Castle."

By April 2, when the trade paper had an ad from Acuff-Rose, quoting Tulsa DJ Bill Taylor saying "Lovesick Blues" was "the greatest string record in years," it was at No. 3, right behind Eddy. By the sixteenth, it had dropped down again to 6, then caught a second wind and the next week—when yet another cover appeared, by Red Kirk—rose to No. 2, still behind Eddy. Then, with still another cover out, by Rusty Gilbert & the Louisiana Swing Boys, it fell to No. 4, only to rally again, hitting No. 2 and making the list of records most played by disk jockeys.

Finally, on May 21, there it was, sitting at No. 1, crowding out Nashville's fair-haired boy, Eddy Arnold. Hank, who was too busy or disinterested to keep track of these doings, was nonplussed when the *Shreveport Times* had reported in March that the record "probably tops the list" of most-played jukebox songs "in this section of the country." But he nearly keeled over when Tillman Franks showed him *Billboard*, with "Lovesick" perched at the top of the folk chart. As Bob McNett recalled,

He laid the magazine down and he sat there silent for hours and hours and I believe he was scared, really scared. He was overwhelmed. I think he felt he was stepping into the unknown, and he was frightened . . . in the clouds a bit. I've often thought that what went through his mind was, "I am the same country boy that I was back in Montgomery, Alabama . . . and now they think I'm something else; they think I'm a big star."[23]

"Love Sick Blues," as *Billboard* identified it, was by June 4 also first on the Most-Played Juke Box Folk Records list—and would be so a few weeks later when these constantly renamed lists would, in the June 25 issue, be bifurcated as "Most Played Juke Box (Country & Western) Records" and "Best-Selling Retail Folk (Country & Western) Records." That was surely a signal moment in country history, and would soon give way to the end of the "folk" component altogether. "Lovesick" would stay on top of the former for *sixteen* weeks, and on the chart for forty-two weeks, selling over 100,000 into the next year, and made a tangible crossover breakthrough, rising as high as No. 24 on the Records Most Played by Disc Jockeys list—the lineal forerunner of the pop chart, which wasn't born until 1955 as the "Top 100."

Fred Rose, though, didn't stand pat. He booked a day of sessions in Nashville for March 1, 1949, gnashing his teeth that Hank again insisted on recording with Audrey, who was now seven months pregnant but no less eager to make another long journey to a studio. They and Clyde Baum again drove up, the sessions now having transitioned from WSM to a properly state-of-the-art shop in the ballroom of the Tulane Hotel, where Castle Studios—the informal name used for the studio at the station, which billed itself as the "Air Castle of the South"—was now where virtually all Nashville recording was centered.

This was by necessity since the old WSM setup was an embarrassment; lacking the room for a lathe to cut the vinyl, engineers had to send recordings twelve miles away to where cutting took place, then had to call over by phone to see if a given take sounded good. Now the process was done under one roof, with the first recording made there in October 1947, Phil Rickey's "Hillbilly Jump."

Hank knew the Tulane, its huge lighted sign looming over the roof, and found Rose with a new group of musicians. Hank and Audrey did their duets on "Dear Brother," the bathetic song he had sung with Kitty Wells and Johnnie Wright about telling a brother that "Mama left this world with a smile on her face, whispering the Savior's name . . . for the city where there is no pain." The other, "Jesus Remembered Me," was a clone of "I Saw the Light"—"Jesus remembered me and so He set me free / Once I was blinded but now I can see / Glory to God, He remembered me."

These were clearly too maudlin for Rose, who would soon have an idea how to separate the lachrymose gospel stuff from the country pop he wanted. More in the pocket were the other two tracks, the first "Lost Highway," the blind country singer Leon Payne's 1948 autobiographical tale written while trying to hitchhike. Hank loved the song for sentiments that could have come right from his own songbooks—"I'm a rolling stone, all alone and lost, / For a life of sin I have paid the cost," filling out the journey with a deck of cards and jug of wine, cautioning other boys not to start "ramblin' around" or else wind up on the same road, lost and too late to pray. There were mournful trade-off solos on the break by Turner and Potter, but the saddest instrument was Hank's baritone, always about to cry and carrying out the word *looooooosssst* to the breaking point. Yet the striking thing about the lyrics was a compulsory, and routinely sexist, change he made in them, adding that "a woman's lies" began his descent.

The session concluded with "May You Never Leave Me Alone," showing his maturing writing skills with its delicate but intense imagery of a bird that "lost its mate in flight," "a piece of driftwood on the sea." Again, however, he could not resist, jarringly so, breaking into the mood by intoning, "I believed the lies you told to me, when you whispered, 'Dear I worship thee.'"

After a break for lunch, everyone came back for four more songs. The first, "Honky Tonk Blues," was essentially a slowed-down, reworked "Honky Tonkin'." The next two, "You're Gonna Change

(Or I'm Gonna Leave)" and "Mind Your Own Business" were right out of the poisoned well of his marriage. "Change" was a splendid twelve-bar blues romp, with smooth, bell-clear electric guitar licks by Zeb Turner, and Hank crooning between yodels, "You wore out a brand new trunk packin' and un-packin' your junk." All that, he laid down, had to stop, and "I don't mean please." In "Mind Your Own Business," a brazen, near note-for-note copy of "Move It On Over" with a delightful fiddle break, he issued a screw-off not to Audrey but to the outside world of busybodies:

> If the wife and I are fussin', brother that's our right
> 'Cause me and that sweet woman's got a license to fight

The final track, "My Son Calls Another Man Daddy," written with Jewell House, an Acuff-Rose client and host of the *Hayloft Jamboree* show in Texarkana, went for backwoods bathos, its subject a jailed man whose son wants nothing to do with him—with one line lamenting, "He'll never know my name nor my face. / God only knows, how it hurts me for another to be in my place." Capping off a long day, he sang it with something less than conviction. In fact, all these were merely "good" songs, meaning there wasn't a "Lovesick Blues" in the bunch.

That was especially apparent when four days later "Lovesick" hit No. 1. Two weeks later still, Rose called Hank back—alone—for a session on March 20 at Castle. For the trip, Hank would at Rose's urging take his first airplane ride. He found it a daunting proposition, wiring Rose: "Flight 58 will arrive at 5:45. I hope."[24]

Landing quite safely, he would record Claude Boone's "Wedding Bells" and Slim Sweet and Curley Kinsey's "I've Just Told Mama Goodbye," both of which had already come out, by Bill Carlisle and Sweet. These songs were a little thin, and Hank's recent reliance on other people's songs was a tip-off to Rose that Hank's writing had sloughed off. But he would wave into release "Bells" and "Mama" as the A and B sides of Hank's next release, on May 1. And, caught in the backdraft of "Lovesick Blues," "Bells" ran up the same chart to No. 2, being kept out of the top spot only by "Lovesick."

The record wound up selling 81,813 more copies, while "Lovesick" would still be on the chart in the new year, tacking on another 50,000 in sales of its own.

But what would happen once that titanic hit was played out? And would this success finally reform his redneck habits? To the contrary, record sales seemed to have no effect on his backsliding into booze. It wasn't that he wouldn't reform; it was as though he *couldn't* and still be able to be the same guy who was making those songs so believable. Still, no one could doubt his life had taken a turn for the better, outwardly, at least.

Audrey's, on the other hand, was a morass of prickly heat and imaginary hives. Her torturous pregnancy had made everyone in their circle a little crazy. She was damn near impossible to be around. Three times she thought she was in labor and had Hank take her to the hospital, only to be told it wasn't time. To be sure, it came as a relief to Hank that for most of April and into June, he was called away on a mission from God.

The *Grand Ole Opry* had finally come a-calling.

13

✦ ★ ✦ ★ ✦ ★ ✦

"*NEVER* PUT ME ON AFTER HANK WILLIAMS!"

An appreciable chunk of Hank's cascading record sales came from Louisiana. Having come to the state barely knowing its tastes, or little expertise in Cajun music and the tastes of country being groomed in the Delta, Hank had become immersed in the idioms of the bayou. It helped a good deal that he could sing the blues, and had a cachet that allowed him artistic license. He also had his stage act, and radio act, down by rote, smooth as a butterbean, using many of the same lines that never seemed to get stale, such as leading into a song with "Ladies and gentlemen, to a country boy like me it makes you feel real good when people like a song you wrote . . . like this one I'm fixin' to sing for ya right now." Onstage, his rap was less mannered, sometimes suggestive. His comedy shtick, usually with whoever the bass player was, as he had with Lum York, would go like this:

> HANK: *Well, lemme ask ya, son, if they had to graft some skin when your face got tore up in a car wreck, where'd they graft it from?*

FOIL: *Let's just say sometimes my face gets tired and wants to sit down.*

Out on the hustings one time, for a show he did with Kitty Wells and Johnnie Wright, he "accidentally" let slip a word then verboten from radio, closing by saying he was going to go out and have a "helluva good time tonight," with no care for what anyone in the management offices would think. He had that Peck's Bad Boy charm, for sure, which cut him slack to get away with a no-no. Seeing him bask in the afterglow of "Lovesick Blues," he was compelling, riveting, curiously down to earth for a rising star. Singing certainly was Hank Williams's salvation. Never did he have a worry when on a stage or before a microphone. Tillman Franks once said he asked Hank how he put so much into a song.

"Well," he replied, "I like to hear me sing. I don't care whether they like me or not. I just like to sing, and I give it what I've got. If they like it, well and good, but I don't worry none about it."[1]

He could say that with the humility of a man who knew he had nothing to worry about, though in truth he always did regardless. It was all good; but not good enough for Hank, or Fred Rose. It was clear to them that Shreveport had already served its purpose for Hank. From the moment "Lovesick Blues" and its follow-ups piled up radio plays all across the country, Rose knew the *Hayride* was small time, too small to hold the raging fire that was Hank Williams.

• • •

As though his new upward mobility came with all sorts of rewards, on May 26, 1949—the one-year anniversary of their divorce—Audrey again had severe labor pains. This time, they were for real, and after getting her to the hospital, Hank began freaking out. As Audrey remembered: "It was really a bad scene for Hank; they couldn't get him away from the door once he heard me screaming. When they tried to tell him he had a healthy son, he said, "No, I don't want to see him, I just want to see my wife."[2] The son, born at 1:45 a.m., was a bruiser, ten pounds, three ounces, whose birth Audrey said "practically killed us both."

They named him Randall Hank Williams, and, soon after, Hank nicknamed him "Bocephus," since he thought the baby's moonlike face was the spittin' image of *Opry* comedian Rod Brasfield's prop puppet of that name.[3] (He had taken to calling Lyrecia "Jughead" for the way her ears jutted out.) Hank dashed off a telegram to Fred Rose reading: "10-pound boy borned this morning at 145. Both doeing fine." Audrey, though, was already calling him by a different name, one that seemed to put a twinkle in Hank's eye. On a radio broadcast from that period, after Audrey had gotten back into singing with him, he said, "Folks, in case you didn't know it Audrey is my wife. And Audrey, I'd like you to come up and tell the folks about Randall."

"You mean Hank Jr.?" she replied in the affected, high-pitched little-girl voice she saved for such moments in the public eye.[4]

His paternal feelings for the boy filled in at least a few of the gaps in his soul. He again laid off the booze and didn't linger at the bars after his radio shows. As he would say in his new sign-off, after hoping the creek wouldn't rise, "Don't worry, Bocephus, Daddy's comin' home to see ya." Yet when the child was born, he was by law a bastard, since Audrey's divorce papers were never rescinded and she and Hank were legally not married.

When this occurred to them, the proper papers were finally filed. It took three months for Randall to be legitimate in the eyes of the law; on August 9, the circuit court in Montgomery that had approved the divorce annulled it as *nunc pro tunc*, with Hank ordered to pay all court costs. There was still the matter of whether the marriage was actually legal in the first place given Audrey's marriage at the time, but no authority ever intervened in the issue, and as of the summer of '49, the Williams clan was one happy, and legally conjoined, family. In fact, Hank now seemed light-years removed from the bounder who came from Alabama.

With the birth of Randall, Hank did the family-man thing,

bouncing the little fella on his knee, feeding and changing him, sleeping next to his crib. Lillie, W. W. Stone, and Irene came down from Montgomery, and the Williams family seemed closer than they had ever been. Perhaps this was one reason why Audrey felt a little distant from her new son. Whether it was the swarming of the Williams clan, postpartum depression, or her eagerness to get back in those tight cowgirl outfits and up onstage again, she seemed to be less fixated on maternal matters.

"Mother was not what you call a doting parent," Lycrecia Williams said. "Daddy did a lot more coddling . . . but she wasn't the type to be tied to the house because of the children. Whenever Daddy needed to go, she wanted to be able to go with him. Mother was always trying to figure out ways to make Daddy bigger or to get bigger bookings for him. She was just a business-minded woman."[5]

Thus it must have eaten at her that Hank was out on the road so much alone during her difficult pregnancy. He and his latest edition of the Drifting Cowboys, who agreed to migrate from Montgomery, were constantly on the go. He and his "boys" were earning up to $1,000 per concert—actually, *they* were still locked in at $60 a week, a pittance beside what Hank took home—while selling out shows across the region and across the country, blessedly free of having their ears bleed when Audrey sang.

Fred Rose during this period was also busy, working behind the scenes to bring him to Nashville and the *Grand Ole Opry*. So was Hank, who figured his days of waiting it out were over. He figured he could barter himself getting in with a heavyweight like Oscar Davis, who managed Ernest Tubb. The last time Davis had heard from Hank, Oscar had told him his version of "Lovesick Blues" was an earsore. Now, having proven the *Opry* seer wrong, Hank had a proposition: he would give Davis 25 percent of his booking fees *for life* if Oscar convinced the *Opry* bigwigs to let him onto their stage. Rose had already begun negotiating with the *Opry* to bring that about. As a kind of trial, not so much of his talent but of his ability to stay out of trouble, the *Opry* included Hank on a very big six-week tour of major cities in Hank's wheelhouse—Texas, Oklahoma, and Louisiana—starting in April 1949, a month before Audrey gave birth.

Unlike on past *Opry* tours, he wasn't just a guest performer but a headliner, billed with Tubb, Minnie Pearl, Red Foley, and Cowboy Copas, none of whom would earn much; Rose could not barter his way to anything but scale for Hank, around a hundred dollars a show. But he was so big in these parts that he superseded even Tubb and Minnie, whose goofy homespun monologues filled with fictitious hillbilly characters and wild stage moves made her a huge fan favorite. Yet being arguably the *Opry*'s biggest name meant little down in bayou country once it was clear the fans down there came out just as much to see the guy she had last seen as a dirty-booted, bedraggled young singer hanging out at a Montgomery radio station. As she sized him up now, "He had a wonderful wardrobe and a clean hat, and shiny boots. He looked great." Watching him perform for the first time, she recalled, "An excitement seemed to spread through the crowd. . . . By the time he got to his last number the excitement had grown to a fever pitch. The crowd would not let him leave the stage. . . . After umpteen encores they finally got Hank off and me on. It was not one of my better shows. They still wanted more of Hank! And I didn't blame them. The man had something indefinable, something that made an audience crave more. I told Oscar after the show—and every other promoter after that—'*Never* put me on after Hank Williams!' And I never followed him again."[6]

With his earnings, Hank had bought another car, a seven-seat Packard touring car limousine with a chrome grille and a matching hood ornament that seemed more like a battering ram. He took over the loan payments from a guitar player in Ernie Tubb's Texas Troubadours, and just like it had done for Ernie and his boys, this vehicle would provide first-class transportation for Hank . . . to the Ryman Auditorium.

Other legal maneuvers also worked to Hank's benefit. Through the rise of "Lovesick Blues," which would spawn still another cover version in July, by Mervin Shiner, Hank had no conception of what it

all meant financially. Shortly after Hank became a dad, in a deal bro-
kered by Fred Rose, Frank Walker tore up Hank's original contract
with the company and gave him a new one, for two years, at a higher
royalty rate—from three to five cents per every record sold, both as
artist on every song and writer of those that went on the market. It
was a 66 percent bump, translating into thousands of dollars for each
successful record. The icing was a sure sign that Hank was no longer a small-time talent—a $1,000 bonus. Little wonder that MGM,
wanting its generosity known in the industry, bought a half-page ad
that would run in the July 30 *Billboard* showing a stick figure of
Hank shaking hands with one of a tuxedo-clad MGM lion holding
a contract, CONGRATULATIONS! HANK! ON YOUR NEW M-G-M RECORDS
CONTRACT! above and blurbs for his records below, and copy reading:
"Week After Week, Hank Williams Leads 'Em All!"

Not by coincidence, that new deal was inked on June 15, four
days after Hank Williams had elevated himself into a *very* big-time
talent. Not that he wasn't already, but the reception he got on the
Opry tour underlined his marketability and the need for the *Opry*
bosses to welcome him into the country glitterati. There was, of
course, some gravely serious talk in the boardroom about Hank's
drinking—the same kind of concerned hogwash that filled the room
when many other, maybe *most* other *Opry* stars were discussed.
The compact with the *Opry* was that they had to at least keep their
boozing in abeyance and pretend to be on the straight and narrow.
The contract Oscar Davis procured from the *Opry*/WSM brass was
based on a promise Davis personally made that Hank would stay
sober for a year.[7] As well, Roy Acuff and Ernest Tubb renewed their
own recommendations to sign him.

Rose was playing every card he could. He gave Harry Stone and
Jack Stapp counterfeit writing credits on a new Rose song, "Chattanoogie Shoe Shine Boy," working off "Chattanooga Choo Choo,"
providing an enormous bonanza to come. All his pimping paid off,
too. The terms of the agreement also included giving Hank his own
early-morning program on WSM. Only a darned fool could blow

such a sweet deal. Not even waiting for his *Opry* debut, Hank arranged his farewell from Shreveport. He informed Henry Clay of his impending move to Nashville, recommending his early-morning show at KWKH be given to country singer Red Sovine, whom Hank had befriended on the *Hayride* and had helped land a contract with MGM; soon, Sovine, too, would join the *Grand Ole Opry*.

The only thing left to do was bid adieu to the *Hayride*. Hank's final show there on June 3 was billed as such and sold out in minutes. His reception that night was overwhelming. He came on at 10:30, read some telegrams, many requesting songs, then broke into "Lovesick Blues" and, amid the hysteria, was called out for *seven* encores. Horace Logan would later say he never allowed anyone more than seven encores, to preserve Hank's record. Now, with an eye trained on Nashville, Hank could tell the audience: "I want to thank y'all from the bottom of my heart, and I'm making you a promise right now. One of these days I'm gonna come back."

He had given Logan the same promise, but considered his work done in Shreveport. The guy who had given northern Louisiana its musical identity—and as Logan said, "the first real star we had" on the *Hayride*—was ready to blow out of town. Mere months after moving in, he made plans to sell his home in Bossier City, though Audrey, Randall, and Lycrecia would remain there until he secured a place in Nashville. As for his current band of Drifting Cowboys, they were free to fend for themselves. On the eve of the *Opry* tour he basically dismissed them all, as Bob McNett would recall, as coldly as a man could.

"I'm going to Texas tomorrow," he told them. "If I call you, you have a job. If I don't, you don't."[8]

• • •

On Friday, June 10, he got in his Packard and made his way to Nashville. To Hank, it must have felt like he was a king in a gilded carriage. He checked into the posh Hermitage Hotel, where the *Opry* had booked him a room.

There was no time for any real rehearsal for the *Opry*. Nor did he believe he needed one. He was slotted, still with a degree of caution, not on the portion of the show broadcast nationally on the NBC network at 10, but rather on the first of the half-hour "pregame" segments that started at 9 p.m., carried only on WSM. Fred Rose had sent over sheet music for the house band, two songs; as on the *Hayride*, if he was received well he'd be brought back later in the show on another nonnetwork segment—at 11, sponsored by Allen Manufacturing—for one more.

The band was made up of some old pros and fresh-faced kids. Hank could be comforted that Zeb Turner from Red Foley's band was its core, Red being the emcee of the *Opry*. Others included Billy Robinson, a nineteen-year-old steel guitar player, Grady Martin and Jimmy Selph on electric guitars, Ernie Newton on bass, and Jimmy Riddle on accordion. Robinson in particular became a highly sought-after session man for decades, a testament to the power of the *Opry*, something Hank learned quickly.

If Hank was a man of means and distinction in Shreveport, now he felt what real power was, even if it emanated from within the walls of a building that country performers thought of as a sinkhole. The turbid brown brick facade of the place gave it a somewhat ominous look, and the hall was cramped and dirty, smelling of urine leaking from stuffed-up bathrooms and of sweat. Regularly, patrons would faint and need to be carried out into the lobby just to breathe. Performers' dressing rooms were basically hooks on the wall in a cluttered backstage area, leading Roy Acuff in future years to buy a building down Broadway just so he and the other acts could dress in privacy before coming back to Ryman to sweat through their fancy clothing as they sang. They'd then split, taking relief in Tootsie's Orchid Lounge across the alley.

After decades of suffering there, Acuff wanted nothing to do with the effort to preserve the Ryman as a landmark. "I never want another note of music played in that building," he said in 1971 after the *Opry* moved to decent digs. "Most of my memories of the Ryman auditorium are of misery, sweating out here on this stage, the audience suffering too. . . . We've been shackled all of my career."

But none of these hardships conflicted with the growing majesty of the *Opry*, even if there had been no heightened anticipation before Hank made his debut on June 11, 1949. While "Lovesick Blues" was known broadly, it was the *song* that was so familiar, not the *singer*. Many, even in the *Opry* crowd, would only realize who he was when he broke into the first bars of his song. What's more, on this night, Ernest Tubb would also be on the earlier portion of the show before taking his regular place on the Prince Albert–sponsored main event, though the official name of the entire show was the "Prince Albert *Grand Ole Opry*." Now, much like Minnie Pearl back in Shreveport, it would be Hank who would have to follow the biggest nova of the troupe.

Undaunted as always, Hank put on his grin, adjusted his string tie, and stepped up when Red Foley called him out, rhapsodizing, "Well, sir, tonight's big-name guest is making his first appearance on Prince Albert's *Grand Ole Opry*. He's a Montgomery, Alabama, boy, been pickin' and singin' about twelve years, but it's been about the last year he's really come into his own. We're proud to give a rousing Prince Albert welcome to the 'Lovesick Blues' boy, Hank Williams!" At that, the 3,574 people in the hall applauded rather sedately. When Foley told him he'd be around the place for a good long time, Hank, all aw-shucks, said, "Well, Red, it looks like I'll be doing just that, and I'll be looking forward to it."

By the time he cranked up, the house was roaring. Many aped his yodeling; others took pictures, the flashbulbs popping in the dark. Done, he took a half-bow, waved, and left the stage, in triumph. Chet Flippo, extrapolating and then some, wrote that at this pinnacle moment of his career, all Hank could think of was the cynical advice old Rufus Payne had dispensed him as a child in Greenville. Backstage, as Hank was being glad-handed by other performers and *Opry* bosses, wrote Flippo,

Harry Stone and Jim Denny just looked at each other. There was no need to talk. They knew who was the new star of the Grand Ole Opry. [Hank] had a tight grin on his face; he knew he had just shown the tight-ass Opry clique what a real star was. . . . He found his guitar and stomped down the concrete steps and across the alleyway to a honkytonk next door [Tootsie's, where the Opry big shots gathered]. He was ready for them if they liked him and he was equally ready for them if they didn't like him. Fuck them. Who were they, anyway. [They] demanded that you bust your nuts for them. Like you were a trained nigger. Tee-Tot had told him that once in Greenville.[9]

In truth, while there surely was a wide gulf between Hank and the Nashville in-crowd, nothing suggests he harbored anything like this sort of enmity against them, and he was more than willing to accommodate the other musicians. Indeed, though Flippo maintained that Hank detested county singer George Morgan, for unknown reasons, a photo exists in which Hank's arm is draped around Morgan's shoulder.[10] Perhaps the only singer he had a beef with was Slim Whitman, who in the early '50s rode his own, almost comical yodeling trill to fame. Hank was once quoted as saying: "He ain't no damn hillbilly."[11] Neither, it seems, did Hank have any feeling of rebellion after conquering the *Opry*. For once, the high of a show *was* enough for him, and maybe he intended to keep his promise to stay sober. When a deejay named Bob McKinnon offered him a drink that night, Hank held off.

"No, I quit," he said. "I can't handle it. I don't ever expect to take another drop."[12]

. . .

Biographers have written of his debut at the *Opry* with hyperbolic flair, most notably the fable that he gave six encores that night. Actually, there were exactly no encores. The applause went on for a good

minute, and Hank took several curtain calls, but even that was pushing it. Such extended encores were kept out of the *Opry* protocol,
the priority being to keep the show running according to a strict
timeline; getting all the commercials in was paramount. Even so, it
was no exaggeration that Hank had killed that night. Another elec-
trifying reaction came when he returned for his second song later
that night on the 11 p.m. postbroadcast segment. He sang "Wedding
Bells" to a similar reaction, all the proof the *Opry* needed to commit to a regular spot for him, booking him to appear the following
Saturday on the prime-time broadcast. Rather than head back to
Shreveport, he hunkered down at the Hermitage that week, during
which he signed with the *Opry* and WSM, where he would begin
an early morning show by midsummer. On that Saturday, the eigh-
teenth, he appeared for the first time on the main Prince Albert
show, again doing "Lovesick Blues" and bringing down the house.

With his triumph in Nashville under his belt, he drove back
down to Shreveport. And while Flippo claimed that Audrey's reaction was not to share his excitement but rather to ask, icily, "What
about me?" she had much to be happy about. This, after all, had
been as much a victory for her as it was for Hank. And now that he
had standing in Nashville, and as she would soon be able to fit into
her stage costumes again, she was sure she would take every step
forward with him. There would also be money on the way, which
she considered her reward for pushing him to this success and sur-
viving all the psychotic scenes.

The Drifting Cowboys also were rewarded. While Fred Rose
held firm on his edict against using them in the studio, Hank could
have them play backup at the *Opry*. "Meet me at the Hermitage,"
he said to Don Helms. "I always told you when I started to work
on the *Grand Ole Opry* I was gonna take your ass with me."[13] The
ever-changing lineup now also included Nashville fiddler Jerry Rivers. He had been in a branch of Ernie Tubb's Texas Troubadours
called the Short Brothers, and was doing some work in a band led
by Big Jeff Bess, who was married to Hattie Louise Bess, the owner

of Toostie's Orchid Lounge. Rivers, also just twenty-one, had played on some gigs in south Alabama that also included Hank, previously turned Hank down when he asked him to leave his bands and come to Shreveport. Now he jumped aboard, and brought with him a bass player, Hillous Buel Butrum, who had at age sixteen played in the *Grand Ole Opry* house band for a short time. The newest edition of the Drifting Cowboys came from all points to Music City on Monday, July 11, whereupon Hank met up with them at the Hermitage; then they all went to WSM, where they rehearsed a bit, and on Thursday, they were performing their first gig at a club downtown, as a warm-up for Hank's next *Opry* appearance on Saturday.

Rivers, who had seen him onstage before, recalled feeling "awe-struck" watching a more polished, cool and confident Hank sing "Lovesick Blues," adding, "I gained a humility I had lost somewhere along the line." He recalled all the times he had told skeptical people in the sticks that this Hank kid would be a star one day. Now, he thought, "By God, he is."[14] Hank was prepared to keep his new gaggle at his side. He catered to their egos, dubbing each with one of those Hank-like nicknames—Helms was "Shag" for his long hair, Rivers "Burrhead" for his lack of same, McNett "Rapid Robert" for his string-pluckin' speed, Butrum "Bew" after his middle name. Hank paid them fifteen dollars for each show they performed with him, far less than the boys in Shreveport had gotten at their peak, but a good five bucks above union scale. He also allowed them to pad their pockets by selling Hank Williams songbooks and sheet music during intermissions, just as Hank had done in the early days.

Hank, for himself, knew he was stepping up even further on the earnings scale, though being under the banner of the *Opry* came with the understanding that the show was not, in itself, going to earn performers a living—rather, it was the exposure that would open up other avenues for them. But the giant shadow of the *Opry* loomed large; while Hank's asking price for an outside gig was set cautiously at $250, or more, if he performed on an *Opry*-arranged tour, the Nashville overlords would exercise their 15 percent commission. By now, though, Hank had a steady income stream. The first really big gusher of royalties from his hit records would come early in 1950, and Fred Rose made that gusher even bigger. With "Lovesick Blues" and "Wedding Bells" still selling, MGM had released the "Move It On Over" clone "Mind Your Own Business" backed with "There'll Be No Teardrops Tonight" in July, and it too caught fire, running to No. 5. Then, in September, came "You're Gonna Change (Or I'm Gonna Leave)" backed with "Lost Highway," and they went a notch higher, with "Lost" going off on its own to No. 12.

It had taken very little time for Hank to be cast into the *Opry* stratosphere with Acuff, Tubb, Foley, and Pearl. And everyone in the troupe would be happy because he made them outside money they never did at the *Opry* show, although for the veterans there might well have been a seed of jealousy growing that he was upstaging them. All that summer they were out tracing a wild checkerboard route that had them hitting venues in the Midwest, in Canada, and on the West Coast; whenever possible, they would backtrack and hurry back to Nashville for the Saturday *Opry* shows. Plans were also made for a *very* long trip, halfway around the world, in November, when the troupe would play for soldiers and fliers on military bases in Europe. One thing that was clear was that if the *Opry* could have made a buck out of it, they would have sent Hank to the moon.

· · ·

The summer *Opry* tour, a glorious roster also featuring Tubb, Acuff, Copas, Pearl, and Bill Monroe, ran through the Midwest, meaning Fred Rose could slide Hank into the Herzog studio in Cincinnati on August 30, with the same musicians who provided the backup the last time he was there. The Drifting Cowboys were still cut out of the studio sessions and could only stand and watch as Hank laid down four tracks—"I'm So Lonesome I Could Cry," "A House Without Love," "I Just Don't Like This Kind of Living," and the curveball of the bunch, his old favorite "My Bucket's Got a Hole in It."

Rose was pleased the first three were written by Hank and owned by Acuff-Rose, the best of them "I'm So Lonesome I Could Cry."

The last had been intended as part of a collection of spoken-word gospel songs Hank wanted to record early in 1950, its lonely despair reaching as far into his soul as anything he had written or would ever write. He had taken it to Rose's office in Nashville, showing the lyrics to Acuff-Rose staff songwriters. One of them, Jimmy Rule, recalled, "Hank handed me a piece of paper and said, 'Do you think people will understand what I'm trying to say when I say this?' The line was 'Did you ever see a robin weep when leaves begin to die.'" Rule thought it was the lament of a man whose heart beat in pain. "Hank had this lonesome streak, and I think it was largely caused by his marital problems. I think he wrote it out of a feeling of loneliness that stayed very much with him. He would be the natural person to write 'I'm so lonesome I could cry.'"[15]

It was unusually florid for a Hank song. With its pastiche of falling stars lighting up a purple sky, weeping robins, and midnight trains whining low, there is a very real possibility that Rose had as much to do with its writing as Hank did. As well, its tone was almost theatrically doleful and melodramatic, just barely staying on the Hank balance beam. Rose, however, always refrained from taking writing credits, even if he deserved them. Vic McAlpin, a fellow Acuff-Rose staff writer from Defeated Creak, Tennessee, who sometimes went on fishing/writing trips with Hank, once described Rose as "a hell of a touch-up man. When I saw a fancy word or phrase in one of the songs, I'd tell Hank, 'Fred just about wrote that song, didn't he?'"[16] Hank, though, had long ago swallowed his pride on this matter. An Acuff-Rose executive, Bob McCluskey, once said, "Hank told me frankly that most of his songs couldn't have been commercially successful without the aid of Fred Rose," and yet Rose, remarkably unconcerned with seeing his name on the records, was more than comfortable knowing a windfall was ahead because of the work he did polishing up the raw gems Hank turned in to him.

Even in its rough form, the genius that birthed it made Hank proprietary about the song once its sheet music got around. Holding it for himself, he told Rose not to license it to anyone else, because "I think ol' Hank needs to record this." Rose molded its perfect verse-chorus-break-verse-chorus structure and set it to a tempo brighter than the mood of the piece. Hank worked in a quiet half-yodel around "I" and "cry," wringing real heartbreak out of them, and the steel guitar and fiddle mewled along with him, toward a last echoing note of profound finality. It still echoes as a requiem to this day. Sadness, loneliness, isolation, these had always been a bedrock of hillbilly music, yet there'd never been something as personally grim and ominous expressed so poetically. Usually a song like that had a bit of uplift, a hint that all would be okay. Not this one. Was it *too* sad, too close to real pain?

Rose wanted it on the market but hedged just a bit—in a way that showed how far black-rooted blues had come, especially in country. Hank's version of "My Bucket's Got a Hole in It" had been one he'd waited over ten years to record, since Rufus Payne had introduced him to it. He sang it in the minstrel blues dialect, lowering his voice from its usual trill. There was plenty of twang in the song, but the bass notes were rounder and deeper than usual, and Hank handled the funky guitar solo on the break, the only one he ever played. Rose had taken his red pencil to the original down-and-dirty Clarence Williams lyrics, also striking Hank's reference to a Ford—brand names were out, lest competing brands, in this case a different car company, wanted to sponsor his radio show. Fred left intact "I can't buy no beer," jive talk like "Doin' the be-bop-bee," and "I got a woman in the bossman's yard."

Per Rose's directive, MGM released it as an A-side with "So Lonesome" on the flip the first week of November 1949, with "Lovesick Blues" and "Wedding Bells" still in the Top 5. It was quite visionary, as "Bucket" had fed the blues habit of many a singer, and when Hank's song was on the country chart by month's end, climbing to No. 2 by the new year, another version of it by country veteran T.

Texas Tyler had beaten it into the Top 10. This helped open the door for one of the song's variants to fly as an early rock and roll standard, Little Richard's "Keep a-Knockin'" It also helped "So Lonesome," which when the jockeys turned the record over went off on its own path to No. 2.

As Hank liked to say introing his songs on the radio, they surely would help to buy him "beans and biscuits."

14

PETTIN' PARTIES, CIGARETTES, AND GIN

Fred Rose had forwarded Hank enough advance money on royalties for him to begin looking for an appropriately living-large home in Nashville. He put a down payment on a three-bedroom, $21,000 ranch house on a rural tract of land just south of Nashville at 4916 Franklin Avenue, and down the road from the new office of Acuff-Rose, paid for in large part by Hank's sales. With three rolling acres, a man could really kick back and breathe. There were no railroad tracks in sight, only leafy woods and those whippoorwills he sang about. When the sale closed in early September of 1949, Hank had already made it palatial, the wet dream of an Alabama country boy who had grown up in shotgun shacks and rooming houses. He had hired contractors to enlarge the place, where something would always be under construction.

Hank and Audrey would spend any money that came in, Audrey mostly on the house. There would be a new master bedroom, a two-car garage off the kitchen, expensive Oriental furnishings, shiny crystal chandeliers. Four new bedrooms were added, a two-story ballroom, a fully equipped bar, a wrought-iron fence carved with musical notes from "Lovesick Blues," awnings on the windows inscribed with a *W*. The master bedroom had white velvet walls, a white shag carpet, a white bed with a heart-shaped headboard. There would be six and a half bathrooms, all with marble sinks. The entire house was painted gold. A nurse named Audrey Ragland was hired to tend to Audrey, Lycrecia, and Randall. Hank bought several horses—he named his, a magnificent strawberry roan Tennessee Walking Horse, Hi Life—and he and Lyrecia rode around on brushy trails. The horses would require the building of a stable and the hiring of grooms. It was, in every way, a portent of decadence soon taken to a slightly higher level in Memphis by one of his lineal descendants in American culture—Elvis Presley and his Graceland—but unlike the fellow with the spit-curl, Hank had no inclination to luxuriate on a velvet throne in his bathroom. All of this culture stuff was the doing of Audrey, and it would nearly bust him.

Seeing it happening before his eyes, Hank seemed only to see *her* profligacy as a problem. A confidant of Hank who shared that opinion once said that "when he made 75,000 dollars, she was at home spending 110,000 dollars—widening their big driveway. . . . He'd say something like, 'What d'ya think of a woman who'd take a mink coat and just throw it in the front yard?' I don't think Hank did anything about it. But a guy with an income like me would just had to've backhanded her."[1] As it was, Hank was loath to even set his fanny down on one of the delicately cushioned chairs, instead preferring to plop down on the floor. Audrey would go tsk-tsk at his unbreakable boorishness. She was, in her mind, a *lady*, no longer a hick. While he would spend hours down at the fishin' crick with a buddy, she would be holding court at the country club in the neighborhood that he avoided like the plague. Moreover, after having driven Hank as if with a bullwhip to get to the *Opry*, she rarely went to the Ryman herself, not just because the bosses wouldn't put her on that stage with him but because she despised the cattle-pen nature and stench of the scene there.

She was gung-ho to get on tour with him and loved when he called her up onstage in some honky-tonk in the sticks. But the *Opry* crowd? If Hank thought they were high-falutin' phonies save for Roy Acuff and Minnie Pearl, Audrey despised them for the opposite reason; they were churls, manipulated by avaricious businessmen. She would rather sit home in her immaculate living room than deal with those pigs. The irony was that, in her figments, she didn't notice that the upscale matrons she longed to fall in with still regarded her as a churl herself. Hank, on the other hand, fully accepted that he would always carry the dirt and scent of the Alabama he never really left behind. And all of it, including the fact that Hank professed love for her while clearly hating to be anywhere near her, was becoming too much for Audrey to hide even with a pricey Oriental rug. Fame and success notwithstanding, they were once more on borrowed time.

· · ·

Hank's skyrocketing stardom was played to the hilt by the Nashville overlords. Even when he went out on his own, with the Drifting Cowboys, he carried an *Opry* sanction. His frequent opening act, Big Bill Lister, given him and paid for by the *Opry*, was in tow. Lister, however, once said that "a naked lady coulda rode an African elephant behind him and wouldn't nobody have noticed. . . . I often wondered why they hired me to warm the crowd up—they didn't need no warming."[2]

Hank would begin his radio duties at WSM in the late summer of '49, squeezed in between legs of seemingly endless *Opry* tours. When the Midwest jaunt ended, he had only a few weeks to enjoy the new house before he was off again, to the Pacific Northwest, southern Canada, and California. Hank had surely gotten into the swing of Nashville etiquette, and his star was on the rise so fast that he could help set a sartorial trend.

When they pulled into LA in September, Hank's first time in La-La Land, he happened into a clothing store, Nudie's of Hollywood, which sold Hollywood-style cowboy wear. This was mainly spangled, fringed, jewel-embroidered jackets with the brand name of Nudie, after the store's owner, Nuta "Nudie" Kotlyarenko, a Ukrainian-born tailor who as a young man ran with gangster Pretty Boy Floyd. He then opened a New York City clothing shop with his brother, Julius, unveiling Nudie's for the Ladies underwear. They relocated to California in the early 1940s, designing and making the glittery garb in his garage. In 1947, as Nudie Cohn, he opened Nudie's Rodeo Tailors and convinced Tex Williams to buy him a sewing machine and wear the clothes. Williams became the prototype of the "Rhinestone Cowboy" and Nudie the prime clothier of country singers. For Hank, those flashy sequined cloth, leather, and lamé suits in every imaginable color was the image he was looking for. He purchased a few suits, then would keep up a steady supply of orders from Nashville, his favorite the jackets with bedazzled musical notes and scales embroidered on them.

Having put his stamp on Nudie's, Hank did the same with WSM, though as with the *Opry*, he had to pass an audition, in this case a trial period by recording eight fifteen-minute shows that the management would determine whether they wanted to put on the air. The show came with a sponsor, an over-the-counter palliative called Hadacol, invented in 1945 by a self-promoting Louisiana state senator, Dudley LeBlanc (after a previous "medicine" of his had been banned by the FDA). LeBlanc's new snake oil proved quite popular, no doubt because of its alcohol content—20 percent. At $1.25 a bottle, it was about the cheapest booze one could buy. WSM called Hank's 6:30 a.m. program *The Health and Happiness Show*; the station wanted to syndicate it nationally and thus Hank would not mention the sponsor or sing jingles about it, so that local stations could plug in their own sponsors' ads. Still, because of the enormous popularity of the flagship Nashville show, Hank would become synonymous with Hadacol—often doing tours it sponsored that drew Roy Acuff and other major stars. Several country songs even used its name in the title, such as Bill Nettles and His Dixie Blue Boys'

"Hadacol Boogie," covered later by Jerry Lee Lewis. Based on "Rum Boogie," it went:

> *A-standing on the corner with a bottle in my hand,*
> *And up stepped a woman, said, "My Hadacol Man"*
> *She done the Hadacol Boogie, Hadacol Boogie, Hadacol Boogie*
> *Hadacol Boogie, Boogie-woogie all the time*[3]

Hank, his option at the station eagerly picked up, helped sell quite a few of those boogie-woogie bottles for two years, propping up the company's profits, which grew by leaps and bounds. When LeBlanc, who liked to be called "Coozan," bayou-speak for "cousin," appeared on Groucho Marx's radio show *You Bet Your Life*, the rapier-witted comedian, another LeBlanc client, asked what Hadacol was good for; LeBlanc happily replied, "It was good for five and a half million for me last year." However, he was playing a little too fast and loose, spending way too much on advertising and living the high life. After just one year, he owed $300,000 in back taxes. He would need a quick way to make money to save the company, or at least keep it propped up for enough time for him to sell it to a sucker. How he did this would soon be evident, and very much involve Hank Williams.

• • •

Playing off the rough hillbilly edges, Hank was a perfect morning host. At the beginning of his WSM tenure, the show was a folksy "Mr. and Mrs." morning coffee klatch, Hank placating Audrey by having her as a co-host, singing and making light-hearted banter. That, however, lasted only four shows, the station's directors perceiving her off-key warbling and ditzy Gracie Allen–type persona as undercutting the "high-class hillbilly" image they wanted for the star. He did the last four trial-run shows alone, to the delight of the station and no doubt Hank himself, and after they had run, he began working solo on a permanent basis, though he would periodically bring Audrey on, at her urging.[4]

Hank never would make much dough directly from the radio. Harry Stone later said he'd be surprised if Hank pulled in even a hundred bucks a week, though indirectly he did, as each play on the air earned a royalty—but just like his regular appearances on the *Opry*, this was really a base of operations for a much wider net. The latter, with its ten million listeners every Saturday night, was the beau ideal of his profession, its Talent Bureau booking agency now as powerful as any such agency in the business; combined with the radio show's intimate setting that allowed him to attract local gigs that could put thousands of dollars into his pocket—he could also command hundreds in advances on the gate—he was virtually a turnkey operation, grinding away in almost ruthless fashion. That was the good part. The not-so-good was the almost athletic-level endurance he needed to have to be able to accommodate it all and still write and record quality songs. By late 1949, it had gotten to the point where Fred Rose stopped waiting for him to send demos or even get an idea for a song and simply wrote down titles of songs, nothing more, on scraps of paper, from which Hank was to erect entire melodies and lyrics, just like that.

It would become a hellacious grind, both in Nashville and on the road, where he might play up to four shows a day, leaving him little time for sleep to recover from the night before. Minnie Pearl and her husband, Henry Rolfs Cannon, a World War II fighter pilot who began his own charter plane company in peacetime, became close to Hank over these years. They would charter a DC-11 and later a Beechcraft private plane to each stop in style, taking Hank with them. Still, he could have used some Hadacol, preferably with a bourbon chaser, for his aching body. The almost literally back-breaking burden was obvious to all around him. If Hank got through any given day without falling off the wagon, they all let out a sigh of relief. But what about tomorrow?

. . .

The *Opry* tour of Europe was another gauge of Hank's and country's rise, and the egos that came with it. USO tours were common, with the biggest stars entertaining the troops at Thanksgiving. Bob Hope, of course, made a cottage industry out of it. However, with so many Southern boys in uniform, by the late '40s country music had become the most popular musical fare heard on Armed Forces Radio.

The tour was booked for theaters and air force bases in November 1949 over two weeks to run through Turkey Day. Wives and husbands came along, which for Audrey meant having to mingle with people she detested. They landed first in Paris, then went on to Wiesbaden, Germany, met by a German oom-pah-pah band playing a Bavarian version of "Dixie." They visited wounded airmen on the hospital base, then took off for Berlin, playing shows in theaters and dance halls, then for Frankfurt, Munich, and Vienna. Some of the shows were recorded for broadcast back home on the *Opry*.

Hank, who had given his first homecoming concert in Montgomery on a show with Bill Monroe two days before, apparently was dry on the trip, not even sampling any German beer, taking no chances of sullying the *Opry* brand during a mission of high import. He was, as in the States, the clear favorite among the troupe, called out for encores of "Lovesick Blues" at each stop. This would be the one and only time he would stand on foreign soil other than Canada and Mexico and he and the others were speechless as they walked through bombed-out ruins one day and breathtaking mountains the next in the land where yodeling had begun.

Hank and Audrey were the unquestioned royal couple of the interlude, being mobbed in each city by Americans stationed on the bases and tourists who recognized them on the streets. In the glamour derby, no one else came close to them, Hank in his snazzy Nudie suits and lizard-skin boots, Audrey in her fur coats and long blond curls cutting a Greta Garbo–like image. They smiled and waved, seeming to revel in the attention, while top stars like Roy Acuff were all but unrecognized. Hank, however, was generally bummed out, unable to stomach the Bavarian food—he'd call out for someone to bring him some ketchup, which not even the best eateries had, sending him into fits of cursing—and like everyone else he was being worked to exhaustion.

The *Opry* announcer Grant Turner later spoke of the troupe being awakened in their hotel rooms early each morning for a round of publicity photos with local officials, then touring hospitals and bases all day before the hectic routine of the nightly shows. "We were going all the time. Finally the husbands and wives all got mad at each other"—something, of course, that was never very far from happening with Hank and Audrey but now became common as the entourage descended into a hornet's nest of backbiting and petty jealousy, revealing the *Opry* crowd not as kin but as social-climbing vanity cases. "We had some really knockdowns and dragouts," Turner said of the squabbles within the troupe.[5] Naturally, none of this was public knowledge; the trip was spun as a real coup, which it was. Before they set out for home—another endless trek with stops in England, the Azores, and Bermuda—the troupe posed for group pictures, smiles frozen on their faces. And yet, though few could have seen it in this ironic light, in a broader prism the hard feelings and bad blood were the real signs of country's arrival as a big-league franchise in entertainment.

For a few uneasy moments, though, it seemed the vital core of country music might all be lost. Flying home two days after Thanksgiving, the plane experienced violent turbulence over the Atlantic and plunged several thousand feet. The passengers gasped, cried, and began saying prayers before the plane leveled off. The venerable *Opry* announcer George Hay would later say on the air that Hank "swore that if he ever got back home, he would kiss the ground. When he got off the plane at Nashville airport, he did just that. He kneeled over slowly and kissed the ground."[6]

· · ·

Before the new decade arrived, the relief over Hank's sobriety ended. Walking back his vow to Bob McKinnon, he apparently began tippling right after he got back home in one piece. On another long, winding *Opry* tour, important dates were set for the week of December 8, 1949, at the Hippodrome Theater in Baltimore, which booked them for four shows a day over a week. Then Hank and Cowboy Copas would branch off and do a two-man show at the Roosevelt Hotel in DC. But Oscar Davis had a problem on his hands. Winding through the Midwest, Davis found Hank in the bar of a hotel in Des Moines, pounding back bourbons. Not having seen Hank like this, Oscar didn't realize that Hank could get cheeky. When he slurred that he wouldn't play at that night's show, Davis growled, "You'd better or you'll never play any other place. I'm gonna tell Jim Denny, 'I don't ever want this sonofabitch to ever play the *Opry* again.'"

"Aw, hell, I was just kidding," Hank laughed, perhaps amused to tweak the *Opry* honcho. Later, after the show, Denny stationed a guard outside Hank's door to make sure he didn't return to the bar and no one would bring him booze. But Davis didn't realize how industrious Hank could be. He apparently fashioned a makeshift transport system, tying a laundry bag to a rope and lowering it four floors to the ground, where a fellow hotel guest put two bottles of bourbon in it before giving the rope a tug. Davis and the hotel dick found Hank passed out drunk on his bed. The next night, in Moline, Illinois, hungover, he was sent onstage. A woman in the audience later related that "two men brought him out, one on each arm, his guitar around his neck, and stood him at the mike. He didn't say a word, not even howdy. He was like a zombie. He sang great for an hour and then the two men came and got him and took him away." She later saw him backstage, propped up in a chair and "smelling like a brewery . . . probably didn't know his name or where he was. But you talk about a performance. He never missed a note."[7]

Davis was fuming. Again that night, Hank slipped the knot and was plied with booze during a craps game. When the troupe got to Baltimore, he couldn't be propped up or sing a note. For those who'd joined up with Hank recently, like Jerry Rivers, these demented scenes were the first time they'd seen him sloshed, confirming all that they'd heard from others.[8] Soon enough, Davis didn't even try to keep him clean. Though Hank's vow to Oscar that he'd keep dry for a year was inoperable, his place secure because of his popularity, Oscar took him off the Hippodrome shows. Told to stay at the hotel, Hank bribed a bellhop to smuggle up booze in a water pitcher. He also was said to have gotten some of the girl square dancers on the show to smuggle him miniature bottles of booze in their hoop skirts. Davis had no recourse but to call the boss—Audrey Sheppard Williams. He told her to come to Baltimore and drive Hank home. Bob McNett and Don Helms picked her up at the airport and took her to the hotel. She was not happy.

Recalled McNett: "She said, 'I am so upset and discouraged, I think I've lost all the love I had for Hank.' I didn't believe her then, and I still don't. But right at that point you could see there was such a strain on that marriage. It was very important to her for him not to drink."[9]

Audrey knew she would be the first one to feel the sting of Hank's backslide. Even when he was dry, life with him was a trial. Being dismissed as co-host of his radio show didn't help matters either, nor being stuck at home with a baby to feed and change while he was out all over the map playing star; she wasn't particularly sympathetic to his complaints that he was overworked and underpaid, and that too many people wanted "a piece of him," as he would put it. Not when she had to go to enormous lengths to keep him from missing shows and other *Opry* business. Once, when he had an *Opry* function scheduled, he decided to go fishing instead with Jerry Rivers on Kentucky Lake. Tracing him there, Audrey chartered a *seaplane* to land on the lake and gather him and help him into his good clothes on the trip back to Nashville for the dinner. Rivers, who, like Hank, could hardly believe his eyes, was finding out Audrey *was* the real boss. As Rivers recounted this incredible sight, Hank's reaction was priceless.

Looking incredulously at the plane, Hank, he said, shook his head and, almost whining, pealed, "I can't get *away* from this!" Added Rivers: "He said, 'I'll see ya later,' and left me sitting in the boat out in the middle of Kentucky Lake."[10]

Lycrecia Williams once candidly remarked that "Mother was a little too ambitious, maybe," not only individually but about Hank's career, while he "just wanted to let [things] kind of happen. If they happened, fine, but if they didn't, that was all right, too. . . . Even though I think Daddy needed that direction, he would have wanted her to be a plain little housewife and stay home. But Mother couldn't do that. She did that in her first marriage and her husband ran off and left her when she was pregnant." At the same time, Audrey realized that if she stayed home, "Daddy wouldn't have gone any further.

McNett never told Hank what Audrey had said, figuring it would kill him, and remove the only ballast he had—indeed, only five days after Davis called her to get him out of Baltimore, she had sobered him up enough for him to rejoin the tour in DC. And the crazy thing was that they often *were* the loving couple. At home, Hank would often sit beside her on the couch, put his arm tenderly around her shoulder, and hug her tight, though Audrey, being far less affectionate, would stiffen up like a board. A photo snapped of them on the long plane ride to Germany shows Hank sleeping cozily on her lap, a blanket pulled up under his chin.

There was, as well, the issue of how she felt about being assumed the dirtiest of his dirty laundry and target of the insults in his songs. Audrey was always guarded about that, saying after his death that "Hank wrote the songs himself—whether or not I was an inspiration, I will leave that up to other people. . . . I know within me and I know what Hank told me on a number of occasions . . . but I've been criticized on some songs—it's so unjust, it's unreal."[11] She also knew that, because of those songs, she would eternally be blamed by some for Hank's drinking, the most unjust of assumptions. As Minnie Pearl said years later after both had died, "A number of people in country music were critical of her. They thought she aggravated Hank's alcohol problem. But I think his sickness went way back to childhood, long before Audrey came into his life. I always liked her."[12]

Still, probably not far from Audrey's thoughts was that if she did stick it out, the value of her community property in a divorce— *another* divorce—might be potentially staggering. These kinds of considerations had been on her mind from the start. For example, she refused to allow Hank to adopt Lyrecia out of an abiding fear that he might somehow gain custody should the marriage collapse. And so even as she contemplated leaving him for good, getting all she could in the meantime overrode it for now, keeping her place in the Hank Williams brand.

• • •

Fred Rose, for his part, was no longer much interested in lecturing Hank about domestic life and drinking his way out of success. "Lovesick Blues" and "Wedding Bells" were followed by a conveyor belt of follow-up country hits—"Mind Your Own Business," backed with "There'll Be No More Tears" (No. 5), "You're Gonna Change (Or I'm Gonna Leave)"/"Lost Highway" (No. 4), and the last song released in '49, his twangy cover of "My Bucket's Got a Hole in It" (No. 2), and the first release of the new decade, "I Just Don't Like This Kind of Living" (No. 5), another of his marital confessionals, this one mocking Audrey's presumptions of his ill-doing—"You ain't never been known to be wrong, and I ain't never been right."

Rose didn't need to worry about Hank relying on other folks' songs anymore. Fatherhood and stardom seemed to put Hank enough at ease to unleash songs that, ironically, cried harder than ever. A cynic might have said Hank's songs of lonely desperation and endlessly brittle and agonizing love, while real enough, also were a good gimmick, and that he excelled at channeling real pain into comfortably commercial ditties. This seemed especially so now that his writing was more of an assembly-line process itself than an undefined process without time limits. Almost diffidently, as if in meek compliance with Rose's cold, impersonal methods, he told a news magazine called *Pathfinder* in 1952, "People don't write music, it's given to you, you sit there and wait and it comes to you. If it takes longer than thirty minutes or an hour, I usually throw it away."[13]

This, of course, was nothing like the way he had written in the past, when he had filled notebooks with scribblings and kept songs in his head for months, *years*, building each one piece by piece as it emerged in concept. If he had washed that process away, he was also washing away much of what was real about him and turning into a human Hadacol.

Whatever he sang surely made people feel better, even if the songs were about feeling worse. Although the temperature in Nashville that fall of '49 had hit a record low of 36 in September, Hank was *hot*. Every day it seemed somebody was covering one of his songs, as if buying a ticket onto the country charts. Roy Acuff did "Jesus Died for Me"; Milton Estes, "House of Gold"; Bill Monroe, "Alabama Waltz."

After "Honky Tonkin'" was covered by Rose Maddox, it would become the first Hank Williams song ever to be recorded by a mainstream pop artist—eighteen-year-old Teresa Brewer, an erstwhile child singer. At around the same time, another budding thrush, nineteen-year-old Polly Burgin, a Tennessean, also covered it on the KEM label in a more authentic hillbilly diva style, yodeling and all, completely alien to her future soft pop songs as Polly Bergen. Brewer would also make a movie-theater short film singing the tune in '51.

Then, too, in a blast from the past, Braxton Schuffert, who had found work in Montgomery as a driver for Hormel Meat while doing a radio show on WSFA that the company sponsored, ran into Hank on one of his periodic visits to pay off Lillie, and the two sat down and wrote some songs. Hank, again flexing his muscle, instructed Rose to pitch Frank Walker on recording Schuffert, who agreed— the angle being that Schuffert could be marketed as a Hank Williams protégé and part-time co-writer.

Walker, who detested Audrey and having to release those duets

with Hank, no doubt figured an actual performer with a Hank connection wasn't a bad bet. Hank then sent Schuffert train fare to
Nashville, put him up at his home—Brax was flabbergasted by the
place, playing with the automatic garage-door opener for hours—
and got him backstage for an *Opry* show. Then, with Rose on the
board, Brax went into Castle Studio on February 8, 1950, and, playing Hank's guitar with the Drifting Cowboys, cut "Rockin' Chair
Daddy," his high-pitched voice and vibrato a throwback to vintage
country, along with standard weepy fare, "Teardrops on a Rose,"
"Why Should I Cry," which dated way back to 1941, and one from
Rose's Acuff-Rose drawer, written by Johnny Anglin, "If Tears Could
Bring You Back."

   "Rockin' Chair Daddy" got the play as a release, under the name
"Braxton Shooford," but didn't do much, selling around 3,500
records. Still, it was all part of the Hank whirlabout. And Rose, clearing the field of these diversions, had booked his meal ticket for studio
time at Castle on January 9 and 10. This time he could not stand in
the way when Hank came in with Rivers, Helms, and McNett, joining holdovers Jack Shook and Ernie Newton. That Hank also played
seemed to make for a four-guitar setup, but Hank's instrument by
now was mainly for show onstage, not studio purposes. Rose did
not put a microphone on the guitar, only one by his mouth. Shook
carried the rhythm, McNett and Helms adding the high, twangy
electric accents.

   Hank came in with three new songs, "Long Gone Lonesome
Blues," "Why Don't You Love Me," and "Why Should We Try Anymore," and would take another crack at "My Son Calls Another Man
Daddy," the song he'd written with Jewell House. The priority was
"Long Gone Lonesome Blues," a song that, like others, sparked a
claim of a stiffed writer's credit. This one came from Vic McAlpin,
who had co-written Eddy Arnold's 1947 No. 1 country hit "What Is
Life Without Love" and wrote other hits into the 1980s. McAlpin
maintained that "Long Gone" was one of those that "we'd start fool-
ing around with . . . and when we got something, he'd give me five

hundred dollars for my half, and I'd stick the money in my pocket and forget it. He wanted the credit for everything." Out on the way to Kentucky Lake, McAlpin remembered,

> [Hank] said, "I gotta have me another blues to record, somethin' like 'Homesick Blues.'" All of a sudden he started singing something like, "She's gone along, gone along blues." He hummed it over a couple of times, then he dropped it. Well, we got in the boat, and I threw my line out. He was fussin' with his bait. You could tell his mind wasn't on it. I said to him, "You come here to fish or watch the fish swim by?"
>
> "Hey, that's the first line," he said.
>
> "Huh?" I said.
>
> He said, "Watch the fish swim by." I got the idea and said, "Okay, but why not say the river was dry?"
>
> "Yeah, okay," he said, so we put the song together.[14]

Hank's line became the first one of the first verse, McAlpin's the third line.

But nowhere on the record would there be Vic's name. If Hank slipped him five big bills, it seemed like a hell of a day's pay for one line, even if in a few months it would seem paltry next to what a credit would have netted him. Indeed, for Hank it was worth five hundred because he heard a hit in his head.

Hank, like Jimmie Rodgers, had a way of making the familiar fresh, with the turn of a phrase and the inflection of his voice. The phrasing was the key, and for that he always needed a good, clever hook. He said it himself, in a thirty-five-page booklet written with Jimmy Rule, *How to Write Folk and Western Music to Sell*. While Hank could get away with telling people that "God writes the songs for me," his thirty-minute time limit reflected a far more cold and calculating writer. In the booklet, issued in 1951 by a local publisher, he noted that the chorus—the hook—was the starting point, "the part of the song sung most," and should be "simple and easy-flowing,"

Growing up bouncing from shotgun shacks to boardinghouses across the bleak South Alabama landscape, Hank could never have dreamed that the rundown wood-frame house where he lived in Georgiana would decades later be restored in splendor as the home of the Hank Williams Fan Club House, one of several museums displaying childhood memorabilia of the future king of country music. (© BILL BACHMANN / ALAMY)

Hank's earliest performances were as a street singer, beginning as a child after his mother, Lillie Williams, bought him a guitar. By his early teens, the frail-looking kid with glasses was wowing crowds on the busy streets of Montgomery, the capital city where his family moved to accommodate his big dreams, and where at age thirteen he began to seriously indulge ever-growing addictions to drinking and trouble. (ALABAMA DEPARTMENT OF ARCHIVES AND HISTORY, MONTGOMERY, ALABAMA)

If walls could sing, this A-frame boardinghouse at 324 North McDonough Street in Montgomery, shown here in 1954 before it was razed, could have spun some awesome country tunes. One of two such boardinghouses Lillie operated on the block—which many suspected were in fact brothels—this was also a home for Hank and his early bandmates. Later he secretly stashed here a girlfriend he impregnated, who after his death gave birth to a daughter. The identity of her father was kept from her for decades. (ALABAMA DEPARTMENT OF ARCHIVES AND HISTORY, MONTGOMERY, ALABAMA)

Looking more like backwoods hillbillies, Hank's first band—called "Hank and Hezzy's Driftin' Cowboys"—pose for an early PR shot, circa 1938. Hank, just fifteen and already hosting his own radio show, wears a black hat and a sheepish grin, standing to the right of his older sister and travel companion, Irene. The other musicians are bassist Smith "Hezzy" Adair and guitarist Braxton Schuffert. The two young girls were probably neighbors invited into the shot. (ALABAMA DEPARTMENT OF ARCHIVES AND HISTORY, MONTGOMERY, ALABAMA)

Although the long road took him far and wide, there was always time for a gig in his native Alabama. In this wide shot circa the late 1940s, Hank fiddles up a storm at the opening of a Chevrolet dealership in Luverne. The band now included Audrey Sheppard, whom he married in 1944. "Miss Audrey" insisted on singing in the act, her ambition and adultery clashing with his but also stoking his songs of cold, cheatin' hearts. (ALABAMA DEPARTMENT OF ARCHIVES AND HISTORY, MONTGOMERY, ALABAMA)

Even before he made his first recording, Hank had written dozens of songs, the lyrics of which in 1946 he paid to have bound in a volume called the *Deluxe Hank Williams Song Book*, which he sold from the stage and on the air on his earliest radio program, at WSFA in Montgomery, earning him a reputation that helped propel him to stardom. (ALABAMA DEPARTMENT OF ARCHIVES AND HISTORY, MONTGOMERY, ALABAMA)

HANK WILLIAMS   exclusively on   M-G-M Records

Hank's first big break came in March 1947 when he was signed to MGM Records, which ran ads such as this boasting of its new find once he proved himself. It didn't take long. The first song he cut for MGM, the suggestive "Move It On Over," peaked at No. 4 on the country chart in August. Seven years later, it would be reworked and renamed, without credit given to Hank, as "Rock Around the Clock" by Bill Haley and His Comets, often regarded as the first rock and roll record. (ALABAMA DEPARTMENT OF ARCHIVES AND HISTORY, MONTGOMERY, ALABAMA)

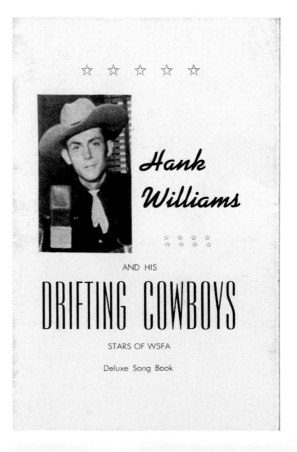

☆ ☆ ☆ ☆ ☆

Hank Williams

☆ ☆ ☆ ☆
☆ ☆ ☆ ☆

AND HIS

DRIFTING COWBOYS

STARS OF WSFA

Deluxe Song Book

HANK WILLIAMS
THE DRIFTING COWBOY

Hank's success recording in the country music capital of Nashville earned him the early morning slot at WSM, the top country radio station in America, which broadcast the *Grand Ole Opry* on the NBC network. Billed as "The Drifting Cowboy," despite his popularity he was soon fired for often showing up drunk, sometimes not showing up at all, keeping the *Opry* door closed to him. Fed up, he moved to Shreveport and instead headlined on the *Louisiana Hayride*.
(ALABAMA DEPARTMENT OF ARCHIVES AND HISTORY, MONTGOMERY, ALABAMA)

Moving back to Nashville in 1949, Hank made his belated debut at the *Grand Ole Opry* and became its top act. But he was starting to break down. In this publicity shot circa 1950, looking bony and wan, his famous impish grin seems tempered. By now the constant pain in his back could only be eased with more and more booze—and, soon, lethal drugs ominously prescribed by a quack doctor he kept on his payroll. (ALABAMA DEPARTMENT OF ARCHIVES AND HISTORY, MONTGOMERY, ALABAMA)

In this 1949 photo, the first family of country music strikes a happy pose, "Miss Audrey" holding her and Hank's infant son Randall, aka Hank Jr., and her daughter Lycrecia at left. Yet Hank and Audrey's endless civil war soon blew the marriage apart. Amid dueling charges of cruelty and infidelity, Audrey won half of his earnings in perpetuity, and when she herself died in misery in 1975, she was buried next to him, eternally Mrs. Hank Williams. (PICTORIAL PRESS LTD / ALAMY)

Despite his declining health and self-destructive tendencies, which included firing a gun at Audrey, Hank dominated the country music genre. But his recklessness carried over to business matters, as he rarely read contracts, which perhaps explains his sardonic look here at another of those signings. The biggest deal he ever made, to star in Hollywood movies, fell through when he broke the contract. And though he was earning a fortune, he would squander almost every penny. (ALABAMA DEPARTMENT OF ARCHIVES AND HISTORY, MONTGOMERY, ALABAMA)

Hank's trademark what-me-worry grin and shambling body language spill off this candid shot of him, cigarette in hand, taken in the WSM studio in the early '50s during a break from his radio show. (ALABAMA DEPARTMENT OF ARCHIVES AND HISTORY, MONTGOMERY, ALABAMA)

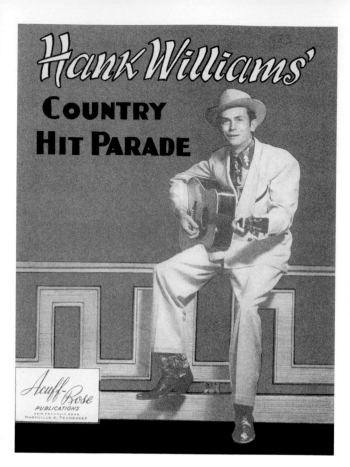

Just one example of the whirlwind that was Hank Williams: a country music magazine with his mug on the cover. Hank's enormous popularity and streak of No. 1 country hits kept him on these covers as well as in the pages of national news magazines, and on the new medium of television, guest-starring on top-rated variety shows hosted by Perry Como and Kate Smith. However, his life degenerated into a mess of booze, drugs, physical problems, and mental instability. (ALABAMA DEPARTMENT OF ARCHIVES AND HISTORY, MONTGOMERY)

Attesting to the fruits of success, Hank proudly poses in the early '50s with fellow country singer Mel Foree in the driveway of his Nashville home beside one of Hank's ever-expanding fleet of long, shiny, chrome-wheeled automobiles bought on a whim, sometimes two at a time, for himself and Audrey. It was in the back seat of these cars where he spent most of his time, writing a good many of his songs during interminable road tours. (PICTORIAL PRESS LTD / ALAMY)

Paralleling his rise, the Drifting Cowboys had gone from an ever-revolving band of transients to a steady, polished unit of top-shelf pros making big money. The most enduring edition of the group, shown here in 1951, included, flanking Hank, bassist Howard Watts and steel guitarist Don Helms, and in front, fiddler Jerry Rivers and lead guitarist Sammy Pruett. By the end of 1952, only Rivers and Helms remained with him, the others unable to tolerate his drinking. (PICTORIAL PRESS LTD / ALAMY)

In the summer of 1952, after being fired by the *Grand Ole Opry*, Hank spent a few days at the secluded Kowaliga Beach resort lodge in the Alabama backwoods with girlfriend Bobbie Jett, including an overnight stay in the local hoosegow after a drunken disturbance. Although he had gotten Bobbie pregnant, he would marry nineteen-year-old Billie Jean Jones in New Orleans in October, taking vows in a sold-out arena. But his master plan was to reconcile with Audrey. (ALABAMA DEPARTMENT OF ARCHIVES AND HISTORY, MONTGOMERY, ALABAMA)

The last photo ever taken of Hank Williams, on December 28, 1952, at a benefit for the Musicians Union at Montgomery's Elite Cafe. While he appeared healthy, when he set off two days later for a scheduled New Year's Eve gig in Charleston, West Virginia, in the back seat of his Cadillac convertible, he told people, "Jesus is comin' after me." On the way he wrote the final song of his life—"I'll Never Get Out of This World Alive." (ALABAMA DEPARTMENT OF ARCHIVES AND HISTORY, MONTGOMERY, ALABAMA)

Hank was right about that. In the wee hours of January 1, 1953, after a circuitous ride on cold, icy roads, his body filled with beer and lethal drugs, he was found dead by his driver in the back seat of the Cadillac just outside of Oak Hill, West Virginia, the cause officially given as heart failure. At his funeral, the biggest ever seen in Montgomery, there was a massive outpouring of emotion by thousands of fans who lined the streets outside the Municipal Arena. (ALABAMA DEPARTMENT OF ARCHIVES AND HISTORY, MONTGOMERY, ALABAMA)

Never averse to publicity even as they mourned, Lillie and Audrey, holding Hank Jr., allowed photographs to be taken of them going through hundreds of letters from Hank's grieving fans, stacked on his old bed in Lillie's boardinghouse. It was a rare truce between the two women, who despised each other as they vied for control of Hank's estate. Lillie had control until her death in 1955, whereupon Audrey sued Irene Williams to become executor of the estate. (ALABAMA DEPARTMENT OF ARCHIVES AND HISTORY, MONTGOMERY, ALABAMA)

Billie Jean Williams remarried another country star, Johnny Horton, but was widowed again in 1959. Older and more business savvy, she was so incensed by her portrayal in a Hank movie that she sued and won a settlement, then took Audrey to court for control over Hank's lucrative royalties and the title of Hank's rightful widow, winning on both counts. Here, during the long courtroom battle, she explains her position to a reporter in 1974, a year before Audrey died, vanquished and near penniless. (ALABAMA DEPARTMENT OF ARCHIVES AND HISTORY, MONTGOMERY, ALABAMA)

Guiding Hank Jr.'s career as a country singer following in Hank's giant footsteps, Audrey had him sing the soundtrack of the first Hank Williams movie, *Your Cheatin' Heart*, in 1964, which earned him his first of many gold records, and make appearances in other films like *A Time to Sing* in 1968. But Hank Jr. bridled at her control as his father had and became estranged from her. He coped with the pressure by nearly killing himself with booze and drugs long into his thriving career as a raucous redneck. (PICTORIAL PRESS LTD / ALAMY)

When Audrey was laid to rest next to Hank at Oakwood Cemetery in Montgomery, necessitating Lillie's remains to be moved several feet away to the right, the Williams family plot was a sprawling expanse, its twin columns towering over the burial ground. Later, as crowds continued stream-ing to the site, benches were installed for their comfort and Hank Jr. would erect a sign warning against desecration of his father's "sacred" grave. (ALABAMA DEPARTMENT OF ARCHIVES AND HISTORY, MONTGOMERY, ALABAMA)

The most compelling link in the chain of Hank's legacy is his grandson Hank Williams III. Unlike his father, Hank Jr., he is an authentic outlaw, departing from country's traditional doltish redneck fare to sing countrified punk called "hellbilly" or "psychobilly," both solo and in the punk-metal band Assjack. Songs like "Trashville" and "Dick in Dixie," rife with lyrics about his hard drug use, trace back to Hank Sr.'s fearlessness and courage to go his own way, with a twang, a screech, and soul. (IMAGEBROKER / ALAMY)

In 1993, Hank was honored on a postage stamp. By then, as well, another piece had been added to his legacy—his long-lost illegitimate daughter, born five days after his death, who, when she learned of her father's identity in her thirties, changed her name to Jett Williams and won coequal control of his estate with Hank Jr. Now in her mid-sixties, she performs as a country singer, sometimes with bands under the name of the Drifting Cowboys. (HIPIX / ALAMY)

Though late to honor him due to lingering gripes about his conduct and lack of proper deference to the country music establishment, Nashville finally got around to giving the "King of Country" his props at the Country Music Hall of Fame, where one of his guitars, a Martin D-28, is on display along with other items of his storied life. Many of his most cherished possessions, though, were donated to various Hank Williams museums in sweet home Alabama, where he rose from impoverished obscurity. (RICHARD ELLIS / ALAMY)

So entrenched is he in the culture of country music, and in the imagination of the public, that more than sixty years after he took his big sleep, his burial ground is officially known as the Hank Williams Memorial Cemetery. His iconic image, engraved on the sign at the graveyard, is a familiar sight on streets and highways all around Alabama, his signature line "Praise the Lord, I Saw the Light" cause to raise a glass and say, "Amen." (ALABAMA DEPARTMENT OF ARCHIVES AND HISTORY, MONTGOMERY, ALABAMA)

devoid of "a lot of trick phrases or impossible chords" and one that "people will naturally want to hum after they have heard it."[15]

As with the later rock and rollers, until the Beatles, the assumption was that lyrics made a song, not the melody. Hank never had the need to play his guitar with a flair. When Frank Page was learning guitar, he remarked to Hank one day, "I've learned C, D, and G." Hank, he said told him, "Shoot, that's all there is." He was also supposed to have said a lot of good guitar players had "educated themselves right out of a job," and that composers who try to write like Shakespeare "will be buried in the same grave with him."

Fortuitous indeed was that while magnetic recording tape was starting to be used in well-equipped studios such as at Castle, the process was still archaic, recorders carrying only one track of tape; whatever was on it was pressed right onto a lathe-cut black lacquer master disk. Even if Rose wanted to add something later on, some extended part or flourish, he couldn't. It had to be right the first time. Simple, but right.

But then, Hank could freely violate his own rules. Another expressed in the booklet was that one should never offend "any religious groups or races" and should avoid lines that had "double meanings or could be interpreted in any indecent manner"—never mind the sly double entendres of "Move It On Over" and all that "Honky Tonkin'" beer chugging and night crawling. And with "Long Gone Lonesome Blues" he did live up to the moniker of the "Hillbilly Shakespeare," though the melody was *very* familiar, all but indistinguishable from "Lovesick Blues." Hank put a fresh face on it by shifting blame for his lonesomeness onto the woman who walked away from a relationship, sending him to the river to go down three times but only come up twice. There was a harder edge to the steel intro, but the medium tempo was the same and the yodeling so frenzied it was almost parody.

If his voice, his timbre lower than usual, seems to be especially bell clear, it was purely intentional. Fred Rose had finally gotten the hang of what and who Hank was—a voice that begged to be heard. And so at a time when records were being smothered in strings and bathed in echoes, Rose took a minimalist approach. Going by how Hank had his band play in concerts—when he sang high notes they played low notes, and vice versa, to separate and accentuate the vocal—Rose instructed Don Helms to play his steel guitar at the highest range.

"Don't ever go below this mark," he said, putting his finger on the corresponding fret. "You want to make it cry, and to be heard on a jukebox."[16]

Rose understood that the hub of Hank's sales was not fans who went to record stores but rather jukebox operators, who sent out orders for the machines with records inside ready to play. There were around 400,000 "boxes" in existence in 1950, and the 5,500 or so operators would buy 150 records a week to play in juke joints. Getting repeat plays in there guaranteed a song almost perpetual life, spawning more record sales. Not for nothing was Hank the ideal match for a jukebox—the derivation of that word being the ancient Creole "juke" or "jouk" or joog," for music, dancing, drinking, and generally disorderly behavior, and in a more modern frame, a roadhouse or brothel—or sexual intercourse.[17] It was those mighty chrome-plated Wurlitzers that made "Lovesick Blues" an enduring hit, and how they belched out a song would be Rose's focus in the studio.

Hank's latest original songs were the latest examples of converting his bitching and moaning about Audrey into commercial gold. "Why Don't You Love Me," for example, was an up-tempo, fiddlin', yodelin' plaint about being treated "like a worn out shoe." And "Why Should We Try Anymore" was a weepin' ballad with a yearning, tremulous vocal in the mold of "I'm So Lonesome I Could Cry." These, and the revamped "Daddy," were all Rose could get out of him before Hank switched over into gospel mode for the vanity project he'd been bugging Fred to sign off on for months, recording not songs but semi-sung, mostly spoken recitations in the manner of a preacher man in the pulpit on Sunday morning.

The last thing Rose wanted was pastoral tunes or for Hank to counter his own puckish persona, but he knew that persona always had an undertone, sometimes flat out, of pleading to Jesus for redemption. But here, too, the jukebox operators entered into the equation. They bought records unheard, on the name of the artist alone, and if some of those would be a man speaking about God, they'd never be played and club owners would pitch a fit. The same applied to the disk jockeys. At the same time, other examples of "talking blues" *had* succeeded. Hank had made his recitations a regular part of his radio shows, going back to Montgomery, and never was he as emotionally invested as when he performed on them, often weeping as he went along.

Rose could hardly turn down a man who *cried* when he performed the songs he loved. But the only way he and Walker would sign off was if Hank recorded these monologues under a pseudonym. Rather than being turned off by the notion, Hank went for it, knowing that the name he chose—a hybrid of religious and secular, Luke the Drifter—would be a thin disguise. So he and Rose came back the next day, and Hank laid down four mordant poems with a stripped-down backup, with only Helms, Bew Butrum on bass, and a church-style organ played by Bradley.

Of the songs recorded during the session, only "Everything's Okay" was an original. And Rose could not have been happy that Hank, who became weepy singing these songs of broken faith and fallen women, fell back on the colloquialisms Fred normally would not have let him get away with in a song. In "Beyond the Sunset," a hymn from the 1910s, he said "soon I'll *foller* you," and in "The Funeral," taken from a pre–Civil War poem, he told of looking through the *winder* as the mourning black couple at the funeral of their son sat in *sorra* while a "sad old colored preacher" eulogized a "little boy who has gone and run away." Of less concern was what today are patently racist words in "The Funeral" describing a black boy with an "Ethiopian face," "curly hair," and "protruding lips," who bore the "ignorance and wisdom of a crushed, undying race"—and conditioned sexism in the other song cut at the session, co-written by Tin Pan Alley titan Billy Rose, "Too Many Parties and Too Many Pals."

Worse for Hank and Fred were that these records stiffed, but Hank would make them familiar, performing them regularly on the radio, mirthfully carrying out the con nobody bought for a second, that Luke was "a relative of mine" or a "half-brother." Frank Walker had no problem releasing the first Luke the Drifter record, "Too Many Parties and Too Many Pals," as sort of half-brother of "Long Gone Lonesome Blues," which came out in early March of 1950, backed with the mushy "My Son Calls Another Man Daddy," winning a typical rave in the March 25 *Billboard*—"One of Hank's top-notch country blues efforts, side should hit fast and hard."

Little Hank could do came up snake eyes. By April 22, "Long Gone" was second on the country chart to Red Foley's recording of "Chattanoogie Shoe Shine Boy." On May 6, Hank's original had leap-frogged over both Ernest Tubb's "I Love You Because" and "Chattanoogie" to occupy the chart penthouse, where it would stay for eight weeks of a twenty-one-week run on the list, its sales estimated at 150,000, rivaling "Lovesick Blues." And "Too Many Parties"—which had been beaten onto the market by another country version by a new western swing band from Chester, Pennsylvania, Bill Haley and the Saddlemen—tagged along, selling some 20,000 without benefit of the jukebox dynamic. So did "My Son Calls Another Man Daddy," which broke out and went to No. 9. "The Funeral" sold a decent 6,600 records of its own. The memorable gems aside, it's doubtful anyone else could have racked up so much with so little.

• • •

During the *Opry* years, he was by far the most popular artist on the franchise's roster, his two or three songs on the Saturday night broadcast for many nonhardcore *Opry* buffs the only reason to tune in. Under these circumstances, the mystery is why the guiding powers there didn't use him far more than on the show they did. Other than the week in 1950 when Red Foley took a vacation at Easter and Hank was given the job as fill-in emcee was he allowed that position, one he clearly deserved and likely would have done better with. He also was loyal to a fault. Despite his personal wariness of the *Opry* caste, he went along when Fred Rose, as an inducement for the *Opry* to take on Hank, in April of '49 let Oscar Davis become his de facto manager, whereupon Davis had given over all his time to booking dates for him.

Although Hank had proven on the radio how personable and disciplined a host he was, and Davis was beginning to feel out the possibilities of him appearing on early TV shows, there was always a hedge about Hank, as too backwoods, too prone to speaking his mind. And, of course, there was the matter of the booze. The irony of that concern was that the *Opry*, for all its tony pretensions, was foisting on its audience crude, burlesque-style stereotypes of country that Hank might have winced at. A typical show from that period began with announcer "Cousin" Louie Buck barking, "Welcome to the capital of country music around the world—the *Grand Ole Opry* . . . Take it away, boys!" The band struck up, frenetic fiddles firing, and Red Foley, introduced as host, ambled on and sang "Shortnin' Bread," then did a comic bit with Rod Brasfield, delivering some wince-creating lines like "I ain't got an enemy in the world—all my friends hate me." Then Foley—who of course had a stake in Hank's success, his band having been essential to his recent records—intoned, "It gives me a great feeling to say howdy to that great Montgomery, Alabama, singing personality—Hank Williams!"

Hank moved on out, did a quick bow, and lit into "You're Gonna Change (Or I'm Gonna Leave)," the words tumbling out with precision and an especially long yodel—"You wore out a brand new trunk packin' and unpackin' your junk. / Your daddy's mad, he's done got *peee-eee-eee-ved*," to hoots and hollers from the house. Next came Wally Fowler and the Oak Ridge Quartet for some "real spiritual singin'," as Foley said, then Minnie Pearl, shouting "How-*deee*!" and then breaking into a tale about a fictitious boyfriend—"He said, when I try to kiss you I can't figure out why you always yell stop. [I said] What I can't figure out is why you do [stop]!'"

> BRASFIELD: *"Minnie, did I ever tell you I had a goat farm?"*
> MINNIE: *"Yeah, I got wind of it. . . .You know something, Rodney, gals say they don't like to kiss a feller with whiskers. When they make up their mind, they ain't gonna beat around the bush."*

The format constrained Hank, as one of a troupe of players, and he would only be able to squeeze in one or two songs per show. But it quickly became evident that when the announcer opened each broadcast by shouting "It's *Grand Ole Opry* time!," for many it meant "It's Hank Williams time!" Placards were drawn up for the lobby of the Ryman, and ads run in the trade papers, labeling him "Mr. Lovesick Blues" or the "Lovesick Blues Boy."

Not blind to Hank's star power, Jim Denny, the *Opry* general manager, tried to be not only a boss but someone Hank could trust. Denny had gone through a hard life himself—working himself up from the mail room at National Home Life Insurance and the aisles at the *Opry*, where he was an usher—and believed he could meld with Hank as a poor boy made good. "I never knew anybody I liked better than Hank," Denny said in the late 1950s, "but I don't think I ever really got close to him. Don't know if anyone really could. He was so bitter. . . . He thought everybody, in the final analysis, had some sort of angle on him. I suppose that's why everybody had misinterpreted him. Because despite it all, he was very kind and generous and very determined to be the top man in his profession."[18]

Minnie Pearl, on the other hand, was able to gain that trust. He was, she said, "actually one of the funniest men I ever knew. He had a wry sense of humor . . . and he loved to tell stories on other people. He never played the star."[19] He didn't need to play it. As far as he had come, he couldn't avoid being swathed in more stardom than he could handle.

15

✳ ✳ ✳ ✳ ✳ ✳ ✳

"IT'S *NEVER* TOO COUNTRY"

When Hank had conquered the *Grand Ole Opry*, his future in Nashville seemed assured. This was something he must have believed when he opened an envelope from Rose early in 1950 and saw a check for over *$10,000*, just one installment of a yearly total of over $15,000 from MGM and $8,000 from Acuff-Rose, and that might have been severely clipped from what he actually had earned—which, *Variety* noted, was something around $65,000. If so, both Walker and Rose had found all sorts of ways to stiff him on "expenses" and deductions for studio time and records that were returned by store owners. Even though Hank would clear almost $20,000 more in royalties in 1950, he likely never made nearly what he was owed.

Beyond simple exploitation of artists, a related matter was that MGM had taken a loss on its pressing plant in New Jersey after it began cutting the smaller 7-inch, vinyl 45 RPM records, following the trend set by RCA of releasing lightweight disks that would take the place of seven or eight bulky 78s.[1] MGM hastened to release Hank product for the first time on 45, and as the record houses scrambled to make the transition with all their artists, jukeboxes would switch over to the 45 format in '50. Once the transition was under way, it was far more expensive to operate this new equipment. MGM needed to massage the bottom line any way it could.

Meanwhile, early in the year, Hank had sold the Shreveport house at a profit, putting another ten grand in his pocket, and the *Opry* assigned him a business manager, Sam Hunt, an executive with Nashville's Third Avenue Bank. Hank, though, would not agree to have any of his stash tied up and out of immediate reach. He toted sacks of bills to the bank for deposit himself. He would pile them up at the window. The teller would ask how much it was. "How the hell do I know?" he'd say. "My job is to make it. Your job is to count it."[2]

Lycrecia Williams recalled one breakfast when Hank and Audrey began talking about cars. Audrey had gotten in her head that she wanted a gold convertible.

"You don't need a convertible," Hank said. "You're a married woman and don't have any business with a convertible."

"I don't care," she told him. "I want a convertible and that's what I'm going to get."[3]

Not only did Audrey get what she wanted—a canary yellow Cadillac drop-top—he came home with one of those for himself, in emerald green.

He was apt to leave ten-, twenty-, even fifty-dollar tips on meals that cost a fraction of that. Or drop a C-note into a hotel clerk or bellhop's hand. They would usually begin to make change for him, but he stopped them. "You need it more than I do," he'd say.

• • •

"Why Don't You Love Me" promptly became Hank's third No. 1 in the early summer of 1950. By then, his whirlwind tours had touched down all over the map, logging thousands of miles with the Drifting Cowboys, lurching from Kansas City to a Southern tour with stops in Jackson, Mississippi, where he did a brief turn on a radio show on WSLI, Mobile, and Pensacola, then back out to Springfield, Missouri, and into Chicago to sing at the important Jukebox Operators Convention.

At the latter, he was photographed for the cover of the March 25, 1950, *Billboard* grinning in the middle of a group of faceless industry suits suddenly eager to "glad-hand" him, as the caption read. In the group were six regional MGM "reps," the association's lawyer, and, hardly by coincidence, Fred Rose (" 'pubber' of Williams' songs") and Oscar Davis. Hank then doubled back to Florence, Alabama, and then made for Nashville, for a job only a performer as elevated as he was could have made a reality—a session not for him but for Audrey.

This had been one of her long-held goals, and Hank, who placated her at almost every turn for the sake of holding the fragile marriage together, had Rose work on it. Frank Walker was out, having made it emphatically clear he wanted no part of Audrey on his label beyond the few duets with Hank, and shooting down her contention that Hank had implicitly signed with MGM as a team. And so Fred, as he had done with Hank in the beginning, called around. Paul Cohen, the A&R boss at Decca, who had passed on Hank, but now, like many of his peers, fancied a scenario that would one day bring him to his label. If the price for that was giving Audrey a one-off deal, with perhaps some spillover of the Williams brand leading to some sales, he could live with that.

On March 28, 1950, Decca reserved time for her at Castle Studios, and she recorded four sides, two written with wishful thinking by Hank—"Help Me Understand," "How Can You Refuse Him Now"—and two by Audrey alone, the less seriously themed "Model T Love" and "Tight Wad Daddy." On April Fool's Day she cut three more, her cover of "Honky Tonkin'" and two others of hers, "I Like That Kind" and "Who Put the Pep in Grandma?," the last a novelty about Hadacol, its hook a repetition of the product's name.

MGM went out with "Help Me Understand" / "How Can You Refuse Him Now" in April billed as "Audrey Williams Singing with String Band." Nothing much was expected of them given her strained voice that was rarely on key but she was smart, not trying to be technically sound but engaging. While Hank couldn't sing on another label's product, he could pitch it on the radio, guaranteeing sales, but more importantly giving Audrey a fix of solo stardom that hopefully would suffice. And Rose helpfully timed the release of two more Hank-Audrey duets, "Jesus Remembered Me" and "I Heard My Mother Praying for Me," in the fall. Audrey must have been in hog heaven. But none of this calmed the turbulent sea of the marriage. Indeed, Audrey became more annoyed when Hank would punish or reward her based on whether things were going well or not. On her part, Hank's drinking always set her off; she saw it more than ever in terms of wrecking not only his career but hers.

When Hank got home from a tour that same April, Audrey, having been told that he'd been drinking, locked the door to the house and wouldn't open it for him. She told him to go to a hotel and sleep it off, and he checked into the Tulane, collapsing into bed with a lit cigarette in his hand. He blacked out, and the next thing anyone knew, the room was in flames. The fire department put out the fire and pulled him out of the room, unscathed, but cops arrested him for causing the blaze, and he spent the night drying out in a jail cell.[4] Sam Hunt had to write a fat check to the Tulane to cover the damages, but Hank had cheated death, and not for the first or last time. Sprung from jail, he went right back to his out-of-control life, the details of which were kept from the public—nothing of the arrest was in the papers, and he would continue to be portrayed as a fine family man with a loving wife. Those who knew better must have laughed out loud at that. Or cried.

• • •

He was back at Castle on June 14—three days before "Why Don't You Love Me" hit No. 1—with three of his favored sidemen, Sammy Pruett on lead guitar, Don Helms on steel guitar, and Jerry Rivers on fiddle, along with Jack Shook on rhythm guitar and Ernie Newton on bass. He cut Leon Payne's "They'll Never Take Her Love from Me," an extraordinary plaint of guilt and regret about having done his woman wrong. The song was so visceral, his voice such a throbbing wound, that Rose used it as the B-side of the next single, "Why Should We Try Anymore?," which went out in August 1950 and topped out at No. 9 on the country chart, before the jocks turned the record over and "They'll Never Take Her Love from Me" went to No. 5.

Behind the scenes, however, there were serious rumblings at the *Opry* about how much more Hank they could put up with. Oscar Davis had had enough of putting out the figurative and literal fires Hank started wherever he went; the last rip was when Hank demanded a higher personal appearance fee on the *Opry* tours, for which he had to take much less than on his own tours. To make matters worse, he had one of those dustups on the road that the *Opry* always prayed wouldn't get in the way.

It was on, of all days, July 1 when Hank and the Drifting Cowboys were the headline act at the Watermelon Festival in DeLeon, Texas, near Fort Worth. Hank was in no shape to go on. He arrived in a stretch limo, remaining in the back seat when a guy who said he was Hank's road manager got out and informed the promoter, W. B. Nowlin, who also happened to be the mayor of the town, that Hank was too ill to perform. Nowlin, who had a full house of people sitting on the grass waiting for Hank, did not take the news well. He called in the chief of police, who proceeded to handcuff the road manager and had two cops pull Hank from the car and carry him onto the stage. As they held him upright, Nowlin told the crowd, "Hank Williams' manager says Hank Williams is too sick to perform, but if you were standing as close to him as I am you would know what he's sick from."[5]

As he spoke, Hank sagged almost down to his knees, but if Nowlin hoped he could shame Hank into going on, he was wrong. When the cops let him go, he stumbled off the stage and back into the limo, which drove off, leaving Nowlin to refund several thousand folks, and to dun Davis for every dime of it. If this was exactly the kind of behavior that made people wary of Hank, he didn't give a damn about his bad reputation, and never would. Hank had resolved not to sell his soul to the *Opry* and soon believed he might not even need that gig anymore, and that they needed him more than he did them. Moreover, Hank was too big for the *Opry* booking agency anyway. An item in *Billboard* announced that the Jolly Joyce Agency of Philadelphia had booked Hank and the Drifting Cowboys for an October 27 appearance at the Mutual Arena in Toronto.

Indeed, the *Opry* had to accept that Hank replaced Davis with any number of "road managers" he'd find in local bars. For a time he made Jerry Rivers his "general manager," and for other bookings hired A. V. "Bam" Bamford, a Cuban businessman who in the 1930s sank his money into several Southern radio stations, helping to establish country on the airwaves. Bamford was also a tireless promoter of himself and country artists who performed on his stations and at state fair concerts he booked, such as Hank in the Shreveport days. In fact, Bamford was yet another who would claim it was he who convinced the *Grand Ole Opry* barons to sign Hank. Bamford, too, migrated to Nashville in the late '40s; he was not affiliated with the *Opry*, yet was given the authority to book Hank on tours with *Opry* stars, doing so immediately by grouping Hank with Minnie Pearl and Ernest Tubb on another swing through Texas and the Deep South.

Neither did Bamford shy away from demanding a higher percentage for Hank, whose power surely did seem to transcend that of the *Opry*. The old vows to keep dry were almost laughable, with the *Opry* impotent to do a thing about it. No one had ever made those arrogant Nashville cutthroats crawl like Hank, and they would make sure no one ever would again. As he continued gaining elevation, characters shady and otherwise filtered through his life. One of the more intriguing was an erstwhile ex-Chicagoan, Jack Rubenstein—who went by the name Jack Ruby. He managed a Dallas nightclub called the Silver Spur and had reputed mob ties, but Hank had become tight with him and committed to playing a gig at the Silver Spur.

Hank flew to Dallas in Henry Cannon's plane, but as the gig neared, he was either too sloshed to go on or perhaps just wanted to stay incognito, the better to keep the gig from the boys in Nashville.

Jerry Rivers would later tell of seeing Hank getting into the elevator at the Hotel Adolphus, where he was not registered, wearing a white cowboy hat and dark glasses wrapped around his face, obviously trying to keep from being recognized.

"Hey, isn't that Hank Williams?" Rivers asked a bellhop.

"Oh, no, sir," he was told. "That's Mr. Herman P. Willis, in room 504."[6]

Rivers laughed to himself, that being the pseudonym Hank used jokingly, often calling someone by that name to rag on him. Rivers made his way up to the room and found him nearly out cold and not eager to make the gig. But he made it anyway, a wise move indeed, keeping Jack Ruby happy. Hank, of course, would not live to see Ruby leap out of the shadows one November day in 1963 to gun down the alleged killer of a president. All he knew, said Jerry Rivers, was that "Ruby was a good old boy. He was a good man to work for."[7]

Rivers also related that at the next stop, in the old stomping grounds of Greenville, Hank was so drunk that frantic calls were made to get Hank Snow to come down from Nashville and sing with the Cowboys, there and also in Little Rock. As his band backed another star, "Herman P. Willis" went back on Henry Cannon's plane and flew home to Nashville, caring not a whit that he was really starting to push boundaries that could only push back.

In November, meanwhile, Irving Mills's lawsuit over the writing credit on "Lovesick Blues" had gone to, amazingly enough, Frank Walker for arbitration, Walker's stolid reputation being such that it overrode any appearance of favoritism to one of his artists. Indeed, Walker played it straight and narrow, ruling that Mills's name was to be printed on all succeeding copies of the record, and that he would collect every cent of the writing royalties for them. Mills would also split all future publishing royalties with Acuff-Rose. And they were lucrative. By year's end, *Billboard* made "Lovesick Blues" the top country and western hit, and "Wedding Bells" was fifth, "Mind Your Own Business" twenty-fourth. It also named Hank the No. 2 Top-Selling Folk (Country and Western) Artist behind Eddy

Arnold. The other trade paper, *Cash Box*, still a bit behind the country curve, named "Lovesick Blues" the Best Hillbilly Song of the Year
in a poll of jukebox vendors. In the year-end roundup in *Billboard*,
Hank came in third among the hillbilly singers, behind Arnold and
Red Foley, and ahead of Roy Acuff and Ernest Tubb.

Once, these kind of designations had meant little. Now, country
music, thanks in large part to him, had detonated, lending its stars
godlike dimensions.

• • •

An odd, brittle sort of god. Hank's mischievous grin and dimples
were trademarks of his youth, but a closer inspection would reveal
a man in deterioration. He always looked malnourished, his 150
pounds stretched across his six-foot frame, the booze and all his
platters full of ketchup never putting an ounce on it. His skin was
sallow, ashen at times, especially when he wore big white cowboy
hats that matched his complexion. He would refuse to take off the
hat, knowing that his hair was thinning rapidly, a bald spot on the
crown of his head widening by the day. His cheeks were hollow,
and his lower teeth serrated from yanking too many caps off beer
bottles. More ominously, his back now was almost always making
him wince, and he would need to sit for long stretches; coming offstage, he sometimes needed to be helped to a dressing room or his
car by members of the band. And, to his great dismay, he couldn't
ride Hi Life, the pain of being on horseback intolerable. Lycrecia
would take the nag out on a run, to give it some exercise. He was,
for all intents and purposes, an old man, in deep pain. And booze
and regular pain pills and powders were not going to be enough to
take it away.

Little Jimmy Dickens, who with Minnie Pearl was constantly on
the road with him, became something like a stand-in Audrey trying to
get a helpless Hank into performance condition. Dickens, a shaver of a
man who stood barely five feet and was nicknamed "Tater" by Hank,
after Dickens's song "Take an Old Cold Tater," once recalled that

Mr. Nudie made his clothes, but Hank could wear the most expensive suit and it'd still look like a sack because of the way he put it on. He'd wear a dress tie with a Western suit, which didn't work, and he'd tie those real old-fashioned long knots. The tie would be off to the side and I'd straighten it up for him because he went out on the stage, but he'd pull it right back over there and say, "You're too particular." He figured those old country boys that came to see him would like him the way he was.[8]

For Hank, the endless rinse and repeat of performing and pocketing big bills was a salve, if even just in his head. But he had other elixirs that rinsed away the boredom and despondency of being out on the long road. Women, of course, were on top of the that menu, and Hank's way of courting friendships with the police in whatever town he was in had the dividend of being allowed not only to skate on a bar brawl or two or speed through the no speeding signs but also, in effect, to use them as pimps. Early Hank biographer Roger Williams wrote that Hank was so fixated on finding loose women that "he relied on the local cops [working in the arena] for accurate information on [women]. He'd cozy up to an officer, ask him a few questions about his pistol, and then say casually, 'Know any goin' women around here?' More often than not the cop did know some, right on the premises, and Hank would be fixed up for an after-the-show engagement."[9]

Williams quoted Nashville songwriter Jimmy Rule saying that among the bulging bags of fan mail that would come into the *Opry* office was one from a California woman that read: "Please come live with me, I can love you twenty-four hours a day and stand up to it."[10] Still, as sophisticated as the system of solicitation furthered by the men in blue was—and as portentous as it would be for future generations of rock and roll stars who took to similarly "scouting" the house picking out women to invite to postconcert activities—an even less savory dimension of it was that often his taste was for not-yet women, commensurate with Hank's creed about sex apparently being "old enough to bleed, old enough to butcher."

Not that there weren't complications. During one swing through California, Hank was said to have fled his motel room in a panic after a fling with a waitress. An unnamed friend of Hank recalled:

All of a sudden, the door flies open and Hank comes out, hoppin' along with one leg in his trousers, He jumps in the car all excited and says, "Come on, come on, let's get outta here!" The guy driving figured it was somethin' good, so he dawdled with the keys. Hank gets even more agitated and shouts, "Hurry up, durn it!"

"What'sa matter, Harm?" we asked him. Well, he wouldn't say at first. But it turns out that after he'd gotten his, he dozed off, and when he woke up her pussy was right in his face, like she was expectin' somethin'. That was too much for an old country boy like Hank. He got the hell out of there.[11]

Still, if Hank didn't do *everything* in bed, he did more than a country or city boy could have been called on to do in a lifetime. Which may be why it wasn't enough to keep him from becoming bored with that, too. Out there on the road, he would go looking not for women or girls but for trinkets of some kind. Often, it would be a gun, or multiples of guns. Jerry Rivers remembered when Hank obsessed on a trip in California on a pair of Colt .45s he'd gotten a tip about. He spent a couple of days locating them and reaching a purchase price. He loved the Colts so much that even when he found out he'd been ripped off—one was a .45 and one a .44—he held on to them, sometimes carrying both of them in his waistband, loaded, making people extremely nervous, especially when he would get loaded himself. It was miraculous that he never fired off any of his guns, nor wound up shooting himself, given how out of control he could get and how obsessed he was with guns, or practically anything with a gun as a motif. He even bought twelve pairs of cufflinks that were mini scale models of a Colt .45.

Nothing, however, could take the place of a good, stiff belt. Although Jimmy Dickens, a major elbow-bender himself, insisted he never saw Hank drunk, "he was very moody [and] his moods were probably related to alcohol. . . . I know what he went through to be an alcoholic, and it's very, very difficult when you drink as much as I did or he did, not to take that first drink before you go on stage. It becomes a part of what you do."[12] Indeed, it was that *first* drink that was the problem, the one everybody feared. Because while Hank could go days, even weeks, sober and clear-headed, all it would take was one shot and he was gone. And the problem was that not even Ike Eisenhower's army could have prevented him from getting to that one shot.

. . .

To Audrey, he was nothing like his confident stage persona. She described him as "extremely nervous before each performance, and each time he went on the stage, it'd take him about three minutes to really relax." In essence, she said, he was "a loner. Well, it was really shyness and loneliness together." She would often see him in arenas or clubs sitting off by himself, like a little boy lost.[13]

That he was still able to crank out songs of great personal meaning and intensity, as well as commercial viability, was downright amazing. He went back in the studio on August 31, 1950, with the same musicians as the last time, but with a notable addition—a drummer, for the first time, Farris Coursey, who not only drummed in Owen Bradley's band but was Bradley's business manager. Coursey would soon be *the* drummer in the Nashville scene, one of a coterie of sidemen known as the "Nashville A Team." Still, the *Opry's* resistance to drumming, and his own methods of having his backup musicians keep a steady beat, made drumming a novelty for Hank. Then, too, as open as he was to trying something new, his mien was basic, unvarnished country blues. Once during a session, when a musician asked Fred Rose if he had played "too country," Rose, reflecting Hank's rock-ribbed tastes, said, "It's *never* too country."[14]

The session at Castle produced another four songs, three written by Hank, "Nobody's Lonesome for Me," "Moanin' the Blues,"

and "Help Me Understand." There was one by Rose—the Cold War
curio "No, No, Joe," the patriotic diss of Joe Stalin that Hank for
some reason thought complementary with his Luke the Drifter
talking blues litany. "Help Me Understand," an allegory of a broken
family "I once knew" and their daughter "Sue," left adrift after "one
word led to another and the last word led to a divorce," was the
best. But it wasn't what Rose thought was A material, so the play
went to "Moanin' the Blues," a literal moan, and a hell of a catchy
one. Hank had written it with Jimmy Dickens as a preemptive plea
should Audrey up and leave, training his yodel and vocal bathos on
his latest tale of woe about "lovin' that gal for so doggone long, I can't
afford to lose her now." Rose consciously kept Hank's colloquial can-
ter by titling the song with the dropped *g*, stoking the down-home
authenticity of the blues feel.

MGM pressed "Moanin'" for an October release, though Hank
wasn't sold on the drum, believing it might be too sharp a sound for
his tastes, and would keep the drum off his sessions, save for one of
the last songs he recorded, "Kaw-Liga." Still, on December 2, it was
at No. 5, and at the end of 1950, "Moanin'" leapfrogged Hank Snow's
"I'm Movin' On" to put Hank back atop the heap.

· · ·

Still, if ever moanin' the blues seemed the framework of his life, it
was now. With spectacular timing, a month before the song came
out, in September 1950, Audrey learned she was pregnant. It was an
accident, for sure, as close as it was to Randall's birth and as torn as
she was about the marriage; her defenses would always be weakened
when he began cooing in her ear, even if all the booze and drugs left
him often unable to finish the job. Thus, Hank was overjoyed he had
sired another child. Audrey was not nearly as happy about the news.

Mindful of how torturous her last pregnancy was, and seeing
how Hank all but ignored the son who would soon become aware of
the sins of his alcoholic father, and not *wanting* another bond to him,
she came to the gut-wrenching decision to have an abortion. When

Hank went out on the road, she found through underground sources a doctor who would agree to perform a procedure that could put him, and maybe her, in jail for many years at a time when the word "abortion," like "pregnant," was almost never used in public. Nothing would ever be known about the identity of the doctor, only that it happened in the Williams home and that after the fetus was aborted, Audrey came down with an infection, likely the result of the abortionist's utensils not being fully sterilized. Bleeding and with a high fever, she was rushed to St. Thomas Hospital in Nashville.

Hank came off the road as she was recovering, and after being told Audrey was in the hospital, he apparently learned from the doctors, or Audrey herself, what had put her there. He would never really talk about it to the point of saying whether he was livid that, as a God-fearing Christian, he believed she had committed one of the ultimate sins. It's also possible that, his faith aside, had she told him her intention he might have agreed to pay for her to travel under cover to a better doctor rather than risk her life, avoiding the possibility that whole messy event finding its way into the newspapers. Indeed, that was something they now would need to work hard to prevent; they were able to perpetuate the con in interviews that Audrey had been hospitalized for unspecified but hardly serious reasons, and it only mattered in the context of how it prompted Hank to write his next big song.

This was something Audrey posited in 1973, leaving some details rather vague, saying that she went into the hospital for "some minor little something," and when Hank showed up at her bedside, he brought a fur coat for her, apparently as a make-good gift after an argument they'd had before he left town. Still steamed at him, she threw the coat on the floor. That night, she said, Hank went home and told Hank Jr.'s nurse, "She's got the coldest heart I've ever seen." And, proving that not even the most painful of personal matters could turn off his instinct for turning pain into commercial gain, he then went into the den and composed "Cold, Cold Heart." For Audrey, who took it as a personal affront, it would prompt her to deny the cold heart was hers. "He got so jealous of men, God knows why. I wasn't doing anything except staying in the background and trying to help him if I could. There were so many stories told. The bigger he got, he always had such a fear of losing me, and I don't know why. I certainly never gave him any reason."[15]

Audrey's explanations were undeniably self-serving—given what she told Don Helms, Hank had good reason to fear losing her—and that she was well trained to hold to a party line about Hank was evident in the fact that she said this even though Hank had spilled the truth long before.

Audrey, indeed, went right back to the public charade about the marriage, even years later. Neither, too, did Lycrecia Williams mention her mother's abortion in her memoirs. And Hank on his part preferred taking the high road, never saying a discouraging word about Audrey until he had to, soon enough, by way of self-defense when he was put under oath.

As soon as Audrey's infection was healed, their shared silence about the abortion notwithstanding, their walk through hell continued. Not even Lillie could get him out from under Audrey's thumb. Lillie for years had been pecking at him that he had a good-for-nothing wife, that she spent too much of his money, that she dragged him down whenever she got herself into the act, that she had to be steppin' out on him, that she was the reason he drank. Lillie's take on the hospitalization was that Audrey had tried to kill herself—and she was crazy enough to try it again if he went on with her, and drag him down with her. To be sure, he didn't disagree with any of it. He'd tell people on the sly that when he'd come home with a thousand dollars in his pocket, he'd by rote give Audrey half, and then spend the rest of the night listening to her try to get the other five hundred. He also said he'd opened a few bank accounts she knew nothing of, and would run to one of them after a show to sink his cash in it.

Audrey, for her part, opened unlimited charge accounts *he* knew nothing about until the bills came in to his business manager of the day. She would appear backstage wearing a $1,000 dress with a big *A* sequined onto the front, flashing her $3,000 diamond ring. During an *Opry* show she attended at the Ryman, Hank told Jim Denny, "I got a reason for drinkin' and here she comes up them steps right now."[16] Yet there they stood, still fused together, making more plans to spend, together and separately, each spending what the other didn't. Never did they look ahead to the next day. That was always a day too far.

16

✸ ✸ ✸ ✸ ✸ ✸ ✸

A BRAND-NEW RECIPE

"Cold, Cold Heart," for all its harrowing genesis, developed in the usual manner. A demo made in November 1950 was given to Fred Rose to make grammatical and literary refinements. Hank, of course, kept secret the ugly origin of the scalding lyrics. When he was interviewed for a 1951 *Wall Street Journal* article about the growth of country, a quite important signpost, he went with his half-chuckled, one-size-fit-all tripe about sitting down and waiting until God wrote it for him.[1] As if the good Lord could have crafted lines that dripped with venom such as

> *I tried so hard, my dear, to show that you're my every dream*
> *Yet you're afraid each thing I do is just some evil scheme*

Other daggers of blame followed. Unlike in previous indictments of her, there was no obligatory mea culpa to dilute blame, no begging for a second chance; his only hedge was to ask *himself* what was holding him back from cutting the cord—which of course was in reality a lifeline. As harsh as these lyrics were, they bore no resemblance to anything he would ever tell her to her face. He still *needed* her, which was the answer to his question, and singing these words must have been quite comforting to the *other* Hank, the whipped one. So comforting that when Rose's old bugaboo—the mismatched meters—arose again, Hank stood firm. The problem was that when Hank came in to record it on December 21, he held the vocal two beats too long to be in meter, or cut it off two beats too quick.

"Hank, it's not in meter. There's a two-four bar here on 'heart.' If you're dancing, your foot's in the air. On 'apart,' I suggest you hold it two more beats."

"Mr. Rose," he said with exasperation, "I don't know nothin' about no meter," repeating the same thing he had told him before, about how he fancied holding notes that he liked. Then, "You'll just have to watch me."[2]

Rose once more stood down. He had no choice now. But Fred's ear was again vital to the song's success. He heard it as the most honest of Hank's blues numbers, and the lyrics were so acrid that it might also have been a fine choice for the Luke the Drifter catalog had the melody Hank set it to not been so bluesy itself, a nice easy tempo with wonderfully smooth chord changes.

A new addition to the crew of sidemen, if only for this one session, would one day be regarded as arguably the greatest electric guitar player country has ever known, Chester Burton "Chet" Atkins. Born in Luttrell, Tennessee, in 1924, he would in his life win fourteen Grammy Awards and be inducted into the Rock and Roll, Country, and Musicians Hall of Fame, and as an executive he would open country to the mainstream. Atkins arrived in Nashville after stints with swing instrumental groups and after passing an audition for Red Foley when Red had his radio show on WLS. He joined Foley's band, then the *Grand Ole Opry* in 1946. He'd had a record out, "Guitar Blues," one of the overlooked gemstones of country, taking the idiom into jazz-band territory with the inclusion of a clarinet solo. In fact, in an example of *Opry* provincialism and utter stupidity, he was fired from the show, and then from his next gig, on a Springfield, Missouri, radio station—for not being "country enough."[3]

Atkins's style derived from Merle Travis's bluegrass method of picking with thumb and two, sometimes three, fingers. It was a gift to country, in that Atkins could blend in with any type of arrangement or meter, adding depth and color without one note out of place or even heard—in other words, the ideal studio sideman. True to form, one cannot distinguish Atkins's guitar in the tightly fused instrumentation, and it was mainly Helms's pedal steel intro that let Hank come out of the gate with a real edge, perhaps the most strident he ever sounded, the teary throb and clipped yodels not sad and sentimental as much as weary, even defeated.

Hank was *angry* when he sang it that day, and he didn't care if it was obvious. Maybe a little *too* obvious for Rose. When the time came to pick an A-side for Hank's next release, Fred went with another song of retribution recorded that day, "Dear John," written in 1949 by Texas songwriter Aubrey Glass. Tex Ritter bartered for a writer's credit on it by promising Glass he would get the song recorded, cashing in when it was cut that year by the Texas swing band Jim Boyd and His Men of the West. While it didn't get anywhere, Rose had wanted Hank to cover it for a year, its infectious grooves right up Hank's alley.

The remaining two songs were recorded as Luke the Drifter entries, "Just Waiting" and "Men with Broken Hearts," the former a cynical parable of various life losers waiting for the next day of routine despair. Hank once explained to the Montgomery newspaperman Allen Rankin, "Don't know why I happened to of wrote that thing. Except somebody that's fell, he's the same man ain't he? So how can he be such a nice guy when he's got it and such a bad guy when he ain't got nothin'?" Yet it was so lugubrious that even Hank confided to Rankin, "Isn't that the awfullest, morbidest song you ever heard in your life?"[4]

This was the Hank that confounded people who knew him. The same guy who while drunk could so easily break a bottle over someone's head, the same guy whose philandering was so brazen, and who could humiliate a band member for hitting a wrong note, would go to pieces in the studio reciting some of these admittedly morbid tearjerkers. At least he wasn't lost in the muck of only recording "hit" material; if he had something to get off his chest, it went in a song, even if it had no shot at success.

Since he wrote almost all his songs now while sitting in the back of his car as it drove through the quiet night on some back road, he had little else but loneliness on his mind. And to those who saw him come apart as he performed the saddest songs, he was a sad sack indeed, someone who couldn't be happy, someone who needed to be protected from his own depths. Roy Acuff used to observe Hank in the studio during such moments. In one session, Wesley Rose remembered, "Roy and Hank spent the whole time singing each other's songs. Hank would cry when he sang one of Roy's, and vice versa. When I drove Roy back to town he told me, 'That's a good boy, Wes, You watch out for him.'"[5]

. . .

"Dear John"/"Cold, Cold Heart" went out with an ad in the February 17 *Billboard* that featured Hank's image and copy screaming MGM'S ALL-TIME CONSISTENT BEST SELLER! above blurbs for "Dear John," "Moanin' the Blues," and "Lovesick Blues"—all three of which would be on the country chart once "John" moved into the Top 10 two weeks later. That the B-side was something more was obvious when "Dear John" became just one of a number of versions of the song, among them the original by Jim Boyd and His Men of the West and an R&B version by the marvelous Dinah Washington, which would go to No. 3 on that chart. Hank's cover sat second among songs listed as "coming up," and by March 24, when "Dear John" had peaked at No. 8, the jocks discovered "Cold, Cold Heart" and were turning it over so much that it replaced "John" as the A-side, soon by frequent request by listeners

Clearly, the buying public cared not a whit about its anger. Like "I'm So Lonesome I Could Cry," "Cold, Cold Heart" showed there was no boundary that Hank couldn't step across in unburdening his

sad, sad heart—or to profit his larcenous heart. The song shot up
to No. 1 on May 12, ahead of Hank Snow's "Rhumba Boogie" and
Lefty Frizzell's "I Want to Be with You Always." That was when
the writer of "You'll Still Be in My Heart," Ted West, who had been
unilaterally removed as writer of record by two other tunesmiths
when T. Texas Tyler recorded it, saw his song now connected to a
Hank Williams chart-topper. He sued not Hank or Fred Rose but
the other two guys. But while the suit was waiting to be settled,
royalties would be frozen on it. Rose would pay Hank his royalties
of $32,000 in mid-'51, but because of that lawsuit, something like
$22,000 more would be held up in the meantime. As it happened,
Hank would never see that chunk of cash because it took until 1955
for the case to be settled, not in West's favor. Such were the repercussions of a whirlwind like Hank. People who normally would let
things lie would fight like hell to get some of the spoils of jamming
in on his success.

• • •

The chart rankings and money figures that accrued from his records
were what kept the flickering flame between Hank and Audrey
burning, not any lingering chemical attraction. Chet Flippo had it
that Hank once cracked wise to a fishing buddy that Audrey was
"just like this damn fishin' boat. She's got a flat bottom, she got no
top, and she smells like fish."[6] Yet he had long grown to depend on
her, and the formula of writing songs about her, and Audrey finding
a modicum of stardom through him not only kept them on track,
however uneasily, but created a gusher. According to *Billboard*, Hank
had earned over $400,000 in an eight-month period ending April
8, 1950. Some of the box office highlights that year were eye-pop-
ping, even by today's standards—10,500 in Kansas City, 16,750 in St
Louis, 18,500 in Amarillo, 13,600 in Toledo, 16,500 on New Year's
Eve in Indianapolis. Then, too, as if he needed it, his sheet music
sold in the thousands every year. Even more impressive was the stol-
idness of the road show.

Even under insufferable duress and a killing schedule, the Drifting Cowboys kept on grinding it out, the cast the same save for the bass men. The trade-off was that they lived like stray dogs, hand to mouth, road sign to road sign. With no time to find motels or restaurants, they were almost entombed in Hank's limo, the boss the most uncomfortable of them all. "With all of his back problems," said Don Helms, "Hank rode the car in misery."[7] His diet was inferior to a stray dog's. Big Bill Lister, touring at times with him, recalled that "Hank was the only person I ever saw could put ketchup on his oatmeal. Out on the road, none of us ate properly. We'd stop to get gas, and at the same time, we'd get a gallon of milk and a dozen doughnuts or cupcakes. We didn't even have time to order hamburgers. There were many weeks that we'd maybe check into a hotel twice— the rest of the time you're driving."[8]

Looking for more ways to squander the constant stash of money, the Williamses could easily keep up with the Joneses—or, more accurately, the Tubbses. Ernie Tubb had opened a record shop near the Ryman in '47, making good side money from it, and Hank and Audrey took that as a cue to open a western clothing store similar to Nudie Cohn's, Hank & Audrey's Corral, at 724 Commerce Street just down the block from Ernie's store. It cost Hank $160 a month to rent, and he put over $7,000 into stocking and furnishing the joint. It was quite a sight, the windows bordered by logs that no doubt took Hank back to his childhood and Lon's logging trains. A huge sign with the couple's images flanking the name of the store in neon lights jutted from the building. A wagon wheel loomed over the front door. The shelves were stocked with boots, kerchiefs, hats, saddles, shirts, and suits designed by Hank and Audrey, as well as Hank's records and sheet music. All that was missing were Daniel Boone–style coonskin caps.

On the day the store opened, Hank did his morning show there, singing with invited guests such as Roy Acuff backed by Lister, Sammy Pruett, and Howie Watts. Fans mobbed the place, causing security concerns, and soon he and Audrey did a Saturday night show from there on WSM before the *Opry*, just like Tubb did with his radio show at his music shop. Musicians mingled with patrons. Hank would send out for burgers for everyone and press twenty-dollar bills into the hands of anyone with a sob story. He had stationery printed with HANK & AUDREY'S CORRAL as the masthead, which he used when he replied to fan letters.

He sold leather holsters, but one accessory he *didn't* sell off the rack, wisely, was guns. While they fit the motif, they made Audrey nervous, with cause, as she was living with a man who had enough guns to build an arsenal and flew into rages directed at her. Indeed, more and more, guns had become a frightening part of the mayhem always about to erupt in the Williams home. A couple who had been their neighbors in Shreveport, Zeke and Helen Clements, had seen them argue, fuss, and fight but never saw Hank with a gun. When they moved to Nashville, Hank seemed not to care who was around when he began menacing Audrey with one or another of his pistols. Audrey tried at first to pass it off as bravado. When Helen told her, "Audrey, I don't like this," Audrey tried to laugh it away. "He won't hurt you," she said, "he likes you." However, when the Clementses stayed over that night, Helen again came across Hank toying with a gun. "Audrey," she said, "I'm getting out of here. You can stay if you want, but he's violent." As she and Zeke were leaving, Hank crept right behind them, holding his gun, a crazed look on his face. This was the image of the man that was now becoming common. Helen had also not seen Hank put his hands on Audrey. That had changed, too. During an argument at the house, Audrey ran into the bathroom to get away from Hank, who followed her in and locked the door. Helen heard a *thwack* and called out, "Hank, open this door. What are you doing in there?"

Sounding calm, as if nothing were awry, he called back, "It's all right, Helen, I just slapped her so she'd stop and listen to me. That's all I done."[9]

But Audrey could dish it out as good as she got. Helen was with them in Hank's car driving home after an *Opry* show when they began spatting as usual. Audrey stopped the car and ordered Hank out, in the middle of nowhere. "Audrey," Helen said, "you're not going to leave him out there on the side of the road like that?"

"Well, I am, too," she told her, starting up the motor again. "I'm not goin' back."

After driving about a mile, though, she did go back. Didn't she always? Their entire life together was one sick scene after another, a perpetual war interrupted by brief lulls in the hostilities, as if to gear up for the next round. But the collateral damage was becoming more than she could handle. Helen Clements told of Audrey finding bottles he had strategically hidden around the house and pouring them down the sink. "One time she was cranky, and she said, 'Let him drink all he wants,' and she went and got him three fifths. He was already so drunk he couldn't get off the couch, but he drank it all and we had to take him to the hospital."[10]

Audrey could be so turned off to him that her crusade to keep him off the bottle was waning, so turned off that not even money could make things better. Before leaving for a gig one time, Hank put a stack of shriveled bills in Helen's hand—$500 in all.

"Give these to her," he instructed her, "but don't do it until I've left."

Helen did, but Audrey wasn't having it. "I don't want them," she said.

"Well, what do you want me to do with them, Audrey?"

"I don't care what you do with them. You can keep them, you can tear them up, but I just don't care!"

That, granted, was rare for her. But it was a marker that she was reaching a breaking point. For now, though, he could still tug at her heart, whenever he would crumble into a pile of pity. As Audrey once looked back:

Everybody always said, "He's gonna kill you one of these days." He'd do these things and when he'd come to his senses, he'd put his head on my lap and cry just like a baby. He'd say, "Why do

I do that to you? I know better 'n that. Why do I do it? Why do I do it?" I begged him to go to a psychiatrist. "We'll just close up the house, and we'll rent an apartment, and we'll stay close to you." He told me, "If you ever have me put anywhere, I'll kill you." He needed help so bad, and I just couldn't do it.[11]

The more abuse and self-destruction he and Audrey could punish each other with, the more it seemed they could suck up in order to keep the business partnership intact. Symbolically, Hank neatly typed a song on a sheet of that stationery, dated October 9, 1951, titled "Heart Filled with Hate," which was an all but rewritten version of "Cold, Cold Heart." Under pictures of Hank and Audrey's smiling faces, the lyrics, in capital letters, read in part, "my love came to [sic] late," and "I'm wed to a heart filled with hate."

Although Fred Rose never put in for a copyright, nor was it ever recorded, these thoughts were always swimming in his head, and laying them out on paper seemed to have a cathartic effect, as if just *seeing* them were a victory over her. For Audrey, the same effect could be had by smashing a piece of crockery or throwing a fur coat in his face. As they struggled to make it through 1951, it seemed like a triumph of love, or maybe just spite, that they were both still in one piece.

. . .

Hank was still affiliated with Hadacol but would freelance around the WSM schedule as well, on short-lived shows with other sponsors, including Duckhead work clothes and Aunt Jemima pancake mix (those shows were recorded but never aired). Then, in late 1950, the station changed the sponsorship of his 7:15–7:30 a.m. show, it never being hard to find one eager to ride him. This was Mother's Best Flour, a perfect tie-in to the demographics of the audience, mainly housewives as they went about making breakfast and shoving baked goods into their ovens. Paid a hundred bucks a week now by WSM, he never missed a show, even if he was on no sleep when he came in. And these were some of the most enduring hours of his career, eighteen hours over seventy-two shows recorded on acetate for replay when he was out on the road. Striking, too, was that he would find a place for Audrey on many shows, singing duets with her or letting her perform solo with the Drifting Cowboys on songs like "Last Night I Heard You Crying in Your Sleep," "Four Flusher," and "Blue Love (In My Heart")."

These were far more polished broadcasts than the transcripts of the Johnnie Fair shows in Shreveport, Hank a master of easy banter and smooth segues from cornpone to his mournful hit songs, gospel hymns, and talking blues, closing each show with a solemn religious number. Most Luke the Drifter numbers he made sure to perform on the air, helping sell those oddball anomalies not heard on juke-boxes. After a tremulous rendition of the talking blues song "The Funeral" on his radio show, Hank, no longer perpetuating the thin joke of his alter ego, informed the audience, "We make quite a few records under the name of Luke the Drifter . . . just a flock of 'em, Luke the Drifter, MGM Records. Nine cents. I don't care if you buy 'em or not 'cause I don't need the money no more. But if you buy one of 'em and notify the folks I owe, they'll send you a congratulations card, I guarantee ya."

Unlike Hadacol, Mother's Best contracted to sponsor the show if it was picked up by stations around the country on a network feed, and Hank and his band posed for publicity photos holding big bags of Mother's Best flour. He also was called upon to weave in commercials for the product, usually with Cousin Louie Buck, and wrote a theme song that went:

> *I love to have that gal around*
> *Her biscuits are so nice and brown*
> *Her pies and cakes beat all the rest*
> *Cause she makes them all with Mother's Best*

As good as he was at injecting quite nearly subliminal plugs into any small talk he did, he would preface a song onstage by saying

"Here's a song that's bought us a lotta beans and biscuits." When he would flirt with the ladies at home by cooing, "Hey, good-lookin', if you've got anything cookin', just make sure you're cookin' it with Mother's Best Flour," it wasn't only a good line—it was good for sales. And of course, it would be good for a song that soon would be heard on just about every radio and jukebox in the land.

This was a Hank at the top of his game, even as his home life was falling apart, the depth of his natural and created personality evident in what are by turns humble and swaggering charm and withering empathy, the stuff of which sold his records. And his range of material on these shows revealed a remarkable sweep of musical knowledge, his selections darting in machine-gun style from a familiar hit to the unknown.

No dummy when it came to business, he made sure to play the standards all the time, "Lovesick Blues" and "I Saw the Light" always in the rotation. And Mother's Best was the single most repeated phrase of any show. After Hank began with a few bars of "Lovesick Blues," he would cue "Luigi" for Buck's typical intro, at which point Hank would interrupt, "Cousin Louie Buck! Beat ya to it." Then, "You fellers are just so wide awake and scrappy this morning, I don't know what I'm gonna do with you. How 'bout comin' in, everybody, and sitting down. I'll fix ya up a mess of biscuits." Or, "Get over in the corner, get your apron on, and stir up a batch of that Mother's Best Biscuits. Give me a chord in A, everybody. [Breaking into a makeshift melody] *Yessir, it's Mother's Best biscuit kind. . . . Here we go, we're gonna go down to Louisianer, Louisianer, I said, where the red river flows. Let's go. . .*" He then began a spirited, fiddlin' version of "Where the Old River Flows," yodeling mutated into ten-second falsetto riffs. He delighted in singing "a song I wrote about my home state," the slow, sinewy "Alabama Waltz."

It was intimate, fun, homey, revealing. There was not a slurred word or flat note—except by Audrey. Indeed, one of the great finds in cultural archaeology was when someone at WSM in the late 1970s happened to see the acetates for all the shows, which included an amazing 143 songs, in their original casings discarded in the trash, waiting to be dumped into the next garbage pickup. Fortunately, someone picked them out, and decades later they formed several retrospective albums of unreleased Hank songs, one of which was nominated for a Grammy as Best Historical Album.

If only he'd known what he was doing was *historical*. For Hank, it was all just a day's pay.

• • •

On March 16, 1951, Hank assembled with Rivers, Helms, Pruett, Shook, Newton, and Owen Bradley on piano and recorded four originals—"I Can't Help It if I'm Still in Love with You," "Howlin' at the Moon," "Hey, Good Lookin'," and "My Heart Would Know," one of the most productive sessions Hank ever had, as well as one of the most carefree. As though he had gotten all the bile out of his system about Audrey, the abortion, and Lord knows what other bugaboos he was carrying inside, he had created these songs with a dose of wishful thinking, and just had fun with them.

After he sang the word "moon" on the second tune, someone in the band bayed an *ow-wooooon* and the arrangement was an upbeat fox-trot beat, as Jerry Rivers pegged it. "That was when all the records said 'Fox Trot,'" he said. "Personally I never knew what the fox trot was, but I knew that tempo."[17] Of course, so did Fred Rose, and it was just what he wanted, and would release as the next single. But the others were top shelf, too. "I Can't Help It" and "My Heart Would Know" were wailing ballads that exposed the same nerve of love no matter what, the former sighing that if his lips could tell a lie, his heart would betray him.

"Hey, Good Lookin'" was the biggest lark he ever sang, Hank having appropriated the title and hook from the 1942 Cole Porter show tune "Hey, Good Lookin' (Something for the Boys)," changing the rest to a litany of corny courtin' cliches and double entendres about things like a "hot rod Ford" sung in eight-to-the-bar blues tempo.

If ever Hank had actually *enjoyed* being in love, or just the thought of it, it was when he scribbled the lines of this song, intending it as the sort of change-of-pace, pop-friendly, see-I-can-do-it dance record that Fred had longed for from the beginning as an entree to the crossover pop market. Rose let some backwoods patois go unedited (though this was one of the few Hank sessions where he didn't officially produce, his influence was still felt), but the yodeling was all but gone now, as Rose consciously turned toward breaking Hank into the more generic fold.

As part of the bargain for the nagging in his gut that told him he was indeed still in love, he was back at Castle on March 23, 1950, to cut two gospel duets with Audrey, Johnny Bailes's "The Pale Horse and His Rider" and Hank's "A Home in Heaven." And his star was of such magnitude that, with Paul Cohen having fulfilled his obligation to release two records by Audrey, Hank had prevailed on Frank Walker to sign her as a solo act to MGM for two years, a minor concession by Walker and a small price for keeping her from crimping any more of Hank's sessions with those cursed duets. Audrey cut her first two MGM solo records at that same session, both written by her, "Leave Us Women Alone" and "If You See My Baby," the latter notable as the title of a different song sung years later by Merle Haggard.

Hank, meanwhile, did indeed seem to be crossing over to a place in his own head in which he could live without all the usual stress and strife. Though the clothing store would lose thousands before they shut it down, it didn't deter him from sinking $60,000 more into a 507-acre farm as a getaway in Carter Creek over in Franklin, buying it from a widow named Lois Brown. The grounds were even more Graceland-like than the Franklin Road estate, an old cotton plantation anchored by an alabaster-white antebellum mansion built in 1856, called Beechwood Hall. The property sat on a hilltop, offering sweeping vistas of the Tennessee Valley. Even though the place had fallen into disrepair and needed tons of work, with bales of hay stacked up in the manor house, Hank believed he could dry out in a real country setting more distant from the web of Nashville, and give Audrey another reason to feel like a queen of the manor, masking the mutual loathing they now had for each other when they were alone. With all that he'd spent on keeping her around, it was just some more good money thrown after bad. And, as always, it could only be so long before that Band-Aid broke, too.

✶ PART FOUR ✶

1950–1953

17

✳ ✳ ✳ ✳ ✳ ✳ ✳

"DON'T HE KILL
AN AUDIENCE?"

By the summer of 1950, with "Howlin' at the Moon" en route
to No. 3 on the country chart and "Hey, Good Lookin'" just
released, Fred Rose was pounding the pavement in New York looking to broach the pop market with Hank's songs. This was not a
new idea; songs of the country-folk genre had become crossover
hits during the '40s, such as Bing Crosby's covers of "You Are My
Sunshine" and "Pistol Packin' Mama," and Ernest Tubb had taken
"Walking the Floor over You" and three other songs into the pop
Top 30. Tin Pan Alley had fashioned its own version of country—
for instance, "Chattanooga Choo Choo," with which Glenn Miller's
band reaped a huge hit in 1941.

As much as country had jumped into the industry pool, though,
it still was corded off in a corner of it, its big sales figures a fraction of
the overall bottom line for the major record houses that drained the
pop market. And Hank was a tough sell. Wesley Rose once recalled,
"I beat on everybody's door with 'Cold, Cold Heart' and I got the
same answer everywhere: 'That's a hillbilly song,' and there's no use

kidding yourself into thinking otherwise.'"[1] The main problem was not country *songs* so much as the stigma of "hillbilly" singers, Hank now being the most famous. If Nashville had developed a "sound," it was only because the Northern crowd had wanted no part of recording it in their studios.

Rose did get one bite, from a most unlikely ally but one who respected country, Mitch Miller, the A&R head of the pop division at Mercury, and as such the man who had waved "The Tennessee Waltz" into release. Having rolled to Columbia in 1950, Miller shared Rose's idealism about country's niche in pop, but he had his critics, including some of his own talent. Frank Sinatra believed Miller sought gimmicky, novelty songs rather than ones of substance. An autocrat, he demanded his own name as leader of the Columbia house orchestra, producing nearly identical-sounding sing-along standards like "The Yellow Rose of Texas." He would ride this schtick a long way, hosting an enormously popular TV show in the '60s. He would also produce country talent like Marty Robbins.

However, Miller had no country act in 1950 and needed an appropriate singer to sing the song he'd bought from Fred Rose, "Cold, Cold Heart." His choice, looking back now, was pure genius—Queens, New York–born Anthony Dominick Benedetto, a former singing waiter and veteran of the Battle of the Bulge, who when he performed in a club with Bob Hope was given a new name by the comedian, Tony Bennett. He was then and now a ridiculously talented and instantly likable man. That Miller freely associated a bombastic Italian with a hillbilly song seemed bizarre, though Bennett had only made one recording, in April, the bluesy ballad "Because of You," which hadn't yet been released when he went into Columbia's New York studio on May 31, 1951, to have a crack at "Cold, Cold Heart." Convincing Bennett was the tough part. When Miller waxed eloquent about the inherent poetry of Hank Williams's song, Bennett had heard little else but the turkey-in-the-straw fiddling and yodeling vocal on Hank's record. Almost pleading, he told Mitch, "Don't make me do no cowboy songs!"[2]

Years later, Bennett would recall that country music to him then was "something that stayed in the Bible Belt"; he told Miller, "It's a great song and Hank Williams is a great songwriter, but I'm a city boy, I wouldn't be able to sing a country song." Miller replied, "If we have to tie you to a tree, you're gonna sing this song, whether you like it or not."[3] He would cut it as a pop song, displaying his vibrato and emotionally intense style, holding high notes for long moments rather than Hank's way of yodeling them, and Miller coated it with dense strings in an orchestral arrangement conducted by Percy Faith. Miller loved it. And Hank? The story was told that he played an advance copy over and over on his turntable at home, dragging people into his parlor and exclaiming like an excited kid, "Hot damn!" as it played. He then placed a call to Bennett.

"Tony," he said, affecting a tone of disfavor, "what's the idea of ruining my song?"[4]

Bennett was taken aback for a second before realizing he was being pranked. Hank then told him how much he appreciated the job he did on it. What could really be appreciated was the timing of the record. Between the session and the April 4 release of "Cold, Cold Heart," "Because of You," which was heard in the movie *I Was an American Spy*, burst out and became Bennett's first hit, going to No. 1 for thirteen weeks. "Cold, Cold Heart," originally released as the B-side of "While We're Young," was reviewed simply in *Billboard* as "a straightforward pop warble of a fetching country ballad," but the combination of Hank's watermark and Tony's bombast was explosive. When the jocks flipped it over, Columbia shifted the song to the A-side, and it took off on an impressive run, going to No. 1 on the pop chart in July, spending twenty-seven weeks on the list.

As Bennett said, "Before that, country just had a certain instrumentation and it never broke out of that 300,000 record sales that Hank Williams used to do. We had the first crossover hits from country music . . . the first country song to sell internationally, all over the world, two million records."[5]

To be sure, it was nothing like Hank's original version. But even if it was only incidentally a country song, the lesson was clear: a good song can't be confined to one set of ears, and now everyone knew that a country song could be a damn good song, even a *great* one. And it officially made Hank Williams a *great* songwriter. Two other covers of "Cold, Cold Heart" dropped that autumn, one from no less than Louis Armstrong, then Donald Peers and Dinah Washington. Gene Autry would croon it in his 1952 movie *Apache Country*, and another pop diva, Joni James, made it all the way to No. 2 with her cover in 1953. It has been covered endlessly ever since, most recently by Norah Jones in 2002, and can only be described as being a *pop* classic.

· · ·

Once, Hank had wondered how it was that Roy Acuff could earn $5,000 a week. Now he was on that very same stratum. One newspaper dubbed him "Hank Williams, $100,000-a-year folk singer."[6] The Drifting Cowboys weren't hurting, either. Hank had bumped them up to $50 each per gig, a good $15 higher than the going union rate for musicians.[7] Then, with so many gigs, he just put them on salary, at $200 a week. If Hank saved a few dollars by doing this, the Cowboys gained more than a few, and peace of mind, since he would have to pay them every week regardless of whether he had taken time off, or was spending some in a dry-out tank.

To further accommodate the band's comfort, he bought a second touring sedan, a '50 Cadillac in canary yellow, to carry their instruments and all of their outfits, though for Hank cars were strictly temporary. That he had little respect for the money in his pocket was obvious. Jerry Rivers recalled that Hank once saw a squirrel dog on a farm and just had to have it, trading the farmer a wristwatch with "several diamonds on the face."[8] He took the dog, rode around with it on a road trip, then brought it back home to Nashville. Rivers maintained that little of material value meant much to Hank. Cars were disposable, even people. The only things he seemed to hold on to over the years were his Colt .38 and .45, his dog, and his horse.

Although performing on the road was the spine of Hank's income, the radio slots, the Saturday night *Opry* shows and his three-hour sessions at Castle Studio were his bread and butter. But Fred Rose's new plan was to make him the biggest country music name in all the land by having him go Hollywood as the new king of the singing cowboys. Rose and Frank Walker had been engaged in discussions with MGM Pictures, knowing they had a lot of leverage as Hank's patrons, having fattened up MGM's overall bottom line and turned him into a pop culture figure since "Cold, Cold Heart." MGM had the contractual right of first refusal on any movie work Hank might branch into. But if Hank had images of living large as a movie star, his life on the road was that of a man afraid to stop touring, ingrained since he was fourteen to feel like a failure if people in dive bars or arenas didn't fill his pockets.

He simply never slowed down, always itching to go out again, instructing Bill England to book him wherever, whenever. Almost always, he went out with another country star, as though needing to know he could still run anyone out of the building. In early '51, he went on a six-day tour with Lefty Frizzell through Little Rock down to Monroe, Louisiana, and to Baton Rouge. After Hank did a solo gig in his old stomping ground at the Shreveport Municipal Auditorium with *Hayride* bluegrass singer Mac Wiseman, the two of them met up again in Corpus Christi, Texas, then concluded the tour at the New Orleans Municipal Auditorium. And Hank never let Lefty forget who sold out all these buildings.

Five years younger than Hank, Lefty was clearly a threat to him. Born William Orville Frizzell in El Dorado, Arkansas, his similarity to Hank was in his yodeling, vowel-extending voice—and his penchant for the bottle and getting himself in dutch. At nineteen, in 1947, the married Frizzell was thrown in jail for having sex with an underage fan. When he got out, he signed with Columbia, which put out his first hit, the two-sided "If You've Got the Money (I've Got the Time)" and "I Love You a Thousand Ways." His subsequent "I Want to Be with You Always" went to No. 1 on the country chart.

Yet Hank, who made a habit of slavishly praising most country singers, couldn't hide his contempt for Lefty as a pretender, lumping
him in with Slim Whitman

"Here, boy, why don't you just stay down in Texas, this is my
territory up here," he told Frizzell once in Nashville, possibly mis-
stating where Lefty came from intentionally.

"Hank," Frizzell replied, trying to placate but not shrink from
him, "the whole damn country is the back yard of both of us, can't
you realize there's enough room for all of us?"

Hank then broke into his famous grin. "Well, I was just kidding.
It's good to have a little competition. Makes me realize I gotta work
harder than ever, and boy you're the best competition I ever had."[9]

But Hank continued to twit Lefty, mostly because he hadn't been
invited to play the *Grand Ole Opry*, something Hank also wouldn't
let him forget. Finally Lefty had enough. "Hell," he shot back, "I just
got a telegram from [Tin Pan Alley music publisher] Hill & Range
on having number one and number two, and I got maybe two more
in there, and you say I need the *Grand Ole Opry*?"

Hank again backed off. "You got a hell of an argument," he con-
ceded, having once made that same argument himself.

The two troubled cowboys forged an uneasy alliance that week,
sharing close quarters as Lefty, Hank, and Big Bill Lister, the only
musician to accompany him, were driven to and fro by Lefty's father.
Lefty later insisted Hank stayed sober the whole time. Not so Lefty.
Between shows, he put a bottle of bourbon on a table between them.
"Hey, I'm gonna have a shot," he said. "How about you?"

"If I was to have what you're fixin' to drink," Hank told him, "I'd
want another and first thing you know I'd be gone."

As the tour went on, Frizzell said, Hank "never sounded better. He was in good shape. He didn't take a drink—and he put on
a show." A footnote to the brief liaison was that Hank apparently
profited from Lefty's store of angst and songs. "All Hank thought
about was writing," said Frizzell, and apparently Hank wrote one
called "I'm Sorry for You, My Friend" after hearing Lefty's tales of

woe about his own marriage. Lefty also agreed to let Hank have a song he apparently had to have, "I Ain't Got Nothing but Time," a wishful title indeed for Hank. It was never known if Hank gave Lefty anything in return, either one of his own songs or perhaps some cash, but they parted with Hank having gotten more out of the tour than Lefty, who, while he would get to sing at the *Opry* and would remain a presence in country music, died in 1975 of a stroke at age forty-seven, and was posthumously elected to the Country Music Hall of Fame.[10]

. . .

If Hank was the clean one on that tour, the sobriety didn't last long. One drink during an *Opry* swing through Canada—for some reason, very fertile territory in the growth of country music—in May 1951 led to an alarming moment. During a show in Ontario, he began weaving around and, unable to judge the distance to the front of the stage, tumbled off it. He was lucky, breaking no bones, but did serious damage to his back and couldn't finish the tour; Big Bill Lister drove him back to Nashville. Lister would recall that on the way back, Hank seemed in such pain that he didn't eat a thing. However, after Bill paid for some food for himself at a fry place and came back to the car, Hank was gone. "In the middle of the next block," Lister recalled, "a big sign said 'Cocktails' and I just broke into a dead run, and by the time I got there, he'd already had him one. I paid the bill and drug him back to the car. It just broke your heart, but I knew I had to get him home."[11]

But that was nothing compared to what happened when, nearing Nashville at the break of dawn, Lister stopped again, to call Audrey. "I'm at the edge of town, and I got Hank with me and he's in pretty bad shape," he told her. Audrey, nothing like the affable and ditzy Gracie Allen character she put on when she did his radio show, or the pastoral, Madonna-like guise of her duets with him, had no sympathy.

"I don't care what you do with the son of a bitch, just don't bring him here," she hissed.

Lister, not knowing where to bring Hank, who was passed out in the back seat, called Jim Denny at the *Opry*, who directed him to one of the sanitariums that Hank was taken to at times like this, the closest one in Madison, Tennessee, out by Cumberland, in the Green Hills eight miles north of town. Once he had booked Hank in, Lister took Hank's cash from the tour and locked it away in a safe in Jim Denny's office at WSM. Then, as if on cue, Audrey, who had been calling around town, located him at the station, though she seemed to have little interest in Hank's health.

"What'd you do with my money?" she demanded to know.

"Lady," an exhausted and disgusted Lister replied, "as far as I know you ain't got no damn money. I gave *Hank*'s money to Jim."[12]

• • •

It wasn't really the drinking that Hank judged to be his problem; it was his back that caused him to seek out relief in a bottle. He had, of course, been tortured by his back since childhood, and while he could plow through the pain as a young man, the undiagnosed spina bifida was unrelenting, damn near crippling him at times. As a result, he had another problem now—the pharmaceutical kind. He had become quite familiar with Nembutal and Demerol, and would confide in people that it was easier to get them on the outside than a bottle of booze. He'd get the stuff from any number of connections along the music circuit; when he did, he would pop them like Good & Plenty, not just the downers but the uppers. He knew which was which only by color—"white-up/red-down," meaning the white ones had the speed, the red ones the knockout drops; the booze, well, that was the delivery system, for both.

While he was laid up in the Madison sanitarium, where Audrey would continue to send him so often that the band had a nickname for it—"the Hut," because patients would be housed in cottages— doctors would pump him full of these drugs. Still, he hated the confining nature of it. When Audrey or Jim Denny would order him to dry out, Don Helms was often given the privilege of getting him there, without letting him know where he was headed. When they pulled up, Helms said, "he'd raise up and look out and say, 'Aw no, aw no, there's that damn Hut!' They'd put him in the cottage and close the door. He'd get sober there, though, because there wasn't nothing to drink. We'd call and ask him, 'What do you need, Hank?' and he'd say, 'Cigarettes, candy bars, and funny books.' "[13]

With the heat on him in Nashville, in April 1951 he decided to go where he felt in his element. That was *not* Montgomery, where he knew he'd be hectored by Lillie about money, about Audrey, about why he was so sickly. He figured he'd have to go to the only place where he ever felt wanted, Shreveport. After making the drive, squirming with intense pain every mile of the way, he checked into a hotel, but when hotel personnel saw him barely able to get up the stairs, they worried that he might not make it through the day and called an ambulance. He was out cold when the medics crashed through the door, scooped him up, and took him in an ambulance to the North Louisiana Sanitarium, which was actually one of the places he had slept off his binges before.

According to hospital records, he was put in room 215 and tended to by Dr. G. H. Cassity, who when Hank told him he felt fine except for his aching back shot him with a hundred milligrams of Demerol. Because Hank also looked dehydrated, Cassity's diagnosis was "acute alcoholism," though he noted that while Hank "has been drinking about four days" he "otherwise seems in good physical condition" and added that Hank "seems to think he has a lot of mental worries." Amazingly, Cassity was probably the first doctor to seriously examine Hank's back, and it was only now that Hank learned exactly what had caused him so much pain through the years; he found a "herniated intervertebral disc" and a "possible rupture of the fourth or fifth lumbar disc." However, further inspection of the lesions on the lower back was a bigger problem: X-rays showed that he had spina bifida occulta of the first sacral segment of the lower spine.[14]

Hank, of course, had never heard those strange words before and had no idea what they meant. The doctor tried to explain that it was a birth defect and that after being untreated for so long, there was little chance of it being cured, or the pain made any less brutal. Cassity did recommend that Hank be fitted in the orthopedic department of the hospital for a lumbrosacral brace, and he was. It was big and bulky, made of metal and leather, and probably weighed twenty pounds. Worn under his baggy clothing, it put a tremendous strain on his legs and was horribly uncomfortable, but at the least it let him stand and sit upright. Discharged on May 24, he wished he didn't know now what he hadn't known before, the examination confirming one of his pet lines about the medical profession—"Ain't no country boy seen a city doctor and lived to tell about it."[15]

· · ·

Hank came back to Nashville pronouncing himself dry and ready to get back to the grind again. And, as usual, Audrey once again let him back in the house, and the two carried on their pantomime of marriage. Sober again for the time being, he went into Castle Studio on June 1 to record four more songs, all slated to be Luke the Drifter numbers. It was a pain in Fred Rose's back, or close to it, that he would have to waste more time on Luke. Yet one of the compositions that came out of the session, "Ramblin' Man," would be the most haunting and immediately identifiable Hank Williams song ever recorded. It was a lament in the vein of "Lovesick Blues" but more pungent and pessimistic, every bit as convincing as any Lead Belly ever sang in his jail cell, or Johnny Cash's later dirge about being stuck in Folsom Prison, with no regrets for having lived the life the Lord meant for him before calling him home.

Although it was meant as a Luke the Drifter entry, he and Rose decided it would sound more authentic as a blues refrain if he sang it in a low, noir-ish burr, in a slow, steady, inexorable cadence, as if marking time on a life where time didn't count anymore. Hank's trembling falsetto and subtle yodel transitions, his holding of syllables, the *chuck-a-chuck* guitar beat, and Don Helms and Jerry Rivers's dead-man-walking interplay of pealing steel and strings could not have been executed any better.

The other three cuts that day were also quite clever, though doomed to minor appreciation as Luke the Drifter material, their bathos not as relieved as "Ramblin' Man." One, "I Dreamed About Mama Last Night," was adapted by Rose from an Edgar Guest poem. "I've Been Down This Road Before" was Hank's paean to learning life's hard lessons, even if it cost him a few teeth in bar brawls. The last, "Pictures from Life's Other Side," was an allegory of youth and beauty spoiled by mortal sin. Still, Rose dutifully released all four. Meanwhile, Hank hit the road again. He played before an enormous crowd on July 4 in Huntington, West Virginia, backed by the Texas singer/pianist Moon Mullican, whose robust boogie blues netted him a half dozen Top 10 country hits including a No. 1 in '51, "I'll Sail My Ship Alone." Hank went out not only in his Tin Man back brace but with a rug on his head. Audrey had been pecking at him for months to hide his bald spot—which few if any ever saw, given that his hat may as well have been surgically attached to his head— believing he'd look more handsome and manly. He thought wearing a piece was sissy stuff but as usual acceded to her. He consulted a wig maker in Nashville, shaved off all the hair on the back of his cranium, and affixed the swatch of dark brown with spirit gum. Self-conscious as he was, he was even more embarrassed when the primitive air-conditioning system in his Cadillac sprang a leak right over his head and doused him, dislodging the wig, which he proceeded to throw out the window.[16]

· · ·

It almost seemed like a coronation when Hank was invited by the Montgomery Junior Chamber of Commerce to perform on July 15, 1951, in what would be a massive celebration back in the town where he made his bones. Though he had played in the city periodically after moving out, the event was billed as Hank Williams Homecoming Day, and he would open the newly completed Cow

Coliseum, the informal name of the W. W. Garrett Agricultural Coliseum, a futuristic lime green edifice with 12,500 seats. The arena still stands, not far from the Hank Williams Museum and the Montgomery Zoo, and to this day those festivities are still the biggest thing that has ever happened in the place. When Hank agreed, it was front-page news; the *Advertiser* ran a headline reading HANK WILLIAMS ACCEPTS MONTGOMERY'S INVITATION.

Yet Hank had a strong ambivalence about the city, having nursed a grudge about the town never having been kind to him on the way up. Still, being able to feel at last appreciated was certainly appealing to him, and for the show he enlisted Hank Snow, Chet Atkins, Big Bill Lister, Brack Schuffert, and the Carter Sisters and their mother, Maybelle. The troupe would give a show at the Veterans Hospital; then Hank would ride in a parade in his honor up Fairgrounds Road to the Coliseum, stopping to give a speech about how much he loved all the city had done for him. He played his native-son part well, recording radio ads pitching the event—which needed no pitching to quickly sell out all 9,000 seats, then the capacity of the arena, saying he was "plumb tickled to be comin' home . . . and grateful as can be to the Jaycees for puttin' on this how-dee-doo," which he promised would be a "humdinger."[17]

During the parade, he sat in the back of a convertible with a proud Lillie Stone, who was miffed that she had to share space with Audrey, who had Randall on her lap and Lycrecia beside her. Still, Lillie had to be happy that this trip was a rare opportunity for Hank to slip her some cash.

Hank put on a smile and waved to crowds that lined up three deep along the route. Then, at a ceremony in front of the arena, Mayor W. A. Gayle handed him a proclamation and a key to the city. Lillie and Audrey were given bouquets. The Jaycees presented Hank with a gold watch as "Alabama's Goodwill Ambassador."[18] At Hank's insistence, the Jaycees also gave Lillie a gold watch. Audrey had only her bouquet. In the excitement, Hank had forgotten to take his guitar with him, so before the show his cousin Walter McNeil drove him to French's Music Store. When Hank walked in the door the owner nearly fainted, and wound up giving him a guitar, free. When Hank came back out to the car, he had a cynical grin. "Ten years ago," he said, "I wanted to buy a guitar on credit and they wouldn't sell it to me. Now they want to give me one."[19]

Hank had not forgotten about his father. Lon Williams was invited to come up from McWilliams, producing uncomfortable vibes with Lillie. As territorial as ever, the woman who once told people her first husband was dead made only grudging concessions now. When Lon tried to pick up Randall, never having seen his grandson before this day, Lillie snatched the baby out of his arms. She also refused him a seat in the lead car. He rode several cars behind, no one knowing who he was.

Lycrecia Williams recalled that a teenager named Lamar Morris found his way backstage and asked Hank if he could go onstage and sing "Hey, Good Lookin'," which was climbing toward No. 1. Hank, she said, had planned to sing the song himself but took the remarkable step of allowing Morris to perform. Fate works in mysterious ways. A few years later, Lycrecia would marry Lamar Morris.[20]

However, the show itself was a disaster, the speakers malfunctioning and people far from the stage not able to hear Hank sing. Angered by it, Hank seemed to hold Bill England responsible; when they returned to Nashville, England was fired and Bam Bamford again hired as booker. But on most counts the event was a success, and for years folks in Montgomery told children and grandchildren they'd been there to see Hank. It surely did nothing to slow him down. Indeed, Fred Rose had just about nailed down the two biggest deals he ever made for Hank. The first was the renewal of the MGM contract that ran out in early July, which Frank Walker agreed to sweeten with another two years at a boosted five-and-a-half-cent royalty rate, rarefied air for an artist, nearly Sinatra territory. But a bigger deal was still in the works, one that would make Hank Williams a movie star.

· · ·

While those details were being negotiated, Hank came back to Castle on July 25 and recorded four songs, though it was again more than a little disconcerting to Fred Rose that Hank's songwriting had taken a dip in quality as so much attention roiled around him. Three were written by Hank, "I'd Still Want You," "Baby, We're Really in Love," and "(I Heard That) Lonesome Whistle." The last was co-written with Shreveport singer/songwriter Jimmie Davis, an early country pioneer who was elected as the "singing governor" of Louisiana twice as an antisegregationist, serving 1944–48 and 1960–64.[21] The fourth, "Crazy Heart," was written by Fred Rose. With a heat wave outside, the studio was sweltering, leading Hank to peel off his shirt as he sang, his bony torso sopping, pouring an extra dose of emotion into his plaintively yodeled peaks on "I'd Still Want You," which seemed to admit need was a stronger pull than love.

The song has some of the same effect as "Move It On Over," its rhythm and poetic structure later appropriated by a rock and roll landmark, Carl Perkins's "Blue Suede Shoes." And Hank's vocals were wonderfully rich and nuanced on the throwback train ballad "Whistle," the title borrowed by Nashville country writer Paul Craft in his song "Midnight Flyer," later covered in the '70s by the Eagles. Yet there was little in these songs to rival "Lovesick Blues" or "Hey, Good Lookin'" as hit material. "Baby, We're Really in Love" had seemed like the best bet, but somehow the acetate was lost or damaged beyond repair—it was never really known which—and the first to go out from the new sessions were "Lonesome Whistle"/"Crazy Heart," each of which broke out for a Top 10 ride, the former to No. 8, the latter to No. 4 late in '51. Good, but not good enough for a man who'd had seven No. 1s and only one lower than No. 5 among his A-side releases since "Lovesick Blues."

Needing more, Rose would have him back on August 10 for four more sides, one a redo of both "Baby, We're Really in Love" and "I'd Still Want You," Hank's hand-wringing, hypocritical lament about Lefty Frizzell's broken marriage, "I'm Sorry for You My Friend," and Curley Williams's "Half as Much."

Rose settled on the singsong, old-time country vibe of "Sorry," bringing Hank back a day later to recut it in a cleaner fashion. But these songs, too, were a notch below Hank's best, though a side benefit was that anything he wrote or recorded now was bait for other singers, country and pop, it being imperative to get *something* with the Hank stamp on vinyl. Even the famously bland bandleader Guy Lombardo wanted in, and his cover of "Crazy Heart" was a Top 20 pop hit.

The rub was that to some industry bigwigs, Hank Williams might as well have been the only name that mattered in country. Because Curley Williams was an Acuff-Rose writer and recorded for Columbia, Fred Rose wanted to give him a little push, producing Curley's "Half as Much" and having it released in November, three months before Hank's would go out. It did well enough, but in 1952 Rosemary Clooney had a No. 1 pop and No. 2 country hit with it for Columbia, and Hank's version went to No. 2 on the country list in early spring. Mitch Miller was delighted. "Ol' Hank's done it again, hasn't he?" he told Wesley Rose, who reminded Mitch the song was actually written by Curley, not Hank, Williams. Miller blinked. "Who's Curley Williams?" he asked. Wesley had to remind him, "A guy that's been on your label about seven years."[22]

Even so, not for a moment did Hank believe he could afford to turn away from his kind of music. He still kept the pledge he began with—"It can never be *too* country." Neither did he tire of the grind of spreading the gospel and making more and more money for Audrey to spend. Nashville seemed to be a mere stopover on his constant schedule of touring, and he could be forgiven if he was looking ahead to his next trek, when he would be the most popular attraction among literally a trainload of America's biggest and whitest names.

18

✶ ✶ ✶ ✶ ✶ ✶ ✶

"THE GUN SHOT
FOUR TIMES"

In mid-August 1951, Hank Williams was on the marquee of a medicine show like no other. It was a lavish, star-studded, ten-week affair sponsored by the snake oil he sold on the radio. Called the Hadacol Caravan, this decadent traveling show was Dudley LeBlanc's second such venture pushing his 20 proof miracle cure. In 1950, drunk with success, and perhaps Hadacol's main ingredient, he had put together the first, a procession of 130 trucks all painted white with the letters HADACOL in black, playing on one-night stands throughout the South, the Midwest, and the West Coast.

Tens of thousands of people paid admission with multiples of twenty-five-cent Hadacol boxtops to see talent LeBlanc had paid top dollar for. At each stop there would be a parade through the center of town to the fairgrounds, the trucks separated by giant blow-up balloons shaped like elephants. Bands played, chorus girls danced, circus acts flew through the air with ease.

Seeing even bigger profits, LeBlanc traded the trucks for a seventeen-Pullman-car train called the *Hadacol Special*. The shows featured bicycle giveaways, beauty contests, and clowns selling Hadacol just like Hank used to sell snake oil off the back of a truck. In what was an amorphous mélange of names that changed almost daily, the stars might be Bob Hope for a few shows, then Milton Berle, then Jimmy Durante, then Jack Benny, supplemented by Dick Haymes, Rudy Vallee, cartoon voice actor Candy Candido, Cesar Romero, and Benny's stage butler, Eddie "Rochester" Anderson. The band was Sharkey Bonano and His Kings of Dixieland, which featured a comedy act by two shucking and jiving black men called Pork Chops and Kidney Stew. Other acts included "the world's tallest man," dancers from the Chez Paree nightclub in Chicago, acrobats, magicians, clowns, and beauty queens. Former heavyweight champ Jack Dempsey was given a spot urging crowds to buy Defense Bonds. Minnie Pearl was back for the country set, and with LeBlanc owing a debt of thanks to Hank's radio pitching, now the biggest hillbilly singer in the land was signed. Hank was allowed to bring with him his Drifting Cowboys band and Big Bill Lister, and permitted to leave on Saturdays to be flown by Minnie's husband back to Nashville for the *Opry*, then catch up with the caravan on Sunday mornings.

The tour was scheduled to run through early October, hitting eighteen states, playing on county fair and bandshell stages for the most part, in murderous heat and humidity. It was far bigger and more hectic than any tour Hank had done with the *Opry* or the Drifting Cowboys, a showcase of high-voltage, vaudeville-trained stars, many of whom were enlisted for Hadacol print ads. LeBlanc was not content to do anything halfway. Hadacol was the second-largest advertiser in the country, behind only Coca-Cola. LeBlanc used the profits to sign up the famous names, boasting that he had spent half a million dollars. Rather than to bring entertainment to the masses, however, the tour was designed as his last gasp to pocket scads of money before he would lose the company, which had become mired in FDA and FTC investigations of possible fraud and mismanagement.

LeBlanc had spent so much on advertising that even the thousands of bottles of snake oil he sold couldn't keep him in the black, and he was having discussions with wealthy investors about selling the company. The stars trusted him even though only Bob Hope was paid an advance, of around $30,000 for what would be exactly two shows. LeBlanc had promised to issue checks to the others periodically along the route, big checks, when the coffers were swelled by teeming crowds. This was okay by Hank, who even with his natural wariness of showbiz egomaniacs was quite taken with LeBlanc.

Before the caravan began on August 14 in LeBlanc's hometown, Lafayette, Louisiana, Hank and Bill Lister visited LeBlanc in his state senate office and knocked back a few shots of Old Forester whiskey from a stock of the stuff bottled just for LeBlanc. As it happened, this was two days after "Hey, Good Lookin'" went to No. 1, and LeBlanc knew he had to use Hank as the closing act of the show. But no one, least of all Hank, appreciated how wildly popular he now was, and that the crowds would swoon over him even as the caravan rolled through non-Southern venues, attracting crowds of 15,000 to 30,000 sweltering in the summer heat. When Bob Hope wasn't around, which was almost always, the emcee role alternated between Benny, Berle, and Romero, none of whom understood why Hank got the coveted closing spot, nor had any idea what sort of ruckus he could cause when he performed.

When Hope hopped on board in Louisville, for the show there and another in Cincinnati, he received his own education. In deference to the comedian, whom he was paying so much, LeBlanc gave him the closing privilege. Hank had no objection, but when he came on as the penultimate act, the typical overheated reception unnerved Hope. When Old Ski Nose walked out to close the show in Louisville, he must have felt the crowd had been deflated. Then, in Cincinnati, Lister recalled:

> Hank encored five times and that crowd wasn't gonna turn him loose, and they were trying to introduce Bob Hope over all this hollerin' and clappin'. They got the crowd quieted down, and

somewhere in his wardrobe Bob Hope had this old hat that he'd used in Paleface, I guess, and he wore that out and just stood there, and when the place quieted down he said, "Just call me Hank Hope."[1]

Minnie Pearl knew this scenario all too well. As she remembered, Hank had not wanted to upstage Hope, and after his fifth encore came back out onstage, without his guitar, and calmed the crowd, saying, "Folks, I thank you a lot, but we've got a mighty big act waitin' to come on, so I'd better leave."[2] However, "Hank Hope" was not as appreciative or affable about it, and told LeBlanc the same thing Minnie had told Oscar Davis: Don't ever make me follow that guy again, ever. When LeBlanc explained the situation to Hank, there was just one condition Hank had. "That's fine," he said. Just pay me what you're paying Hope."[3] That was wishful thinking. Hope left the caravan that night and never returned, putting that bit of static to a stop. Still, Hank was not particularly impressed with any of the Hollywood crowd that Fred Rose was trying to make him a part of, and was offended by the most obnoxious of them, Milton Berle, who hopped onto the caravan in St. Louis for a few days. Berle's faded vaudeville career had been revived by TV, his uproarious slapstick antics as host of the manic Texaco variety show already legend, such as mincing around the stage in drag. But worse was that "Uncle" Miltie popped up uninvited and mugged and preened as others performed, at times delivering crude insults about them. Only Berle thought this was funny. Watching with Hank offstage as Berle ruined someone's act, Bill Lister said, "If that joker comes out doing that when we're out there, he's really gonna mess things up. If he wants a good laugh, I'm gonna get this ol' guitar and crown him with it." "If you do," Hank said, "I'll buy you any guitar you want."[4]

A few weeks later, Hank would tell *Billboard* that he had been invited to appear on Ed Sullivan's *Toast of the Town* Sunday night TV show, but that he turned down an offer to go on Berle's show. "The last time I worked with him, in St. Louis," he said, "there like to have been a killing"[5]—Southern parlance for "there was almost a killing." As it turned out, he did neither show, perhaps blowing smoke about Sullivan. Not that that sort of thing mattered to him. His job was still, as he saw it, not to act like a star but to sing for his supper. When he did, Minnie Pearl once reflected, he seemed to have a singular kind of appeal.

In the end, though, the Hadacol Caravan could not be saved, by him or anyone else. Midway through the tour, LeBlanc simply ran out of money. When the caravan dropped anchor in Montgomery, Brack Schuffert climbed aboard the train car Hank was in and found him glum.

"Hank, how you doin', boy?" he greeted him.

"I'm doing no good at all," Hank said.

"What's the matter? All them pretty movie stars on the train, Hank."

"I don't have nothin' to do with 'em. They think they're better than I am."

Hank then unfurled a pink-colored check made out to him for $7,500. "Ever'body on this train has got one of these," he said, "and they all bounced."[6]

He kept his commitment to the show, drowning his ire in booze. At a stop in Columbus, Georgia, a newspaperman named Ray Jenkins sidled up to him hoping for an interview. Hank didn't shoo him away but was of no help. "I couldn't figure out if he was drunk or what, but he didn't say much," Jenkins said later, "and I couldn't make sense of what he said. I didn't even write a story about him."[7]

When the caravan stopped in Wichita in mid-September, Hank and Minnie flew back to Nashville for the *Opry*. They considered not going back, but, not wanting to shortchange fans who had paid for tickets, they did, flying to Oklahoma City on Sunday the sixteenth, Hank writing on the way a song called "Heart of a Devil, Face of a Saint," something that could have applied to many people. The next day the troupe got to Dallas for a show in the Cotton Bowl. That was when tour officials sent word through the trains that LeBlanc had sold Hadacol. The tour was over. Instructions were passed to report to the office car of the train to collect tickets back to their homes. Jerry Rivers recalled "a scene of near panic. Everyone was rushing about trying to get his personal belongings, and at the same time looking for friends made on the tour for one last goodbye."[8]

The performers asked anyone with any connection to LeBlanc, who seemed to have vanished, about being paid. The ticket department braced for what would be a tidal wave of angry people demanding refunds. The next morning, LeBlanc was seen calmly eating breakfast in his hotel. Hank and Lister saw him in the dining room and sat down at his table.

"What did you sell Hadacol for?" Hank asked, meaning *why*.

"Eight and a half million," LeBlanc replied, the only way he knew to answer such a question.[9]

Hank probably was the least surprised of anyone that LeBlanc took the money and ran—though not far, as it happened. The new owners of Hadacol inherited the morass of legal problems faced by LeBlanc and declared bankruptcy a year later, leaving LeBlanc to settle for $2 million from a $10 million sale. "Coozan" Dud would thereafter run for governor of Louisiana four times, all unsuccessfully, but serve four terms in the state senate before dying in 1971 at seventy-seven. Hank could only hope he had learned something from the Hadacol tour. With nothing in his pocket to show for it, he went home to Nashville, wiser and more cynical, but with no self-pity about being taken to the cleaners by a grifter like Dud LeBlanc. With all that was going on in the real world, there was no time for regrets.

• • •

Hank arrived back in Nashville to the news that Fred Rose and Frank Walker had closed the deal with MGM Pictures to make him a movie star. That very weekend, he would sign the contract backstage at the *Grand Ole Opry*, with newspaper photographers there to capture a moment everyone expected to be a landmark for country music.

Walker would come down from New York for the occasion and be able to bask in the same spotlight, as would the *Opry* brass, led by Jim Denny, who no doubt construed it as reward for sticking with Hank through so much toil and trouble. Thanks to the MGM public relations department, word had broken in the press of the deal, with Walker proudly pimping the new MGM movie-star-to-be by saying no one had ever before been signed to a movie deal without an audition or screen test. Even the biggest names in country, like Acuff, Tubb, and even Gene Autry, had to go through that process before they appeared in the movies. Walker had reason to pop his buttons. The year before, he had scored a movie deal with MGM for Billy Eckstine, who now was filming the musical *Skirts Ahoy*.

However, Hank wasn't so sure he was up to the movie star thing and had held off signing; then, when he had gone on the Hadacol tour, he said it would keep him from going to Hollywood for an audition, which he had no desire to do, regardless. But by stalling he gained some remarkable concessions that showed how prepared the top rank at MGM were to get him under their tent. And even though they, Rose, and Walker wanted him to sign early, MGM kept pushing for better terms, and got them: a five-year contract, a weekly salary of *$5,000*, and a $10,000 guarantee for every movie he was in, at least one per year, requiring no more than four weeks of work.

One new producer at MGM, a Hungarian immigrant named Joe Pasternak, had specialized in making musicals like *Summer Stock* but saw in Hank the chance to add country music fans to the MGM demographics and had already offered him his first picture, the third studio version of *Peg o' My Heart*. Pasternak had cast Esther Williams and wanted Hank to costar, not as a singer but rather a down-home good guy. As reported later in the October 27 *Billboard*: "Joe Pasternak, of MGM, has planned parts in big films for Williams, with no horse-opera parts scheduled." Hank was unconvinced he could pull it off but finally signed up, surrounded by Fred and Wesley Rose, Frank Walker, and Jim Denny. A photo taken of the signing shows Hank seated at a table, pen in hand, clad in a cowboy suit and smiling up at the flinty Walker, who peers through horn-rim glasses at the camera, cigar dangling from his mouth, looking less than ecstatic—perhaps imagining all the ways the deal could go wrong. *Billboard* broke the story on October 13 this way:

HANK WILLIAMS INKS PACT

New York, Oct. 6—Hank Williams, who has been one of hottest oatune artists on wax the past two years, signed a five-year movie deal with MGM pictures, parent company of the MGM disk diskery which records him. Williams is one of the regulars on the "Grand Ole Opry" show. Frank Walker, MGM Records' prexy, represented the flickery for the inking of the singer.

That made it official in the world of showbiz, but it was squeezed into a small space on page 16, meaning it was hardly news that would make the earth move. The Nashville papers gave it a lot more space, and in country circles it seemed to augur a new era, when their stars would be doing more than the guy-saves-gal-from-the-railroad-tracks level of the Roy Rogers films. Given that only a small slice of America outside of the South knew what he looked like, Hank might just have a kind of antiheroic quality, since he always seemed to hint at something dark underneath the grinnin' cowboy facade. But the next move was left to Hank, which was never a good idea.

• • •

As if warming up for mass exposure, Hank would make his first mainstream media push not on the big screen but the small one. Not by chance, TV also beckoned, its own adopting of country an important staple in the early years of the tube, when it was fighting a war against the Hollywood studio heads, who believed people would stop going out to theaters if they had the choice of watching movies at home. For years they fought to boycott the TV networks before understanding how symbiotic and mutually beneficial these two mediums were; and while movies were in short supply, TV found its first pillars in vaudeville-like variety shows, wrestling and boxing matches, kid shows, and cowboy series. Within another few years, the *Grand Ole Opry* and the *Louisiana Hayride* would have TV versions—too late for Hank.

Instead, he began on a low rung, when in 1950 WSM broke into the TV game, performing with the Drifting Cowboys on irregularly scheduled music spots, and though there are photos of them, Audrey, and Louie Buck on a set in Studio C designed to look like a living room, any kinescopes (films made of live broadcasts) were lost in a flood in the building in the early '80s. But Hank took a major step up in nationwide recognition when he was given a shot on a network show, invited to appear on no less than the *Perry Como Show* on Wednesday, November 14. He would be paid the going rate for stars of his magnitude on the big shows, between $3,000 and $5,000, and the Drifting Cowboys, with Big Bill Lister, would get union scale of $70 each, for a few minutes of work—not a bad deal.

That Monday, he drove up from Nashville with the Cowboys and Lister to rehearse for the CBS network program hosted by the always relaxed, bordering-on -narcoleptic "Mr. C," as he was announced on the show. Como had as sharp an eye as Ed Sullivan for talent across the board, and had already given country a prime-time network welcome when he had Eddy Arnold as a guest in April 1950. But Hank's crossover appeal was a big leap for harder-core hillbilly pop. A cynic might say Como made TV safe for country by presenting it as an idiom as bland as his usual fare, which even with showstoppers like Peggy Lee, Patti Page, Lena Horne, and the Mills Brothers came out vapid and flavorless.

As Lister recalled, Como took to Hank and his boys, spending idle time with them shooting pool at a table that would be a prop on the show. The other main attraction with Hank was the McGuire Sisters. Sadly, any kinescopes made of this show have been lost, and the only trace of Hank performing the one song he sang, "Hey, Good

Lookin'," is a still photo of Hank and Como. But he must have made quite an impression , because the next week Como opened the show with a relaxed pop treatment of "Hey, Good Lookin'," which he seemed to believe was far inferior because he semi-jokingly apologized to Hank for it.[10]

To Hank, though, even a nice guy like Como had an angle to play by courting him, something he assumed practically everybody on Broadway was doing to *somebody*. During rehearsals, Lister said, Como had wanted Hank to sing, with no extra pay, the jingle of the show's sponsors, Chesterfield, but Hank couldn't get the melody down and told him, "Well, we'll just have to give up on that." Wanting to split as fast from the Big Apple as he could, he and the boys packed up quickly. On the way home, Hank remembered the jingle thing and giggled. "I didn't come all the way from south Alabama to sing a commercial," he said.[11] Not unless the sponsor was directly paying *him* for it, that is.

· · ·

The Como show had also been booked to coincide with the release of Hank's first-ever album. Fred Rose and Frank Walker had come around to the still-not-universal assumption that albums were helpful in selling records other than operas, film soundtracks, or Broadway musicals. Rose in particular had been a holdout, believing that single releases needed to be discrete products, that fans and the jukebox vendors would only go for those and leave a pricier album, even if hits were on it, in the sale bin. Indeed, there would be no set album chart in *Billboard* until the mid-'50s, no country album chart until the '60s, and only then did the Beatles prove that albums could be recognized as synergic with singles, stoking greater sales and placing an artist's music into a context, or *concept*.

But Walker couldn't be left at the gate when the era of the 10-inch, 33⅓ RPM, vinyl Gramophone "LP" began in 1949, virtually overnight replacing the oversized 78 RPM and 45 RPM albums, which really were albums, four or five records bundled into one package. The first MGM LPs were rereleases of movie soundtracks. Even new material put out by Billy Eckstine, Jimmy Durante, Sarah Vaughan, and Lena Horne on the 33⅓ format were still concurrently released on old formats, four 45 RPM and four 78 RPM records, as *Hank Williams Sings* by Hank Williams and His Drifting Cowboys would be. Rose committed to the LP tentatively. Indeed, carrying the 10-inch catalog number E-10,[12] it was a pallid work, culled from vaulted songs from pre-1950, a couple of hits ("A Mansion on the Hill," "Wedding Bells," "Lost Highway"), the belatedly popular "Wealth Won't Save Your Soul" "I Saw the Light," and the little-heard oldies "Six More Miles (To the Graveyard)," "I've Just Told Mama Goodbye," and "A House Without Love."

As for the more recent smashes, Rose had no intention of "giving them away" at less than full price. Neither did he fret much when, either because he was right about albums, or because he had slapped chaff onto it, or because MGM put almost no promotion behind it, *Hank Williams Sings*, released November 9, 1951, was indeed left in the bins, while the newest single, out the same month, "Baby, We're Really in Love," became Hank's fourteenth Top 5 country hit.

Rose was more concerned with the singles he could draw on in 1952. On December 11, Hank came into Castle Studios and recorded three tracks, none for new songs but stronger remakes of "Let's Turn Back the Years," "I'm Sorry for You, My Friend," and "Honky Tonk Blues," a strong hint that Rose was still waiting for Hank to get back into his hit groove, having seen nothing new that excited him.

Hank was struggling to keep pace with the incredible productivity that left people breathless. He was just plain tired of the grueling pace that had helped make him such a wealthy man, and it showed. His back pain, despite the brace and the painkillers, had grown so excruciating that he could neither stand nor sit even in the back of his limo without doses of tranquilizers so heavy that it would have been impossible for him to stand without crumbling. Onstage, he would wrap himself around the microphone stand like a snake to keep upright, and if he was zonked out, he couldn't even remember what to sing. The brace was so bulky that it felt like he was carrying a refrigerator under his Nudie suits. The worst of it was when he had to sit in his car, bolt upright, every pothole in the road sending sharp pain stabbing up his back. Yet, like always, he pushed on, self-medicating, grateful if he woke up after blacking out only with a hangover and not hurting so bad he'd need help rising from his bed, or floor.

The drinking for several years now had been for little else than chasing away the pain, and he had little interest in nourishing himself, food having no taste or function. Pictures of him off the stage in 1951 and '52 show a shockingly emaciated man, skeletal, stooped, anemic, almost refugee-like. He had dropped hints about his condition, and as early as the March 31, 1951, edition of *Billboard* there was an item that read: "Hank Williams is suffering a spine disorder and will probably take six weeks off soon for surgery." But "soon" turned into months, carrying through the Hadacol Caravan and the Perry Como appearance.

In December, when he repaired to his farm after recording in Nashville, he somehow believed going hunting would be good for his back. He invited Jerry Rivers over, and they toted their rifles to the woods. Just his luck, his dog Skip—the same pooch he had traded his gold watch for—took off after a groundhog, and the two men followed and tried to hurdle a gully in the woods. Jerry made it. Hank didn't. Landing awkwardly, he yowled as he slipped in the ditch and his back gave out. He lay there, unable to move a muscle.

Rivers was able to get him to his feet and drive him home, but his back was stiff as a board, and in a few days he went to see a doctor, who took one look and checked him into Nashville's Vanderbilt University Medical Center on December 13. Two osteopathic surgeons, Ben Fowler and George Carpenter, were assigned to him, and Hank all but begged them to end the agony.

"Cure me or kill me," he told them. "I can't go on like this."

There was no cure, but both doctors agreed surgery was necessary to correct and realign his battered spine. It was impossible to repair damaged nerves, but an operation might prevent further damage, drain excess fluid, and keep infections at a minimum. Such procedures had not been available when Hank was a kid, and for years he had resisted any sort of invasive therapy after the condition was diagnosed. Now he had to answer for that, by being anesthetized for the first time, and Lord knows what he was thinking when he was counting backward from one hundred breathing through an oxygen mask and losing consciousness. Could he even on some level have hoped he wouldn't wake up?

Carpenter, the surgeon that day, didn't know the extent of the problem until he opened Hank up. As Hank would later tell it, "He found a lot wrong that he hadn't anticipated before," and "I had what you call a spinal fusion. I had two ruptured disks in my back. The first and second vertebrae was no good, it was just deformed or broken when I was a child, or wore out or something."[13] The surgery was extensive, and during the four hours he spent in the operating room, Audrey, who was controlling the traffic of visitors, apparently refused to allow anyone into the waiting room. When it was over, he came out of it fine, but doctors were up-front with him, saying he was to be confined to his hospital bed until February, lest he throw his back out all over again. The next day, Lillie Stone, whom Hank had told of the operation only the day before, made it to Nashville and tried to see her son. However, Audrey apparently shooed her out of Hank's room, as if in a demonstration of her authority. Hank, who was out of it, found out about it when Lillie told him of the snub after he got home, and he was livid.

It all happened so fast that when *Billboard* reported the surgery "for a back condition" in the January 12 issue, Hank was long past the procedure, and flat on his back recovering. He would have to cancel a string of holiday shows booked by Jim Denny for the *Grand Ole Opry* troupe that would lead up to a New Year's Eve engagement in DC, a nonstop procession through Raleigh, Spartanburg, Charleston, Baltimore, and Washington. Denny gritted his teeth when Hank was laid up yet again, even if this time for something *other* than a hangover. When he visited him in his room, he found Hank itchy and feeling like a caged animal. Bravely, Hank said he'd make the Baltimore and DC shows if he could fly to each in a plane fitted with a stretcher. Denny said no and instead brought in two replacements for him. One was Jimmie Davis. The other was the ambitious, long-suffering woman with whom Hank shared a bed and professions of love, though with less and less frequency.

• • •

Though it seemed like a good idea for Audrey to fill in—at least until she would sing—Hank was genuinely upset having to miss those shows, and even more so at Audrey because of how she had handled Lillie's visit. At the time, "Cold, Cold Heart" was still sitting at No. 2 after forty-one weeks on the chart, about to be declared the top country song of the year in *Billboard*, and "Baby, We're in Love" was moving up. Crowds were lining up to buy tickets for the DC-area shows. Worse, because of the natural inclination to assume Hank wasn't there because he was drunk, Denny had him record announcements in his room to be played on DC and Baltimore radio stations and also over the loudspeakers at the concerts, explaining in detail his back surgery, assuring the good folks at those concerts that they would surely enjoy "my wife and my boys," and thanking "my good friend Jimmie Davis for pinch-hittin' for me." He went on: "I'd like to say thanks to you for buyin' my records and listenin' to 'em and I'd like to promise you that just as soon as I get up out of this bed I'm gonna try to get up to Washington and make an appearance. Till I see ya, thanks a lot. I know you gonna have a great big time at the show. Thank ya a lot."[14]

It was a humiliating exercise for a star like him to force out. Worse, Audrey would be taking his bows in DC. He was ticked as it was that Audrey had agreed with the doctors that he should stay in the hospital until February. For her part, Audrey reckoned such exposure was just desserts, given that she was not part of the Hadacol Caravan or invited to go on TV shows with him. Not once was she considered to have any part of movies that might await Hank, even though she was his queen, his Dale Evans. Furthermore, Hank had become tart about her in interviews, once calling her "my War Department"—ostensibly a compliment about how she would go to war for him, it could be taken as a veiled reference to their domestic strife. And privately, he was more so. Once, while having drinks with Hillous Butrum, he boasted that he could get Butrum a recording contract.

"You can't do that, Hank," the guitar player said. "I can't sing."

"The hell I can't," Hank barked. "I got Audrey one. If I can get her one, I can get one for anybody."[15]

Digs like that could always spark more fireworks, the residue of which now bled over into their joint appearances. During a *Health and Happiness* broadcast, Audrey screeched a song she wrote, "I'm Telling You," which was an answer to Hank's "You're Gonna Change (Or I'm Gonna Leave)," another of his empty threats, vowing "I'm gonna pack up and go home and live with my mamma." Audrey's riposte made the same threat, which she sang while glaring at him. "Thank you, ma'am," Hank said, a little unnerved, when she was done, "I don't know whether you's kiddin' or not."[16]

There was no doubt that Audrey had grown fed up hearing herself vilified in song, the only thing missing being her name as the antagonist. And their mutual adultery was a sort of take-*that* game of escalation, a game with no winners and two losers. Looking back years later, Frances Preston, the president of BMI, who had worked at WSM in the '50s and answered most of Hank's fan mail, remarked that Hank and Audrey "had a way of torturing each other."[17] And Lycrecia Williams said that besides blaming each other for their adultery, they took to pinning blame on anyone they could, believing that "a lot of people in Nashville" had "made trouble" for them. "Someone would tell one of them this and someone else would tell the other one that, and it created a lot of friction between them. I'm sure some people would have liked them to split up. As big a star as Daddy was, I'm sure there were other women who would have liked to see Daddy free."[18]

For a man as casually adulterous as Hank, he was insanely jealous that Audrey was cheating on *him*. Chet Atkins would recall being with Hank late at night. "He would call his wife at two o'clock in the morning and she would be out catting around. And that drove him to drink, of course. He never stopped loving Audrey. Men tend to fall in love with women they can't control."[19] Audrey, on the other hand, had stopped even pretending that love was their bond. Lycrecia Williams acknowledged that her mother almost certainly would have left Hank earlier had it not been for the children, which made Lycrecia feel terribly guilty. "I didn't want it to be my responsibility if she stayed with him when they were unhappy. I told her, 'Don't stay with him because of me.'"[20]

• • •

When Hank checked out of the hospital early, in mid-December 1951, and came home to Franklin Street in an ambulance, hobbling on crutches, he was pricklier than usual. And Audrey had no desire to cater to him. The painkilling drugs only added to his unfocused impulse to lash out, and his jealousy now became the stuff of hallucination. At worst, he would "see" her with other men and confront her about it, scaring her, which was why Audrey wanted him to stay in the hospital. Lycrecia remembered that "Mother fussed with him for leaving [the hospital] early, and . . . Daddy got angry and threw a chair and had to go back to the hospital again,"[21] apparently having re-injured his back, fortunately not seriously.

Hank was out again Christmas week. Two days before the holiday, he physically assaulted her, and she fled the house, leaving the kids in the care of the housekeeper. She was then told by a neighbor, a Mr. Harlan, that Hank had been waving around a gun and was in a "terribly foul mood." Fearful for the kids, Audrey came back and took them to stay with a family in the neighborhood, the Garretts. Then, the day before her New Year's Eve date in DC, Audrey tiptoed into the house to pack her show clothes for the trip, with the help of three women friends. As she remembered years later,

Three elderly women whose husbands were Nashville businessmen came with me. I knew he was acting up, but I was just hoping I would slip in and out. . . . So we were just easing around—I
knew he was very edgy—and as I walked out the door, a gun shot
four times. I could hardly walk. I thought the woman who was
driving me would never get the car started because she was completely scared to death. I don't know if he was shooting at me, or
wanting me to think that he was shooting himself.[22]

Hank was in the den at the time, and the shots had gone through
the bay window of the house as Audrey and her friends exited the
front door. The fact that the slugs' direction had been altered by the
glass may have saved one, two, or three lives that day—*if* just scaring
her had been his intent. Of course, even if it had been, the wildly flying bullets might have accidentally struck any of the women regardless. In any case, he got lucky, and *they* even luckier when, after
making sure they were in one piece and that he hadn't done himself
in, Audrey and her friends scrambled off the grounds.

Audrey was somehow able to calm her nerves, fly to DC, and
perform with Jimmie Davis, happily assuring the fans that Hank
was doing fine at home and thinking of them. Just before the clock
struck midnight and a new year rang in, she called Hank. It wasn't to
say Happy New Year. Rather, not knowing if he was even coherent
enough to understand her or make out her words, she unburdened
in one sentence.

"Hank," she said, tears running down her cheeks, "I'll never live
with you another day."

• • •

Because Audrey did not call the police—perhaps by doing so she
would have missed her flight and the gig in DC—the shooting incident was just another unreported Hank Williams crime. While
Audrey was taking his place in DC, he remained stewing in his
manic thoughts, draining bottles of painkillers the doctors had given

him and likely feeling abandoned at the most depressing time of year. He was visited only once, by Jack Anglin, Johnnie Wright, and his wife, Kitty Wells, who were shaken when they saw the screen door and window shredded by bullet holes and one of Hank's guitars wrecked on the patio floor. Inside, Hank rambled on about Audrey's perfidy. "That busted my heart," he said.

Although word of the shooting caper got out, for the record Hank would never admit publicly to firing even one shot. And he apparently didn't believe, even now, that the marriage was over. He hoped Audrey would pity him, and that she would at some point confess her sins and beg *him* to come back. He also planned on convincing her once and for all that he would go sober, and told people he had turned a corner, physically and mentally, with all that time to think about his life over the holidays. Rather than a time of madness, he swore, those holidays by his lonesome had been "the happiest time of my life."[23]

Without a drop during the exile at his home, he would get all misty when he thought about how little he had seen of his son over the holidays. Little Bocephus wasn't so little anymore; he was approaching three, and he hardly knew his father. Brack Schuffert related how during happier times Audrey and Randall were in a car outside the house waiting for Hank to come out for a trip to the airport. Little Bocephus, seeing his dad walking to the car, started climbing out an open window. Said Schuffert: "Hank grabbed him and tears were just running down Hank's cheeks. He was just crying out loud. Then he had to give the baby back to Audrey and go on that plane to leave." Later Hank said of having to say goodbye to a young son so often, "That's just not right. It'll kill you."[24]

On January 3, he could move around easily enough on his crutches to leave the house in accordance with Audrey's demand to clear out. She had delayed coming back to Nashville until he was gone. Hank somehow drove himself not to the farm but to the Andrew Jackson Hotel. But now Audrey felt sorry about his being alone, or maybe she pitied him, and called his cousin Marie McNeil in Montgomery and asked her to drive in and take him to his mother's boardinghouse to recuperate. He was there for a couple of weeks, then returned, again not to the farm where he'd be all alone but rather to bunk with Ray Price, with whom he'd become friendly. Hank saw him as a protégé, and as Price made strides in the industry, writing several country blues hits for Lefty Frizzell like "Give Me More, More, More of Your Kisses," he pulled some strings to help Ray land a recording contract with Bullet Records. Price's first record, "Jealous Lies," was about as Hank-like as a song could get. Soon Hank was promising Price he would get him on that *Opry* stage, which he did, and he even loaned Price the use of the Drifting Cowboys.

He owed Hank, and so Price allowed him to dwell on the ground floor of his rented two-story brick home at 2718 Westwood in a clearing on Nashville's Natchez Trace, a leafy forest trail that led all the way down to Natchez, Mississippi, and was once traveled by Native American traders. Even today, the Trace is a wonderfully isolated habitat, and Hank could all but keep himself lost to the world here. Price, whose given first name is Noble, may have been accommodating partly out of what Hank could do for him, but he also worried that Hank was in real peril now, a man in effect waiting to die. He reached this dire conclusion when Hank related to him how he had responded to Audrey when she had called and told him she'd never live with him again. Said Price years later, his deep, resonant voice still breaking up telling about it:

He told Audrey, "If you don't come back to me, I won't live over a year." And that was New Year's Eve of '51. That's all I'm gonna say.[25]

19

✳ ✳ ✳ ✳ ✳ ✳ ✳

"ALMOST A CONTINUOUS NIGHTMARE"

On January 10, 1952, Audrey Mae Williams filed papers, a second time, for "separate maintenance"—i.e., divorce—from Hiram "Hank" Williams. Claiming "cruel and inhuman treatment" and abandonment, she revised history, a *lot*, in her bill of complaint. Somehow confusing the year of their marriage as 1941, and taking credit for saving his career by taking him out of Montgomery to Shreveport, she said the reward for all that was being "embarrassed and humiliated" by his "mistreatment" of her. After she had been "comparatively happy" for a time with him, she argued, his conduct became "intolerable." Yet, as if holding to some kind of implicit compact not to reveal *too*-ugly details of Hank's life that might damage his—and, by extension, her—future earnings, she omitted any reference to her abortion, his drinking, their adultery, or the shooting incident over Christmas, modifying the details of it to say only that he was "prevented from inflicting more violence upon her only by [her] hurried departure." Still, she did relate that, two days before that he was "cursing and abusing her," and had struck her with such force and violence that she would have been knocked to the floor had she not caught on a desk to prevent herself from falling. This cruel attack occurred in the presence of the complainant's two young children. . . . Defendant is a man of violent disposition when aroused, and this violence is particularly aggravated when the complainant, herself, is the object thereof. [He] does not hesitate to make a physical attack upon [her].[1]

With a good bit of chutzpah, she slagged him for "engaging in the wildest extravagances" and that he had left the house leaving her "no funds whatsoever" and that she was "confronted with numerous bills." She asked that a "reasonable part of the Defendant's income" be "sequestered" for her and the children. Hank, who never thought Audrey would betray him like this on the record, would answer in early March after retaining a lawyer. He shot back—this time figuratively—that she was in fact guilty of the very charges she leveled against him, and was the cause of anything untoward he ever did, going back to before their first separation, denying "any misconduct on his part" led to it. His cross-complaint, in the third person, admitted only that he

has [not] been perfect. He has perhaps been guilty of indiscretions. . . . However, he [will] show to the Court that [her] conduct has made life so unbearable and miserable for him that it has been almost a continuous nightmare.[2]

He traced back to their early days what he called her "inattention . . . to her home and husband," and her insistence "that she, too, was . . . a singer of ability [and that Hank] build her up as an entertainer despite the fact she had neither voice nor musical ability," and he claimed she had cost him "many jobs" because venues wouldn't allow her on the stage, while he kept "plugging ahead trying to better their conditions." Yet he loved his wife, despite her weaknesses, rages, flights, and attacks upon him . . . and [the fact that she] indulged in every extravagance she could possibly stretch his income to cover. . . . Her hunger for clothes, jewelry, automobiles and luxuries . . . kept them drained dry financially. . . . [In 1951 alone she cost him] a total expenditure of approximately $50,000.00. Just at one store, . . . Weinberger's, [she] spent $900.00 for evening gowns. She paid $350.00 for one dress.

Rolling on, he told of her calling him a "son-of-a-bitch and many other names too vile and vulgar" to repeat, "before various friends and relatives, including their children" and "his own mother." She had, he said, "on innumerable occasions flown into rages of temper and fits, and cursed and abused him and struck him, scratched him, thrown furniture and articles at him. . . . He has appeared in public appearances time after time with scratches and bruises upon his face and body as a result." She "told him that she did not love him, that she hated him, and that she didn't expect to live with him . . . and has condemned and castigated him for showing any affection or love for her whatsoever."

Although Audrey had not brought up his cheating, he had no such qualms about hers, linking her to unnamed men she was "going openly and notoriously with." Clearly having done his homework, through a hired detective, he said one was "a young man" who had "worked for the Highway Patrol of Tennessee" whom she had visited in "Bowling Green, Kentucky and other places." Another, Hank said, she had been with in early January when she

was apprehended by police officers in an automobile on a side road in Davidson County, Tennessee, behind the Municipal Airport . . . in company with an automobile dealer . . . in the arms of this man who was loving and kissing her.

A third man, he maintained, was "another member of the Tennessee Highway Patrol," with whom she had "been to various tourist courts

and secluded places" and who had "visited her on innumerable occasions in [Hank and Audrey's] home" apparently when Hank was out
of town, but even "when her own mother was in the house and it
was necessary for her to slip him in the back door." She had, he
added, "had dates with various other men" and was "currently infat-
uated with a man here in Davidson County" who was seen driving
around in the Cadillac Hank had bought for her as recently as the
day before. And while she had claimed he'd failed to provide for her,
Audrey, he said, had "just returned from a trip to Miami . . . for the
purpose of going to the races."

He also made sure to get in Audrey's botched abortion as proof of
why she was "positively unfit to have the custody and control of her
minor child." Furthermore, Audrey hadn't "spent one full day with
their child since it was born." Randall had "spent three-fourths" of
his life with people who weren't his mother, and it was his nurse he
called "Mama," Hank said—not adding how many of those fourths
were due to his own frequent absences. He grandly offered to take
custody of Randall, bizarrely, since he himself didn't intend to take
care of him; instead, the boy would be "given a good home with
[Lillie]" and "raised under clean and Christian influences." He didn't
mention that such a Christian home might be a place where men
paid to have sex. And, with more gall, he offered to raise *Lycrecia* in
this manner, even though they shared no blood.

Audrey, he summed up, had "been guilty of such cruel and inhuman treatment and conduct towards him as renders it unsafe and
improper for him to further cohabit with her." Since it was Audrey
who had split from *him*, this was rather ironic. Yet the filing was
perhaps his most bravura performance, without his voice ever being
heard, each word stabbing Audrey right in the heart. But she had her
own gumshoe work, having uncovered all the sources of his money
and the ways he had diverted it, and added as co-defendants Acuff-
Rose, WSM, Loew's Inc., First American Bank, and Third National
Bank, holders of the mortgages and leases on his properties, the
clothing store, and his automobiles.

As hard as it is to fathom now, this mud fight was not made public knowledge by any reporters. In those days before *TMZ* and *National Enquirer*, it was the sort of personal matter the courts rarely leaked to the media, which even when they did sniff it out, often provided further protection by keeping it off the front pages in deference to stars, and politicians. Whether or not anyone was insulating him, or just by luck, Hank could *still* pretend he had that happy marriage the magazines always wrote of, along with the credulous opinion that his songs of loneliness and heartbreak were not directly connected to his home life. For Audrey, there were considerations of her own in keeping it private. Having soaked up the applause of a big crowd in DC, she did not want to disconnect from Hank's star. She even tried convincing Frank Walker to go on recording her as a solo act, as "Mrs. Hank Williams." Even as they wrangled over the terms of the divorce, they could seem permanently joined on some pathologically disturbed level. Despite needing to fight back against her, Hank never believed they were through. What he told Ray Price was right; without Audrey as a constant presence, he really *was* lost, another day older and closer to death.

. . .

But that didn't mean he took any vows of celibacy waiting for Audrey to get this divorce out of her system. Addicted to her love as he was, he had moved rather easily enough to another playmate's bed, having been messing around for months with a woman named Bobbie Webb Jett. Almost a year older than Hank, born on October 5, 1922, she was pretty and dirty blond, with big brown eyes, frizzy hair, and pale skin. Her family was relatively wealthy, and her uncle was a sheriff in Denison County. But after her parents split she was abandoned by her mother, Antha Pauline Jett, who migrated to California and left her to be raised by her grandmother Ocie Belle Jett. As a young woman, she apparently followed her mother to the West Coast, where she danced in a vaudeville chorus line for a time.

When she returned to Nashville in '49 with a daughter named

Josephine—who she claimed, some biographers have said, was sired
by rodeo singer Monte Hall—she went to work for the Selective Service and as a nurse, caring for the elderly Ocie Belle until her death.
As it happened, that skill and her soft spot for country singers may
have drawn her closer to Hank, who was introduced to Bobbie by
her uncle Willard Jett, a major buff of the *Grand Ole Opry*. They
became serious either late in '51 before his back operation or during
his convalescence.

As it happened, she lived only a few houses away from Price on
Natchez Trace and spent time there with Hank, who told people she
was indeed his nurse. Bobbie was pretty and sexy without needing
to get painted up like Audrey. For Hank, the clincher may have been
that Bobbie had a kid, there being something about motherhood that
activated what may have been those Oedipal underpinnings from
growing up effectively fatherless—which had also been elemental in
taking up with Audrey.

Bobbie began to travel with him when he was able to. Late in January 1952, Bam Bamford booked a show in Norfolk, then two in Richmond as headliner of the first "Hillbilly of the Month" show. Hank
would be backed by Ray Price and brought with him Don Helms and
Howie Watts, using local musicians to fill out the band. He wore a
back brace, but on the way he became racked with pain and began
drinking and popping pills. As a result, he was unable to play the
Norfolk gig, which was canceled. By the time he got to Richmond,
promoter B. C. Gates insisted on hiring a guard to shield him from
booze—a tactic that he always seemed to be able to outfox. Hours
before the first show, he called room service in his hotel and ordered
tomato juice and some rubbing alcohol, the only kind he could wangle,
so he could rub his back with it. The guard let it through, whereupon
Hank mixed the juice and the alcohol, getting so violently ill that he
puked his guts out. Somehow, he made it to the hall, the Mosque
Theater, where things got worse. As dumb luck would have it, a writer
for the *Richmond Times-Dispatch* was there to cover the show—one of
the very, very few contemporaneous reviews of a Hank show.

The writer, Edith Lindeman, knew about music—a part-time songwriter, she would write "Little Things Mean a Lot," a No. 1 pop hit for Kitty Kallen in 1954, and "Red Headed Stranger," a signature hit later for Willie Nelson—and was appalled at what she saw and heard. Hank actually didn't want to go on and kept motioning Price to stretch his set. With the crowd chanting for Hank, Ray preemptively told the audience about Hank's operation and said he "wasn't feeling too well so you'll have to forgive him." After he introduced him he waited onstage in case Hank crumpled. As Lindeman wrote, "His spine most certainly was not holding him erect. He sang 'Cold, Cold Heart,' but did not get some of the words in the right places. Then he sang 'Lonesome Blues,' with a good deal of off-key yodeling." As he pushed on, people began to leave, and seventy-five of them demanded refunds at the box office. "Pretty soon," she reported, "10 policemen appeared and the man in the box office went off with the receipts to take them to B. C. Gates . . . who was reported to be ill at home."[3]

During the intermission, Gates's hired guard tried to fully awaken Hank, walking him in the cold air outside and force-feeding him a sandwich and coffee. There were still people chanting for Hank, and he came back out on the stage. This time, wrote Lindeman, "his spine seemed to be better." Coherent now, he addressed the crowd, saying, "I wish I was in as good shape as you are." Knowing that many would assume he was sloshed, he went on, "Hank Williams is a lot of things but he ain't a liar." Then he asked for any doctors in the house, saying he would prove he'd had surgery by showing his scars. "And if you ain't nice to me, I'll turn around and walk right off." Price, fearing that Hank would lift his shirt and dip his pants, rushed out and interrupted, "We all love you, Hank, don't we, folks?" The house broke into applause—a rescue mission for which, Lindeman noted, Price "deserves some special place in hillbilly heaven."

Hank was able to finish the show, sounding "pretty good," she agreed, then he made for his "big yellow automobile with a chauffeur to drive him home." The next night, having seen the scathing review, he said he would dedicate a number to a "gracious lady writer" and pointedly launched into "Mind Your Own Business."

As adept an escape artist as Hank was, the negative review did nothing to stop the bookings, which led him north of the border, to a show in Peterborough, Ontario, promoted by Oscar Davis. Again in a haze, he stumbled out, sang a facsimile of "Lovesick Blues" a few times, introduced his band by getting all the names wrong, then, when he was unable to pick a song he could remember the words to, he simply exited the stage, serenaded by boos. So worried was Helms that angry Canadians would follow them to get their money back, he asked for a police escort to and across the border. According to Chet Flippo, a car forced them off the road and four guys got out, one demanding that Hank be let out "so I can beat the shit outta him."[4] Whether that happened or not, these sorts of grisly scenes were getting all too common, giving Helms, Watts, and other Drifting Cowboys every reason to be relieved to be working mainly for Ray Price now. And Ray himself was becoming seriously conflicted, not having known what he was in for when he took in a decaying Hank Williams.

• • •

In early February, Hank and Bobbie, who left her daughter with relatives, stayed in the boardinghouse at 318 North McDonough Street. While Lillie was always appalled at her son's tastes in women, unlike the icy discord between her and Audrey, she got along well enough with Bobbie, if only because this one wasn't a threat to her in controlling Hank. Bobbie's role as his nurse also eased the static, since *anyone* offering her son relief from the wicked witch from Banks was acceptable to Lillie. However, things would get a lot more complicated for the pair. In early April 1952, their carelessness led to Bobbie becoming pregnant, a development they kept between them. Hank, of course, was elated once again that he would be a father, and there would most definitely not be an abortion this time. Yet almost as quickly as things had heated up with Bobbie, they would cool down, soon creating a ridiculously tangled situation built on silence, money, and lies, much of which would not be known for decades. Bobbie Jett herself would remain a mystery. When the first biographies of Hank appeared in the '70s there was no mention of her. No pictures seem to exist of them together, and very few of Bobbie alone.

Hank never lived with her, nor was he faithful to her, and carrying his child didn't change that. He was quickly running around with other women, none serious to him except one—Anita Carter, the eighteen-year-old, youngest and comeliest of the three Carter Family daughters. At the time, Hank had been turning to country music's first family, who were known for their kindness and hospitality, for comfort. The middle Carter sister, June, was friends with both Hank and Audrey, later saying of their marriage that "it was a love with such possession, power, jealousy, and hate that it consumed [them] like a fire. It was burning him alive."[5]

While Hank was suspicious that June had helped talk Audrey into divorcing him, he saw Anita as an angel in white. He was knocked out when she sang some of his songs at the *Grand Ole Opry* and since then had found his way over to Pop and Maybelle Carter's home for some of their family dinners, knowing Anita would be there, and he would feast his eyes on her, making everyone uncomfortable. He would call her late at night, drunk, just to hear her voice. June, who had married Carl Smith that year, was alarmed seeing Hank pursue her baby sister. She also would become caught in the line of his derangement. Once, driving to the Carters' house, Hank thought he saw Audrey in a car ahead of him on the road out front being driven by June. Thinking June was taking sides with her, he tried to run the car off the road, the women screaming in horror. Only then did he see that it wasn't Audrey in the car but Anita. The incident terrified Anita and June and enraged Maybelle Carter. When Hank came into the house, he tried to explain his actions.

"But Mama—" he began, before she cut him off. "Don't you call me Mama!" she barked.

Helen Carter remembered that was the angriest she ever saw her mother, and that Hank shuddered as she dressed him down. Yet June, seeing how far gone he was, would sit with him, seeing him cry his eyes out as he said he still loved Audrey, even as he kept professing his love for Anita. He was pathetic, off his rocker, and quite dangerous, but the sisters were frightened to death that he was walking his last mile. Prone to teenage crushes, Anita became attracted to him when she heard him perform "Cold, Cold Heart" at the *Opry* and dissolved into tears, later saying, "I thought it was one of the saddest and most beautiful things I'd ever heard." Knowing how she reacted, Hank waded deeper in, even giving Anita a "friendship" ring. But now he had June to get through.

"This is ridiculous! And it's just wrong, morally wrong," she told him.

Hank, of course, let advice like that go in one ear and out the other. And June was going to have to endure even more frightening moments down the road.

• • •

As messed up as Hank's life was, it almost seems logical that the Carters, for all their dread of him, shared another of his breakthrough moments. On Wednesday, March 26, 1952, Hank was seen on the nation's TV screens for the second time, on NBC's 8 p.m. *Kate Smith Evening Hour*, solidifying his vanguard role as a transcendent hillbilly at a time when TV reordered Americans' leisure-time attentions and habits. In this maw, Roy Rogers would become a staple on the young medium, and old oat-burning serials from the 1930s were being watched religiously by kids who toted lunch pails with Roy and Trigger on them to school.

In Nashville, it was imperative to clear the way for the *Grand Ole Opry* to get its own TV showcase, preferably a simulcast of the Saturday night spectacles at the Ryman, and various barn-dance and hootenanny shows were already sprinkling local markets. It was not an easy sale. The networks, dominated by Northern businessmen, had little affinity for hillbilly entertainment. Indeed, it would take until 1955 before the "outsider" network, ABC, took on the *Opry* and the *Country Music Jubilee*.

Back in 1952, what progress the *Opry* was making was largely due to Hank. Gene Autry must have recognized this, too; in his movie that year, *Apache Country*, he sang "Cold, Cold Heart." It's unlikely that when Jim Denny began pitching NBC to do an *Opry* program, he would have gotten anywhere without Hank as the main attraction. That was what clinched the Kate Smith gig. The producers agreed to give over a half hour to *Opry* acts, and big ones, like Roy Acuff and the Carter Family, if Hank was guaranteed to perform.

That Hank's puckish charm was a fit for the tube was evident on the Smith show. It didn't hurt that the pleasingly plump Smith, a veteran of the band era, radio, and Broadway, also recorded for MGM, her bombastic rendition of "God Bless America" to become a ritual at sporting and other events well into the next century. But Hank had pull, too, bringing not only himself but Acuff into a prime-time network slot. Roy was tapped to repeat the same job he had at the Ryman, as master of ceremonies keeping the acts moving on and off. That's what he did on the Smith show, with the Carter Sisters and Mother Maybelle and a troupe of *Opry* square dancers and musicians flitting through on the small screen in all their rustic charm. But it really was Hank who stole the show with his rendition of "Hey, Good Lookin'," and the show went so well that Smith and the network signed off with Denny on a follow-up, with the same cast to return for an encore on April 23. Before then, though, some major events would unfold for Hank.

• • •

On April 3, he and Audrey agreed to terms for the divorce. After fighting like a cornered rat in his rebuttal to Audrey's claims, he now seemed resigned, even eager, to end the case on a note of conciliation. Knowing he had no chance at keeping Audrey from being given half of his earnings, and that she knew all the ways he had used to hide money from her, he fought no longer, agreeing to all of Audrey's demands. However, Hank had done some preparing for this. When Audrey's lawyer Carmack Cochran had examined Hank's finances, he found little of what Hank had boasted of in the papers, the singer apparently having hidden most of his assets—Cochran claimed that Hank had opened numerous bank accounts under bogus names bur had drained them all, leaving only $725 in their joint account.[6] But rather than squirreling away a fortune, the rest was shriveled by debts, with $10,000 still left to be paid on the Franklin Avenue house and $45,000 on the farm, where Hank had dropped another $15,000 on a herd of white-faced cattle; even her '51 Cadillac convertible had a $706 note.

Despite Hank's overestimation of his worth, and Audrey's claim that he had earned $92,000 in 1951 and was on the way to more than that in '52, she did not press for a large lump sum, accepting a cash payout of just $1,000, as well as possession of the house and Caddy, assuming the remaining payments on each. She also retained custody of Randall, giving Hank liberal visitation rights and allowing Randall to live with him over the summer of 1953. Hank, who also agreed to pay her court costs of around $4,000, would get the farm and his two Cadillacs, all of his road earnings, and the clothing store, which he would sell at a loss within weeks. Audrey's big score wasn't immediate material possessions—it was that she was given half of all of his future royalties, in perpetuity, meaning that the woman he had painted as an avaricious, adulterous, shrieking banshee unfit to raise a family or run a lemonade stand would be enriched long into the future, including from songs not even written yet. The one catch to this, and in Hank's mind his victory, was that this spigot would be closed if she ever remarried.

For Audrey, who had become accustomed to bedding men just fine without being legally attached, and despite the tsk-tsking of the Lord, this was a no-brainer. For Hank, it left the door ajar a crack for when she might return to him for more mutual punishment, a pipe dream that he needed to believe. No matter that, on his part, he would take no such pledge himself. As would become all too evident.

• • •

In mid-April, after months of inaction, Hank gave in to the siren song of Hollywood, but only because he was reminded he had signed a contract with MGM Pictures—something that he either forgot about right away, or wanted to. Slim Whitman, in fact, would remark several years later that Hank "couldn't remember he'd done it, because he wasn't sober when he'd signed for all that money."[7]

Now, the early stumbles of his return to performing and the divorce over with, a trip to LA was scheduled, during which he would meet with the MGM brass on their home turf. Blithely, Hank had made his pick for his big-screen debut after Joe Pasternak offered him another role, that of a sheriff in *Small Town Girl*, in which he would sing four songs. It sounded good to him, and the April 26 *Billboard* ran an item headlined INK WILLIAMS FOR MGM PIC reporting his "first definite picture with the MGM flickery." Jerry Rivers and Don Helms would be in the movie with him, as would the Nat King Cole Trio. This was wildly exciting to the country crowd, who would be able to see Hank up close and personal and revel in country now finding a place in the mainstream alongside pop and R&B acts.

While on the coast, he would also play a few gigs and stay with Tex Williams, the talking blues pioneer, in LA. Before that he'd make it to gigs around Fresno and Oakland and then with Ernie Tubb in Bakersfield. He would then go to LA to meet the MGM brass, do some gigs around town, then finish up the California trek with Ernie in San Diego for a show with Minnie Pearl.

The first order of business was the Northern California leg of the journey. While in the Bay Area next, he gave a notable interview to Ralph J. Gleason. Thirty-five at the time, the future *Rolling Stone* co-founding editor had joined the *San Francisco Chronicle* as a jazz writer in 1950. As he would recall in 1969, "I really didn't know doodley-britt about Country-Western Music except that I dug Ernest Tubb and T. Texas Tyler and thought that 'You two-timed me one time too often' was a great song." Gleason, who in truth had written the year before about Eddy Arnold, said Hank "was by God popular, and a fat-ish man with big glasses named Wally Eliott, who doubled as a C/W disk jockey under the nom de disque of Longhorn Joe was presenting Williams in several one nighters, So I went to talk to him." A born New Yorker, Gleason was no naïf, but his first sight of Hank at Oakland's Leamington Hotel took him aback. Hank, he said,

> came out of the bathroom carrying a glass of water. He was lean, slightly stooped over and long-jawed. He shook hands quickly, then went over to the top of the bureau, swept off a handful of pills and deftly dropped them, one at a time, with short, expert slugs from the glass. . . . I was a little surprised by the pills, but then he looked pale and thin, and had deep-set eyes and might have been hungover for all I knew. . . . He threw the pill boxes in his suitcase, and we went down to the coffee shop, Hank Williams talked and ate breakfast, and I wrote it down.[8]

Gleason would be a power in rock music, helping organize the epochal 1967 Monterey Pop Festival, when these sorts of details were *expected* of a music scribe. But in '52, he was still working in a frame when drunkenness and drugs were hushed in deference to performers. Keeping those details out, his story still gave Hank heft, charting his history, his homage to Rufus Payne, and his definition of his work as "folk music." Gleason caught Hank's show that night, on April 15, at an old barrelhouse out past El Cerrito called San Pablo Hall, where he noted that Hank's pickup band was "terrible" and that Hank "squeezed himself to get the notes out sometimes," yet "he had that *thing*. He made them scream . . . and that audience was shipped right up from Enid or Wichita Falls intact." The later memoir related that at intermission, "it was impossible to talk to him. He was a little stoned . . . and the party was beginning to get a little rough. They were whiskey drinkers, so I gave them room, looked around a while and then went back out."

Gleason, whose story ran on June 1, reported that Hank had gone on about how he loved his farm and that his ambition was to retire there and watch "them cattle work while I write songs an' fish." As he later wrote in *Rolling Stone*, "He never did, of course. I had no idea how tortured a man he was when I saw him. It came through more in his performance. He didn't cry but he made *you* cry."

Hank played the gig with Ernest Tubb in Bakersfield; then they made their way down to LA on the sixteenth. After meeting up with Tex Williams, he confided in him enough to talk about the gunshots he had fired at Audrey; since he missed, he said, he'd just have to get it right and "kill her" next time. Tex figured he was just pulling his leg, but with Hank, who could really know?

For the MGM bosses he managed to clean himself up real pretty and put on a powder blue suit and hat. Wesley Rose had flown in so that a business adviser could accompany Hank in his meetings with the big shots, and they were taken first to see Joe Pasternak, who, as if inspecting a heifer, had Hank stand up and turn around, no doubt shocked himself how dissipated he was. Worse, Hank had been told he needed to wear a toupee, that a balding cowboy wasn't the image Hollywood wanted, leading him to go have another made to replace the one he'd thrown out the car window. Pasternak asked him if he had any hair under his hat. "Hell yes," Hank replied, "I got a dresser drawer full of it," a funny line that Pasternak reacted to with a face of stone.[9]

He was then ushered into Dore Schary's office, a seat of Hollywood power. Schary had won an Oscar for writing the screenplay for *Boys Town*, before working his way up at MGM and RKO. A Jew born in Newark, New Jersey, Schary knew little of country music and seemed to like clashing with people. Esther Williams later skewered him in her memoirs as imperious, crude, and cruel, with "an uncanny instinct for failure."[10] Sensing hostility immediately, Hank, rather than bowing to a baron known to put cold fear into actors' and writers' blood, barely spoke a word and wouldn't meet his eyes as Schary interviewed him. Later, Wes Rose would say that Schary was mortally offended that Hank refused to remove his cowboy hat and had put his cowboy-booted feet on Schary's big white-painted, crescent-shaped oak desk, not caring that it was completely disrespectful. There was also the possibility, too, that Hank had uttered some anti-Semitic remarks in Schary's presence.

But it is also entirely possible that Hank was acting the fool with a purpose—to kill the whole deal, without it looking like he had wimped out of it. Schary, who had heard of Hank's reputation, thought he was drunk and ended the meeting without shaking his hand. Outside the office, Hank saw a black shoeshine boy and stopped for a shine. Wes Rose, who had held his tongue, confronted Hank about why he'd acted like such a schmuck.

"You see this kid here?" Hank said, slipping a twenty into the boy's hand. "This kid here is more of a man than that guy in the office will ever be."[11]

Hank didn't seem eager to go through with it, quite likely because he thought he would embarrass himself if he tried. He had so many reasons not to be happy with himself that he didn't need one more, and to be on the hook for five years might not be worth any amount of money to him. He was expected back in June, when shooting would begin. Hank knew he wouldn't be there.

With the chore of either impressing or turning off the movie crowd done, he returned to the gigs. The next one was at the Riverside Rancho dance hall, just north of Hollywood. The crime novelist John Gilmore, then a teenager doing bit parts in movies, was able to hang with him. He recalled years later that Hank "was in rotten shape" and "his face looked like a dead man's." In the parking lot, "he started sharing [his] Johnnie Walker Red with me and Barry Bowron—son of L.A.'s then-mayor Fletcher Bowron—and another pal, Mike Paley, a Hell's Angels biker." Tex Williams, mixing metaphors, told Gilmore that night that "Hank's a funny bird. He's got a truckload of troubles hitched to himself. Cut off like he is from Nashville, he's a salmon in the desert. The damn guy's running headlong at disaster, but nobody can figure it out." Shaking hands with him, Gilmore recalled,

> his hand felt like bones, long and sinewy, and hard as though made of something other than skin. And icy, as if he didn't have any blood in his veins. . . . He gestured to pass the bottle along . . . and I gasped. When Hank tipped it back, he seemed to just pour it down into himself as if swallowing water. . . . There was a trickling sound, and I thought the liquor was leaking out of the sack. But it was Hank pissing in his pants as he drank. The urine trickled through his trouser leg to form a puddle around his double-eagle boots. Hank apparently didn't notice it. . . . When he saw the puddle at his feet, he said, "Well, sonovabitch!" and spat down at the ground. . . . Then Hank started to laugh. It was a heehawing sound like a donkey, and he rubbed his forehead hard with the fingers of both hands. He looked like a zombie.[12]

Hank changed his pants in the back of his Packard, then went onstage in the old ballroom, and the crowd ate it up. Gilmore was struck by the fact that, among the hits, Hank sang a new song he'd recently written but hadn't yet recorded, called "I'll Never Get Out of This World Alive." For emphasis, he sang it twice.

. . .

In San Diego, his gig was promoted by old friend Bam Bamford and his wife, Maxine. But he and Ernie Tubb nearly didn't make it. They were traveling in Ernie's car, and it broke down on the way. With the crowd and the Bamfords growing restless, Minnie Pearl had to go on alone. After fifteen minutes, they finally arrived. Minnie looked into the wings and was shocked at Hank's appearance. He was, she later said, "pathetic, emaciated, haunted-looking, [a] tragic figure of a man being assisted through the stage door—not too gently—by a male nurse. . . . It upset me to see my friend handled that way. [Hank] was like a pitiful lost child to me, and I had never seen him in as bad shape as he was that day." So, she said, "I ran to him and hugged him. He threw his arms around me and clung to me, crying. I tried to comfort him, to tell him everything was going to be all right, just as you would try to comfort a child crying in the dark."[13]

However, A. V. Bamford faced the same cold reality as every promoter—including himself a few times—who sold out a concert because of Hank only to see him either show up late, not at all, or stinking drunk: thousands of dollars were at stake, and their own reputation, not to mention Hank's. Would it do him any good to put him onstage if he was unable to perform? Maxine was determined not to be one of the increasing number of promoters burned by Hank. Backstage, she and the male nurse forced coffee on him, walked him around, dunked his face in cold water, then dressed him in his Nudie suit and pushed him onto the stage. Minnie remembered it as "so cruel" and "pathetic," saying that "it tore me apart to see him out there trying to sing, his voice cracking, hanging onto the microphone for dear life, a sickening caricature of the superb, magnetic performer he had been."

The audiences let him have it, making Minnie even angrier that a man who, she said, "belonged in a hospital" was put in this situation, "even if the illness was self-inflicted." Worse, that was only the first of two shows booked for that night. And between them, the Bamfords' plan was to drive Hank around, hoping he'd sober up. Minnie, not wanting him to be alone with "people who didn't love him and saw him as a piece of merchandise" got in, too. It was, she said, "the longest automobile ride I've ever had in my life." Hank, having been off booze and pills for around five hours, was craving more. Dumped into the front seat, his back brace torturing him, gripping his stomach with his hands, he begged them to stop the car and, oh God dear Lord, let him out so he could scrounge up *something* to drink. Minnie thought there was only one way to get his mind off it.

"Come on, Hank, let's sing," she said, breaking into his cry for redemption, "I Saw the Light."

He tried to sing along, his voice cracking. Then he stopped and looked at her, putting his hand on hers.

"That's just it, Minnie," he wheezed. "There ain't no light. It's all dark."

The words crushed her heart. He seemed at the end of the line, on borrowed time. That's when she understood his ills went far beyond addiction. "The pills and alcohol," she said, "were the instruments of his death, not the cause. The cause lay somewhere deep in his psyche, and only God knows what went on there."[14] Still, Hank always seemed to be able to get himself together. He played the second show that night, with no reported glitches or audience disfavor, and nothing that Jim Denny heard back in Nashville slowed down the bookings of Hank and the *Opry* stars on upcoming tours. Already, the troupe was set to go on a mid-May tour through the South and the desert oasis of Las Vegas. Hank had his *Opry* shows, his radio shows, and the encore appearance on the *Kate Smith* show right after he would get back from his California journey. Even for a guy who considered the road a reprieve from a dead-end life, it was daunting.

Before he left California, he popped into the LA radio station KMPC for a quick interview with the country DJ "Cottonseed" Clark. At one stage Clark asked him why he sang so many sad songs. "Well, Cottonseed," he drawled, "I guess I always have been a *saddist*."[15] Never did he utter a more accurate sentence in his life.

· · ·

The second Kate Smith show, which was so important to Jim Denny, was only so for Hank for one reason—it would give him a chance to sing to Anita Carter, having insisted on a duet with her. On Monday, April 21, two days before the show, Hank, Roy Acuff, the Carter Sisters, and Mother Maybelle again drove to New York, the stakes again high for country. After Smith lavishly praised the country stars for their "wholesome entertainment," Acuff smoothly did his turn as the master of ceremonies, bringing on a number of supporting acts and square dancers from the *Grand Ole Opry*. The proceedings quickly turned into a nationally televised hoedown. Kate also belted out a few country numbers herself, such as "Feudin' and Fightin' Again." The high spot was when Hank was introduced, Acuff calling him a "fellow you folks enjoyed so much here the other time, a fella that writes as many songs as anybody in the country, and sings 'em just as well when it comes to the country style of singin'—Hank Williams!"

Hank ambled on with Helms, Rivers, and Pruett, and boyishly prefaced a song "that's been awful kind to me and the boys, it's bought us quite a few beans and biscuits, it's the best song we've ever had"—playfully drawing out the next word—"*fi-nancially*, a tune called 'Cold, Cold Heart.'" Not only would Hank and Roy make a splendid impression on the show, but June Carter may have walked away with it, recasting herself, as Audrey tried with less success to pull off, from a serious young woman into a mini Minnie Pearl, squealing and squeaking in a Betty Boop voice and displaying her frilly long johns under her flower-print dress.

After Hank was done, she had to introduce the duet between Hank and her "little baby sister," no doubt with gnashed teeth, saying Anita was "awful stuck on the way Hank Williams sangs pretty little songs, and the last I seen her she's over yonder in a bunch of straw singin' one of 'em herself." The scene then shifted to Anita, seated in a makeshift hayloft. She began the song Hank had picked for them, "I Can't Help It if I'm Still in Love with You," one quite apt for the occasion. As she sang in her delicate soprano voice, a smirking Hank appeared, with his guitar, in a white Nudie suit with embroidered musical notes. Anita, who had become torn about him, gazed into his eyes like a lovesick schoolgirl, and the electricity was palpable.

For the finale, the cast, gussied up in their Sunday best hillbilly outfits, gathered for a group sing-along of "I Saw the Light," with Roy and Hank trading off on the verses; then everybody broke into a square dance as they sang Acuff's "Glorybound Train," Hank finding his way through the crowd to reach his hand out to Anita for their own dance. At the end of the segment, Acuff told the audience, with his signature closing line, "Good night, neighbors."

After the show, Hank dodged June's watchful eye and squired Anita around town, a tricky matter since she was underage and, worse, seemingly prone to his affections. When Anita said she'd heard Peggy Lee was playing at the Copacabana nightclub, Hank shmeared the doorman some cash to let them in. Peggy happened to be singing one of his songs, and Hank swept Anita onto the dance floor, feeling no pain as he kicked up his heels in a spastic two-step that made Anita wish the lights would go out. Other patrons were having a good laugh at the redneck, until Peggy, who recognized him, called Hank up and introduced him, to hearty applause, as he basked in the limelight of city slickers.[16] Not known is how the night ended, but once the troupe returned to Nashville he seemed to lose interest, as was his wont with women. Either reason prevailed for both of them, or Mama Maybelle and June laid the law down, or something less than magical transpired when, and if, they tried to consummate the romance.

Hank and June still had one more go-around, over her friendship with Audrey. A few weeks later, when Hank invited himself over to Mother Maybelle's house, Audrey was there. Seeing him, she ran out the back door, but Hank caught a glimpse of her and asked June to tell her he wanted to go back with her to the Franklin Street house for a talk, vowing, "I won't hurt her. I promise I won't." Audrey, though, was petrified. "He'll kill me before I even get there," she said.[17] June believed it was a good idea for Hank and Audrey to talk. She said she'd accompany her and told Hank to wait for them there. He was waiting in the driveway when they arrived. Audrey recognized his look as menacing and ducked down to the floor of the car. Hank approached.

"I know she's in there," he growled. "Tell 'er to get 'er ass up."

June assured Audrey she'd be all right, that Hank was just woofin', but Audrey refused to leave unless June shielded her. She did, but when they got out, Audrey ran for the door, with Hank in hot pursuit. June wedged herself between them and pushed him back. "You can't come in here like that," she screamed.

"The hell I can't," he barked. "It's my house."

Of course, it wasn't, not anymore, but in Hank's world, he owned the house, and still owned *Audrey*. He returned to his car and then walked back toward them—a pistol in hand. Audrey had seen this movie before, but not June, who now was rightly trembling in fear. As she yelled out to him, "You cannot *do* this, Hank!" he took aim and pulled the trigger. As in the incident months prior, the shot flew high. It "rattled my head," June would later say, and before she could even think, *another* shot rang out. By instinct, the two women fell to the pavement, not knowing if they were hit or not, screaming, reaching blindly for the doorknob before he could shoot again. Audrey realized she was uninjured, but June lay still on the ground. Hank stood lifeless, the gun at his side, as if paralyzed.

"You've killed her!" she bellowed at him. "You've killed June!"[18]

Snapping out of it, he took the coward's way out, sprinting to his car and driving off, not stopping to see if June was dead or alive. Within a few moments, she began to move, too scared to cry. She had believed she was in God's hands when she went down, but she too was unhurt, at least physically. And once more, Hank Williams, now officially off his rocker, was cut slack; neither Audrey nor June reported the incident to the police. For Audrey, part of the reason was financial; for June, it was more human. As she saw him, Hank was walking dead and needed sympathy for it. "I realized he was crazy," June said. "We knew he was going to die, and he was going to die soon."

Hank did try to make amends. A week later, he came to the studio as the Carter Family did their radio show on WSM. "I have to talk to you," he told June. "I'm sorry. I'm . . . I'm desperately sorry." She said later that she forgave him. Because, by now, it was impossible to look at Hank Williams and not feel anger being dissolved by overwhelming sadness and pity.

20

✳ ✳ ✳ ✳ ✳ ✳ ✳

HURTING FROM INSIDE

Although the California tour was a loud warning signal, Jim Denny went ahead with ambitious plans, with Hank in the middle of them. He booked *Opry* tours in late April through early May 1952 with a troupe that included Ernie Tubb, the Carter Family, Carl Smith, and Danny Dill. They wound through Texas and veered all the way to Toronto before heading back home for the *Opry* broadcast. Hank posed no major trouble and in fact seemed to have lightened up after his dark revelations to Minnie Pearl in San Diego, and his protestations of deep regret following the frightful incidents with Audrey and June. He brought Lillie up from Montgomery on Mother's Day, and a remarkably forgiving Audrey allowed Randall and Lycrecia to spend the day with him. Denny then put together another tour that would alight in perhaps the worst possible venue, given Hank's parlous mental and physical condition—Las Vegas.

A two-week engagement was booked to begin on May 16, Hank being the only *Opry* biggie on the bill, no other big star wanting to make the long trip. By the early '50s, the city of lost wages had grown from an isolated desert oasis for gamblers into a tight coterie of hotels, some rumored to be bankrolled by mobsters, with a steady schedule of performers to entertain the gamblers and tourists between trips to the slot machines and craps tables. The *Opry* pooh-bahs naturally saw this spigot of excess money and greed as a good bet to extend their own avarice. And though the slogan that best explained the city's appeal was still decades off, it might well have occurred to Denny and his minions that if they were going to send Hank here, it would be helpful indeed if what happened in Vegas would stay in Vegas.

The show would be in the Last Frontier, built in 1942 around an existing hotel called the Club Pair-O-Dice. The second casino on the Strip, it was popular as a one-stop locale where you could either marry or get a quickie divorce and then gamble. The troupe would play in a lounge called the Ramona Room, as part of a monthlong country gala billed as "Helldorado," apropos as it turned out. Hank was supposed to fly to Vegas but, coming off a bender, missed the flight. Jerry Rivers and Don Helms, who would be driving out there, were called by a frantic Denny at the last minute and told to pick up Hank and take him with them—and to take every step they could to keep Hank from booze.

As Rivers would recall, Hank "looked like any old derelict you'd see on skid row. He would've drunk anything. In fact, Don thinks he tried to drink some anti-freeze on that trip. . . . We'd avoid stopping at filling stations that had beer signs out front. One time we caught him trying to bribe the colored boy who was wiping off our windshield. He had some money out, and he was asking the boy, 'You got anything to drink here?'" Rivers said Hank arrived in Vegas "mean as a snake but stone sober."[1] Denny had ordered them to pay two burly hotel dicks extra, with *Opry* money, to keep Hank off the sauce, working in twelve-hour shifts. One of them shook hands with Hank and told him, "We're gonna be the best of buddies. But if I see you take a drink of anything, I'm gonna knock you flat on the ground."

There were few high rollers around, mainly transients, and only familiar names would bring them into the lounges. When Hank took the stage for his first performance, the patrons could barely fill a barn, which is where they belonged. "The crowds were mostly farmers, cowhands, and hotel employees," said Rivers. "They'd buy one ninety-cent Coke, watch the show, and leave," not stopping at the slot machines or tables. The hotel promoters could only take so much. The irony was that Hank had stayed dry—but so had the audiences; if booze did not flow, the hotel made no money. Taking the gig seriously, Hank had gone to the extraordinary length of renting some jukeboxes from a Vegas vendor to set up in the lounges and stocking them with his records, but they were barely played. After one week, the engagement was canceled and slapstick vaudeville comedian Ed Wynn brought in to replace the hillbillies. Hank didn't mind at all. "I could see a sigh of relief come over him," Helms recalled.

Now, with the gig done, Rivers and Helms took the leash off. As they were leaving Las Vegas, the three of them stopped to catch Rex Allen, the movies' "Arizona Cowboy," perform at the Thunderbird Hotel, and Hank got stinking drunk. Neither did Helms and Rivers keep him from boozing all the way back to Nashville. But at least Denny couldn't blame Hank for the debacle; that was on him, for misreading Vegas and overestimating the reach of the *Opry*. The only positive was that he may have thought he had finally gotten a handle on his problem child. As Roger Williams put it in his seminal Hank biography, when it came to keeping Hank clean, "Jim Denny had at least one notable success, in Las Vegas."[2]

But *was* it? Lycrecia Williams by contrast recalled this trip as anything but a success. Denny, she said, had sent "an ex-policeman named Charlie Sanders to keep tabs on Daddy," but he still "arrived drunk," and "as things got worse, the club management decided to cancel the contract after only five days."[3] While in Vegas, she related, he was "locked in his room, but he tied his boots to a bedsheet and lowered them. A bellboy filled them with bottles of liquor, which Daddy then reeled back up." She quoted Danny Dill saying that Hank, similar to the Hollywood deal, "blew it deliberately. . . . He was one of the first hillbilly singers to go to Las Vegas [but] I think the man was scared." She also quoted Denny's wife, Dolly, as calling the trip "the straw that broke the camel's back," convincing Jim that he could no longer put up with Hank. As it turned out, it wasn't the last straw, not yet. Still, however Denny regarded Hank's conduct on the trip, there was now little margin of error left for the top country star in Nashville.

• • •

In late May 1952, even after the awful meeting with Dore Schary, MGM Pictures sent Hank a contract meant to officially sign him for *Small Town Girl*. "You are to report to us at our studios in Culver City, California, on or before" June 16, it read, signed by the Loew's vice president.[4] But the space under Hank's name would remain blank, the contract unreturned. When the movie began in mid-June, it still was. Without telling anyone, Hank had changed his mind. Not having memorized a single line of the script, he treated the project like it didn't exist. Without a personal manager as a conduit, and Fred Rose and Frank Walker never able to lean on him, the studio couldn't wait. Nor did they want him anymore. Another letter was sent, dated June 17. It read:

> Dear Mr. Williams:
> Referring to that certain contract between you and us dated September 22, 1951, covering your employment by us as an actor in such roles and in such photoplays and/or other productions as we may designate, this is to notify you that, for good and sufficient cause, your employment under said contract is hereby terminated.[5]

Hank had already moved on by then, in effect terminating *them*. He left so much ill will that Schary, for one, would insist later that there had never been a signed contract between Hank and the studio at all, no matter that the termination letter referred to that very contract. There would never be a Hank Williams movie, a real pity for future generations who could only appreciate his talent on grainy home movies and TV kinescopes. Tex Williams, on his part, believed Hank "could've done better than Bob Wills, who wanted to be a movie star more than anything. [But] Hank never said a thing about movies, because he didn't care about 'em."[6] It was a pity for Rose and Walker, too, all that negotiation for naught, and greater profits for Hank's songs perhaps now just a sidebar.

Maybe Walker did foresee this at the signing, his grim look indicative that if Hank did mess it all up, there would be nothing he could do about it. Which is exactly what happened.

• • •

On May 28, the final divorce papers came to Audrey's and Hank's lawyers, needing only the signatures. They both went in and signed, a note of finality that Hank accepted begrudgingly, though not necessarily permanently. For him, nothing lasted forever, not a marriage, not a divorce, not life. Only love and death were permanent. He was clearly not over Audrey, and may indeed have believed he would not survive much longer without her if she didn't come back, a fairy tale he refused to dismiss. When his lawyer told him he still didn't need to sign away half of his future royalties, Hank said, "I want to." Ray Price, who was with him, interpreted that as Hank wanting to "show her he loved her and wanted her to come back."[7]

Still, his lovesick blues did not stop him from moving on to his next victim—er, partner. His happy roving cowboy eye was not near dead. Needing a warm set of curves to keep from fixating endlessly on Audrey, with Bobbie Jett now existing solely as the incubator of his next child, and with Anita Carter over, he soon began circling like a vulture around someone as young and pert as Anita but with a ton more baggage. This was Billie Jean Jones Eshliman, who in August would turn nineteen. Hank had actually spent his Shreveport days just yards from her on Modica Street. Her father was a Bossier City cop, and the family lived a few houses away from Hank and Audrey, though they had never met. When she was sixteen, she met a corporal in the air force stationed in Shreveport named Harrison Eshliman. She dropped out of school, and they married in June 1949. A year later, he transferred to Lubbock, and they had a daughter, Jerry Lynn Eshliman. As the marriage fell apart, Billie Jean moved back home and began working as a carhop and an operator for the phone company.

She was a knockout, with long legs, a classically beautiful face, full pouty lips, and a flowing mane of auburn hair. As Webb Pierce once said, "She was so beautiful cars would wreck when she walked by."[8] He was far from the only member of the *Louisiana Hayride* to notice. Billie Jean, who liked to frequent the *Hayride*, was a catch, and the first to grab her was Faron Young, who was discovered by Webb the year before. The short, darkly handsome singer revered Hank, having started out as a pop singer until he heard Hank one night on the *Hayride*. Young joined Pierce's band and won a contract from Capitol Records before moving to Nashville, where he earned a spot on the *Grand Ole Opry*, Hank helping him along by giving him a song to record called "Goin' Steady." Young became an item with Billie Jean and brought her to Nashville the night he made his *Opry* debut on June 14, 1952, which would be an auspicious night for Hank for several reasons.

Headlining the show as usual, after being introduced by Red Foley, he told Red, "I got a brand-new song that ain't never been aired."

"Ain't never been aired"? Red said, following the script.

"No, and it might need airin'." Hank winked. "It's 'Jam-bal-*eye*-oh on the *Beye*-oh.'"

With that, he broke into "Jambalaya (On the Bayou)," helping send it through the country music roof. And then, backstage, he first caught sight of Ms. Eshliman. Faron Young had seated her in a glass booth with other relatives of the performers, and when Hank came in to say hello to them, he was hit by a thunderbolt. Seeing her in a tight, off-the-shoulder dress with a plunging neckline revealing all he needed to know, he ambled over to her and with no subtlety asked if she was married.

"No, sir," she said.

"Well, who you with?"

When she told him, he sent a staffer to fetch Young. When he came in, Hank asked him, "Boy, you gonna marry this girl?"

"No sir, I don't think so," Young replied. "She's got too many boyfriends for me."

Young was kidding, but Hank leaped into the breach.

"Well, boy, if you don't, I am," he said.

That became the theme of the night for Hank, not to steal Billie Jean from Faron Young but to take her off his hands. Big-heartedly, he said he'd fix Faron up with the woman he himself had brought to the show, whom he described as "that ol' black-haired gal in the front row with the red dress on."[9] The four of them went to a club called the Nocturne, but Billie Jean begged off going inside. She had never been to a nightclub before or taken a drink of alcohol. That was an opening for Hank. "Well, I'll just sit out in the car with you," he said, "and Faron and my girl can go in and dance."

He then made small talk that turned heavier. He was amazed that she lived so close to him in Shreveport. He listened to her go over her marriage and being a mother—again, making him very interested. She told him she had made plans with Young to marry but that "I couldn't get along with Faron. No one can." She giggled and told him that when she was a younger teenager, she had told her mother she would marry Hank Williams. That's when he made a vow. As Billie Jean would recall decades later, the conversation went like this:

"You know, ol' Hank's gonna marry you."

"No you ain't. I'm not getting married. I'm ain't ready to get married. . . . You don't even know me, and I don't know you."

"That's awright, I'm gonna marry you."[10]

She didn't know if he was serious. She did know she wasn't ready to marry and that these randy country singers were bad news. However, like Audrey, like Anita Carter, like almost *all* women, she gave in to his little grin and big swagger. They went into the club and sat together, on condition that he drink only coffee. Don Helms, who was also at the Nocturne, said later that "Hank left with Billie."[11] Faron Young's version of what happened next was that

> we went out to Hank's house, and Hank got a big suitcase and opened it, and it was full of guns. I've never seen so many pistols. And Billie was sitting there. [She said] "Oh, Hank, what is this?"
>
> "That's a .38."
>
> "And what's this?"
>
> "That's a .45"
>
> And so I wasn't paying no attention. I was sitting around and having a beer or two. I got to thinking, watching the way he kept watching her, cuz she was a beautiful, beautiful girl, Billie Jean was.
>
> I went in the back [of the house] and here come Hank, and there was a pistol pointed right at me. . . . He said, "Well, boy, I don't want no hard feelings but I think I'm in love with that girl."
>
> I said, ". . . you can have that girl. You can put that gun back in your pocket, cuz I ain't gonna die for her."[12]

However, in other recitations, Young spoke of the "switch" being made more casually, with no gun pulled or required. Billie Jean really left him, he said, because Hank simply had more money. Others made the case that Faron revered Hank so much he stood aside out of deference. In any case, he soon moved on, entering the army for his hitch later that fall. In boot camp he met his staff sergeant's daughter, Hilda Macon, who happened to be Uncle Dave Macon's great-granddaughter, and they married before the end of the year, when "Goin' Steady" became Young's first big hit—and not a bad souvenir for having had a brief encounter with Hank Williams.

Billie Jean never admitted she dumped Young for a man with more money. But neither did she ever speak of a gun threat being involved. After Young had receded, she and Hank became closer. She moved into a ten-dollar-a-week room in a boardinghouse on Shelby Street, and Hank proudly took to calling Billie Jean "my French girl," something this full-blooded Irish lass was definitely not, except in his imagination.

. . .

By early summer 1952, the *Opry* brass was still cutting Hank slack. With their blessing he was given a new radio gig at WSM on Sunday evenings for more money. The brass also kept overlooking his missed gigs on the road, which Hank usually, and smartly, kept limited to his own bookings, not those of the *Opry*, the overlords being far more zealously proprietary of their own brand than of Hank's. As drunks will do, he also became wily about making excuses for himself, not that he needed to exaggerate how painful his back was. Don Helms, who still was playing some dates for Hank in and out of the studio, his steel guitar so elemental in striking those weepy or kicky chords, recalled driving to one gig when Hank moaned in the back seat, "Ohh, my back." As much as he knew Hank was hurting, he could tell he was milking it to get him to stop and buy him booze somewhere, so he kept driving.

"Ohh, my back," Hank repeated, a little louder.

Helms still didn't stop, and felt a sharp boot kick from the back seat.

"Dammit!" Hank yowled, "I said, 'Oh, my back,' and when I say 'Oh, my back,' I mean 'Oh, my back.'"[13]

That was code for *get me some booze or you'll lose these high-paying gigs*. Still, Helms and Jerry Rivers would soon split from him completely rather than put up with the bullshit and madness anymore.

The irony was that on a broad level, Hank seemed pristine. Once he had broken through the crossover wall, selling over a million records in 1950, the consumer print media "discovered" his idiom, only about two decades late, and Hank, of course, was a major point of reference for the Northern-based literati, who still used broad strokes addressing country with ingrained condescension. While the *New York Times* stayed away completely, never covering the idiom, *Collier's* July 28, 1951, issue brought a story titled THERE'S GOLD IN

THEM THAR HILLBILLY TUNES. The *Wall Street Journal*, always up for a good capitalist success story, patted country on the head with the title HILLBILLY TIMES BOOM. *Billboard*, arguably the most respectful and helpful of the major press sheets when it came to country, nonetheless used the same template even as its reporting was a marker of where the idiom now stood. Page 1 of the August 19, 1950, issue featured a four-column story headlined THERE'S GOLD IN OPERA ROW just above a two-column-wide story by Jerry Wexler headlined B'WAY PUB TURN SONG REVENOORS BUT HILLBILLIES GOT ALL THE GOLD. Wexler wrote that pop publishers were streaming to Nashville to get a foothold only to find the country songs already owned by Nashville interests. "The reason is simple," he wrote. "The top hillbilly performers write almost all the country hits."

The stories on Hank were fluff, and sometimes fluffed Audrey, too—"Yes, girls, Hank is married to lovely and listenable Miss Audrey, featured on his program," read a note in December 1951, the month when the marriage blew apart. Yet if one could read between the lines, some hints about his mood might have surfaced in a cover story on him in a June 1952 interview when he said his favorite song was "Death Is Only a Dream," a very bleak work by the bluegrass Stanley Brothers, written after one brother nearly died in an automobile accident.

No one can know if Hank on some level wished for that dream to come true, if he was just plain tired of living and being exploited, at least as he saw it. "They're slicing me up and selling me like baloney," he would tell people, this from one of the greatest baloney salesmen there ever was.[14]

If so, that was the price for hauling country onto the top shelf of American music, which with great irony happened as the South was devolving. Superhighways began replacing the old Southern plantation fields, oil rigs dotted what was left of open land, and factory smokestacks belched into skies that once were so blue. The rock-and-roll-loving teenagers adopted the "mobile culture" spawned by these infrastructural changes, turning hot rods and motorcycles into sacred instruments—something Hank had portended in "Hey, Good Lookin'" with its images and patois of "hot rod Fords," "goin' steady," and "cookin'" in the back seat. Not for nothing did future generations look back at Hank as "the most important person in the history of country music."[15] MGM Records may have even owed its very existence to him, Hank's chain of hits having pushed them into "the big six" with Columbia, RCA Victor, Decca, Capitol, and Mercury. He was the hub of a wheel with many spokes. But he himself was spinning out of control.

· · ·

As the summer fell in Nashville, Hank Williams had a child on the way and a nubile young lover, yet he was already pining for the woman he had lost, and damn near killed a few times. Audrey Mae Sheppard, who still identified herself as "Mrs. Hank Williams" and would go on doing so, seemed indeed to be permanently wedded to him on levels deeper than statutory law and terms of divorce. June Carter recalled that when she, her husband, Carl Smith, and Hank went to see a baseball game that summer, Hank became more and more fixated on a woman in the stands, who he thought from a distance was Audrey. Said June: "He could always see her somewhere," even if only in his mind.[16] When Hank spoke of marrying Billie Jean, wrote Lycrecia Williams, "he would say, 'I wish it was Audrey.'" He seemed to be living out the song he had written foreseeing their split, "I Can't Help It if I'm Still in Love with You." And while Audrey was cooler about it, her daughter believed that "neither would ever be free of their love for each other."

Audrey indeed seemed to have moments of ongoing feelings for him. While he was staying at the Andrew Jackson, she was at the movies with a friend one day when, seeming distracted, she checked her watch. "Hank will be at the hotel for about an hour and a half. I'm going to call him," she said, and rushed to the lobby phone booth. The Williams's housekeeper, Audrey Ragland, would say of her that "deep down in her heart she was hurting [but] she didn't want people to know her real feelings." Hank, by contrast, didn't try to hide his hurt. Ray Price could hear it his voice, see it in his eyes, smell it on his breath. For all the goofballs and losers who came through the house, Price said that Hank was "a lonely person," and when he wanted to talk,

> he'd call all over the country trying to find me. I think he drank because he wanted people to pay attention to him. He wanted people to show him they loved him, and this was his way of testing them. He was doing real fine when he thought she wasn't actually going to divorce him. . . . But when the divorce came it got real bad. He went off the deep end. Don Helms and I wound up taking him to a sanitarium up in Madison. Then . . . he started raising cane again.[17]

It was possible to see the drinking in a broader light now; as a way for Hank to keep people pitying him, enough for him to be able to measure their loyalty. But now fewer of them were even around, making him turn to booze even more as a salve. Sometimes, it was all he seemed to care about. It frightened Ray to see Hank wasting away as a result. "He had no interest in food. If he ate and the food came flying back up, he'd take another drink right away. Naw, he wasn't a public drunk. He'd do all his drinking right in a room. The problem was to get him out once he got started." Helms would say that Hank was "ashamed at his own behavior," but when Audrey was gone there was no chance he was ever going to stop it. When a reporter from the *Nashville Tennessean*, H. B. Teeter, came to WSM to begin a series of interviews with him that summer, Hank's remarks bordered on morbid.

"I'll never live long enough for you to write about me," he said at one point, adding, "God comin' down the road after me."[18]

With no fresh Hank product, all Fred Rose could do was release another album, giving it more thought than he had the first. He picked from among Hank's bluesier songs and alloyed eight of them, this time including three No. 1 hits ("Lovesick Blues," "Long Gone

Lonesome Blues," "Honky Tonk Blues") and two more Top 10 hits ("Moanin' the Blues," "I'm a Long Gone Daddy") in a kind of seminal "best of" compilation, and as such a collector's-item-to-be.

When Rose finally got Hank back in the studio on June 13, 1952, it had been six months since he'd last laid down a note. Writing had been the last thing on his mind, and the best Rose could do was cobble up four songs, none of them written solely by Hank, the only session he ever did without at least one of those. One was co-written with Rose, the terribly prophetic "I'll Never Get Out of This World Alive," which Hank had made a fixture in his act. Another was a joint effort with Hank's pudgy, piano-playing buddy Moon Mullican—"Jambalaya (On the Bayou)"—during a ride on Minnie Pearl's husband's plane, the song he had already performed at the *Opry*. It was an homage to Hank's ancestral roots—and it too was prophetic, since the hook "Son of a gun, we'll have big fun on the bayou" would shortly be his hope of salvation.

A third cut, "Window Shopping," covered a 1914 early country song by Marcel Joseph fleshed out with cute metaphors of a straying woman—a natural theme for Hank. Rose collaborated on the last cut, "Settin' the Woods on Fire," with Tin Pan Alley songwriter Ed G. Nelson. Hank brought in Jerry Rivers and Don Helms to team with Chet Atkins and old friend Charles "Indian" Wright of the Willis Brothers on bass, a reunion of his first Sterling recording session. The arrangements for the four songs cut that day had the sharp, chiming electric guitar riffs that had crept from the background of earlier rhythm-and-blues country rags like "Move It On Over" to stamp nascent rockabilly.

Arguably, the most optimistic *and* pessimistic of Hank's recordings came out of this session—"Jambalaya" and "I'll Never Get Out of This World Alive," though the latter, a sad blues rag, wasn't nearly as depressing as "I'm So Lonesome I Could Cry" or as dour as "Ramblin' Man." The steel guitars and fiddle rang out in the style of a New Orleans funeral as Hank, returning to yodeling accentuation, made fatalism almost trippy, not in frustration but in resigned amusement that "I've had a lot of luck but it's all been bad," crowing that he would live high "until that fatal day," because "no matter how I struggle and strive, I'll never get out of this world alive."

"Jambalaya" must have been exactly what Hank's fans were waiting for, another merry tune like "Hey, Good Lookin'." Its cyclical melody was borrowed from an old Cajun rag by Chuck Guillory, "Grand Texas," but the lyrics were a follow-up to Hank's previous dip in the Pontchartrain, "Bayou Pon-Pon," a Delta blues stomp written with Jimmie Davis. "Jambalaya" was like a pontoon tour of Cajun country, its native dialects, its flat-bottom boats and epicurean delights, and the Delta women Dickey Betts would later swear thought the world of him.

Alas, Hank couldn't really manage the French Cajun tongue, which was more pidgin Alabama backwoods, but he sure sounded comfy with lines like "Thibodaux Fontaineaux the place is buzzin' / Kinfolk come to see Yvonne by the dozen," and colloquialisms like "Goodbye Joe, me gotta go" and "me oh my-oh" as rhyming mechanisms with "on the bayou" were dead-on perfect. Rose deserved a lot of credit for recognizing its appeal beyond country, producing the song in a folk style, with a very tight meter, technically perfect and highly danceable, with Hank in a yodel-less, pop prism. Rose was aiming at that market, as he also would with "Woods," and "Jambalaya" came rolling out as hip-hopping, twangy country pop, Atkins's bass-deep guitar chords the very essence of rockabilly.

It had been a trying session. Hank was burnt-out and capable of only maybe one good take. Atkins recalled that "after each take, he'd sit down in a chair. I remember thinking, 'Hoss, you're just not jivin',' because he was so weak that all he could do was just sing a few lines and then just fall in the chair."[19] Under these circumstances, it's nothing short of amazing how vibrant these records sound. Rose knew "Jambalaya (On the Bayou)" would be the first one released, and it went out on July 18—with only Hank listed as the writer, Moon Mullican being given surreptitious royalties because Fred Rose was loath to leave Mullican at the mercy of his label. The ditty only whetted the public's appetite for Hank songs, sung by whomever. Mitch Miller had Jo Stafford cover "Jambalaya" as frothy pop. Bandleader Art Mooney covered "Window Shopping." MGM had Fran Warren cover "Settin' the Woods on Fire." And with his desire to record having been awakened, Hank was back at Castle on July 11 to record a quartet of songs. This time they weren't sweet and light, but more than ever mirrors into his empty soul, emptier now with the divorce having become final one day before. The first, the bitter "You Win Again," had him seething that "trustin' you was my great sin."

The next, "I Won't Be Home No More," was another, now moot, empty threat about leaving her. The last two were tear-jerking Luke the Drifter semi-raps. "Be Careful of the Stones That You Throw" was written by Bonnie Dodd, an Acuff Rose client who had penned hits for Tex Ritter and Little Jimmie Dickens. The final number, "Why Don't You Make Up Your Mind," was a not-so-coy suggestion to Audrey of the pain she created for him, moaning that "there just ain't nobody knows what I go through." Yet this was actually one of the most amusing numbers he'd ever written, with sly references to her having "a big policeman carry me back home." His impish tone gave it the feel of satire, but the last line came down hard. Pausing for effect, drawing up all his frustrations, he intoned laconically, the music going silent behind him:

What in the confounded cat hair you want me to do?

"You Win Again," the B-side of "Settin' the Woods on Fire," would branch off to go Top 10 country and be covered by, among many others, Johnny Cash, Jerry Lee Lewis, George Jones, and Bob Dylan on his unreleased 1967 *Basement Tapes*, which also covered "Be Careful of the Stones You Throw." Clearly, there was still a market for thoughts and confessions that most men would prefer to keep private, at least if they came from Hank Williams.

• • •

As the summer of '52 was broiling Nashville, the hours in the studio and the intimate moments with Billie Jean were about his only pleasant respites. And then he managed to piss off Billie Jean.

To be sure, Hank didn't seem to know how to have a normal relationship with a woman. The innocent coffee meetings they had early on had lapsed, and Hank was now drunk much of the time, his mood swings frightening her. He still professed his love for her, but it was a peculiar kind of love. For one thing, she would relate in future years that they shared a bed but not intercourse. Later, when such things were judged fair to say aloud in a tell-all culture, Billie Jean, by then a weathered, weary sort of belle, had no hedge in saying of Hank and sex, "It was on his mind, but, as my momma always said, 'If it can't get up, it can't get out.'"[20] She said this was the result of his back operation, not making it clear if she meant that he was in too much pain, or that opiates and the slew of other painkillers he used in conjunction with booze to relieve that pain had rendered him impotent.

However, if this is true, it creates at least the possibility that Bobbie Jett may have been impregnated by some other man, given that she became pregnant in March, well before Hank met Billie Jean and only two months following the operation. Among the many mysteries in this man's life, the identity of children born in proximity to him is the most intriguing, and sordid. Witness his cousin Marie's son "Butch" Fitzgerald, who swore until his dying day that Hank was his father. Of course, it is possible that Billie Jean assumed a bit too much about his ability to perform offstage, with other women if not her. But in the summer of '52, whatever the nature of their relationship, the matter of procreation was just one of the plethora of complications about to further muddy up his soiled life.

• • •

It had not taken long for Hank to piss off Ray Price. He had turned the quaint Natchez Trace dwelling into a combination brothel/honky-tonk. People of all sorts constantly shuttled in and out, music blasted from the radio, and God knows what was going on in there, with alarming normalcy. As Price noted, when the pain would be unbearable Hank would simply call a doctor willing to aid him and "go get a morphine shot, just like that." After a while, all the furniture was ruined by cigarette smoke and burns; garbage was always strewn all over, unwashed dishes in the sink, empty bottles even in the bathroom.

A physician friend of Hank's, Dr. Crawford Adams, who scrupulously did not ply him with any drugs, would come over with his wife and leave disgusted with what they saw going on, which Adams thought was Hank's way of dealing with losing Audrey. "He'd try *everything* to forget Audrey," he said, "women, parties, everything. He'd get to thinking about Audrey and he wouldn't give a damn. He'd just drink like it was water."[21]

The "sponges," as Adams called them, would eagerly help Hank throw his money away. This flotsam would stream through Price's house at all hours, unnerving Ray and his girlfriend upstairs, and the noise and carousing downstairs woke them up every night. When Ray had allowed Hank to crash there, he expected it would be temporary, so he wouldn't be alone on his farm without Audrey and Randall. But Hank seemed not to want to leave, and one day had the temerity to tell Ray to find another place to live because he wanted the house to himself. Rather than be offended, and tired of being his nurse and doormat, Price jumped at the chance. He began packing, taking no chances Hank would accuse him of taking something of his by calling Mac McGree over from the Corral to verify each item wasn't Hank's. Hank then came into Ray's room and asked why he was packing up.

"I just can't take it anymore, Hank," he said.

"Don't leave me," Hank replied, a line he must have practiced a thousand times on Audrey.

"I got to," Ray told him.

"You know I didn't mean it, Ray," Hank said, giving it a last try. "You don't have to go."[22]

   As much as it pained him whenever Hank seemed small and
needy, Ray left, and would only return to his own house when Hank
was gone from it. Not just from the house but gone from Nashville.
That would happen sooner than anyone thought, least of all Hank.
Only something radical was going to bring his life into some semblance of order, and about the most radical thing fell on him like
an anvil when, before that stifling summer was over, a decision was
made that had been building for three years, one that would shake
up the new realm of country music.

21

✳ ✳ ✳ ✳ ✳ ✳ ✳

SO FAR GONE

Before that summer of '52 had ended, the sky had seemed the limit for Hank Williams, no medium beyond his reach. He could have been a movie star, a TV star, a Las Vegas star. In July, the first national TV show hosted by a country star, a landmark moment to be sure, went on the air when not Hank but Eddy Arnold—who had bid adieu to the *Opry* of his own volition—hosted a summer replacement variety program in Perry Como's time slot. It is conceivable that could have been Hank Williams's program, had he not managed to scare half the world with his self-destructive habits and drive himself into a ditch of personal agonies. Not just his boozing but his mental stability was an open issue now, and it was only getting worse. Listening to his songs, people would shake their heads and wonder how a man that talented could be so suicidal; not that there weren't clues in those lyrics.

One of those people was Jim Denny, though one of his big plans for the *Opry* brand that went awry had nothing to do with Hank. It came as the result of the triumphant *Kate Smith Show*. He arranged for the *Opry* to go white glove, booking a sixteen-week engagement through September 13 in the Big Apple, at not just any nightclub but the rooftop ballroom of the chic Astor Hotel. It was a nifty idea; each week a different *Opry* star would headline the act, with Hank finishing the run as star of the final week. The attraction ran for four weeks, to dwindling audiences, before by mutual agreement the show was canceled, and before Hank got to appear. The irony of the failure in the Big Apple was that by the time Hank's star turn would have come around, he was already gone from the *Opry*.

His sacking came after three years of mounting insubordination, but in a tighter frame around three months of extreme insubordination. Hank went out on the road for the *Opry* icon in late July with Ernest Tubb and Minnie Pearl in El Paso. Though he was well received, Minnie worried even more about him falling deeper into an abyss since his heartbreaking lament in San Diego about seeing "no light." He had also failed to show up at WSM for many of his radio shows, forcing the station to replay shows that they had already repeated when he was out on the road. He did keep his commitment at the *Grand Ole Opry*, wowing audiences as usual and pumping "Jambalaya" into a monster hit. He dutifully performed it, "Window Shopping," and "Honky Tonkin'" at the Ryman on July 12. But even the *Opry* wasn't good enough for him to be a good soldier to a corporate entity. In the midst of his latest malaise, he was scheduled to appear at the *Opry* on August 2, as well as the following Friday, when a "Friday Night Frolics" radio hullabaloo was booked for the *Opry* troupe in Reading, Pennsylvania. Instead, he missed the *Opry* appearance to perform in Sunset Park in West Grove, Pennsylvania, on Sunday the third.

Two days later, when he got home, the lean, lanky Denny drove out to Natchez Trace with Carl Smith to tell Hank in no uncertain terms the line had been drawn. Finding Hank semi-coherent, he told him his position with the *Opry* was hanging by a thread; the bosses at WSM and the *Opry* wanted Hank fired, but he had gotten him one last chance to straighten out. Naturally, ultimatums like these made Hank's jaw clench and his rebel streak rise. But it was also bad timing, coming as the roller coaster ride that was his personal life again headed straight to hell.

. . .

Actually, things had seemed to be turning around for him only weeks before. Wanting to make good on his intention to marry Billie Jean Eshliman, he got down on one knee and asked her to marry him sometime in September. Having been worn down by his charm, she said yes. Even with so much *Opry* business pending, he made plans to drive down to Shreveport so that he could meet her parents. Hank bundled their luggage into his Cadillac convertible, and with a hired driver at the wheel they headed down Route 31. He was feeling so good about himself, and so renewed, that he wrote thirteen songs, dictating them in the back seat to Billie Jean, who wrote them in his notebook—a high privilege indeed. "Write this down for ol' Hank, baby," she recalled him telling her, and "he'd call 'em off as fast as I could write."[1] Apparently, at one point, he felt compelled to tell Billie that, in contrast to Audrey, "One thing about you, babe, Ole Hank could never be ashamed of you."[2] Hearing himself say that, he had yet another song for the notebook.

When they got to Modica Street, Billie Jean saw her mother emptying trash outside the house and introduced her fiancé to her. "Mamma," she said, "I want you to meet Hank Williams." He was wearing a grungy white shirt, dusty slacks, and a baseball cap, looking like a hobo. "Son of a bitch," she said, "you ain't no Hank Williams." Grinning his grin, he pulled off the hat, took his guitar out of its case, put a foot up on the fender, and broke into "Lovesick Blues." All doubt removed, they had a pleasant time.

Chivalrously, while Billie Jean slept in her parents' house, he and the driver bunked at her newlywed brother Sonny's home across the street. Hank drank no liquor at meals and sing-alongs in the backyard, but his incontinence reared up and, according to Chet Flippo, "he wet the bed that night," upsetting the Jones family, who "didn't like to see a grown man pissing on new furniture. . . . That was the first time Billie Jean knew that Hank was having that kind of problem, and she wrote it off as something alcoholics do."[3]

Still, Hank charmed the family with studied manners and some impromptu singing and strumming. The Joneses loved him, and he made sure to tell them how much he loved their little girl and how good he'd be to her. He promised he'd marry her as soon as she could get a divorce from her husband. After two days with the future in-laws, he loaded back up and they headed home so he could make his *Opry* appearance three days hence. Back in Nashville, Hank stopped to buy five pounds of fish his driver would fry up for them out at Hank's farm. However, when they got there, Hank was again victim to his recklessness, the first sign of which was the glass in the front door smashed. As Billie Jean recalled:

> One of his girlfriends had moved in, literally bag and baggage. She broke the door out and moved in. Here I am with my fiancé, and this blonde moved in. He asked her to leave and she wouldn't. That was the only kind of people that was around him. I said, "Well, I'm leaving. Just have the chauffeur drive me home." I said, "I'm tired of the blondes, I'm tired of the whiskey, I'm tired of the whole bit."[4]

She said he became enraged at the bimbo and tossed her down a flight of stairs and out the door, whereupon she picked herself up and marched back in and began rasslin' with Hank as Billie Jean and the driver watched, not knowing what to do. If that wasn't bizarre enough, when they broke their clench, Hank acted as if it were the most normal thing in the world to deal with a scorned woman at his own house, and thought nothing of having Billie Jean *and* the blonde together in his car, dropping each off at a different location. Billie Jean was dropped first, with no way of knowing if Hank even took the other girl home. She recalled:

> I was mad. He said he was gonna get rid of that broad but was gonna take her to a club first. I told him, "That's it, I'm gone. I'm history. I ain't puttin' up with this crap no more. . . . The rest

of that week, I packed. He got rid of that sucker and came back over. I said, "I'm going back to Louisiana. This is wrong and I don't want any part of it."

As much as Hank could charm a rattlesnake, and as much as Billie Jean had been sweet-talked into accepting his proposal, she was a tough polecat, with sharp claws, and no man could tame her. When she said, "Just do me a favor and let me alone. I've enjoyed all of this relationship I can stand," he did. The next day, Billie Jean was on a Greyhound bus, a long gone momma, en route for Shreveport. But to Hank it was a small wrinkle. Just as with Audrey, he believed he'd get her back. He had no doubt, he told people, that given time he'd still marry that "French gal."

· · · ·

In the aftermath of Billie Jean's departure, the *Opry* was about the last thing he gave a hang about. Following Jim Denny's ultimatum, he did make it to Reading for the hullabaloo event but was so drunk he couldn't go on, and promoters angrily complained to Denny that they'd lose their shirts after refunds. A day later, August 9, the brass nervously paced as the *Opry* show neared and there was no sign of him. When the curtain went up, still no Hank. The show went on without him, leaving yet another crowd disappointed when Cousin Louie Buck announced the lineup for the show and didn't mention Hank.

The next day, Sunday, Denny felt personally betrayed, and nothing could keep him from what he had to do. The *Opry* politburo called an emergency meeting upstairs. Everyone who mattered was there: Denny, WSM president Jack Dewitt, head of advertising Irving Waugh, program manager Jack Stapp, chief studio engineer George Reynolds, and the president of National Life, Edwin Craig. Also there was a man who had warned Hank long before Denny did, Fred Rose.

Either a vote was taken to fire Hank, or the decision was made alone by Jack Stapp, who took responsibility for doing so for years.

He wanted to do it that day, but Hank was again incognito. The next day, Monday, August 11. Hank made it back to Nashville—how he didn't really know, since it seems he lost his Cadillac somewhere in Pennsylvania. When he woke up at Natchez Trace, Johnnie Wright was there with him, having gotten him home from Pennsylvania. Hank was hung over but sentient when the phone rang, a call he surely knew was coming after his wild weekend. According to Stapp, it was he on the other end, summoning Hank to his office at WSM. When he arrived, "all the guys sat there" on a long, green couch as Jack told Hank he was "suspended"—not fired—from the *Opry* and WSM. Stapp maintained that Hank took the news calmly, saying little, and left, perhaps relieved, or too hung over to care.[5]

Another story, told by the WSM station manager, Harry Stone, who oddly wasn't at these meetings, was that as he came into the building later that morning he saw a car parked behind it, "with a hillbilly at the wheel." He peered in the window, and "there in the back seat lay Hank Williams. He was the most pitiful-looking thing I'd ever seen." He said Hank saw him and said, "Mr. Harry, they just fired me."

"The hell you say," Stone replied, evidently not having been consulted. "What for?"

"For drinkin'," Hank acknowledged.[6]

Denny, though, would for years swear that it was he who did the dirty deed, not in the office but on the phone, and that "it was the toughest thing I ever had to do in my life."[7] That version was backed up by Ernie Tubb, who said he was in the office at the time. You have to "prove to me" you can get straight, Denny told Hank, and then "you can call me in December and I'll let you know about coming back to the *Opry* next year." When Denny hung up the phone, Tubb said, "he had tears in his eyes." Tubb soon after ran into Ed Craig in the parking lot; he related Denny's call and said Jim was trying to get Hank straight.

"I'm sure Jim means well," Craig told him, "but it may work the other way. It may kill him," meaning Hank.

Ernie would later say, "I was feeling the same way."

Johnnie Wright also confirmed Denny's climactic call. He said Hank had no interest in begging or apologizing and defiantly said to Denny, "You cain't fire me 'cause I already quit."[8] When Denny told Hank to call him back in December, Hank's veins popped. "Check the fucking *Billboard* charts and then call *me* back" was his comeback, a damn good one.

Wright said Hank decided on the spot to get out of Nashville. He began packing the old trailer he kept in the driveway at the farm, HANK WILLIAMS AND HIS DRIFTING COWBOYS painted on each side. He then hitched it to Johnnie's Chrysler limousine and they drove to WSM, where he sent Johnnie up to the office to pick up a $300 check due him from the station. Roy Acuff and Owen Bradley were in the office that day, too, feeling terrible about Hank getting the gate, and not a little pissed off at Denny about it. When Wright told them Hank was downstairs in the car, they hurried down to see him. Hank was half in the bag but told them he was leaving town. They asked where he was headed, but it was obvious to all who knew him that there was only one place he could have gone. He was on the road to South Alabammy once again.

. . .

Wright agreed to drive Hank to Montgomery, and on the way out of Nashville Hank said, "Johnnie, get me some whiskey." Wright stopped at a liquor store, cashed the check, and bought a fifth of bourbon for the ride. When they got to Lillie's boardinghouse, Hank was out cold. Recalled Wright: "We pulled his clothes off, put him to bed, and talked to his mother 'til he woke up. Hank acted like he didn't care he'd been canned."[9]

Meanwhile, the news that shook country to its cowboy boots had broken in the Nashville papers. The reason given for the firing was that Hank had "failed to appear on a number of personal appearance dates and Opry programs in the past few months." It was also reported in the August 23 *Billboard* with a small item on page 31 headlined OPRY BOUNCES HANK WILLIAMS—but, curiously, it was datelined August 9, meaning that someone at the *Opry* must have fed advance word to the trade paper of the firing. Still referring to him as a "hillbilly star"—thereby explaining why it was not major news in the showbiz galaxy—the item said that Hank's immediate plans were "unknown" and that "it is believed that the singer will return to his home in Montgomery, Ala."

But within days, feeling a backlash from their patrons, *Opry* people began spreading the fable that Hank was merely taking a sabbatical because he was "sick." It seemed the *Opry* was protecting its behind, not willing to play the heavy. Hank, meanwhile, simply didn't care. Reflecting his attitude, Billie Jean would say that "I don't believe he was fired, I think he just didn't wanna show up. If he didn't wanna go he wouldn't go. He didn't seem to be concerned one way or the other about the *Opry*. His heart wasn't in it anymore. He didn't see performing on the *Opry* as a big deal."[10]

He would waste no time getting back on the road, and, when he did, he'd use the firing as a one-liner, drawling with that grin, "Well, they fired me from the *Opry*, but ol' Bones always closes the show." Bam Bamford was still booking for him, and plans for another "homecoming" were made, this one in Greenville, on August 15.[11]

Even so, this was no shining moment for Hank Williams, and he knew it. Bravado and even relief aside, he had screwed up. Perhaps it added to his desperado scent, although he was anything but proud that being a drunkard and a screw-up was ruining his life. Don Helms happened to see Hank just before he left Nashville, when he returned a shotgun and a watch Hank had given him to hold for him. "I'll be seein' you boys around," he said jauntily, adding one of his Hank-isms that, this time, made perfect sense.

"Don't worry about anything," he said. "Nothin's gonna be all right anyhow."[12]

. . .

The Greenville homecoming on August 15, 1952, was just what Hank needed. Protecting his reputation, the local papers underplayed the firing as a medical issue, a leave of absence to recuperate from "blood poisoning." Feeling much at home, he bought a new car to ride in the parade, a four-month-old, powder blue Cadillac Series 62 similar to the tan Coup de Ville he'd misplaced, paying $3,818 toward the sale price of $5,083.

Although he needed a loan from the Third National Bank to afford it, he wanted his wheels to reflect his status, *Opry* or not. It had all the plush extras: black pleated leather seats, spotlight, continental kit, and a gold-plated *V* beneath the Cadillac symbol on the hood, which graced only the most expensive models. He got plates with Alabama number TL-1469 and filled the tank for the trip to Greenville. It wasn't a car as much as a ragtop tank, its 30-hp engine enough to bulldoze a brick wall. Enough to save a man's life out on a bad road.

During the two-day celebration, Lon Williams was once again called up from McWilliams, and like clockwork, Lillie wouldn't permit him to ride in the open car during the parade, which proceeded past an estimated 8,500 people, three deep in some spots. Hank, in his white buckskin Nudie suit and hat, smiled and waved, a hero on his home turf again. Some stories would have it that he went looking for Rufus "Tee Tot" Payne, unaware he had been buried in an unmarked grave since 1939. After the bash, Hank returned to Lillie's boardinghouse, to contemplate his next move.

Bobbie Jett was already there, living in secrecy during her pregnancy, and it's not entirely clear how she fit in during this interim. However, when Billie Jean went back to Shreveport, Bobbie and Hank may have had some sort of rekindling, since when Hank chose to get away to the country for a few days, she was with him. The venue was provided by Bob McKinnon, the DJ he had known in Nashville who had since left and taken a job with a radio station in Alexander City in Tallapoosa County, some sixty miles northeast of Montgomery. One of McKinnon's relatives owned a secluded fishing lodge in the wooded marshlands of Kowaliga Bay out at nearby Martin Lake. This was as backwoods as one could get in Alabama, where

Creek Indian names still define the few roads and landmarks and their tribal mythology runs as thick as the moonshine.

McKinnon drove Hank and Bobbie, who he was told was Hank's nurse, to the cabin. He dropped them at around 4 p.m. on Sunday the seventeenth and left. The hours that followed must have been manic indeed, because at midnight, eight hours later, McKinnon's phone rang in Montgomery, and at the other end was a police chief named Winfred Patterson, who told him Hank was in the Alexander City jail. It seems Hank had taken Bobbie to the Russell Hotel in town, where she still was. The chief explained that Hank had gotten drunk and created a disturbance, running through the hotel screaming about protecting the lady guests from some guy who was "whupping them."[12] McKinnon drove up, collected Bobbie from the hotel and came over to bail him out.

A photo was apparently taken of Hank when he was arrested, and it would come out later on, showing him standing in front of a jail cell in baggy jeans and a hat, his shirtless chest mere skin and bones. His eyes looked a tad deranged, his mouth struggling to complete that patented Hank smile. No charges were filed, and Hank took it so lightly that he joked with Patterson, "I been in worse jails, and better ones."

McKinnon found him in his cell asleep. He hoisted him over his shoulder like a rag doll and deposited him in the car outside. He then drove Hank and Bobbie down Dadeville Highway to another motel, put him to bed, and drove Bobbie back to the lodge to pick up some items. While there, McKinnon would recall, "I heard her crying and throwing up. I asked her what was wrong, and she said she was pregnant."[13] At the time, it made McKinnon one of maybe three or four people who knew that secret.

The next day, Hank had McKinnon drive to a bank in Alexander City, where he was able to withdraw some money to buy clothes; then they went back to the lodge in Kowalinga. McKinnon by now had reported back to Lillie about Hank's condition, and she hurried her way up to Tallapoosa with a detective named Louis King, bringing with her bottles of medicine prescribed by her doctor for Hank that supposedly countered the effects of alcoholism. Another person who showed up was Cowboy Bob Helton, perhaps Hank's closest friend in Montgomery. He had been one of the few people Hank had introduced to Bobbie during their stay at the boardinghouse in February, and he would later recall that when Lillie saw Bobbie in the lodge, she had a question for her son.

"Hank," she asked, "isn't that Bobbie and isn't she pregnant?"

"Yes, old eagle eye," Hank confessed. "I'm the father, and I'm taking the baby."[14]

• • •

Lillie undoubtedly had a lot more questions. But for now, Hank told her to go back to Montgomery. He then went back to getting wrecked. He, Bobbie, and McKinnon ran across a bootlegger in Kellyton and drank moonshine all night, even the pregnant Bobbie. Feeling no pain, on the ride back to the lodge, Hank began banging out a rhythm with his fists against the dashboard and chanting, Indian style, *"Kowaliga! Kowaliga!"* That was enough to compose a song called "Kowaliga," a sad tale of doomed love based on one of those Creek legends. He also completed one of those songs Billie Jean had transcribed for him on the car ride to meet her parents, "Your Cheatin' Heart," a sort of sequel to "Cold, Cold Heart," inspired by the same residual venom about Audrey. Feeling productive, he wrote one more, "Lonesomest Time of the Day."

He was upbeat about these works, enough to call Fred Rose and tell him to come down to Montgomery and work with him on them. He ended the getaway, with McKinnon driving him back to the boardinghouse. Bobbie was given a train ticket to Nashville and moved into a hotel there with her daughter, her pregnancy now out in the open to Hank's family. Periodically, Lillie would send Marie McNeil to spend some time with Bobbie as she progressed toward her due date in January. Hank, on the other hand, made no effort to be with her, once again turning his thoughts to Billie Jean. But before he could pick up with her, he had work to do. Rose arrived in Montgomery with Murray Nash, a former RCA song-plugger who had joined the Acuff-Rose hierarchy. They all labored long and hard at the boardinghouse to buff the songs, putting a lot of time on "Kowaliga," which Rose thought was ponderous. Liberally rewriting the lyrics, he used as a metaphorical device for Hank's fable a wooden Indian, the kind found in tobacco stores. Rose crafted a deft, tongue-in-cheek ditty that Hank acknowledged elevated it from a curio into a commercial winner. The name was also changed, to the more colloquial way Hank pronounced it, "Kaw-Liga." The content was almost adolescent ("Poor ol' Kaw-Liga, he never got a kiss / Poor ol' Kaw-Liga, he don't know what he missed"), but even here, there was a reference to personality flaws he no doubt saw in himself, the lovesick Indian too stubborn—and made of knotty pine.

The message in the other song they worked on, "Your Cheatin' Heart," veered away from himself and to the woman he could live neither with nor without; her perfidies, he tells her, "will make you weep" and unable to sleep because "your cheatin' heart will tell on you." Perhaps it was his way of warning Audrey that she could only make peace with her cheatin' heart if she came back to his bed for those long nights. Rose on his part was satisfied with what he heard. Hank was back in the groove, he believed, and "Kaw-Liga" in particular offered an excellent comeback vehicle.

His songwriting was back on track, and a good many country music fans, and even more pop fans and industry lords, cared little about his firing by the *Opry*, since his records had transcended that stage anyway. Nor was it of much importance that as the autumn of '52 began, Hank was on the move again and had made his new base of operations in the city that had made him a star—Shreveport.

• • •

Other than returning to Nashville, professionally, this had been the only plausible route for him to take, and certainly so romantically. Indeed, he had excitedly told people the day he left Nashville that his future would be with Billie Jean down on the bayou. In the month since then, he had gone about shedding the properties he still had in Nashville. He sold the farm at half the price he bought it for. He also sold Hank & Audrey's Corral, including $60,000 worth of inventory, to Mac McGee for a mere $4,000, accepting liability for $12,000 in debt—a sweetheart deal that did McGee no good, as he would shutter the store a year later.[15] This helped him pad his wallet, which was fattened to the tune of $55,042 in royalties in 1952. Still, Hank cared little about the money; it was severing all ties with the city he had conquered that gave him so much pain.

Shreveport was in his sights now. As early as August 30, the *Shreveport Times* reported Hank had signed a three-year deal to perform on the *Hayride*. At the same time, as if it had been planned as a gimmick for his reentry to Louisiana, "Jambalaya (On the Bayou)" was screaming up both the country and pop charts. By September 27, *Billboard* had it at No. 3 on the country list and No. 1 among country disk jockey plays. Jo Stafford's cover for Columbia was at No. 5 on the Best Selling Pop Singles chart and was the third-most-played jukebox record, right after her own "You Belong to Me," peaking at No. 3.

That same issue also carried a full-page ad bought by the label, with Mitch Miller penning a column called "The Pitch from Mitch," which was all about Hank—who worked for a rival label. "Man, that's one crazy song-writer," he wrote. "He's cranked out five straight hits in a row, which makes him practically the Conestoga edition of *Rodgers* and *Hammerstein*." Absent in this panegyric was anything about the *Opry* firing; in Miller's worldview that was small-time. Hank's crossover appeal was big-time. Miller took bows for the pop hits made by Stafford alone and with Frankie Laine on "Hey, Good Lookin'g" (No. 9) and noted that Stafford and Laine had just cut "Settin' the Woods on Fire," swooning:

> If there ever was a record made for a night on the town, this is it! . . . The kids have never been in better form, and we're on our way to another big one. Consequently, thanks to Hank Williams!

Of course, Mitch erred in attributing "Woods" to Hank's pen, but it was a natural assumption. Everything Hank touched he seemed to make his own. "Jambalaya" would remain in the country Top 10 right up until nearly the end of the year, and be given a ride to No. 24 on the pop list. And yet Horace Logan and Henry Clay had serious doubts about taking a problem off the *Opry*'s hands only to make it theirs. But both Fred Rose and Jim Denny pulled strings for Hank again, making the case that it would be mutually beneficial for the *Opry* and the *Hayride* if Hank finally got straight, and Rose laid it on thick to Horace how much Hank thought of him—like a father to a prodigal son. With the deal done—for one year, with two one-year options to follow—the price for getting him back being $250 per *Hayride* show, the usual rate being $18. Hank readied himself for the triumphal return, which would coincide with him cashing in on his proposal to Billie Jean Jones Eshliman.

"Baby," he cooed over the phone to her early in September, "this is ol' Hank. I do believe we got a date."

He meant to marry, reminding her that before she'd left Nashville they had agreed on October 19. Billie Jean, unsure if she'd ever seen him again, had not yet even filed divorce papers from Harrison Holland Eshliman. Now, he told her he was coming to town, that she should find him a place and prepare to get hitched.

He was there in early September. By then his Coupe de Ville had been found in Pennsylvania, towed to Nashville, then driven to Montgomery by Marie McNeil. Hank drove to Shreveport with Clyde Perdue, the young man who had promoted the Greenville homecoming; Lillie had talked Hank into hiring him as his new manager. Hank arrived in his blue Caddy and took up residence in a cheap motel on Shamrock Street that was owned by Billie Jean's brother Sonny's father-in-law. He then picked up where he'd left off with Billie Jean, who ready or not was now his fiancée.

His first few days in town, he began tooling around Shreveport, seeking to reestablish ties with the musicians that had played behind him four years before. However, things had changed, people had moved on. The only one outside of the *Hayride* house band he could conscript as a new Drifting Cowboy was Sonny Jones, who played the guitar, and only because Billie Jean refused to accompany him on the road unless Sonny got the job. Hank agreed, and Sonny knew he was one of the inner circle when Hank gave him a nickname, based on Sonny's frizzy hair. To Hank, he was now "Niggerhead."

When she looked back on those days much later, Billie Jean portrayed herself as next to virginal, a naïve girl injected into the life of a madman.

"Lord, I was young and dumb," she said, insisting, despite having consorted with a big star before Hank, that she'd never "been anywhere or done anything," never stayed in a hotel or owned luggage. Even when she began staying in hotels with Hank, "I still carried my shoes in one hand and all my things in a big Kotex box." Hank, she said, found her naïveté "kind of cute," a relief from his own life. To be sure, she described him as "already awful burned out and used up."[16]

However, this was not the Billie Jean some people remembered. Perhaps influenced by Hank, she was not a teetotaler anymore, nor just window dressing. During his resettlement, Hank found an old ally who had also split from the *Opry*—Oscar Davis, who had quit booking his Drifting Cowboy gigs rather than deal with Hank's erratic behavior. Davis had still promoted shows thereafter that starred Hank—including the ones in DC and Baltimore that Hank had to miss when he had back surgery—and the two men remained friendly. But then Davis fell out with the Nashville powers, and he too left town. He was promoting way out in Vancouver when Hank traced him and asked him to come back to work for him in Shreveport. Letting bygones be, Oscar agreed and made the long trek to the bayou. Davis would recall being nearly knocked over when Hank introduced him to Billie Jean in a restaurant his first night in. Hank, he said, "must have loved those tits because they were tremendous. You could take any of those and compete with a Graf Zeppelin. Plenty big. They used to get drunk down in Bossier City [and] he was living in a horrible, horrible motel. Sparsely furnished. An old

kitchen table and junk all around. Every night we had to go out and
sit and drink."[17]

Billie Jean took a lot of crap from Hank, but gave a lot back.
Davis remembered that Billie Jean "would call him the damnedest names." The two of them always seemed to have some space
between them, their loving gazes through forced smiles. Billie Jean
never really acted like she was committed to marriage, and there
was doubt that it would happen. As one of the *Hayride* sidemen,
guitarist Tommy Hill, recalled, "Hank and Billie Jean left each
other two or three times a day. As far as what I knew, they would
have got along okay if Hank had stayed off the booze. He acted
like he loved the woman. I also seen him beat the hell out of her. [I
saw] him work her over and her work him over."[18] Seeing them in
these bouts, many of Hank's old musician buddies kept away. One,
Hank's old guitarist from his earlier days in Shreveport, Felton
Pruett, told of Hank "treating her bad, cussin' at her, and I thought,
'Hell, I don't need none of this.'"[19]

While the behavior of the couple was an echo of Hank and
Audrey, the difference was that Hank and Audrey loved each other,
hopelessly. Hank and Billie Jean indeed *acted* like they were in love,
but it seemed an excuse to show off, for Billie Jean to elevate her life.
For Hank, it had at least as much to do with showing his ex-wife he
could do what he had legally prevented her from doing. It wasn't love
for Billie Jean—it was spite for Audrey.

• • •

As these events were panning out, another drama, a dark and awful
one beneath the glamour and glitz, was taking shape in the shadows. A drama that more than any other factor in his life at the time
would lay him the lowest. Hank had recently added a new name
to his stable of "doctors," one Horace Raphol "Toby" Marshall. A
slight, bookish-looking forty-two-year-old fellow with beady eyes
that stared through rimless glasses, Marshall had been lurking in the
shadows of his own life, by design, since he was on the run, keeping

a secret. A high school dropout, he nonetheless claimed that he had BS, MA, and DSC (Doctor of Science and Psychology) degrees. BS was right. Marshall would later admit to being a "pathological, constitutional liar."[20] Records show he spent a year in the San Quentin federal pen in 1938 for armed robbery and forgery, for passing a bad $500 check in a card game. He served a year in Oklahoma, then jumped parole in October 1951 and forged a career as a doctor.[21]

He wore the imprimatur convincingly, certified by a diploma from something called the Chicago University of Applied Sciences and Arts, which he later admitted he had purchased for thirty-five bucks from a magazine salesman with a printing press as they filled their gas tanks. He was also a recovering alcoholic, with a smarmy self-conviction, or just a con, that he held the formula to recovery, and he circulated as a country doctor with no office, no address, and no phone number, just a black bag full of drugs, which he obtained at first from a real doctor. Marshall got around, using his skills at forgery by applying for and receiving certification from a board of medical examiners. Marshall's prescription pads bore the homey name "Connie's Prescription Shop," a pharmacy on North Walker Street in Oklahoma City with a shady reputation. (In 1957 it was found guilty and fined $62,000 in a wrongful death suit after a woman died after taking medicine from the shop that contained a lethal poison.)[22]

Lycrecia Williams believed Hank first met Marshall during an Oklahoma City stop in October 1952. Marshall, she said, "had appeared to give him a shot that immediately sobered him up."[23] Billie Jean also recalled a trip Hank took to Oklahoma City around that time, leaving with $3,000 and coming back with $300, explaining that the rest went for "treatment." Apparently it didn't take long for Marshall to follow him to other locales. About a week before the wedding, Hank was playing a show at the Baton Rouge High School when he ran into his old Drifting Cowboy bass man Lum York. Hank invited Lum to play the gig, and as they waited backstage York heard some scary talk. He recalled:

The doctor had given him something to take and had told him, "Now when you take this, do you want to die?" Hank said, "No" and the doctor said, "Well, if you take anything to drink while you're taking this stuff, it'll kill you deader than a hammer."[24]

Blunt warnings like that, of course, meant little to Hank. All he knew was that Marshall had the goods he needed, but on a deeper level he meshed with him. Classic con man that Marshall was, he could fool sick and troubled people, especially alcoholics, into believing he cared on a human level for their well-being. He played on Hank's loneliness, posing as his friend and adviser. Marshall would later relate spending twenty-four to thirty-six hours at a time with patients, "giving the alcoholic the attention his family wouldn't. I'd sit hours. I'd be there when he woke, and I'd talk with him. I'd show him he was wanted. That's how I worked with Hank Williams. He drank without reserve."[25]

Marshall also wormed his way into the confidence of Lillie Stone, whom he met when he followed Hank back to Montgomery after one tour, one of his precepts being that he didn't treat an alcoholic but rather the entire family. Lillie's usual sharp eye for users and abusers of Hank, other than herself, was blurred by Marshall's smooth tongue and seeming authenticity. With her assent, he was soon a favored member of the inner circle.

To be sure, Marshall did seem to have a real empathy for Hank and wanted sincerely to cure him of booze, but curiously, or not, had less concern about keeping him dependent on drugs that he carried in his black bag, which was always filled with needles and bottles of amphetamines and barbiturates. Billie Jean recalled that Marshall followed Hank wherever he went "with a little black bag. Every time my husband went to fill a singing date and got away from me, that guy with the bag would meet him and administer to him."[26]

Nothing in that bag was beneficial in the long run for Hank. But none of what Marshall was "administering" was as ominous as the new drug in Hank's life that he was becoming dependent on—chloral hydrate, an extremely powerful and habit-forming sedative.

The effects were obvious. Hank arrived at Shreveport Municipal Auditorium for the *Hayride* broadcast on September 13. As Webb Pierce remembered, "He'd been drinkin' and you could tell it backstage. His eyes were watery. And that [hard] stare he used to have, that was gone."[27] Still, he knocked off "Jambalaya" and several other hits and was called out for four or five encores.

Four days later, his twenty-ninth birthday, he played a dance hall in San Antonio, the Barn, owned by country singer Charlie Walker. During the show, it was arranged for an eleven-year-old prodigy to sit in Hank's lap and play "Steel Guitar Rag." Everyone thought it was precious, except for the kid, Doug Sahm—who would earn fame as the front man of the fabulous '60s Tex-Mex rock band the Sir Douglas Quintet ("She's About a Mover," "Mendocino"). Years later Sahm's son, Shawn, recalled his father, who died in 1999, saying that Hank's "breath stank of whiskey and there wasn't nothin' left to him," and that Hank kept saying, "Play that steel, boy!"[28]

The night went well, however, with a big birthday cake rolled out and "Happy Birthday" sung to him by the audience, bringing ol' Hank to tears. But when Hank, Billie Jean, Sonny, and Charlie went backstage afterward, a beer-bellied redneck with some sort of grudge against Hank tried to attack him, touching off one of those old familiar brawls. "Git him, Niggerhead!" he called to Sonny, who took the guy down with a punch to the face before Hank finished him off by aiming his pointy-toed cowboy boot several times at the guy's groin.[29] It was as if he had never left the buckets of blood back in Alabama, and he seemed to feel right at home.

Fred Rose, meanwhile, had booked September 23 for the session at Castle Studio that would include "Kaw-Liga" and "Your Cheatin' Heart." The two other songs chosen were a Hank original, "I Could Never Be Ashamed of You," written around the phrase he had used during the ride with Billie Jean to see her parents, and Rose and

Hy Heath's "Take These Chains from My Heart." Don Helms was on pedal steel, Chet Atkins on lead guitar, Jack Shook on rhythm guitar, Floyd Chase on bass, Tommy Jackson on fiddle. For "Kaw-Liga," drummer Farris Coursey, who'd played on the only other Hank record with a drum part, "Moanin' the Blues," was called back. Hank, having worked hard to get the song's keys right, sang with the light-hearted, almost satiric archness Rose wanted, playing off tribal tom-toms in the song and Jackson's frantic fiddling, which ended the song with a fade-out, the only song of Hank's not to end on a dead stop.

Recording "Your Cheatin' Heart," Rose sped up the pace of the demo to keep it breezy, giving a pop feel to Hank's emotional vocal. The third track, "Ashamed," rather than being a valentine to Billie Jean, had emerged, tellingly and ironically, as another *Audrey* song, a wistful admission that when all was said and done, "Darlin', I could never be ashamed of you." The last cut, "Take These Chains from My Heart," was also conciliatory, written for him in the style of his sad songs as a plea to be released from the bondage of love he had created. Rose struck a highly effective theme with the "chains" metaphor, as would be seen when Ray Charles covered the song a decade hence as a country follow-up to his country-flavored hit "Unchain My Heart."

However, it was all Hank could do to make it through the session. As with previous sessions, he tired quickly and frequently needed to lie down on a couch in a studio office to gather up enough energy to complete each track. Clearly, he was running down, his heart too stressed by the booze and pills and malnourishment. His lungs, filled with cigarette smoke and phlegm most of the time, were laboring, his organs punished by toxins. The truly amazing thing was that none of it could be heard in his voice, and the session turned out to be a remarkable one, a buffet of typically tangled, contradictory themes, all fresh, taut, vibrant. All *Hank*. When he left Nashville that night, weak as an old bush dog, he felt as if he still owned the town, though he might not live to see it again.

• • •

Perhaps wisely, Hank had not introduced Billie Jean to the woman who thought no woman was good enough for him, his mother, who would by rote size up any prospective wife as another "whore" and gold-digger. That meeting could wait, lest Billie Jean run away screaming before he could slip a ring on her finger. Neither did Hank find any reason to tell Billie Jean about Bobbie Jett. He did tell her plenty about Audrey, though, enough to scare the bejeezus out of her. He had also gotten Billie Jean to file for divorce at the Bossier City courthouse on September 25, prompting Oscar Davis to concoct a modern-day fairy tale that could be sold to a mass audience and exploit Hank's star power to the max. He said to Hank, "Why don't we make some money out of this thing? Why don't we have a public wedding?"[30] Hank needed no more selling to get on board with it.

They would according to this plan take their vows with thousands of people as witnesses. Hank wouldn't even have to perform; other *Hayride* acts would do that, and the show would climax with the nuptials, with a good time had by all. It sounded so good, so *easy*, and profitable, that Davis got to thinking if one such "wedding" could make a mint, why not *two*? He could sell the first show as a Sunday afternoon "rehearsal," followed by a nighttime "wedding."

According to Billie Jean, Hank asked her, "What do you think?" She said she told him, "Well, it doesn't matter to me where we get married." Shreveport was too small for a royal wedding. Oscar wanted New Orleans, a big sold-out arena, namely, the Municipal Auditorium, the jewel of Deep South cultural art centers.

The prince and his princess bride would enter the 75,000-square-foot hall and say their "I do's" onstage before 14,000 standing-room-only paying guests, twice in one day. Their hope was that the divorce would be final by the date chosen for the nuptials, Sunday, October 19, the first show at 3 p.m., the second at 7 p.m. Tickets went on sale scaled at seventy-five cents to a dollar-fifty, and went like mint juleps in the hot sun. Soon after, Billie Jean was driving to New Orleans to work with Oscar on the preparations and promotion, which as Davis explained it later was mainly for the purpose of getting the couple some bread. Even after selling short all his holdings, Davis said, Hank "didn't have any money, and he needed some stuff to start the marriage with, especially furniture."[31]

But here is where things got murky. Because when the last woman to walk down an aisle with Hank Williams heard about all this, she didn't send her best wishes. Instead, Audrey Sheppard Williams suddenly seemed quite eager to interfere in his affairs. To outsiders, Audrey had seemed to move on well enough from the divorce. She was still trying to continue a singing career with an eponymous country band and living fairly lavishly on Franklin Street. She showed no outward signs of jealousy about Hank's women in his life. As Ray Price related, "Hank said, 'If you don't come back to me I'm gonna marry Billie Jean.' And Audrey said, 'Go ahead.' "[32] Still, Hank apparently made one last play for sympathy, or pity, before marrying. As Audrey told it:

> A year to the night before he died, I told him I would never live with him again. Six months to the day we got our divorce, he told me, "Well, I've done everything to get you back." You know what the problem was? I had these two children. I said, "These children have to have a mother." I could see they wasn't gonna have a father. He got so far gone, God bless his heart, that they just got nervous when he walked in the door. And that's bad on children.[33]

Yet something may have made her take a much more intense interest in his life when he made his wedding plans, possibly thinking of the possible repercussions for her, financially, if a new wife had a legal stake. What's more, she apparently found an ally in Lillie Stone, the woman she had detested bone and marrow, and vice versa.

The two old enemies grew closer than they ever had been, in common fear and loathing of Billie Jean. Audrey even made her presence felt with Bobbie Jett, whom Lillie had told her all about and who could also affect Audrey's slice of the pie. With Bobbie living in Nashville, Audrey began to visit her, without Hank's knowledge. No one knew what they talked about, but they seemed to get along, possibly after Bobbie told her she wasn't going to marry Hank. Still, what Audrey may or may not have been up to caused enormous paranoia in Hank and Billie Jean. When the wedding plans were announced, Audrey and Lillie flew down to Shreveport with Randall and called Hank. Audrey, according to Billie Jean, "told him if he wanted to see the boy, he'd have to meet her out at the airport, and that's what he did. 'Course he came back and he looked like a Mack truck had hit him."[34]

The meeting was in a hotel by the airport, and Hank came out disheveled, a bruise on his face from another fight with Audrey. A *Hayride* musician saw him the next day and asked, "What tiger bit you?"

"Audrey and my mother has been down here," he said. "I don't know what they're going to do in New Orleans."[35]

Audrey had already decided to keep Hank from visiting Randall. She and the boy had also visited him on a gig in Oklahoma City, and a story arose that as they sat in a restaurant he whipped out a gun and shot a hole through a painting on the wall of the battleship *Missouri*, sending diners ducking and the police to be called. When a cop asked why he'd fired the shot, Hank supposedly replied, "Hell, it drew on me first."[36] Audrey once concluded that "he needed help so bad, and I just couldn't do it," and this makes it plausible to wonder if that's really what Hank feared—not physical damage or a stint in in one of his drying-out tanks but that he would wake up inside a straitjacket in a rubber room. To avoid that, he figured he needed Audrey to be the one who looked deranged. Indeed, Horace Logan would say that "Hank's primary interest in Billie Jean was to make Audrey jealous."[37] He even invited Audrey to the wedding. Hank's explanation was that it was the only way Randall could be there, and Billie Jean accepted it. But whatever her plan, Audrey wouldn't take

that bait. She had no desire to attend, nor for her son to. Lillie would
stay away, too, her ultimate signal of disapproval.

Leading up to October 19, Hank and Billie Jean spent a lot of
their time wondering where Audrey would show up next, what corner or bush she would be lurking behind, and what she might do.
And Hank kept pushing Billie Jean to keep her lawyer, whom he was
paying for, working on the divorce.

Meanwhile, Oscar Davis was getting everything ready in New
Orleans. The papers were running breathless advance stories about
it being the biggest wedding(s) in the city's history. But all this went
ahead without the certainty that Billie Jean would be free to marry
on that day. The court hearing on the divorce had been scheduled
for October 17, and the hope was that the judge would gavel the case
to a close then. But Hank was so spooked that Audrey would do
something, he seemed prepared to get married whether it counted or
not. After all, he was a pro at that.

. . .

Hank had moved out of the dive motel and with Billie Jean into
a rented two-bedroom apartment on the same street. As Davis
noticed, it had not a stick of furniture in it. Davis was going to purchase furniture for them that he would be able to put onstage in
New Orleans as prop "gifts." Hank, however, had just one piece of
business to take care of before he married—to make sure Bobbie Jett
would not become another problem he didn't need.

After Hank backed away from Bobbie, his lawyers contacted her
with a proposition that would benefit both of them. Not surpris-
ingly, Lillie had a hand in this, and dominated the agreement that
was drawn up by his Montgomery lawyer, Robert B. Stewart. Hank's
fear had been that Bobbie, after giving birth, would pester him with
financial demands, play the same games with visitation as Audrey,
and perhaps go public with the tawdry story just months after Hank
had married. Thus, he had to take care of her financially and settle
all possible monetary claims legally now. The terms were that Bob-

bie would receive $100 every month until she delivered, $200 if she miscarried.

However, the man who could be brought to tears by the thought of fatherhood seemed to hedge about taking responsibility for the child, the first sentence stating that "Hank Williams *may* be the father of said child" and that "paternity of said child is in doubt." But he would provide for it nonetheless, without tying either himself or Bobbie to the chore. Custody would go to Lillie for the first two years, during which he and Bobbie would have free visitation rights; then, with the third year, Hank would retain custody, and as of the fifth year, share custody with Bobbie thereafter. He would pay all costs in the raising of the child and would keep paying her $100 a month for the rest of her life. Almost punitively, he also would pay for a *one-way* ticket for her to fly to *California* within seventy-five days of the birth. To keep her hermetically sealed until then, Bobbie would live at Lillie's boardinghouse, with Hank paying $172 a month for the room. Last, and most important to Hank, the agreement said this:

> Bobbie W. Jett does hereby release the said Hank Williams from any and all further claims arising out of her condition or the birth of said child.[38]

Hank flew into Montgomery on October 15 to add his signature. Bobbie then moved with her daughter, Jo, into 318 North McDonough Street, keeping her lip zipped for the rest of her life about her time with Hank and the arrangement that would for the child become a Gordian knot.

22

✦ ✦ ✦ ✦ ✦ ✦ ✦

"I SEE JESUS COMIN' DOWN
THE ROAD"

Hank and Billie Jean wound up getting married on October 18, the date Hank had originally chosen, a day before the scheduled spectacles in New Orleans. They did this for one reason, paranoia about Audrey disrupting the grandly staged day of celebration, which led Hank to seriously contemplate eloping.

In this light, the court hearing on the divorce on the seventeenth was irrelevant to him. Billie Jean dutifully went to court on that day, accompanied by her father. She was represented by a Bossier City lawyer, Louis Lyons, whose fee Hank was picking up. Harrison Eshliman didn't bother to show up to contest it, and all seemed cut and dried, but Judge James Bolin said not so fast.

Under state law, another step was required, a technicality, though Billie Jean would insist she never heard any such thing from the judge that day. Years later she recalled, "He failed to tell me that a judgment or something had to be read in court aloud before my divorce was granted." This meant she would need to return to court for that reading, yet when she asked Lyons if she was free to marry, he responded, "Yes, don't worry about it."[1]

If so, that might have been legal malpractice. In truth, final dissolution would not come until October 28. Maybe Lyons misunderstood the judge, or believed Hank wanted to hear only one answer that day. A delay would mean the lucrative New Orleans events would have to be rescheduled, or even dropped. Hank had no intention of waiting. Getting hitched, and fast, was his only option. So he took the most direct route. He obtained a marriage license, and after the *Hayride* show the following night, when he and Billie Jean should have been home packing for the morning trip to New Orleans, he asked musician Paul Howard if he knew of a justice of the peace in the area. Howard knew of one up in Minden, twenty-eight miles east of Shreveport in Caddo Parish. But it was the only place they could go, they figured, without Audrey getting in the way.

Hank and Billie Jean, along with Howard and his wife, rode there in Sonny Jones's green Ford, rather than Hank's Cadillac, just to give Audrey the slip if she was hiding in the bushes watching. They arrived at 1 a.m., waking up Justice of the Peace P. E. Burton, who was unaware that the couple were not legally free to marry. On the drive back, they ran out of gas, and Hank, still clad in his white Nudie suit, hat, and boots, got out and on a pitch-black road thumbed down a ride for him and Howard to the nearest filling station. The stunned motorist who stopped, a soldier in uniform as Billie Jean remembered, must have thought he was dreaming, and an appreciative Hank asked him to stay the night in Shreveport.

"You don't want to do that," Billie Jean said sternly, "not on our wedding night." Paul Howard recalled that this caused a fight between Hank and Billie Jean "for four hours" before she got her way and the soldier was sent away.[2]

With the actual ceremony done, the New Orleans episodes were completely for show, and money. Thinking he had put one over on Audrey, Hank was giddy. "We'll be married and there's nothin' she can do but cause a scene in public," he guffawed. Given that his feelings about Audrey were so twisted, it is possible that he may have actually been itching for a melodramatic scene, as it would prove how much Audrey wanted him back. Considering this kind of thoughts, Billie Jean Jones Williams seemed almost an afterthought.

No one really knows what Audrey was planning to do, if anything. According to Lycrecia Williams, her mother was "humiliated" by the marriage and Lillie Stone was betrayed by it.[3] Lillie still had not met Billie Jean, and didn't know Hank had eloped until days after. Neither was in New Orleans for the spectacle, and they missed a hell of a show. The scene there was worthy of Mardi Gras.

Oscar Davis chartered a plane for them to fly down from Shreveport that morning; a limousine picked them up and brought them to the Jung Hotel, where Hank steadied himself with some breakfast bourbon, before a police escort ushered them to the Municipal Auditorium. In the meantime, the invited guests began arriving at the arena, including Billie Jean's family—her sisters-in-law would be her bridesmaids—but none of Hank's, not even Lon Williams. Hank's best man was *Hayride* singer Billy Walker, who flew in with him and Billie Jean and who would be one of the *Hayride* performers at both shows, along with the husband-and-wife team of Tommy and Goldie Hill. Walker later said Billie was distraught on the flight, worried Audrey would make a scene.

As people began lining up on St. Peter Street outside the arena, the stage was decorated, with Davis having bought dozens of bouquets and bottles of champagne to line it, and a seven-foot cake to be placed midstage. Gifts donated by friends and fans were all around. Billie Jean wore an all-white silk gown and veil bought at a local bridal shop on one of her earlier visits, one of the many very expensive items that Davis billed to Hank, who agreed to give him half of the ticket sales. Hank had also done his part in the promotional work, telling the newspapers, "All the folks want me to get married, and all of 'em can't get in at one time."[4]

Actually, some folks wouldn't have come even if *they* were paid.

That included Fred and Wesley Rose, and everyone from the *Opry* crowd. Not even Ray Price, Don Helms, and Jerry Rivers RSVP'd. Wesley Rose, looking back, winced when he said, "To us, it was no place to get married. My father felt he'd be part of a carnival if he went."[5] Indeed, it seemed almost destined that something would go wrong, and it did, when the preacher hired to perform the service— who had no idea he would be performing any empty ritual—learned that Billie Jean's divorce was not yet final. As she remembered, "He looked at our license and said, 'I can't do this' as the people were stacked in there, hanging off the rafters."[6] The preacher got his hat and left. Another preacher, Reverend L. B. Shelton of the First Baptist Church of Algiers, agreed to do the ceremony and was rushed to the hall.

The show went on, and, with anticipation mounting, Billy Walker finished up his set and began singing "Anything Your Heart Desires." A spotlight was turned on, and a white carpet was illuminated leading from the wings to the stage. Appearing out of the dark, there was Hank, looking like Roy Rogers in dark brown slacks, a cowboy shirt with white and brown fringe across the chest and white trimming on the collars and sleeves, and a white hat.

On his arm was the dazzling Billie Jean, and they strode to center stage, where the wedding party had assembled along with VIP guests, who, although the invitations had promised that "stars of stage, screen and radio will be in attendance," numbered few, the biggest ones being members of the *Hayride* troupe, local DJs, Nudie Cohn, and the dashing mayor of New Orleans, deLesseps Story "Chep" Morrison. Women squealed in the audience; men whooped. It *was* big fun on the bayou. As they stood before the replacement preacher, Hank doffed his hat, his bald spot making the crowd buzz. But even in these moments right before pledging his everlasting love to a woman, he had another woman on his mind.

"I know Audrey will be down to stop this," he whispered to Davis, who thought the strangest thing about how Hank said it was that it sounded *wishful*. As Davis believed, "He was hoping."[7] Indeed, Hank had even sent a chartered plane to Nashville for her. But as he kept one eye open for Audrey, he warmed up to the charade. All went smoothly, the nuptials, the cutting of the cake, the bouquet toss, and the first dance of the newlyweds, met with thunderous applause. Hank felt no pain after imbibing bottles of champagne. He led Billie Jean by the arm to the front of the stage and introduced "my wife." Then, egged on by the crowd, he surprised the musicians by strapping on a guitar and breaking into impromptu renditions of "Jambalaya," "Cold, Cold Heart," "You Win Again," and "Lonesome Blues." Hank, in a newspaper interview two days before his death, fondly noted that "when I played 'Jambalaya' those Frenchmen roared the roof off. They went crazy."[8]

After the last song, Hank and Oscar counted the money. Hank and Billie Jean relaxed at the Jung for a while, then came back hours later and did it all over again. Davis had arranged for the couple to go on a honeymoon, chartering a private plane to take them to Cuba. But they were both too tired after the long day and instead went back to the Jung, with Davis setting up a postwedding meeting with the press there. Hank was too drunk to leave the room, but Billie Jean did. Boy, did she ever. Barefoot, barely wearing a translucent negligee, she assured the reporters that Hank was "resting." She giggled through a few more questions, the picture of saucy innocence, posed for pictures, then said she had a pressing engagement upstairs.

The next morning, they passed up the honeymoon altogether, and it was canceled. Clyde Perdue drove them back to Shreveport, where the furniture and appliances would be trucked and carried into their apartment. Within days, Hank got back out on the road for some local gigs, taking Billie Jean with him. However, the glow of New Orleans dissipated fast. Hank had come to believe that Davis had kept most of the proceeds of the shows, and began pressing Oscar about it.[9] He denied any wrongdoing. But for Hank, the relationship was poisoned, and he broke it off, Oscar Davis becoming yet another burned bridge left behind.

Losing Hank as a client meant little to Davis, who owed him a lot, having been rescued by him in Vancouver, and he never expressed any bitterness. Hank, though, could only go in the opposite direction. For all of the pomp of the wedding ceremonies, he came away hearing whispers that he was so down on his luck now that he would do just about anything for a good payday, even getting married. Similar cynicism greeted his new wife.

The hardest thing for him was that even in bayou country, the old vim and vibe were gone. Not that they didn't still love him, but he wasn't especially of the moment for them anymore. The *Hayride* had moved beyond him, his absences having sent audiences seeking other young stars who became what Hank had been, like Faron Young and Webb Pierce. He felt somewhat distant from the crowds and began dropping hints that he was going to be gone again, retracing his path of a few years before, his destination the same—the *Grand Ole Opry*. For all his pride and bravado, he needed Nashville again in his blood.

. . .

On October 18, Judge James Bolin reconvened the divorce case, looking not so pleased that in the interim he'd seen newspaper stories about the wedding bashes in New Orleans. Bolin asked Billie Jean's lawyer Louis Lyons if he'd seen those stories. Lyons, improbably, said he hadn't. Bolin could have invalidated the marriage for another reason—both Hank and Billie Jean had inexplicably lied about their ages on the documents they signed when P. E. Burton married them in Minden, Hank saying he was thirty, Billie Jean twenty.[10] Bolin ruled that the marriage was indeed illegal and that they would need to marry once again. However, neither of them seemed particularly interested in doing so. They had married *three* times, wasn't that enough?

Even so, legal or not, Billie Jean gave the marriage all she had for a while. She saw Hank as a helpless man-child, never having experienced the tenderness nor the parental bonds of childhood. "He had never been held," she said. "I knew I had to be a lover and a mother to him. We wrestled, had picnics. I gave him a childhood. We held hands, and I'd sit on his lap. I wore short-shorts and T-shirts tied up in the front. I was a virgin in a lot of ways."[11]

What she meant to him, however, was not clear. He still believed the true love of his life was Audrey, but Billie Jean's sexy country-girl "virgin" in cutoffs was surely a breath of fresh air compared with the stale air of Audrey's hard, cheatin'-hearted visage. Billie, he told folks, was "the best thing that ever happened to me. I was way down and she brought me up out of the ditch."

Or at least she tried. Though he made a habit of introducing her from the stage when he went on the road, she went with him not for the attention but hoping to somehow limit his drinking, although the tactics were similar to those used by Audrey, Don Helms, and Jerry Rivers back in Nashville. She allowed him a limit of two cans of beer—one ice cold one after a show or in the evening, another right before bed—no hard stuff, and talked tough with him. "If he got more," she once said, "I'd force milk and raw eggs down him, then I'd call my brothers to pack him off to the hospital. . . . I told him, 'You either walk as a man as my husband, or you don't walk at all.'"[12] Usually he'd be taken, semi-coherently, to the North Louisiana Sanitarium in Shreveport, the new version of "the Hut." Billie Jean said, "He'd go up in the elevator singing, 'Good-by, Joe, me gotta go, me oh my oh.'" The hospital's records show that the first time he was confined there was, fittingly, on Halloween 1952, and that he was unusually frank with the doctors. One, Dr. J. E. Williams, wrote in the records that Hank was

admitted for Rx of acute alcoholic intoxication. States he has been on the road for seven weeks playing various stage commitments and has been drinking steadily for the entire period. Complains of chest pains, especially over upper chest regions. States that deep breathing greatly exaggerates pain. Has had almost constant cold and cough for past several weeks. Has taken many kinds of antibiotics in huge quantities.[13]

Several things stand out here. Ominous things. As early as October, possibly sooner, Hank had been experiencing chest pains. Out on the road, he had told people about it, saying his chest felt like it was about to "bust open" and that he could hardly breathe at times nor sleep. Those "antibiotics"—sedatives and painkillers—had raised his blood pressure, putting more strain on his heart. The doctors evidently didn't look very far into this complaint, even though he was suffering from, among many other maladies, edema, a buildup of fluid under the skin that causes swelling and raises blood pressure, and myositis, an inflammation of the muscles. Hank had likely been broaching a serious heart condition for years, aggravated in every way by his lifestyle, chain-smoking, and malnutrition. There was also in his blood the drug that may have caused more damage than any other, including morphine.

That was chloral hydrate, which he had discovered courtesy of "Dr." Toby Marshall's little black bag and been taking on a regular basis since the early fall. Thus, the drugs pumped into him at the sanitarium were already familiar to his system, including:

Sodium amytal, 1 grain
Vitadex, 5 percent, 1,000 cc
IV drip, adrenal cortical extract, 10 cc
Empirin, unknown dosage
Chloral hydrate, 7.5 grains
Morphine, unknown dosage

Most humans, and some elephants, might have been knocked out for days by this cocktail. On November 1, Hank slept through the night and until around two in the afternoon the next day, whereupon he was given even higher doses of the same chemicals, knocking him out but good for another day.[14] This was par for the course in the treatment of serious alcoholics, a far cry from the meditation techniques and less-addicting detox medicines given celebrity alcoholics at luxury rehabilitation clinics/spas today. Not only was it counterproductive and harmful, for a Hank Williams the hospital was something like a candy store. In fact, he might have been given CH before Toby Marshall in previous sanitarium visits. Doctors did their part to keep him off booze for a few days, but what he did next was all on him; no behavioral modifications or psychological treatment were ever discussed. He only hated these visits because there was no booze to wash down the drugs.

During the Shreveport sanitarium stays, Billie Jean did her part, too. "I brought him every weird, crazy funny book on the stands," she said, "hundreds of them." He would come out sober, shaky but good enough to perform. Each time, everyone would hope he was finally straight, but knew better. There seemed no way to keep him from finding and hiding hootch; too many people were entirely happy to kiss his behind and get it to him. And now, with Marshall providing nonstop drugs, he was at greater risk than ever. He knew this, yet he still couldn't lay off. Once, so the story goes, when Billie Jean came into their bedroom Hank was on his knees, reaching under the bed.

"God damn, baby," he told her, "I was just lookin' for my shoes."

"Hank," she said, "you got your shoes on."[15]

Checking under the bed, she pulled out two cases of beer. As Hank stared helplessly, she opened each can and poured the suds into the toilet.

Only a few months after they moved in, the new furniture in the apartment was pee stained, the result of his incontinence after drinking. Much of the time Billie Jean was changing him like a baby, cleaning him up, and herself—"You're pissing on me, Hank Williams!" Chet Flippo had her scolding Hank one night when she woke up with her pajamas soaked.[16] So assiduous was she in trying to stop the flow of what he was evacuating that she didn't yet realize the lethal potential of the benign-looking pills or believe anything was amiss when he would call one of his doctors.[17] That only continued in Shreveport, and on the road if he could find one of those "doctors"—there was always some telephone number to call that a friend of a friend had given him. He apparently even felt compelled to make a quick side trip to Havana, not for a honeymoon but to rustle up some pharmaceuticals on the cheap.

Toby Marshall was a shortcut to that end. Most people around Hank detested his imperious demeanor and how he seemed to enjoy being able to lead Hank around with just a few words. What's more, his advice began to extend beyond medical issues to Hank's career, marriage, even his songs. But it was either patronize Marshall or suffer in a way few people ever did, his back hurting so bad that, feeling entombed by his brace, he'd slide down in the back seat of his car until he was in a fetal position on the floorboard, sobbing.

If Billie Jean was with him, she'd slide down onto the floor as well, cradling his head, crying with him. However, finding relief now carried extreme peril, since, as Billie Jean would recall, "whatever chloral hydrate was, Hank wouldn't take 'em right. He'd take 'em by the handfuls." With the rhinoceros-like levels of resistance he had built up over the years to alcohol and chemicals, sometimes these megadoses simply allowed him to calm down, numb the pain and send him onto a stage looking like the Hank of five years before. Which of course would lead him to think he could handle the booze like he used to.

Marshall had advised Hank from the start that adding even a drop of booze could kill him in combination with the ultra-potent drugs he shot him with, wanting to keep his hooks so deeply into Hank that he conveniently made allowances. Marshall began giving him shots to induce him to vomit his guts out, so as to clear any alcohol. He was operating by a plainly insidious regimen: drink two beers in the morning, have an injection, puke, guzzle plenty of black coffee and Dexedrine tablets, do a show, drink two more beers, then take bennies to go to sleep.[18] It was living, but it sure as hell wasn't life. Nor did it really work. Rather than being relaxed and in command, said Billie Jean, "he'd be walking across the stage and he would fall. People would think he was drunk, but he wasn't. He'd lost control in one leg, which with the kind of back problems that he had is very common." This, as well as the incontinence, might also have been an early manifestation of paralysis as the result of his edema and spina bifida.

Crowds at one stop generally didn't hear about Hank missing a show at the previous one, nor would they care. As long as he didn't cheat the crowd out of a performance, they'd go wild as usual. But more and more, that loyalty was eroding right along with his anatomy. His face seemed to be slowly caving in, the hollow of his cheeks unable to support his cheekbones, leaving a kind of death mask. Naturally most thought it was because he seemed to almost never eat; his diet for weeks at a time on the road would be eggs smothered in ketchup. Billie Jean would become so alarmed she'd drag him to her parents' for Sunday dinners and fill his plate with meat, potatoes, gravy, and, of course, ketchup. To her relief, he would begin to fatten up, even though much of the weight gain was bloat, likely due more to his mounting heart disease and edema.

Someone was impressed enough to plant an item in the October 18 *Billboard* that read: "Hank Williams has gained 30 pounds and reports he is in the best of health." Getting with the program, when he and Billie would have Sunday dinners at her parents' house, Hank would stock up on all kind of groceries. As happy as Hank was at those times, believing that he was getting healthier and that he had allayed some of Billie Jean and Lillie's worries about him, the ongoing trauma to his heart and organs was worsening. As soon as he would tank up on the chloral hydrate and go into the binge-and-purge regimen, he'd be a scarecrow again. As Claude King said of those days, "He and I were the same age exactly, but to me he was an old man."[19]

He had just turned twenty-nine.

23

✳ ✳ ✳ ✳ ✳ ✳ ✳

"DON'T WORRY ABOUT
OL' HANK"

If October had been a pleasant turnabout, even a stay of execution, November brought him back down. When he left the North Louisiana Sanitarium, Hank was whole enough to get out on the road again. Not incidental was that his money was being bled dry.

Toby Marshall, who was being paid $300 a week just to stand by, made it easier for him to obtain chloral hydrate on the road by giving him a blank pad with scripts signed by Marshall. He also was given a card signed by Marshall that permitted him to receive a morphine shot from a licensed physician,[1] meaning he no longer needed to scour the underbelly of the sticks to get one of those with a dirty needle—which, it is suspected, caused him to contract hepatitis in '52 as well. It all seemed foolproof, and Hank and Billie Jean took to the road, remaining there most of November, Hank having no choice but to take whatever gigs he could, mainly around the crescent of Louisiana and Texas.

The big clubs, *Opry* stages, and glittery national tours were a thing of the past. The man who had run Bob Hope and Milton Berle off stages and starred on the biggest TV shows now was laboring on country's back circuit, being propped up by the *Hayride* for life support. If Oscar Davis had found it harder to book him on solo gigs, Clyde Perdue, with none of Oscar's pull or skill, had to settle for the backwoods high school auditoriums, dance halls, and honky-tonks Hank had once thought he'd never see again. Worse, his attitude was that he was doing the rednecks a favor, when it was really the other way around now. Folks would still come to see him, and a good night's pay could net him maybe $500 after paying off the local musicians. If he felt all right, and could come in sober, he would leave 'em damp and panting. As Billie Jean, whom he would proudly show off to the audiences, said of those times, "He'd say, 'Hot damn, boys, let's pick.' That sucker, man, he'd put on a good show."[2]

But if he'd put some beer into his gut after Toby Marshall had evacuated it with a shot of CH, it was touch and go whether he would make it at all, and if he did, he might embarrass himself, be a mean drunk, screw up a few songs, then go and collect the bread. This, of course, had always been the way he rolled, but now it wasn't only his boozing; it was that he seemed disdainful of the audience.

On a *Hayride* stop in Brownwood, Texas, he broke into the "blue" version of the old folk tune "The Little Old Red Shawl My Mother Wore," singing, "The dirty drawers that Maggie wore, they was torn and they was split / You could see where she had shit." He thought such riffing was innocent fun, even if one was not to say such things in mixed company, yet it drew howls of "Indecency!" Horace Logan, who emceed the *Hayride* tours, yelled from the wings, "Hank, shut up!" and insisted that Hank later apologize. Still another time, in Lafayette, Louisiana, he walked onto the stage, didn't feel it, and asked, "Y'all paid to see ol' Hank, didn't ya?" After the predictable cacophony of *yessss!* he drawled, "Well, you seen him," and left,[3] costing the promoters thousands in refunds.

More promoters begged off him now. The promoters who made the gamble usually were rewarded—but took no chances. Many a night would seem a replay of what Minnie Pearl had witnessed in San

Diego, when A. V. Bamford's wife, Maxine, demanded Hank play no
matter what. And now, the shadowy "doctor" with the black bag was
seen as an ally of the promoters and bookers. Marshall was a "Mr.
Fixit" called in to dope up Hank solely to be able to play. Tommy
Hill often was on those gigs. He would recall, "I said, 'They're killing him.' The booker and the doctor. They were sons of bitches."[4]
Indeed, Minnie herself caught a few shows Hank did in the sticks.

> When Hank was ready to walk on stage, he turned to me with
> that little-boy look, and I said, "Hank, you oughtn't go out there
> and try to work." He said, "Don't worry about ol' Hank, it's gonna
> be alright." He stood out there, trying to sing but not being able
> to. He'd forget the words so often he could hardly get through a
> song. His voice was like the cry of a child or a wounded animal.[5]

Still, Hank brought much of the degradation on himself. Having
to go out and perform just to stay afloat, he did it with a sense of
loathing for himself and his fans. At one *Hayride* gig, he knocked
back a pint of whiskey given to him by a local DJ, then came onstage,
and when the crowd began calling for him to do "Lovesick Blues," he
ignored them. Boos filled the air; then, when he sang, badly, there
were cackles and catcalls. That sent Horace Logan, as it had Ray
Price in the past, onstage to shame the crowd. "You folks have been
entertained by this man for weeks and years," he lectured them.
"You have seen and felt this man's genius and ability. He needs our
help and our sympathy, not our hypocrisy. When he's straight you
all know how great he is. But when he's having problems, I will not
stand for you laughing at this man."[6]

No matter. Afterward, a mob of people formed outside the hall,
found him in his car, and began rocking it back and forth before cops
got them away. Hearing about it, the promoter of the next gig called
Logan and said if Hank wasn't going to arrive sober, he shouldn't
arrive at all. That one was canceled.

Oscar Davis had watched over Hank from the moment he'd

wake him up until he sent him out onto the stage. Now, with Oscar gone, such chores fell to Billie Jean, who came along on most of his appearances. But if Billie Jean wasn't there, he would drink and Toby Marshall would be summoned to give him a shot of something. The breaking point was if he got his hands on firewater. Tommy Hill said that Hank would begin a tour sober, "but if somebody slipped him a drink it was all over. He'd wilt, just wilt from booze. His blood was full of alcohol and he couldn't drink any more. He was a sick man. When he crossed the line, he was a tyrant; the language, the lack of respect for anybody."[7]

. . .

Billie Jean had morphed from arm candy to trying to wield the authority of a wife, though she had to cross swords with Lillie to do it. Late in the fall of 1952, after Hank had taken her home to finally meet his mother—who acted in much the same insulting way she had when he'd brought home Audrey—Lillie told Hank she wanted to buy a third boardinghouse, assuming Hank would stake her the money for it. But Billie Jean put her foot down, threatening to leave if he did. Yet Lillie wouldn't let up. Billie Jean overheard Hank and Lillie screaming about money, several times with pushing and shoving involved.

Of course, those weren't the only secrets being kept from her. Hidden out of sight, stashed away in Lillie's second boardinghouse, was Bobbie Jett, who was quickly approaching her due date and was brought back to Montgomery to give birth. Not for nothing did Hank, according to what Lillie said later, take to singing the Jo Stafford song "Keep It a Secret" around the house, an inside joke between them.

As sure as she was that Billie Jean was out to usurp her and her money supply line, Lillie construed Billie Jean's loathing of Toby Marshall as just cause to bring Marshall further into the family affairs. Incredibly, Lillie so bought into the con that she apparently took his place as Hank's candy man at home. Billie Jean nearly fainted when she walked into the parlor at the boardinghouse one day and observed Lillie sticking a needle in his arm.[8] The explanation, as she had been assured by Marshall, was that the shot was "vitamins." However, it seemed ominous that when Marshall did show up in Montgomery, he and Lillie would repair into a room, close the door, and discuss Hank's treatment, with Billie Jean—and Hank—shut out. As far as Lillie was concerned, as long as it wasn't booze, it was good for Hank, not comprehending that every shot was driving him faster to his grave.

. . .

The last two weeks of November, Hank was on the road again, Bam Bamford having booked dates for him in Florida and Georgia. One stop was Pensacola, where he still liked to spend time with his old mentor Pappy McCormick. He got there on a charter plane, and on the way, said the pilot, James Hutchins, later, Billie Jean told Hank she was pregnant, which would have meant Hank no longer was shooting blanks. However, the plane began running low on fuel, and there was much anxiety that it might have to ditch before landing.

The next day, Billie Jean was said to have awakened in their room at the San Carlos Hotel in a pool of blood, apparently miscarrying. Hank, in a panic, ran out to get her a box of Kotex, but found himself in a bar and didn't return for hours,[9] apparently forgetting about the woman he said he loved bleeding out the child who would carry his name. Billie Jean was able to get help at the hotel, though she lost the child. But, seeing no need to comfort her, Hank was on stage that night at the Diamond Horseshoe Club, with Pappy playing steel guitar.

On the same jag, Hank visited his sister, Irene Smith, who was now living with her husband in the Naval Housing Project in Portsmouth, Virginia, and had journeyed to Jacksonville, where they kept a beach house, to see him. Irene was aghast at how he looked and would later claim that when he left, she had a very uncomfortable feeling. After dinner, he headed for his hotel. As he walked away,

Irene ran to him and hugged him. "Goodbye, I love you very much," she told him. Then, walking back to her husband, she watched his silhouette disappear in the distance. "I will never see him again alive," she said. "He is dying and he knows it."[10]

He was making others believe the same thing. More and more, he was now wheezing and coughing, possibly suffering from bronchitis or pneumonia. When he returned to Shreveport, Billie once more sent him to the North Louisiana Sanitarium on November 27, during the Thanksgiving holiday. He was out in a few days, again narcotized, but not feeling anything close to fine. He made it to Dallas on December 6 for the Big D Jamboree, an *Opry/Hayride*–style show in an arena designed to look like a barnyard, the 4,500-seat Sportatorium, where many Texas singers came to play after gigs at Jack Ruby's three downtown clubs. Hank was so drunk he blacked out on the floor backstage, and the promoter was said to have invited spectators to file past the prostrate figure lying there in a kind of death pose in his white cowboy suit.[11]

Hank got through a gig in Biloxi the next day. When he returned home on December 10, he had a raging fight with Billie Jean and was taken by the Jones brothers for another confinement at the sanitarium. When he woke up, he panicked. He tore the IV tube from his arm, steadied himself as he stood in his hospital pajamas, changed into the snazzy suit he'd worn when he was brought in, pulled his boots on, stuck his cowboy hat on his head, stuck his gun into his waistband, and stumbled down the hall, down the stairs, and out of the building. He wandered the streets, garnering double takes from passersby. Then, after he caused a ruckus outside a restaurant, a cop named H. H. Pittman ran him in. Getting wind of it, on the twelfth the *Shreveport Times* reported, FAMOUS SONG COMPOSER IS ARRESTED HERE, with these details:

> Hank Williams, the singing cowboy, was arrested in downtown Shreveport yesterday afternoon on charges of being drunk and disorderly. . . . Pittman said Williams, who insisted that "I

shouldn't have to go to jail," was dressed in a blue serge suit and a bright green hat with a big feather [and] was carrying a .38 caliber revolver. . . . No weapons charge was filed against him. [He] was released on bond at 9:45 p.m.

As in all other such scrapes, any charges were either dismissed or dispensed. Hank returned to the sanitarium, came out pacified, and waded right into two weeks of touring in the sticks, increasingly drunk, leading to more terrible performances. He made his *Hayride* appearance on the thirteenth, then left for a weeklong Texas swing with a *Hayride* troupe that included Billy Walker, Al Rogers, Charlie Adams, and Tommy Hill and his sister and singing partner, Goldie. He went without Billie Jean. Tommy and Goldie were driving him in his baby blue Cadillac to Houston for the gig at Cook's Hoedown Club in Houston the next night. They were out in Nacogdoches at around two in the morning when Hank, in the back seat, began making ungodly groaning and gurgling noises, then lurched forward and passed out, not an unusual event, except that they couldn't hear him breathing. As Tommy would describe it, "He turned black." Goldie screamed, "Hank can't get his breath!"

Recalled Tommy: "Goldie was hysterical. I stopped the car, dragged Hank out, stood him up, grabbed him around the waist, and bounced him up and down until he started breathing. The windpipe had been cut off."[12]

Relieved that he was breathing again, they proceeded to Houston. At the Rice Hotel, Tommy had porters get a stretcher to take Hank to his room. All the while, Hill said, Hank was adamant about one thing: "He wouldn't go to no doctor." The Sunday night gig at Cook's Hoedown—where Elvis played in November 1954 and a happening place still today—was important, and Toby Marshall was due to meet up with him that day, but when he arrived Hank wasn't at the Rice. Marshall, calling around to the jails and bars, tracked him down to another hotel, where he was three sheets to the wind. Hank was as close to death as he'd ever seen him, and after getting him back to the

Rice he applied his usual treatment of beers and chloral hydrate. Hank, barely coherent and sounding like a croaking toad, took the stage, and the sellout crowd cut him no break. They booed him off. The promoter, Warren Stark, tried pouring black coffee down his throat, but when he came back after intermission, he was booed again. According to a police sergeant assigned to the club that night, Hank told him backstage, "Man, they're killin' me. They're workin' me to death." Echoing Minnie Pearl, the sergeant said, "It just broke my heart."[13]

Booked to play three sets, he didn't show for the third. Back at the Rice later that night, he phoned Billie Jean and said he'd never felt sicker. But Marshall got him to the next stop, in Victoria. And it was here where he may or may not have had a mild heart attack. The details are sketchy—Marshall would later say only that Hank had been "too goofed up" to go on that night—but Marshall was compelled to write a letter addressed to Lillie. He had been coordinating his visits to Hank on the road with Lillie for some time now, at her insistence, and filing reports to her after each visit, along with travel expenses for her to reimburse. Now, however, he suggested that she hire an ambulance and go in it to Houston, clearly implying that the ambulance might be a hearse. Alarmed, Lillie decided she would fly to Texas, but couldn't get there until Wednesday when Hank would be in Dallas.

If it was a heart attack, Hank seemed to push through it. He made all his shows that week, in San Antonio on Tuesday, back at the Sportatorium in Dallas on Wednesday. Hank flew in with Warren Stark, leaving Tommy and Goldie to get there in the Caddy, and when he learned Lillie would be waiting for him, he became angry, perhaps knowing he'd have to stay clean and sober. Indeed, there were no drunken escapades, no crowds gawking at him as he lay on the floor. After the gig, he and Stark, who owned the venue that would close out the tour—the Skyline Club in Austin—went to see Bob Wills perform at a Dallas club, then hit the road for Snook, Texas, then Austin. Lillie and Toby Marshall, who apparently were pleased Hank seemed to be fine, made the trip in a separate car.[14] The tour finale at the Skyline was on Friday, December 19.

Hank, however, seemed to have caught the flu again, and facing two sets that had been contracted for, he stalled going on for an hour. The audience grew restless. And yet when he finally emerged from the wings, looking haggard and sweating heavily, he seemed to feel the need to put on a show to be remembered. His normal set in a club ran around forty-five minutes. But now his two sets each ran an hour and a half, lasting from 9 p.m. until 1 a.m., well after the club's midnight closing time. People were on their feet the whole time.

Tommy Hill, who backed him up along with the house band featuring Jimmy Day on steel guitar, said that "he put on one of the best shows I ever saw. He didn't falter a bit. He done some songs over and over. Me and Goldie have talked about it since. He sung everything he knew, even a bunch of gospel songs,"[15] which he almost never did at a honky-tonk.

He apparently was able to find some booze in Stark's office between sets, and it cooled his temperature. Marshall did not need to inject him with anything. After Hank left the stage, he met up with Lillie and Marshall. However, as the Skyline appearance would be entrenched in history as Hank's last club performance, it's not surprising that there would arise alternate versions of what transpired.

Some swore he actually had played for three hours straight, with no intermission. And according to Jim Grabowske, a local musician who claimed he was hired to play steel guitar at the Skyline that night, "You could tell he wasn't feeling well—very, very shaky on the stage. The first [set], he made it all right. He tried to make the second . . . but he was shaking too bad. And, of course, we all felt sorry for him, but then, evidently, Warren saw what was happening and came and got him."[16]

Stark, he said, called an ambulance, and Hank was taken to Brackenridge Hospital, even though "nobody was aware of it," and Hank's Cadillac was left in the Skyline parking lot for days while he was in the hospital. But this version seems highly suspect, given that Hank was scheduled to be on the *Hayride* the next night, and because Lillie would not have wanted to hang around Austin. The more plausible version is that she, Hank, and Billie Jean left after the show, with Clyde Perdue at the wheel.

When they got back to Shreveport, they checked Hank into Highland Hospital to be treated for what had turned into pneumonia. Lillie then went to see Horace Logan with a request. She had determined that Hank could no longer be left to his own devices, that he needed to leave Shreveport for the security of his real home, Montgomery. Logan was sympathetic. He'd seen Hank fall even harder since he'd left Nashville and harbored the same fears everyone else did that he couldn't survive much longer. He agreed to give Hank an open-ended leave of absence from the *Hayride*; the only condition was that Hank continue on the *Hayride* when he was again healthy.

Hank's stay in Highland Hospital was brief. The very next day, December 20, he was in his apartment, he and Billie Jean collecting the items he needed for what she thought would be no more than a week or two in Montgomery over the Christmas holiday. She apparently had no idea that Hank had no intention of returning to Shreveport, though he did tell her that when he played his next dates he might stop in Nashville and meet with Jim Denny about returning to the *Opry*. Those dates, two of them, had been booked by Bam Bamford back in November, expressly outside of the Deep South, where promoters were less likely to have heard about the recent missed and ill-performed shows. They were fairly modest gigs, a New Year's Eve show in Charleston, then on New Year's Day in Canton, Ohio. All Billie Jean knew was that they were going to spend some time away from the rat race, which Hank needed, even if Lillie's place was a rat's nest.

Though her relationship with Lillie was cold and distant, Billie Jean could be relieved that Lillie would take some of the responsibility of tending to him. But Billie would have to be vigilant that Lillie wasn't draining all of Hank's money, such was the dwindling state of their finances. Indeed, the proceeds from his recent appearances were meager, and practically eaten up by travel expenses and Hank funneling so much money to Lillie.

He had by now sold off much of his gun collection, guitars, jewelry, just about anything of value. About all he had left was around $4,000 he had received in the mail recently, royalties from Acuff-Rose. Everything else, he said, was being tied up by Audrey,[17] a convenient but specious dodge, since she had renounced any claim to his current finances beyond the $1,000 divorce settlement and her ownership of the Franklin Street property. If he could hold out, the next big infusion of funds would come early in the new year when the MGM royalties were due on his massive chain of hits, possibly several hundred thousand dollars.

Wasting no time, late that afternoon, Hank got behind the wheel of his Cadillac and Billie Jean into the passenger seat. Lillie and Clyde Perdue slid into Hank's yellow Cadillac sedan, and the two-car convoy headed for Montgomery, from where he would go straight onto the road for the New Year's gigs. On the drive to Montgomery, Hank still said nothing to Billie Jean about the woman at the boardinghouse who was a full nine months pregnant and might need to be taken to the delivery room at any minute. But he was ready to deal with it should it happen. Indeed, he may have been ready to choose this occasion to make some rather crucial decisions, one being that the marriage to Billie Jean was over.

• • •

As the newest wave of Hank fever swept through the charts, with "Jambalaya" sitting at No. 1 on Christmas and "Settin' the Woods on Fire" at No. 10 ("Half as Much," which had gone to No. 2, would be named the top country record of the year by *Cash Box*), he seemed to spike in enthusiasm. Many of the things he did seemed to be clearing the decks for the new year. For one thing, he seemed to think he was on the wagon by drinking no hard stuff, only beer.

And he was about ready to give up Billie Jean, too, which was a shock to those who had seen or read about that glittering wedding in New Orleans. Indeed, while Lillie refused to accept her as her daughter-in-law, other family members had no such reservations about Billie Jean. During the stay in Montgomery, when Hank and Billie Jean stayed in the same room he had grown up in, Lillie was so rude to her that Billie would leave the house and sit forlornly in a coffee shop. Hank did, however, take her on a side trip to visit his cousin Taft Skipper, who now lived in Georgiana with his wife, Erleen, running a general store and raising hogs. Hank seemed somewhat rejuvenated on the trip, and caused a stir among the locals who saw him drive through town in his baby blue Cadillac and gathered around him as if he were a Pied Piper.

Taft could see why Hank had fallen for Billie Jean. "Some people at church," he recalled, "said she was the purtiest girl they ever saw," and after a meal, "she got right up and cleaned off the table. Hank told me he loved Billie, and that she was a nice girl, too. He said he was gonna settle down and try to lead a decent life and that him and Billie Jean had plans to rebuild his life. The way they talked at supper that night, I believe they'd a-done it."[18]

The two couples went to Christmas Eve morning services at the East Chapman Baptist Church, and Hank gave an impromptu concert at Taft's general store, singing "Kaw-Liga," "Jambalaya," and a new song he'd made a demo of in Shreveport, "The Log Train," a sentimental journey back to childhood riding the trains driven by Lon, whom he wanted to visit and sing for on Christmas Day.

Hank and Billie Jean made the drive to McWilliams, but Lon wasn't at his simple white bungalow nearby one of Hank's early schoolhouses, having gone with his wife, Ola, and their daughter, Leila, to his in-laws' home in Selma. Disappointed, Hank could only pen a note to leave for Lon, along with a gold cigarette lighter for him and a five-pound box of chocolates for the girls.

One of those old acquaintances he caught up with in the backwoods was a woman he used to know in McWilliams who was a neighbor of Lon's, Edna Curry Lamkin, who recalled that Hank "looked marvelous. He was feeling good, too. [But] I believe Hank had a premonition that 'time was running out' on him, and that, unconsciously, he had come to tell us all goodbye."[19] He also dropped in on his aunt Bertha, Lon's sister, in Pine Apple and some local honky-tonks where he had cut his teeth.

After motoring back to Montgomery, he and Billie Jean went with Taft and Erleen to the Blue-Gray Classic, the college football "North versus South" all-star game played each Christmas Day in the Cramton Bowl, a game that for years after was kept segregated by the promoter, the Montgomery Lions Club. It was a cold, blustery day, and Hank couldn't sit long in the stands and left early, heading back to the boardinghouse. In fact, he had been feeling bad the whole trip. Walking across Taft's hog farm one morning, he suddenly reached for his chest and struggled for breath. "He said he thought he had a touch of the asthma," Taft would recall.[20]

The reverie of padding through the muddy backwoods could not hide the cold reality that he and his life were falling apart. Brack Schuffert, on one of his visits to Hank at the boardinghouse, remembered that Hank was "lying in bed with his clothes on. He was sick in bed and Doctor Stokes [Lillie's doctor] had come out. He had a fever. Doctor Stokes tried to get him in the hospital, but he wouldn't go."[21] Billie Jean would say of those days, "He couldn't even sleep in bed then, the pain was so bad."[22] And, despite Hank's tender rhapsodies about Billie Jean to the Skippers, their marriage was another cold reality.

Hank might have tired of the beautiful young thing who laid the law down to him and kept pouring his goodies down the drain. Their fights had become as raucous as Hank's dust-ups with Audrey, and almost as physical. One witness to this was Irella Beach, the wife of Freddy Beach, one of Hank's earliest Drifting Cowboys in Montgomery. She said Hank and Billie were at a bar one night when Hank got up on the bar top and began dancing. As Billie pulled at him, Hank suddenly "hit Billie in the face 'cause she was trying to get him to quit. He was sloppy drunk, and she took off home. She said, 'Ain't no man gonna beat on me,' and she left."[23]

Lillie, working in tandem with Audrey, might have drummed it into him that Billie Jean was impeding his progress and health. Maybe Hank associated her with small-time life now that he had Nashville back in his sights. Maybe she was just too little-girl for him. Or maybe Audrey had thrown him a bone. Over Christmas, Audrey claimed later on, Hank called and asked her if he could come back, and she said yes—a contention that, like many others, was quite convenient and unprovable. Whatever was going on, Oscar Davis, who still spent time with Hank in his role as producer and emcee of the *Hayride* shows, said that Hank was clinging to a storybook ending, with the only family he considered to be genuine.

Audrey and Randall were on his mind all the time in 1952, with misty effects, while he seemed emotionally detached from Billie Jean. He ran into his cousin M. C. Jarrett in Montgomery, who asked him if he had a band. "All I got is a wife and a git-tar," he said dryly, "and I wish I only had the git-tar."[24] When Hank had spoken with Jimmie Rodgers's widow, Carrie, during the holiday, he was already referring to his "last marriage" being over, meaning the one to Billie Jean. His private conversations now were streaked with casual asides about "going back to Audrey." Billy Walker recalled that

> he told me he'd already made the deal to go back to the Opry in February. He said he was going to get rid of Billie Jean and try to get Audrey back and get his life straightened out. He told me that he knew he was in bad shape and he wanted to get away from this doctor whose hold on him was drugs. . . . I think he had been physically attracted to Billie Jean, but he wanted to go home. He told me he could never love no one but Audrey.[25]

Lycrecia Williams, who was by then old enough to understand the disordered yin and yang of the relationship between her mother and ex-stepfather, said that in the last days of 1952, "I remember Mother coming into the back room and telling Miss Ragland that Daddy was coming home, and she wanted them to get the house ready."[26]

. . .

Fred Rose, of course, had planned for him to reclaim his Nashville pedigree all along, and according to what Wesley Rose and several *Opry* executives claimed after Hank's death, it had actually been agreed that Hank would return to the Ryman stage on February 3, though nothing to that effect was written on paper. Hank, believing his penance done, seemed sure of it. "I'll be back with you before you know it," he chirped to Ray Price, who had attended the Sporta-torium show in Dallas.[27]

Toby Marshall wasn't chirping. He was worried that Hank might get *too* well to need his "help." On December 28, Lillie wired Mar-shall that she thought Hank was well enough to make the long New Year's trip alone, a somewhat odd assumption about a man still perched on the edge. That Marshall read into this that the gravy train might be over was obvious by his reaction. He promptly dashed off a two-page letter to Hank, which he would never read. In it, Mar-shall seemed to plead and do a little buttering up. "Boy, I am tickled and pleased as can be [to] know that you feel good," he began. "You will really put on a top-flight performance." Then, getting to the point, he wrote:

There is only one thing I ask, Hank, [that] you morally owe to yourself, me, and your public. <u>If you run into trouble call me</u>. . . . There is nothing wrong with an old boy asking for help when he is sick. And no matter where you are or what the circum-stances might be, I'll manage to get there. And you know I can help you. . . . Sorta miss worrying about you, though, for 18–20 hours a day several days running.[28]

He then assured Hank that he had personally seen to it that an Oklahoma City promoter, Venita Cravens, was offering him a six-show engagement at the city's auditorium, the first on February 22, and though this probably seemed like small potatoes to Hank, Marshall insisted, "This is the sort of thing you need, rather than beer joints and honky tonks, to get you back on top where you belong. . . . If you are going back to the Opry, you need some top-flight bookings to help things along." Marshall then tried to play on his attachment to Lillie. "I sincerely hope your mother recovered. She was really very sick when you [were] at Austin. . . . She is a very wonderful, understanding person." He ended: "Your mother said in her wire that I would 'hear' from you later. I certainly hope you do write me, Hank, or call, or something. Excuse the scrawl—and good luck, Toby."

Written on the bottom was his contact information: "Toby Marshall, M.D., 1333-A NE 19th St., Oklahoma City, Okla, ph: Jackson 53107—home, Jackson 8-2121—Doctor's Bureau (they always know where I am)."

He also wired Lillie back, imploring, "If you feel my presence necessary there for 31st and First engagements imperative, I know immediately to make arrangements here [and will] proceed to Charleston." He even had his reservations made. Grifting motives aside, Marshall's passive-aggressive messages to Hank and Lillie strongly dissented from the rosy optimism that preceded Hank's New Year's trek.[29] And he was not alone. In fact, many who saw Hank that winter remember him in need of help more than ever.

Despite Lillie's diagnosis, he was becoming sicker by the day, living in a kind of altered state, expressing great faith about his future while he himself, and many others around him, were having premonitions about him dying. To Hank Williams Jr., who as Randall Williams did not see his father during those end times but would learn through the years about them, his namesake was, he said, "haunted by his genius [and] his own demons" and became "a parody of himself" as his friends and family "stood by unable or unwilling to help." When Hank Jr. would learn about the three marriages to Billie Jean, he would shake his head and say, accurately, that it was "pathetic."[30]

On December 29, one day after what was his last-ever public appearance, at the annual charity banquet by the American Federation of Musicians local 479 at the Elite Cafe in Montgomery, which he attended with Billie Jean, they had another big fight. Hank had bought a toy train set for Randall, and Billie Jean made a stink about it, perhaps because of the price or because she didn't want Hank to visit Audrey in Nashville to personally give it to his son. What happened next, according to Lillie and Hank's cousin Marie McNeil, who was at the house at the time, was that Hank told Billie Jean they were through. As Irene Williams also told it later, Hank was so steamed that Billie Jean seemed not to care about his son that he suddenly decided that their marriage was "illegal," and upon hearing this Billie became livid and threatened to leave. The Williams family version is that Hank beat her to the punch and, just before leaving for Charleston, put her on a plane back to Shreveport. The story went on that Billie Jean was so upset about the breakup that she took some of Hank's pills and became violently ill.

However, based on subsequent events, this almost surely did not happen, nor did it make much sense, since Hank of course knew about the chancy status of the marriage when they ran off to Minden, at his directive. But it did bolster the family's position, and weaken Billie's, and in the years to come this would matter greatly to each side. Granted, Hank was just devious enough to have held the marriage card in his pocket for when he could use it to his advantage. It was also evident that he wanted to see the birth of his next child, or if not, to hold it without keeping the secret anymore, and Billie Jean would get in the way of that. And if he got back with Audrey, he would surely need to end the marriage. Indeed, it seemed probative that Audrey, on New Year's Eve, would be partying with Bam Bamford's wife, Maxine, in Nashville while Bam would be en route to the shows he had booked for Hank.

Even so, Billie Jean would never agree to any suggestion that Hank had rid himself of her. She did admit to taking a handful of Hank's pills, but maintained that Lillie had given them to her, and "they made me groggy and crazy as a bat. I vomited for two hours and after that felt as if I was in a drunken stupor."[31] But not only was there never a breakup; she insisted that she planned to travel to

West Virginia and Ohio with Hank, until the bad weather forecasts led Hank to advise her to go back to Shreveport to spend New Year's with her parents and brothers. She said she and Hank had made plans to meet back in Montgomery on January 3, and Hank, looking ahead, told her, "Hey, baby, let's us move to Nashville and buy one of them big houses."[32]

His most famous contemporaries—Minnie Pearl, Kitty Wells, June Carter, Roy Acuff, Ernie Tubb, Ray Price, Lefty Frizzell, Claude King—knew all too well of his flaws and madness, but to them he never abated as the best in the business. Nor was he anything less than an idol to the sprouting crop of country stars he had inspired.

George Jones, who was then twenty-one, his budding career interrupted by a hitch in the marines, once recalled the reaction he had when he met Hank. "I just stared," then "I couldn't think or eat nothin' unless it was Hank Williams, and I couldn't wait for his next record to come out. He had to be, really, the greatest."[33]

That was the only Hank Williams many would ever know. At that last show, Sunday night the twenty-eighth, at the Elite Cafe banquet for the local musicians union, the *Alabama Journal* reported two days later, without mentioning his name at first, "the boy who once worked here for eleven dollars" was now "a thin, tired looking ex-country boy with a guitar." Yet he had gotten up "and sang (or howled) a number of his tunes that started out to be hillbilly and ended up as pop numbers," including "Jambalaya (On the Bayou)," "Cold, Cold Heart," "You Win Again," and 'Lonesome Blues." Then, it concluded, "there was thunderous applause as he went back to his steak. He was, of course, Hank Williams."

A photo taken of him that night showed him to be ostensibly healthy and happy. He wore that wry Hank grin, his cheeks fuller than normal, his hair slicked back, looking ready for bear. And once again, the road lay ahead.

24

✤ ✤ ✤ ✤ ✤ ✤ ✤

THEN CAME
THAT FATEFUL DAY

Hiram "Hank" Williams, old before his time and ill in countless ways, was by all measures in no condition to travel long distances in bone-chilling, rainy, blustery weather. He may have wanted to go just as much to get away from the madness in Montgomery, a constant urge whenever he spent any time there. But even if the concert dates over the New Year's holiday were of critical importance— which they weren't—looking back, because no one thought to talk him out of that last ride, or at least make sure he wouldn't be traveling essentially alone in bone-freezing weather, his family and friends *did* let him down. Indeed, after receiving Toby Marshall's telegram, Lillie's only adjustment wasn't to reconsider her feeling that Hank was well enough to travel alone but rather to give Marshall instructions to be in Charleston with his black bag well stocked. This despite telling Marshall that Hank recently had a "highly upsetting emotional incident" that sent him back to the bottle.[1]

Hank's last full day in Montgomery, Monday, December 29, 1952, was especially maudlin. Needing to go to church, an urge he rarely felt, he went to the St. Jude's Hospital chapel, to pray with the nuns. "Ol' Hank needs to straighten up some things with the Man," Billie Jean said he told her.[2] He was even more melancholy when he came into his cousin Marie McNeil's room and handed her forty dollars, which he wanted used to help pay the doctor who would deliver Bobbie Jett's baby. As he left the room, Marie said, Hank told her, "Ol' Hank's not gonna be with you another Christmas. I'm closer to the Lord than I've ever been in my life." Billie Jean recalled that Hank tossed and turned in bed all that night, the pain in his back excruciating. At one point, he leaped out of bed and, she recalled, started shadowboxing, mimicking throwing punches at an invisible target. Startled, she asked, "Hank, what in the world is the matter with you?"

"Every time I close my eyes," he said, echoing what he'd told newspaperman H. B. Teeter a year before, "I see Jesus comin' down the road. He's comin' after ol' Hank."[3]

None of these mawkish expressions seemed to alarm them, having heard variations of the theme before. The next morning, his travel plans still in limbo, he chartered a flight to Charleston for early afternoon. But because of the horrendous weather—a snowstorm had blanketed Montgomery, one of the few to ever hit the city—he'd had to go about hiring a driver days before. Hank could have pulled out of one or both concerts, but because of his reputation for missing shows he couldn't afford more bad publicity. He insisted on going, and had convinced Don Helms on the phone to play at both dates. Helms, with Jerry Rivers, was now in Ray Price's band, and Ray was scheduled to play in Cleveland a day earlier, so Helms signed on to meet up with Hank in Canton, for a $200 payday, and would hitch a ride out with Bam Bamford.

Seeking a driver, Hank first asked Brack Schuffert, but Brack couldn't miss work at Hormel Meats. An old standby in the Driftin' Cowboys, "Beanpole" Boling, was working at a Montgomery cab company, but he too was busy. He then went over to the Lee Street Taxi storefront and asked the owner, Dan Carr, who'd gotten him drivers before, if he could spare someone. Carr recommended his son, Charles, a thin, sandy-haired, eighteen-year-old freshman at Auburn University who was home for the holidays. He had once driven Hank, who thought Charles rode the gas pedal a little hard, but then that was how Hank himself liked to drive. So Charles Carr it was, at $400 for the four-day round-trip.

Carr backed up Billie Jean when he confirmed she was still indeed in Montgomery and far from being disowned by Hank. Right up until he drove away, Carr said, she was asking Hank if she could go with him, but Hank said no. Billie Jean would recall that farewell with more melancholy:

> Hank was in the car. I was back in my room putting my makeup on. And he came back into the room, came up behind me and kissed me on the cheek. He sat down on the edge of the bed. He just looked at me, not saying a word. I stood in front of the mirror, my back to him, and to me he looked like he was already dead. And I asked him if somethin' was botherin' him. And he said, "No, baby, I just wanted to look at you one more time."[4]

• • •

At around 11:30 a.m. Wednesday, Hank and Carr loaded up his baby blue '52 Cadillac convertible. Hank laid his guitar on the back seat and stowed in the trunk a couple of others, along with several stage suits and other things he would need. He was wearing dark blue serge pants and jacket, a white shirt, black tie, navy blue overcoat, white felt cowboy hat, and blue suede shoes. With his pearl-handled .45 tucked in his coat pocket, Hank climbed into his accustomed travel quarters, the well-used back seat of the Caddy. As Carr pulled away, Hank told him to wait and went back in the house, changing into white cowboy boots. Still hoping the plane would be allowed to take off, he had Carr buzz by the airport, but with all flights canceled well into the day, Hank settled in, his back already hurting, for what would be hours on the road.

Before heading out of the city, though, there were some loose ends to tie up. Needing a shot of something for the road, he had Carr stop by a hotel where he'd heard there was a convention of construction contractors going on. Ambling into the ballroom where people stared, their mouths agape, he helped himself to some drinks and left. He then swung by Doc Stokes's office. He was going to deliver Bobbie's child, and Hank also gave him forty dollars, then asked Stokes if he could give him a shot of morphine. Stokes, smelling liquor on his breath, refused.

Hank then tried one of the doctors he'd gone to before with Toby Marshall's card and prescriptions, and the doctor, identified in one account only as a man named Black, shot him up with morphine. Hank walked out, his legs wobbly but feeling fine. He also had several chloral hydrate tables in his pocket, after using the last prescription he had left from Toby Marshall's stash.

Carr then made two more stops, first at a gas station to change a tire, and even the guy who changed it, Cecil Jackson, would enjoy *his* fame for entering the coming drama. Hank then stopped at the Hollywood Drive-In diner and bought some sandwiches, coffee, and a six-pack of Falstaff beer. *Now* he could leave. At around five o'clock, darkness had thrown a veil over the sky and the snow. The Caddy turned onto Highway 31 and headed northbound.

· · ·

The itinerary was to cover nearly a thousand miles, from Montgomery to Charleston to Canton. Posters were printed for the appearances, the one for the Canton show featuring Hank's signature saying "If the good Lord's willing, and the creek don't rise . . . I'll see you at Canton Memorial Auditorium New Year's Day 1953." As it happened, an *Opry* troupe was also playing in Canton on New Year's Day, starring Carl Smith and the Carter Sisters. And Bamford was quite willing to take a few liberties, plastering the poster for Hank's show with the words GRAND OLE OPRY PRESENTS IN PERSON. . . . The show would be the same at both engagements, an early set—8 p.m.

in Charleston, 3 p.m. in Canton—followed by late shows at 10:30 and 5:30, respectively.

Hank would headline on an "All-Star" bill with the cornpone comedy team Homer and Jethro, the Webb Sisters, Alabama warbler Autry Inman, who had played bass in Cowboy Copas's band, and Harold Franklin "Hawkshaw" Hawkins. Most of the acts would play behind Hank, with Helms, and be joined by Bill Monroe's fiddler, Red Taylor.

Because Hank had gotten out of Montgomery late, he decided to stay the night in Birmingham, raising some hell as usual. When Carr parked illegally in front of the posh Tutwiler Hotel, a cop ticketed him and, not moved when Carr told him who was in the back seat, shooed him away. They then booked two rooms at the Redmont, where three women recognized Hank within minutes and spent the next hour in his room. Carr and Hank ordered room service and after a good night's sleep were off early the next morning, New Year's Eve day. They made a stop in Fort Payne, where Hank bought a bottle of bourbon, and made it to Chattanooga by lunchtime and ate in a diner. Hank dropped a dime in the box and played Tony Bennett's cover of "Cold, Cold Heart," then left a $50 bill for the waitress, saying, "Here's the biggest tip you ever got."

By 1 p.m. they were in Knoxville, still three hundred miles from Charleston. He had Carr check on flights. There was one at 3:30 that would get there by 6. Hank bought two tickets, deciding to keep Carr along for company. During the ride up, Hank had gotten along well with the kid; they had sung to keep the boredom away, and he liked the kid's spunk. The Caddy would be left in the airport parking lot until they came back on the return trip.

With time before the flight, Hank found his way to St. Mary's Hospital, where, in mysterious circumstances Carr never explained, he was able to have a doctor give him another morphine shot. The plane boarded and took off on time. But the weather was rough, and the plane was ordered to turn back to Knoxville, landing at 6 p.m. By now, as Carr learned when he phoned Lillie, the two Charleston shows had been canceled due to the storm. Most of the performers were able to navigate the icy roads and get to the theater just as it was being boarded up. Bam Bamford, arriving with Don Helms, was particularly peeved, knowing he'd be refunding two sellout houses of 4,000 people. Bam instructed all of them to get going to Canton for the next night's shows. One other interested party had made it to Charleston as well—Toby Marshall, who called Lillie for his marching orders.

Meanwhile, stuck back in Knoxville, Carr and a dog-tired Hank checked into the Andrew Johnson Hotel. Hank, who had drained the bourbon, could barely stand, and two porters all but carried him to his room. One of them, Emmanuel Martin, recalled that Hank "was very much alive. I talked to him coming in, talked to him coming out, and I remember he made one little statement, 'When you drink like this, this is the price you gotta pay.' "[5] Carr ordered two room service steaks, but Hank was laid out on his bed, kept awake only because he developed nagging hiccups that seemed to approach convulsions. Concerned, Carr also called Lillie again, who proceeded to call Marshall to tell him where Hank was. Marshall then phoned Carr with instructions to have the front desk summon a doctor. Minutes later, Dr. Paul Cardwell rushed to the hotel and, possibly having conferred by phone with Marshall, injected Hank with two more morphine shots along with vitamin B-12. Brought up to speed, Marshall informed Carr not to stay overnight at the hotel and to get back on the road to Canton, and whatever he did, keep Hank away from the sauce.

From this point on, mysteries abound that have never been solved, mysteries with plenty of clues but a lot of doubt. Some have, through the years, advanced the theory that when two porters carted Hank down to the Cadillac at around 10:45 p.m. he was already dead, although the hotel manager would offer later that Hank was still alive albeit looking "groggy." And Carr, for his part, later noted, "If he was dead, it was a dead man walking around when we stopped later."[6]

Over the next eight hours, as Hank sat almost silent in the convertible, which even with the heater blasting was as cold as a meat locker, nobody apparently tried to speak with or check on him, nor heard a peep from him in the back seat. Carr would later say Hank had spent time writing songs and chugging some beer, and noted that the last song they sang was Red Foley's "Midnight," a song that may have matched the mood he was in as he sang for the last time:

> *Midnight, I lie in bed awake and stare at nothing at all*
> *Wonderin', wonderin' why you don't care, wishing you'd call*

• • •

Ensuing police reports and investigations only served to sow doubt and confusion, keeping the Hank legend appropriately, and eternally, necromantic, aptly bathed in a dark, cold, pitch-black midnight.

Charles Carr, who should have known all there was to know, didn't make the enigma any clearer. From what is known, Carr headed through Rutledge Pike toward the West Virginia border, but just before the new year rang in, exhausted, he nearly collided head-on with a highway patrol car while trying to pass a truck in Blaine, notably the hometown of Roy Acuff and Carl Smith. A rookie cop, Swann H. Kitts, was riding with a veteran sheriff, J. N. Antrican, in the car, and after pulling the Caddy over, Kitts later testified, he saw a lifeless-looking man, his collar and hat covering his face, slumped across the back seat, seemingly asleep, and asked Carr if something was wrong with the passenger.

"No," he said, acting very nervous, "he's been drinking six beers and the doctor gave him a sedative to make him sleep."

"That guy looks dead," noted Kitts, who later ventured that he thought the "pale and blue looking" man *was* dead but, inexplicably, did not check his pulse or try to rouse him.

Neither did Carr say who it was, possibly guilty he had not followed Marshall's orders to keep Hank dry. Even more oddly, the sheriff never got out to add his expertise. Adding to the mystery,

Kitts would also recall seeing in the passenger seat a "serviceman" in uniform. Carr disputed this later, as well as the testimony of the manager at the Andrew Johnson, who said that he had arranged for Carr to ride with a relief driver in case he grew too tired, and that the driver wore a chauffeur's uniform and cap.[7] Rather than giving him a ticket, Kitts had Carr follow the police car to a magistrate in Rutledge, who fined Carr twenty-five dollars. He paid out of his pocket—even as, incredibly, a man that a police officer believed was dead was simply left in the back seat outside, still unchecked.

By now, it was 1 a.m., the new year having come during this bizarre interlude, which was nowhere near over. In no mood to celebrate, Carr hit Highway 19, crossed into West Virginia, and stopped at a gas station in Bluefield to fill up. It was around 4:30 now. He asked the attendant if he knew where a relief driver could be found and was directed to a diner, the Doughboy Lunch Restaurant. Here, Carr claimed later, Hank got out and stretched his legs. "I asked him if he wanted a sandwich or something," Carr recalled. "And he said, 'No, I just want to get some sleep.' I don't know if that's the last thing he said. But it's the last thing I remember him telling me."[8]

Carr said Hank did not go in the diner, though waitress Hazel Wells said Hank did come in, said who he was, and also inquired about a relief driver. Carr found a thirty-seven-year-old local cabbie, Don Howard Surface, who was in a booth having breakfast and agreed to take over the driving through the dangerous mountain roads of the Appalachians, in exchange for an unknown sum and bus fare back to Bluefield. Carr would also say that before they left the town, Hank awoke and—contradicting his assertion that Hank had already spoken his last words to him—wanted to find a doctor to give him another shot of morphine, but at that hour it was impossible, and they pushed off again.

Surface was still there when the Caddy stopped for coffee and sandwiches somewhere in Princeton, West Virginia at around 6 a.m. It was still dark and freezing, and Hank was out cold. Carr said Surface left to go back home here, but it was later determined Surface was still at the wheel when they stopped in Oak Hill, in Fayette County, a half hour later to fill up again and get some grub at the Skyline Diner. Only now did Charles Carr think it necessary to pay much attention to the man in the back seat, and only because the blanket Hank had wrapped around himself had fallen off. He was lying still on the seat in a kind of coffin pose, on his back, arms folded across his chest, eyes closed.

As Carr reached back to pull the blanket over him, he touched one of Hank's hands. It felt cold as a stone and stiff. As Carr would put it, "I felt a little unnatural resistance from his arm." Panicking, Carr rushed into the restaurant—it's unknown whether Surface, if he was still there, came inside with him—and came back out with an older man who took a look at Hank and summed up the situation with classic understatement.

"I think you got a problem," he said.[9]

Police reports would indicate that Carr and Surface, if he was there, knowing they had a famous corpse in the back and needing to get it to a hospital, asked for directions to one at Burdette's Pure Oil gas station. Carr asked the owner, Peter Burdette, to call the local police station and tell them a dead man had been driven into his place. Within minutes, a police car arrived, and Officer Orris Stamey confirmed Hank was dead. His body was still somewhat warm, but his extremities were numbed by rigor mortis. Stamey then had Carr and Surface follow him to Oak Hill Hospital. Once there, Carr raced into the emergency room. "I ran in and explained my situation to the two interns," he recalled. "They came out and looked at Hank and said, 'He's dead.' I asked 'em, 'Can't you do something to revive him?' One of them looked at me and said, 'No, he's just dead.'"[10]

The orderlies pulled Hank's body from the car, lifted him by his armpits, and toted him inside. He was laid out on a stretcher, and another intern, Diego Nunnari, listed the time of death at 7 a.m., though Nunnari estimated that Hank had died between two and four hours before that. Carr, walking around in a daze, couldn't face calling Lillie. Instead, he called his father, who told him he had to call Lillie.

No doubt gulping hard, Carr did, and was floored when her reaction was nothing like a mother's anguish over losing a son; rather, she was all business. "Don't let anything happen to the car" were her first words when Carr had finished telling what happened, apparently thinking that if the car was impounded by the authorities, it might never be returned, and possibly could offer incriminating evidence of what Hank was doing to himself, something Lillie wanted never to become public knowledge. Lillie also sent a telegram at 10:33 a.m. to Irene in Virginia, which read perfunctorily, "Come at once. Hank is dead. Mother."[11] As it happened, eerily, Irene had had another premonition during the night that her brother was dead, and had even packed a suitcase so she could go to Montgomery for his funeral.[12]

Toby Marshall, after Lillie called him in Charleston, was ashen but probably not completely shocked. He hopped a bus and arrived in Oak Hill early the next day. By then, Hank's body had been removed to the Tyree Funeral Home. Lillie was already in town, having arrived with Carr's father, flying to Roanoke because the Charleston airport was still closed, then taking a cab. Lillie didn't go right to the funeral parlor; instead, she went to the police station to find out what they knew of Hank's death and the belongings in the car. She was armed with legal papers saying she was his next of kin, and others showing that Billie Jean's belated divorce from Harrison Eshlimar invalidated her marriage to Hank, and she therefore was *not* Hank's next of kin, with no right to his remains and belongings.

"Mrs. Stone made all the arrangements," Joe Tyree, who ran the funeral parlor, said. "She chose a Batesville casket with silver finish and white interior. She went out to his car and chose one of his white cowboy outfits to bury him in."

Tyree recalled that she was a "nice, stately-looking woman, very pleasant and composed. She held her grief."[13]

. . .

Lillie did not bother to call Billie Jean, who had only been home a few hours, at her parents' house in Shreveport that New Year's Eve. She was awakened by the phone at around 8 a.m. As Billie Jean would recall, "The operator asked for Sergeant Jones. I said, "'Daddy, the call is from West Virginia, so Hank must be in trouble.' Usually he would call my dad, if he was stopped for speeding or something. I went and laid back down and I heard him talking to Hank, but it was the chauffeur. . . . My daddy said, 'Oh Lord.' . . . He held me and said Hank was dead, and I was screaming and crying. I said, 'Don't let them touch him. He often pretends he's asleep.' I thought they were going to bury him alive."[14] She and her father made arrangements to travel to Oak Hill early the next morning, with Billie Jean assuming she would claim Hank's s body and bring it back to Montgomery on January 2.

Audrey Williams, who her daughter, Lycrecia, said "was expecting Daddy home soon,"[15] was still sleeping after her New Year's Eve partying with Maxine Bamford when she was awakened in Nashville around the same time by a phone call from a friend who'd gotten the news about Hank. Her housekeeper, Audrey Ragland, would recall, "Mrs. Williams told me he was dead. I could not believe it, but she said, 'Yes, Hank is dead.' Then she went all to pieces."[16]

Not far away, Fred Rose was awakened by a call from another industry man who'd gotten early word of the tragedy, though Wesley Rose's story in future years that his father called him "at 3 or 4 a.m." to break it to him was clearly wrong. "Sit down," he said his father told him, "or this might knock you down. Hank died tonight. Now don't fall all to pieces."[17] Nashville seemed to be paralyzed as more and more people heard the news, and at the *Opry*, they began putting together a tribute to the reprobate who had been fired to air in place of the regular show the next Saturday.

Frank Walker also got the news from Fred. Not knowing what to do, he sat down and wrote an open letter to "Hank Williams, c/o Songwriter; Paradise," which read: "I don't know much about the circumstances and it really doesn't matter, does it? What does mat-

ter though is that the World is ever so much better for the fact that
you have lived with us, even for such a short time."[18] Walker would
run the letter on the back of the memorial album of Hank songs
MGM would soon rush out.

When Bam Bamford arrived at the theater in Canton later that
morning, he called home, and Maxine, crying hysterically, broke the
news to him. Cut to his knees, Bamford, who had already given back
refunds on the two shows in Charleston, had to straighten up and
save these two. People began to gather at the Memorial Auditorium
for the 3 p.m. performance, not yet aware that Hank was dead. Don
Helms, who had gotten into Canton at 5 a.m. with Autry Inman,
went to the auditorium, where, he would recall, Bam met him at the
dressing room door.

"Brace yourself," he said. "Hank died on the way here."

Backstage, Helms broke it to Jerry Rivers; the latter would say it
was "shocking but not unbelievable. . . . It came almost inevitably as
the closing chapter."

Bamford chose not to inform the audience, lest they want their
money back right away. After the curtain was raised, the emcee,
local disk jockey Cliff Rodgers, grimly walked to center stage and,
rather than trying to rouse the crowd, said quietly, "Ladies and gentlemen, I've been in show business almost twenty years, and I've
been called upon to do many difficult things in front of an audience,
but today I'm about to perform the most difficult task I have ever
done. This morning on the way to Canton to do this show, Hank
Williams died in his car." There was a murmur, then some nervous
laughter by people assuming it was a rib about Hank's habit of missing shows. Rodgers went on, "Ladies and gentlemen, this in no joke.
Hank Williams is dead."[19]

Then the lights dimmed, a single spotlight was shined on the curtains, and Hawkshaw Hawkins—who would also die prematurely, in
the 1963 plane crash that killed Patsy Cline and Cowboy Copas—
began to mournfully croon "I Saw the Light." When it was clear it
was no joke, the entire house began to join in, many in tears. The

show went on, the *Canton Repository* writing the next day, "That was the way he would have wanted it."

. . .

In Oak Hill, Hank's body reposed at the Tyree Funeral Home, but had not yet been embalmed. An autopsy remained to be done, but because there was a recent welt on Hank's forehead, an inquest was ordered by the Fayette County prosecutor, Howard Carson, who quickly assembled a panel of six local citizens to serve as the coroner's jury. Officers Janney and Stamey were called into the second-floor room where Hank's naked corpse lay on a table under a sheet, to be asked questions about what had happened; oddly, Swann Kitts was not summoned. Charles Carr and Don Surface were also called. Two state troopers stood guard as a pathologist from Beckley Hospital, Ivan Malinin, and county coroner J. B. Thompson went about the autopsy. One of the citizens on the panel would remember, "Howard Janney took us upstairs to where the body was lying under a sheet. We spent about 15 minutes looking at it, and couldn't see anything wrong at all, just that he was unhealthy-looking. He was very, very skinny. I don't mean to be disrespectful, but there was sort of a comic feel about being there, because we didn't really know what we were doing."[20]

For Charles Carr, it was anything but comical. Carr had reason to be nervous, and not just because of the bruise on Hank's head, which was actually quite common for Hank given the scrapes he got into. Carr's account of Hank stretching his legs in Bluefield may have been meant to blunt his inability to check on his passenger for so many hours and the snail's pace of the journey, which never would have gotten Hank to Canton in time and would put the heat on Carr.

It was a particularly gruesome six hours in that airless room, and as blood and organ samples were taken from the body and readied to be sent to Charleston for analysis, several people nearly passed out. The body itself was enough to sicken an observer; looking at it unclothed, one could see why he was so ill. A ghastly sight, Hank's bones and ribs poked through his pale, scaly skin. His arms were covered with needlemarks, and the clumping of scar tissue and scabbing was so thick that Malinin had a hard time finding a vein he could puncture with a needle to draw blood.

Over the next eight days, the cause of Hank's death remained undetermined as labs analyzed the blood and organ samples. But it was assumed that he didn't just up and die, that he had been slowly killing himself for months, years. Billie Jean, to whom he had predicted Jesus was about to come for him on the road, would provide the coda of his life and death years later when she mused, "They always said he died too young, but he was much older than his years. And he was in too much pain to live."[21]

· · ·

Around the country, word of mouth had almost immediately begun to spread. For many in the country niche, it felt like a deep personal loss. George Jones, who was a young serviceman at the time, recalled that Hank "had been my biggest musical influence. By that thinking you could say he was the biggest part of my life at that time. That's how personally I took him and his songs. . . . I lay there and bawled."[22]

At around 1 p.m., the Associated Press learned of Hank's death and sent the news out on its ticker, and word broke on the radio. Among those on the air at the time was Nelson King on WCKY in Indianapolis. He, of course, had been given a writing credit by Hank on "There'll Be No Teardrops Tonight" and may have been Hank's closest ally on the radio. King stoically delivered a five-minute soliloquy as he read the bulletin about Hank. He then played Hank's "I'm Bound for That Promised Land."

By the next morning, newspapers across the country had picked up the AP story. After having ignored him, save for a few scattered mentions when he was on TV or the radio, the *New York Times* gave him a grudging two-paragraph item with a headline about the late "King of the Hillbillies" on page 4. However, in Nashville, embla-

zoned across page 1 of the *Tennessean* was the headline HANK WIL-
LIAMS DIES IN AUTO. A separate death notice began: "It is a tragic fact
that Mr. Hank Williams was never able to bring to his own life the
satisfaction that he gave to so many others. . . . For all [his successes],
he was never at peace with himself." H. B. Teeter could now write
about Hank's "premonition of death" the year before. In Montgomery, meanwhile, the loss was like family; the *Advertiser* front page
blared HANK DEAD AT AGE 29. Everyone knew who that was.

In Knoxville, the first rippling of doubt about where and when it
happened appeared that same day in a *Journal* article headlined MYS-
TERY SHROUDS DEATH OF SINGER HANK WILLIAMS, citing Swann Kitts's
statement that Hank had "looked dead" when he saw him. The
"mystery" would soon become a subtheme. In Nashville, sad as they
were over at the *Grand Ole Opry*, it was an awkward situation. The
Opry hadn't seen him since August 11 when he came in to cash that
$300 check. But now they embraced him, even if they had to embel-
lish a wee bit—Jim Denny falsely insisting that Hank would have
appeared on the *Opry* show in Canton on New Year's Day (years
later Denny would have the *Opry* poster for that show doctored so
that Hank's name was on it).

· · ·

When Billie Jean arrived by plane in Oak Hill on Friday morning
with her father and brother, she burst into Tyree's Funeral Parlor and
screamed, "Where is my baby, if I can only kiss him, I can breathe
life back into him!" She had to be led out of the room to regain some
composure. When she did, Billie Jean's thoughts, like Lillie's, were
on the car. As she would later say, "[Lillie] had hid the car from me,
taken all his possessions from his body, his billfold, his rings, everything personal, all the money that he had."[23]

Worse, Lillie had all but abrogated Billie's rights as Hank's widow.
Her request to be allowed to take the body back to Montgomery was
summarily rejected by the authorities, who gave all rights to Lillie.
These were the first steps in what would be a decades-long cam-

paign by the Williams family, in conjunction with Audrey, to render Billie Jean irrelevant, even invisible, a rank outsider. In the face of this blatant favoritism, Joe Tyree would swear later that he acted evenhandedly, because "neither the mother nor the wife ever saw the body while it was here."[24] But that seems far-fetched, since Lillie had made sure that when Hank was embalmed and put in a casket for the ride home, he was dressed in his dazzling white cowboy suit.

Also in Oak Hill that morning was Toby Marshall, who like Lillie seemed to be thinking of covering up things. Neither was he overly broken up. When he arrived in Montgomery for the funeral, he had a bill prepared for Lille, totaling $736.39 for his travel expenses and his fee for prescribing some of the last shots that helped stop Hank Williams's heart.[25] Lillie ignored it. With Hank gone, she had no use for Marshall. He then tried to stick Billie Jean with the same bill.

In truth, Lillie really didn't hide the car from Billie Jean, and she couldn't do much about keeping it from the prying eyes and hands of strangers. When police searched it, they found Hank's gun and felt hat on the floor along with several unopened beer cans and notebook pages, one with freshly written lyrics for a song that clearly came from the most tortured crevice in his broken soul, where he was still obsessed with the failure of his union with Audrey. The only lines he had gotten through read:

We met we lived and dear we loved, then came that fatal daylight
The love that fades far away
Tonight we both are all alone and here's all I can say
I love you still and always will, but that's the price we have to pay

These artifacts were of no value to investigators, and most were quickly given to Lillie. The Caddy was then stored overnight back at Burdette's gas station, during which time people gawked at it. At that point the gun and cowboy hat were still inside it, and although the car was supposed to be kept locked, they were apparently stolen. Decades later, Howard Janney told a reporter that Peter Burdette "had the hat and was wearing it around. I went up to get it, and he said that Hank's mother gave it to him."

According to local lore, the hat became a curse for Burdette; after he started wearing it, the yarn goes, his hair began to fall out, and then, spooked by the curse, he committed suicide behind his station.[26]

As for Charles Carr, he had been given a room in Tyree's apartment above the funeral parlor the one night he was kept in Oak Hill. He was permitted to go back home the next afternoon, eight days before he would be officially cleared of any charges. Carr, his father, Lillie, and Toby Marshall crowded into Hank's Caddy for the trip to Montgomery. Lillie had decided there was no room for Billie Jean and her father, who had to get to Montgomery by plane. Grudgingly, Lillie let her stay at the boardinghouse until the funeral, which would be on the following Sunday.

The drive must have been surreal indeed. The car followed a hearse with Hank's body, driven by Joe Tyree and his assistant Alex Childress. Tyree once recalled that "all the way down, we kept hearing [Hank's] songs on the radio. It wasn't until then I realized how famous he was. We'd pull into filling stations and the attendants would wipe the dirt off the license plate and see the West Virginia tags. They would figure it out and comeask me if we were carrying Hank back."

In Montgomery, they took the body to White's Chapel Funeral Home, and at about seven in the morning, Daniel Carr dropped Lillie and Marshall at the boardinghouse, where Billie Jean had arrived the night before, then drove his son home in his car. Carr would not be forgotten. He would come to the funeral, and comfort a weeping Irene Smith.

. . .

When Lillie, the Carrs, and Toby Marshall returned to the boardinghouse, Billie Jean was still seething over being treated so shabbily in Oak Hill. According to what Irene Smith posited many years later, her mother had gone to her room to lie down when Billie Jean went to use the phone on the wall in the hallway just outside the door. "Get up here," Lillie overheard her say, perhaps to her brother back in Shreveport. "This old gray-haired bitch is trying to steal all of Hank's stuff from me." Later in the day, Irene said, "[Lillie told me that] if I did not get [Billie] out of the house, she would kill her."[27] Irene said she acted as a peacemaker between the two, if only temporarily.

Billie Jean—who would insist, dubiously, that *she* had actually brought Hank's body back from Oak Hill, in an ambulance with her brother—had her own take on these moments.[28] At one point, she and Lillie, she said, "were fightin' in the bathroom and elsewhere. She was so big—[a] good six-foot and no less than 250 pounds—and I had to get up on the commode to slap her. . . . All the fighting was taking place because during mine and Hank's marriage she hassled him for money and, hell, she had more than he did because Audrey got it all when they divorced. I put my foot down: no more money." Still, all the decisions pertaining to the funeral came down to Lillie. When Billie Jean wanted to buy a new suit for Hank to wear in his casket, only to be overruled by Lillie, an exasperated Billie Jean gave up. "This is your mother's show," she wearily told Irene, "let her run it."

· · ·

Almost immediately, Lillie began taking charge of the gravesite she wanted for Hank. Oakwood Cemetery, which wanted very much to be his final resting place, gave her wide latitude, allowing her to bury Hank temporarily in one plot while an elaborate mausoleum was built on another. The cemetery's owner, John Hart, anticipating that it would be a tourist attraction, began the process of clearing as much land as he could for the plot. There were two parts to the cemetery, the original, now quite crowded section and a newer, less congested annex. Hank's plot would go into the latter, but only after Hart could arrange with the families of many buried there—including British and Free French soldiers killed while training in Alabama during World War II—to return their loved ones' remains to them. Digging them up would be a horrific task, as many had been buried with no coffins, and those whose relatives couldn't be found would be reburied in a mass grave, all to serve the interest of an alcoholic, philandering country singer.

Lillie began to be inundated by calls from stonemasons around the country—and she knew many, from the years she spent in the Masonic Temple—filling her head with grand and grander design ideas. Willie Gayle, who designed monuments for the Henley Memorial Company in Montgomery, won the job for what he called "a good five figures,"[29] designing a family plot cut from Vermont granite on a two-step pedestal. Among a number of carvings in the stone would be lyrics from "Kaw-Liga," "Hey, Good Lookin'," and "Jambalaya," and notes from "I Saw the Light." There would be a bronze plaque of Hank and his guitar being bathed in pastoral rays from the sun. At the base of the monument would go a marble cowboy hat replicating Hank's favorite in minute detail, under which would be carved the names of some of the religious-themed Luke the Drifter songs. And, pointedly, a poem would be embedded in the headstone, written by Audrey Williams. Titled "Thank You, Darling," it thanked him for "all the love you gave me," for "the many beautiful songs," for "being such a wonderful father to Lycrecia," and "for our wonderful son." Its last lines were:

And now all I can say:
There are no words in the dictionary
That can express my love for you
Someday beyond the blue

As much as it was a poem, it was also a warning that Audrey's preferred status as "Mrs. Hank Williams" was itself being carved in stone. Indeed, with Lillie's benefaction, she already had a reservation to be buried in the family plot as well, right next to Hank and Lillie.

When Hank was interred in the permanent plot, he would go in

a vault that Lillie had secured through Leaborne L. Eads, who handled such things for the Henley company. She demanded only the
best vault and purchased a Wilbert Continental model, lined with
solid steel, asphalt, and copper. Eads made the sale with an observation that appealed to Lillie's desire to keep Hank's remains pristine,
forever. "That's what preserved King Tut," he said.[30]

                              •   •   •

Hank, meanwhile, seemed almost an afterthought lying carefree in
a casket over at White's funeral home, peacefully insulated from the
mayhem brewing at the boardinghouse. By day's end, Billie Jean's
mother and brothers had arrived, and the place had become not the
site of a sad vigil but a snake pit of bad blood and intentions, the Hat-
fields and McCoys under the same roof. It became so intolerable that
the Joneses decided to spend the night before the funeral in a hotel
room, with one bed, the younger ones sleeping on the floor. During
those two miserable days, the Cadillac *was* hidden from Billie Jean
by Lillie and Audrey, along with any other possessions Billie Jean
would have a claim on. While Audrey, who had arrived with Bam
and Maxine Bamford and stayed with Lillie in her room, planned
the funeral, not once did she or Lillie consult with Billie.

Many of the funeral expenses were shouldered by the city of
Montgomery, which volunteered the use of Municipal Auditorium,
and by local florists eager to contribute arrangements in tribute to
the city's best-known celebrity, some extraordinarily ornate, two
fashioned as giant guitars. The entire police and fire department
would be on call to clear the way for Hank's casket to be transported
to the arena. Bam Bamford was called on to use his promotional
skills to create a funeral for a king, much like Oscar Davis planning
Hank's royal weddings in New Orleans—only Bamford had to put
up with what he would say was "terrific friction between Audrey,
Billie Jean, and Hank's mother."[31] All of them acted like scavengers
combing through whatever possessions of Hank's they could find.
"There was a briefcase that they were all looking for," he said, "and

they found it in Billie Jean's room, and they got it while she was in the toilet and gave it to me and I put it in the trunk of my car. The following day I gave it to Fred Rose."

Audrey, who had come with Lycrecia but not Randall, whom she left home with Audrey Ragland, put on an emotional show of mutual grief with Lillie, on some level meant as a message for Billie Jean, to whom neither woman spoke a word. Lillie had to respect the fact that, because of Audrey's divorce settlement, she couldn't do anything about the half-split Audrey owned of all Hank's future royalties or her ownership of his Nashville house. But Lillie did have hegemony over Hank's personal estate, and she meant to control every dime of it for as long as she lived. Still, in order to make herself executrix of the estate she needed to take care of a few more details, cutting out not only Billie Jean but the husband that had been left behind long ago and was dead to her.

As it happened, she could achieve the latter that weekend, when a heartbroken Lon Williams made his way up to Montgomery for the funeral by bus, five dollars in his pocket. As Brack Schuffert recalled, he was at the front door when a bedraggled man in the crowd outside the house inched his way toward the house late on Saturday night and said meekly, "I'm Hank Williams's daddy." Lon told him he needed to buy some flowers for his son, and Brack took him to a local florist, who asked Lon what size bouquet he wanted. "I'm a poor man," the aging, nearly forgotten patriarch said. "All I can afford is five dollars."[32] The florist took pity on him, giving him a large bouquet, gratis. Lillie, though, took no pity on him. When he and Schuffert returned to the house, she refused to allow Lon free boarding for the night. Brack would put him up instead. And Lillie pounced, denying Lon *his* rights as the paternal survivor.

Because Hank had not left a will, Lon was by law the executor of Hank's estate; Hank's own lawyer Robert Stewart had so advised him. However, Lillie also advised him of something—she would drag him through the courts, spending anything necessary, to challenge his standing, telling everyone she could that he had abandoned the family and seen his son only a handful of times. Lon, who had once beaten her in court just to be able to get out of the VA Hospital, had no stomach to go through it again. He told Lillie that the happiest day of his life would be when he died and was rid of her, and within a week he signed away his paternal rights, asking nothing in return.

Lillie did allow him a seat at the funeral, though not with the family in the first several rows but lost in the general seating section dozens of rows behind. Nor did he appear in any of the family photos that day.

However, not all family business had been settled yet. Shutting out Billie Jean wasn't good enough; she had to be *bought* out to avoid future static. As it was, Billie Jean was being shamed by everyone in the Williams family. Toby Marshall, who thought he was still doing Lillie's bidding, he lit into Billie when he heard her throwing around her "old bitch" complaints about Lillie.

Billie, having come to Montgomery without any black clothing, was wearing red slacks. Marshall, whose expertise apparently included sartorial advice, got in her face to say that she was dressed inappropriately and her behavior was unacceptable.[33] It must have taken superhuman will for Billie Jean to let that slide without letting the bogus doctor know what she thought of *him*.

And, of course, there was another sticky wicket: the future heir sitting in Bobbie Jett's womb. Indeed, Lord knows what Bobbie must have been thinking during all this clamor on North McDonough, doing her grieving alone and knowing that she would be giving birth any minute now to a child with no father. Lillie had reminded her that the agreement she and Hank had signed was still in force, that Lillie would still be the child's legal guardian, and Bobbie was still bound by the terms to leave for California. Just in case Bobbie did go into labor when everyone else was at the funeral, Lillie's doctor would be stationed with her in her room and take her to the hospital.

Because so many people began gathering outside both White's and the boardinghouse, Lillie decided to have Hank's silver-and-gold-trimmed coffin carted to 318 North McDonough Street and placed in the anteroom, a quite unnerving sight, especially to Billie Jean, who was allowed only twenty minutes by Lillie to say goodbye to Hank in private. During this interim Brack Schuffert was enlisted as a kind of gatekeeper, allowing a few people at a time to come in and file past the casket, which he would open briefly, offering a glimpse of Hank's embalmed face beneath a protective thin mesh screen. Many of them cried, some as they draped themselves over the casket.

. . . .

Bamford had quickly accepted the city's offer of the use of Municipal Auditorium for the funeral, and invites went out to industry people that almost alone would fill all of its 2,700 seats. Nashville would be well represented, as would the big boys from New York. Oscar Davis and Horace Logan would be there, but for the most part the Shreveport crowd was deemed too small-time. The stage was prepared for a combination funeral and tent show. The voices of Nashville would be there—Ernest Tubb, Roy Acuff, Red Foley, Ray Price, Bill Monroe, the Carter Sisters, Carl Davis, Kitty Wells, Johnnie Wright, Jack Anglin, Little Jimmie Dickens, Webb Pierce— as would Jim Denny, the man who had fired Hank, Oscar Davis, Horace Logan, and Frank Walker.

Bamford, who also arranged for two Montgomery radio stations to carry the event live, carried out these chores, torn up that he had to jazz up the denouement of a man of simple tastes, but it was Lillie and Audrey's call to make the funeral and burial the largest event in Montgomery since the inauguration of Jefferson Davis. At Oakwood Cemetery, the temporary plot had been set aside for Hank to tarry in while Willie Gayle's stonecutters and landscapers erected the permanent plot and monuments in the annex.

On Sunday morning, January 4, 1953, the crowd outside the boardinghouse was so large that some of the pallbearers couldn't get there. Jerry Rivers had driven from Nashville with several *Opry* musicians, who like the big stars had performed the night before at the Ryman in tribute to Hank and were all bleary-eyed. Rivers became a "temporary pallbearer" in taking the coffin to the hearse for the slow ride to the arena. There, the casket was carried through the crowds already massing on the street outside the auditorium, which were estimated at 25,000. It was then set up just under the stage, and again the coffin was opened so the multitudes waiting outside in the bitter cold could file past Hank in his repose, clad in the white Nudie suit. This went on for several hours, during which at least four women fainted when they saw him.

These were folks that Hank would have appreciated. What's more, a distinct number of black fans were in the crowd. Several hundred were able to enter for the service, funneled upstairs into the "colored" section of the mezzanine. Lillie, to her credit, made room during the service for a black gospel quartet, the Southwind Singers, as the chorale during the musical segments.

As limousines pulled up outside and celebrity and important-looking folks alighted, flashbulbs took to popping and newsreel cameras whirring. The teeming crowd heaved in great waves, scaring the police. Then, at 2:30 p.m., the procession to the casket was ended and the doors closed to all but the capacity seating of 2,750 people. The service began, to the harmony of a church organ and women, and more than a few men, sobbing, including Little Jimmie Dickens, who stood backstage openly bawling.

Ernest Tubb opened the program singing "Beyond the Sunset." Roy Acuff, after a brief elegy, began a group sing-along of "I Saw the Light," joined by Foley, Smith, and Pierce. Red then took center stage and sang "Peace in the Valley." He and Hank had made a mutual compact a few years before that whoever died first, the other would sing the song at his funeral, and Foley finished the song in tears. The musicians—Helms, Rivers, Hillous Butrum, Sammy Pruett, and *Hayride* guitarists Felton Pruett and Dobber Johnson— played sad dirges and bouncy foot-stompin' tunes. Looking back,

Helms would say "the eeriest thing I ever had to do in my life" was to "stand up there and play with Hank's coffin right below me" just under the lip of the stage.[34]

Because Lillie and her husband, Bill Stone, rarely touched or even spoke to each other, Tubb lent his shoulder for her to cry on, sitting on her other side during the service. Even now, though, the feuding was not put aside. When Billie Jean and her family got to the auditorium, no seats near the stage had been saved for them. They found some well back, until someone who knew her moved them up to where Lillie, Irene, and Audrey were—though photos taken during the service show Billie in the second row, behind them.

Billie's agony continued when she mistook one mourner, a young Indian girl, for someone else and the girl, recognizing Billie, told her, "I'm not anyone you ever heard of. I'm just a person who loved Hank with all my heart, not a tramp like you that married him for his money," touching off a brief scuffle.[35] Billie also had to put up with Tubb, who in his role as Lillie's paraclete, Billie said, "looked at me like he didn't even know me."

. . .

The service was given by Rev. Henry L. Lyon, pastor of the Highland Avenue Baptist Church, and Rev. Talmadge Smith of the Ramer Baptist Church. Lyon, with a quiet, polished theatricality, spun tales of Hank interwoven with biblical homilies and patriotic fervor. Hank, he said, "has just answered the call of the last round-up," going on to eulogize him as "the man who climbed from the shoeshine stand to the heights of immortal glory. . . . When he played on his guitar, he played on the heartstrings of millions of Americans. They listened to Hank over the radio in their homes, in the bus station, in the office. They listened everywhere—white and colored, rich and poor, the illiterate and the educated, the young and the old. . . . Hank Williams did have something that humanity universally needs—a song with a heartfelt message."

The service done, the pallbearers—among them Denny, Bamford, Jack Anglin, Johnnie Wright, and Brack Schuffert—carried the coffin back to the hearse, which had one more slow ride through Montgomery. More big crowds had waited patiently at the Oakwood Cemetery in the hills overlooking the city, many having brought their young children with them, who could someday tell their own children and grandchildren that they had been there when God called home his ramblin' man. The family and invited guests arrived at around three, Lillie still clutching Ernie Tubb, a pale Billie Jean kept from collapsing by her brother Sonny. Seeing the grounds, she hated the place, and the whole "Hank-a-palooza" nature of the day, which one country chronicle later called an "emotional orgy."[36] She would say:

> It reminded me of the rebirth of the Hadacol Show. Everybody wanted to "sang." And they did. For us who was hurtin', it just left us lingering on for hours, having to sit silently looking at Hank. Cold. Still. Dreading the inevitable—puttin' him in the ground, throwing dirt on him. Dreadin' the coffin lid to shut because you knew you'd never see his face again. . . . If I hadn't been broke, country, a child, ignorant, I would've brought him home to the bayou . . . but as it was, my daddy took me back home from Alabama on the Greyhound Bus. . . . Hank was gone—the buzzards had started to pick at his leavin's. All I wanted to do was get the hell out of there. We did—back to my dad's shotgun house in Louisiana. Sure was dull without Hank buggin' mamma to cook him some biscuits and sorghum syrup.[37]

That claim may have been to some sorghum syrup itself. Billie Jean's lawyer Robert Stewart later said that before she went home, she warned him that "if I didn't have them seven Cadillacs ready for her to take back to Shreveport, her brothers would personally stomp my God-damn teeth down my throat." She might have gone home, but she seemed as determined to stand her ground as was Lillie, and collect as many "leavin's" as she could.

When the mourners had dispersed, one other family figure went home. That was the sad, mostly unrecognized figure of Elonzo Williams. Rather than the boardinghouse, he headed for the bus depot for the next Greyhound to McWilliams, alone, penniless, grieving. He kept his thoughts private, still probably wanting to kick himself for not being at home when Hank had dropped by a few weeks before. Then he went home, where all he had left of his son was the note Hank had left for him that day with a lighter and a box of chocolates, all of which he would zealously preserve in protective cases until the day he died.

· · ·

The medical examiner's autopsy report and the coroner's inquest report were released on January 10. The former—which apparently later vanished without explanation from the Fayette County medical records—was surprising in its omissions but not its conclusion, which was that cause of death was "Acute rt. ventricular dilation," one of a dozen ways of saying *heart failure*.

In layman's terms, it meant a longtime enlargement of the ventricular walls of Hank's heart, making it work too hard.[38] In full, Hank technically had "edema of the brain, congestive hyperemia of all the parenchymatous organs and paralysis of the respiratory center with asphyxia." As well, his seated position on the long ride had raised the level of his diaphragm, another dangerous trigger.[39] It seemed that Hank had not suffered any pain when he died, as other hemorrhages on his tongue suggested an "unconscious death," meaning he had slipped away while he slumbered.

Although coroners didn't test for drugs in most autopsies then, it was assumed that Hank would be so tested. Carr had told police of the sedatives and shots, and the pocket of Hank's overcoat was empty, making it clear that he had taken all of the chloral hydrate tablets. However, out of incompetence, or deference, or maybe fear of Lillie's wrath, no testing was done. While alcohol was listed as being in his blood, it was not said to be an immediate contributor to his death, a cop-out if ever there was one. Lab reanalysis of the autopsy samples in future years would establish definitively that he had alcoholic cardiomyopathy, a fatal toxicity of the blood.[40] The shorthand explanation would be that Hank Williams drank himself to death—a technically incorrect premise, given that his liver was found to be healthy—and when his drug abuse became common knowledge a decade later, that too became part of the equation. Toby Marshall emerged as the chief foil, but dozens of real doctors went along for the ride, for a buck or to succor a famous man they knew could not survive long. All of them had blood on their hands, even if they could brag at dinner parties that they had tended to Hank Williams.

The inquest panel signed a statement in its report to Magistrate Virgil Lyons that read: "We the jury find . . . that Hank Williams died of a severe heart condition and hemorrhage. No evidence was found of foul play."[41] The welt on his head was brushed off, as was the coroner's finding that Hank also had "small subcutaneous hemorrhages" on his back and groin, it being impossible to pinpoint how and when they occurred. The overriding theme of these reports was that nothing was out of the ordinary in the death of a very sick, twenty-nine-year-old "radio singer," as the death certificate would read when it was finally issued on March 15.

Now came a new round of news stories, with hundreds of papers putting a period on the story with headlines such as that in the June 11 *Milwaukee Sentinel*—FIND ATTACK KILLED HANK WILLIAMS, not that speculation and skepticism wouldn't go on, as they still do and likely always will. Still, this was not really major news in America at the time. *Billboard*, which had charted his unlikely rise, relegated his demise to its January 10 issue, on page 13, headlined HANK WILLIAMS, FOLK TUNE STAR, DIES SUDDENLY, and maintained the old nomenclature by calling him "one of the nation's best known and loved hillbilly artists and songwriters."

In Nashville, where disdain for the working-class audiences at the *Opry* and its "hillbilly" stars had kept mentions of him to a minimum, the extraordinary outpouring of grief was sudden cause for deification. Editorials were written about him as a man with "the unusual gift of seeing, and feeling, life's repertoire of deepest sentiment," whose "brief life was nothing short of fabulous," and who despite being "the most lonesome, saddest, and frustrated of individuals . . . never forgot his fans . . . many of whom are found here in Middle Tennessee [where] his death is counted a distinct loss."[42]

Of course, in Alabama they claimed territorial dibs on him—MONTGOMERY'S FAMOUS FOLK SINGER, the *Alabama Journal* codified him—but the loss was felt far outside the South. Way out in Spokane, an editorial titled A GREAT SINGER PASSES concluded: "Hank Williams' tunes went straight to the heart of his hearers, and . . . let it be said that he who writes the songs of a people is greater than he who taketh a city."[43] A paper in Hartford, Connecticut, noting he sang "hillbilly music," went on to offer him his due props, before concluding with faint praise, "It would be fine if American tastes became more widely cultivated to something better. But the opposite seems true. Slowly but surely the cult of hillbilly spreads over the land [and] the hillbilly singer is a new category of national hero."[44]

In Montgomery, people wrote letters to the newspapers every day for months with heartfelt testaments about what he had meant to them. And no doubt the industry barons were moved, too, by a surge in his sales, a common dynamic in showbiz when a star dies, but not to this extent. When he died, "Jambalaya (On the Bayou)" was still No. 5 on the *Billboard* country chart. One week later, it vaulted to number 1 on the newly renamed "C&W" chart, and the prophetic "Settin' the Woods on Fire" would soon grab the No. 2 position, while "I'll Never Get Out of This World Alive" had just hit the chart at No. 3. "I Could Never Be Ashamed of You" was the top country entry on the "Coming Up in the Trade" list, and his face was alive as ever in a big MGM ad for its new releases. On the front page of the trade paper, an article titled FANS CLAMOR FOR DISKS OF LATE SINGER reported the "immediate and tremendous upsurge for all of the hillbilly writer-singer's past records," noting this was "reminiscent of what happened to [Al] Jolson's records after his death." He had not been ranked on top in any of the trade papers' polls for the year just passed, but a year later, readers of *Down Beat* voted him the most popular country and western performer—not for the year but of all time.

. . .

On January 16, when the permanent plot at the Oakwood Cemetery Annex was finished and the remains of those who made way for it disinterred, Hank's body was moved in the dead of night and buried in its vault, with no pomp and ceremony. Seeing men with torches carrying things from open graves, some local citizens called police, thinking someone was robbing a grave. Just as John Hart had figured, so many people would come here that a large sign was needed to direct them to the "Hank Williams Memorial Annex." A stone hat was placed where his head would be if he were lying above the grave. A bench would be added for visitors to sit on. Two concrete vases for fresh flowers every day were put on each side. Two stone-carved guitars were also added. Standing or sitting in silence, stone guitars and engraved sheet music all around, one could hear the romantic sound of railroad-train horns in the distance through the woods, and yet as rustic as the setting is, Billie Jean always thought these stately granite walls would be of no comfort to Hank in his repose.

"Hank was afraid of the dark and graves," she said later. "He wouldn't have wanted to be in that cold, dark ground."[45]

But that is where Hank Williams went, under the imposing granite pillar on which some of his song titles were carved, the eeriest of all being "I'll Never Get Out of This World Alive," looming over a ghostly sketch of Hank Williams with no face, just an outline with empty space inside it. Nothing could have better illustrated a man nobody really knew but for the outer lines, a man who was all too comfortable with the darkness.

EPILOGUE

✳ ✳ ✳ ✳ ✳ ✳

OF MYTH AND MEN

Hank Williams did not die broke, but his tax bracket had fallen considerably. Mostly what he had left was his guitars and his guns. His account at First National Bank of Montgomery had $4,394.80 in it. He also had Nudie stage-costume suits worth $300 to $450, and one white gabardine suit with blue music notes valued at $500. The instruments were a Martin D18 guitar with pearl inlay and case ($322.50), a Gibson SJ with case ($162), and a Martin D28 with case ($258). The guns were a Colt .45 Frontier ($125), a Colt .44 Frontier ($125), a Smith & Wesson .45 ($75), a Colt .45 ($75), a German Luger ($75), a 16 gauge single-barrel shotgun ($100), a 16 gauge Winchester pump action ($100), and a 16 gauge Remington automatic ($100). There were also the two Cadillacs and his wedding ring—none of which Billie Jean was given, teeth-kicking threats notwithstanding; they remained with Lillie. He also owned a stabled Walking Horse named Highlight Merry Boy, having sold off Hi Life. In all, Hank's assets totaled $13,329.25. (In 2009, the Martin D18 alone sold for $134,000 in an auction.)[1]

Most of the smaller and inanimate items were in Lillie's house, as were sundry others such as awards, letters, trophies, scrapbooks, luggage, paintings, guitar picks, a saddle, a fiddle, and a crucifix, which would soon be on public display when Lillie fashioned a kind of shrine-museum in Hank's old bedroom. Of course, the real assets were not in dollar bills but on paper, in those future royalty rights, and the overarching question was who would control the half not owned by Audrey.

Billboard reported that Hank was in line to reap around half a million dollars in royalties in 1953. And the subterranean infighting about money—prefaced by Hank's suspicions about Oscar Davis, who was subsequently cleared of any wrongdoing in an investigation in Louisiana of what happened to the proceeds of the wedding events—began almost as soon the news broke of his death. As purveyors of Hank's songs, even as Fred Rose and Frank Walker mourned him they were taking advantage of the expanded window opened by his death. Rose, tipping his hand, published an open letter similar to Walker's after Hank's death, addressed to the public, and it read like a sales pitch:

> I believe that Hank Williams is just as much alive today as he ever was, and if you will just listen to some of the great songs he has written and recorded . . . I'm sure you will agree with me. Hank's life was, and is, in his great love for country music and I intend to do all in my power to keep his songs alive eternally because I believe that is the way Hank wanted it to be. . . . No, I am not implying that you play Hank's records more than you have been but I am implying that you do not play them any less.[2]

And they didn't. Just a month after Hank's death, MGM released the first of a long thread of posthumous Hank Williams LPs, *The Memorial Album*, containing not just previous hits but unreleased songs awaiting release when he died. Of these, "Kaw-Liga," the tongue-in-cheek novelty written during the wild week on Martin Lake with Bobbie Jett, was put out in late January, and it too sprinted to No. 1 on the country chart, as did its B-side, "Your Cheatin' Heart." "Take These Chains from My Heart" also shot to

No. 1, and "I Won't Be Home No More" to No. 4. Before the year
was out, "Weary Blues from Waitin'" had reached No. 7.

Since Lillie had forced Lon out as administrator of Hank's estate,
she owned all of his possessions and half of his future royalties,
as well as his songs' copyrights, which had reverted to Hank from
Acuff-Rose and would not expire until 1974. The owner of the other
half of the royalty pie, Audrey Sheppard Williams, was also looking forward to feeding off them. But Billie Jean was sure to stake a
claim, and it was unclear what effect Hank's death and lack of a will
would have on all prior agreements. As a preemptive strike, Audrey
quickly filed suit in Nashville against MGM Records and Acuff-
Rose. The suit demanded that both publishing companies continue
to pay her half of the royalties from Hank Williams's records. When
Billboard got on the story in its May 23 issue, it was with the kind
of headline that would become common —FILE ACTION TO UNTANGLE
HANK WILLIAMS ESTATE.

Lillie and Audrey were prepared to slime Billie Jean any way
they could. They were so spooked by her that they believed she had
possession of a stolen cache of unpublished songs by Hank that she
would sell to other singers, perhaps Johnny Horton, a rising *Hayride*
star with whom she was getting very friendly, and who was waiting
out his own divorce. On January 9, the *Montgomery Advertiser* ran
a story headlined LEGALITY MAY BE QUESTIONED IN WILLIAMS' SECOND
MARRIAGE, which could only have been leaked by Lillie or someone
close to her. In the first instance of what would be decades of dueling
lawsuits by sundry parties, Billie Jean filed suit in Minden, where
she and Hank were married, albeit illegally, to prevent Audrey from
using the name "Mrs. Hank Williams" either professionally—as she
recently had in an *Opry* road show in New Orleans—or personally,
asking for $100,000 in damages if she did.

Audrey, who responded that she had been using the name for ten
years, filed her own court papers seeking to immediately invalidate
Hank's marriage to Billie Jean—high irony given that Audrey had
never been validly married to him, either. On January 15, a Shreve-

port judge ruled in her favor, rejecting Billie Jean's contention that, dates aside, she had married Hank "in good faith." That was edifying to Lillie as well. But she was fighting on different fronts to keep control of Hank's legacy. And now, there was another person in the picture.

. . .

Two days after Hank went to that better place, Bobbie Jett went into labor and was taken to St. Margaret's Hospital. She gave birth to a daughter she named Antha Belle, after her mother's first and grandmother's middle names. The only visitors she had were Lillie, Marie McNeil, and her daughter, Jo. Per the agreement, Lillie took the baby home to the boardinghouse, and Bobbie left, first to go back to Nashville with Jo. She returned to Montgomery only to sign papers granting Lillie sole custody, then took off for California. Lillie promptly changed the girl's name to Cathy Yvone Stone— apparently after the line "My Yvonne the sweetest one" in "Jambalaya," though she misspelled it on the papers—and, conspicuously, *not* Williams.

This was to be a terrible mistake. Lillie, grossly overweight and diagnosed with a heart condition, was hardly the ideal person to care for a baby, and Irene had tried to talk her out of it and into giving Antha up for adoption. Irene worried about the scandal that would erupt if it ever got out that Hank had a love child. "Ye Gods," she wrote to her lawyer at the time, if that ever happened "I would feel like changing my name." Still, Lillie insisted that having Hank's child would bring her closer to him in death. Besides, she swore, it was what "Hank would have wanted."

Lillie had the same old spunk, and habit for discarding husbands. In April 1954, she divorced W. W. Stone after taking up with another, younger boarder named Slim Stern, though in the warped reality of the Williams family, Stone went on living in Lillie's next-door boardinghouse.

In the meantime, Hank's widow—the most recent one—did

not stay alone for long. After a rather brief period of grieving, she was ready to marry Johnny Horton, just as Hank had predicted she would during the time he had tired of her and the chubby-cheeked, California-born, Texas-raised singer showed the same kind of interest in her that Hank did when he stole her from from Young. Yet the legal battle for control of half of Hank's estate needed to be settled, lest she lose her rights by doing so. The problem was, it was a tangled case, involving the discrete marriage laws of three states, Alabama, Tennessee, and Louisiana. For Billie Jean, short on money as she was, fighting Lillie in court was prohibitive. Naïvely, she said at the time that if she could get together with Audrey, "we could work this thing out on friendly terms."[3]

Lillie had money, but the perils of losing in the end to Billie were real. And so they settled, with Lillie buying off Billie Jean cheap, $30,000. How Lillie could have had this much cash on hand is another mystery, possibly only explained by her having skimmed an enormous amount of money from her son. Billie Jean, who had acceded to promoters' schemes to sing on the road herself as "Mrs. Hank Williams,"[4] relinquished not only any claims on Hank's estate but the use of the name, thereby lifting the injunction preventing Audrey from doing so. She also had to hand over any of Hank's items still in their home in Shreveport. She retained only her widow's Social Security benefit, despite the Shreveport judge's ruling. But she owned something else, too. What no one seemed to grasp was that Billie Jean now owned those renewal copyrights that had reverted to Hank, which Lillie didn't think to challenge. Neither did Billie Jean realize what that might mean. For now. The deal she made with Lillie was signed on August 19, 1952, with Billie Jean, like Lillie, adopting the phrase that would become a mantra justifying practically any arguable decision. Hank, she said, "would have wanted it that way."[5]

That date officially marked the end of her grieving period. A month later, she wed Horton, putting her on another roller coaster ride. Though it would be a big decade for Horton, who broke out in the mid-'50s with the Hank-like rockabilly songs "Honky Tonk Man" and "I'm a One-Woman Man," allowing Billie Jean to once again preen as the wife of a country star, he brought with him an endless pit of debt, and whatever was left of the settlement after lawyer costs went down that hole. Yet, with it all, she was not out of legal options in the matter of Hank's estate. She would learn this at a time when she was no longer an ingenue but a hardheaded business-woman with a thirst for vengeance.

. . .

In the immediate aftermath of Hank's death, "Doctor" Toby Marshall became front and center of the story. Compounding his emergence as a villain, on March 3 Marshall's estranged wife, Fay, died of a cerebral hemorrhage at her home in Albuquerque. He was unable to lurk in the shadows any longer. No less than Oklahoma governor Johnston Murray personally revoked Marshall's parole. Police raided his Oklahoma City apartment, arrested him, and seized files and a shelf full of bottles of barbiturates. They also found a list of his "patients," one of whom was Hank Williams. Marshall knew he was going to serve prison time for jumping parole, but being found liable for causing two deaths would put him away the rest of his life. Thus, when an investigation was held under the auspices of the state legislature, Marshall, who under oath admitted he not only wasn't a doctor but "never went beyond high school," claimed he had merely tried to shield Hank from "others," unnamed people who were "fair-weather friends" and "parasites who fawned on him, played up to him, kept him supplied with liquor."[6] He somehow forgot to mention drugs.

Marshall also tried another tack to deflect blame, implying that Hank had actually taken his own life. As Marshall said later, Hank's "emotional problems" and extreme loneliness were taken beyond the breaking point by playing "honky-tonk beer joint[s] that he simply hated," and that within six months "he might have been playing for nickels and dimes on skid row." If Hank had decided to commit suicide, he said, derisively, "he still had enough prestige left as a star to make a first-class production of it." This was the man he had claimed he "loved." Marshall also was not beneath a little blackmail, issuing a not-so-subtle reminder to Billie Jean that he still had that unpaid "bill" pending, and that he knew a thing or two about Hank and his family that could prove useful to her if she paid up,[7] and not so much if she didn't. However, Marshall was doomed when Billie Jean, calling his bluff, testified and put the blame on no one but him, blowing the lid off his methods of keeping Hank narcotized with needles and blank prescription pads. Even so, when the investigators called in Dr. Ivan Malinin to go over his autopsy report, no different conclusion was reached, and they went easy on Marshall, who was also cleared by the New Mexico attorney general in the death of his wife.[8]

Marshall was sent back to prison, but only on the parole violation, until May 1954. He then was arrested for vagrancy, possession of barbiturates, and attempting to pass a bogus check at a motel where he had registered as a doctor. He did a year on that rap, then in 1957 was convicted in Denver for dispensing drugs without a prescription, serving six months. He began to claim he'd written a book in which he told the "real" story of Hank's "suicide," several passages of which came to light but never a complete manuscript. Living out his days in accustomed dark shadows, he died in 1972 in Colorado, himself a forerunner, and cautionary tale, of a coming trend in rock music, that of the feel-good "doctors" whose famous "patients" would die under the same sort of circumstances as did Hank Williams.

• • •

Lillie soon began to commercialize Hank's life as a small cottage industry. She opened the boardinghouse to guided tours of his bedroom, which she preserved as a shrine, religiously cleaned, his bed remade every day, his guitars and other possessions dating back to childhood dusted and left exactly where they were; she would inspect the room daily to see to it nothing had been moved even an inch. She also turned to selling her memories of Hank. Hiring

Allen Rankin as her ghostwriter, she published the first book about him, *Our Hank Williams: The Drifting Cowboy*, if one can so call a fawning sixteen-page pamphlet of no real value sold by mail order for one dollar. Her intent was to establish him as a good son who simply got some bad breaks and took refuge from the "ins and outs" of his marriage to Audrey—Billie was never brought up—by coming home. It began:

> I hope you will like this little memento of Hank Williams, "The Drifting Cowboy." . . . It warms my heart to know you are Hank's friend and fan because I am the best friend and fan Hank ever had . . . . Hank visited me several times in those last days. How proud he was that no matter where he went or what he did, he had Mama at home to come back to. He acted gay, kept putting up a bold front to the last, but he was nearly at the end of the line and looking back, somehow he must have realized it.[9]

Lillie, thinking bigger, also made a deal to make a movie about the man who had rejected Hollywood. What's more, it would be produced by none other than Joe Pasternak, who'd known all too well the real Hank. But Lillie drove a hard bargain, not for money so much—she optioned the rights to MGM Pictures for only $2,000, with another $20,000 to come if it was made—but for the studio to agree not to mention Hank's divorce from Audrey, who would still be portrayed as his wife when he died, or Billie Jean.

MGM readily agreed, and Audrey would not have settled for anything less. She now considered her divorce from Hank a mere technicality, her illegal marriages to be sacred, and herself the legitimate widow, the *only* widow. Only twelve days after his death she wrote a bylined article in the *Montgomery Advertiser* that began: "There could never be another love like that of Hank Williams and myself. I felt like that the day I met him in 1943 and I still feel the same"— leaving out quite a bit in between, such as their two divorces, all the fighting, an abortion, and various gunshots fired in her direction.

Any bouts they had during the "good and bad" of their marriages, she said, ended the same—"I always went back."[10] Audrey bore much guilt, believing she could have prevented his death had she not divorced him. As Lycrecia Williams said, "I know Mother often blamed herself for Daddy's troubles, which is what the spouses of alcoholics often do. After his death, Mother devoted herself to his career. That's how she mourned him."[11]

Maybe so, but she found plenty of time to push her own career, and more and more, that of "Hank Jr.," the name she had bestowed on Randall Hank Williams for professional purposes that would damn near kill him the way it had his daddy. The most important thing in her life, Audrey said, was to "try to carry on where he left off. . . . I will try to find happiness in the world in which he found it and gave it to me." Toward that end, she would express in song what she never had when he was alive, when his songs scalded her. One went like this:

Have you told the angels how much I love you
And tho you're gone you still seem so near

Lillie tended dutifully to Cathy, but her health predictably gave out. Unable to leave her bed most days, she had transferred ownership of her two boardinghouses to the now married Marie McNeil Glenn, who also began to raise Cathy, the two of them living in the house next door to Lillie's, though Lillie's carping about everything she did led Marie to not speak to her for months.

On February 26, 1955, Lillie's maid went to clean her room and could not wake her. She called Marie, who ran over. Finding no signs of life, she called a doctor, who pronounced Lillie dead, after fifty-six uncompromising, nonjoyous years. There were far fewer mourners at her funeral, where she too lay in an open casket. But when she went, Lillie might have been at least contented that she would be buried next to her baby boy at Oakwood Cemetery.

Upon her death, which put the Hank Williams movie into mothballs, Irene Smith became administrator of Hank's estate, which Audrey—whose alliance with Lillie disintegrated as soon as Billie Jean was bought out—had unsuccessfully petitioned the courts to name her as Lillie grew more ill. But Marie was not up to adopting Cathy. Irene still refused to do so as well. So Marie located Bobbie in California and said only she could prevent the child from being put up for adoption by strangers. Bobbie, though, turned her back, saying she had married a man named John Tippins from whom she'd kept the secret and who wanted his own family—indeed, she would have *six* children with him.[12]

It was said that Pappy McCormick, one of the few cronies Hank had told about his love child, offered to adopt her but that Irene wanted to keep her from anyone who "knowed anything about Hank," the idea being that if the girl ever found out the truth, and it got around, this would further damage Hank's already dicey reputation. Not incidentally, if Cathy was kept in the dark, she could never stake a claim to his estate. And just to make sure, Irene filed, and won, a motion in an Alabama state court to strip the adopted girl of any claim to Hank's estate.

And so Cathy Yvone Stone, with Bill Stone obediently signing the papers giving her up, was bundled off to an orphanage to await adoption. In March 1955, she was adopted by James and Ilda Mae Cook in Pine Level, Alabama, but that must not have worked out, because a year later she was adopted by Wayne and Louise Deupree in Mobile, who renamed her Cathy Louise Deupree. She was still only three, had been given three different names, and it seemed all but certain she would never learn who her biological parents were. Except there was a small catch. When Lillie's estate was settled, leaving only around $6,000 to her name, it was discovered that she had in her will left Cathy a sum of $2,200, to be paid when she reached the age of twenty-one. No one thought much of it then. But, as with Billie Jean, an opening was provided for another unintended interloper to make trouble aplenty down the line.

• • •

The only *known* heir of Hank Williams began to show by the mid-1950s that he had inherited some of his father's singing chops, and this was something else that his mother could exploit. Audrey became the same kind of ham-fisted, domineering stage mother to Hank Jr. that Lillie had been to Hank Sr. She handled his career, allowing no outsiders. She booked the prepubescent Hank to sing at county fairs and church socials, and thought it would be good PR to pose with him in front of the Cadillac that Irene now kept from her, both smiling inches from where Hank had died so lonely. Hank Jr. had no idea what these rituals were about. Like his father, he only knew he liked to get up and sing for people. With all the details ramrodded by Audrey, he toured with a reconstituted Drifting Cowboys, sang at the *Grand Ole Opry* at eleven, and in 1962, at fourteen, signed a $100,000 recording contract with MGM.

Audrey could bask in his precocious success, and tipple her way through the kind of society parties she loved to frequent in her latest designer outfit. But history repeated itself in other ways. Just as Hank had rebelled against Lillie, Hank Jr. started to chafe at *his* mother's hard-driving demands, and as a result would soon develop the same self-destructive habits that killed his daddy. He also recoiled as his father had against the gentlemen of the *Opry*. When he became old enough, Hank Jr. recognized their self-serving artifices whenever any of them spoke about Hank Sr.

"To hear the tributes," Hank Jr. said, "one would think that the entire city [of Nashville] took turns kissing Daddy while he was still alive. Everybody loved Hank. Everybody worried over his, ahem, 'excesses.' Everybody tried to help him. When he was alive, he was despised and envied; after he died, he was some kind of saint."[13]

Yet not even in Montgomery did they start building statues of Hank Williams right away. In 1954 one was unveiled at the Cramton Bowl, as Ferlin Husky sang "I Saw the Light," that was later placed at the gravesite. There would be periodic "Hank Williams Day" parades. He got a star on the Hollywood Walk of Fame in 1960, and won induction into the Country Music Hall of Fame a year later and the Alabama Music Hall of Fame in 1985. But it took until the '90s for a museum and the statues in Montgomery to be erected.

While Audrey's attempt to perform in the '50s fronting the "Drifting Cowgirls" was another laughable failure, she maintained a semblance of a music career. Frank Walker seemingly felt he owed it to Hank to keep Audrey at MGM, not to mention needing her permission to keep releasing Hank material.

Fred Rose probably profited the most from having been associated with Hank, though he wasn't around long enough to enjoy it. The overlord for so much of Hank's and Nashville's spectacular growth died of a heart attack on December 1, 1954, at age fifty-six. With Wesley Rose taking the reins, Acuff-Rose would become even more the prime conduit of country music. Wesley would continue the partnership with Roy Acuff until 1985, when the company's catalog was sold to Gaylord Entertainment Company, parent company of the *Grand Ole Opry*.

Not only were Hank's songs a mint for their publisher; they resurfaced with each generation. For example, when Willie Nelson needed to jump-start his career in the mid-'70s, he recorded Rose's 1945 "Blue Eyes Crying in the Rain," which Hank had also recorded, in 1951. The song made the *Red Headed Stranger* concept album work perfectly.

Not that there weren't dissenters within Nashville's hypocritical charade of laying on of hands for Hank. Jerry Byrd, the steel guitar player who had worked some Hank sessions, said that when Jim Denny had told him after Hank's death, "We'll never see the likes of him again," Byrd responded, "I hope not." He recalled Denny looking at him "like I'd blasphemed." He then explained, "You're trying to put a halo on him that won't fit." In his view, Hank "had a great chance and blew it" and "did as much to hurt country music as he did to help it—doing shows drunk as hell and insulting the audience. Everyone forgets that. They have short memories."[14]

• • •

Ironically, such honesty might have impressed Hank Jr. more than the hollow tributes from Nashville. But this was a distinct minority opinion, snowed under by the collective guilt of not having accepted him when he was alive. And he would remain in the DNA of country even as it moved ahead without him, and kept finding new assimilation in pop and other genres.

As it was, Hank was still all over the radio, in posthumous singles and pieced-together albums. And when the MGM vaults ran dry of old Hank product after the single "Please Don't Let Me Love You" in 1956 (No. 9 country), it would simply rerelease it all over again in different packages. As late as 1966, "I'm So Lonesome I Could Cry" was dusted off and went to No. 43 (and No. 109 pop), and in '89 the composted "duet" of the song with Hank Sr. and Jr. hit No. 7. The chain went on, and on, the singles to be replaced in the 2000s by massive box sets, all of which would place somewhere on the country album chart. MGM had defined his legacy early, in ads it took out after his death, such as one in the December 5, 1953, *Billboard*, Hank's smiling face beaming under the stirring epitaph "Still King of 'em All."

• • •

Irene Smith, for whom serving as executrix of the estate was a full-time headache, decided in 1958 to leave the rat race of Montgomery. She left the boardinghouses to Marie Glenn (who would soon divorce and marry a man named Ed Harvell) and moved to Dallas with her husband and earned a real estate license. She had also been hired in March 1955 by *Country Song Roundup* to write a column called "Hank's Corner," doing so until 1961. The column, sometimes in the form of a letter addressed to Hank in the great beyond, was mainly designed to dispel the growing notion of him as a drunken

rakehell. Irene, who claimed she had "extra sensory" communica-
tions with Hank in death, and would later hold séances to "talk"
with him, wrote in one column:

> Hank drank, but he did not spend his whole life drunk. He was in
> terrible pain the last two years of his life and was given sedatives
> by his doctors for this pain. But Hank was not a dope addict, and
> as far as I know he never pitched a dope party in his life. Basi-
> cally, Hank was a clean, honest man [and not] the kind of person
> these people are writing about.[15]

She ended one of her letters with "So long, Hank; you and Mama
make a place for me. 'We three,' it always was and always will be."[16]

However, as she alluded to, by the late 1950s it was no longer
possible to pretend that Hank didn't live by the darkest and dirtiest
of impulses, and this made him prime fodder for the salacious pages
of low-grade men's magazines of the era, one of which described
him as an "ill-tempered, surly egomaniac who was only interested
in morphine, heroin, whiskey, and himself—in the order named,"[17]
though heroin had never been on his drug menu. This seedy, noir-ish
quality made him the kind of unmasked, troubled rebel who could
only suffer a tragic fate, like James Dean. Indeed, beneath the rebel
cool of a Hank Williams was the cautionary lesson that emulating
him just might kill you.

George Jones came close. He went on revering Hank, even had
himself introduced to an audience as "Hank Williams." He was
thrilled when, as he recalled, "somebody said I fulfilled the Hank
Williams mystique." But he did so all too well. He wound wind up
broke and homeless, suffering from mental illness, addicted to booze
and cocaine, living in his car and waving a gun around. One day he
was seen "loitering on Music Row, chatting up an eight-by-ten glossy
of Hank Williams."[18] Friends staged an intervention and committed
him to a psychiatric hospital—the very thing Hank refused to do
for himself—saving him, though he would have relapses all his life.

Still, as frightening as it was to envision oneself too deeply in the mold of Hank, he was an ideal subject for a movie.

Even as Lillie's death shelved her movie deal, Audrey had been working to revive it. There were discussions with MGM, and several scripts written, but Audrey had demands—as with Lillie's deal, there was to be no mention of Billie Jean or the divorce from Audrey, and no drinking. Joe Pasternak wouldn't give in this time, nor could they find a convincing leading man, though a young Steve McQueen's name was dropped as a possibility.

Then, in 1964, Audrey maneuvered to finally get a movie deal, partly to commercialize Hank Jr., who she demanded had to sing Hank's songs in the flick, but mostly to glorify herself and enrich the estate she had hopes of controlling one day. Hank Jr. was now fifteen, talented, handsome, and easily manipulated. As he would recall of touring with Audrey's "Caravan of Stars" in the early '60s, "There's a guy named Merle Haggard and one named Waylon and a little bitty kid out there, Hank Jr. And they're wondering which of those two guys is going to make it? And I'm in [Waylon Jennings's] Dodge motor home so I can get over there and sneak cigarettes to get away from mama."[19]

This time the studio agreed to Audrey's whitewashing demands and assigned the project to producer Sam Katzman, known as the "King of Schlock" for his cheaply made B-movies, including *Rock Around the Clock* and Elvis Presley's *Kissing Cousins*. Katzman wanted Elvis to play Hank, but he declined, as did Nick Adams, and the role went to suave, suntanned, distinctly non-Southern George Hamilton, a huge Williams fan. Audrey was given veto power on the script and casting, and was charmed by Hamilton when he pitched himself to her.

The product that came out of this, directed by Gene Nelson, was titled *Your Cheatin' Heart*. Filmed in black-and-white on a shoestring budget of $1.2 million, it was shot in Nashville, some scenes at Audrey's house, and reduced the rich Hank Williams saga to, as Hamilton later said, "quickie drive-in fare that might sell some records in the South and maybe to some crossover *Beverly Hillbillies* fans."[20] Audrey, played by pert Susan Oliver in a cast of mostly character actors, was portrayed as a wholesome, loyal wife still married to Hank when he died, who waited for him with the kids in Canton on that fateful day.

As Katzman sheepishly understated, "We didn't go for any art in it. We had to exaggerate a lot . . . just to get a story out of it"—a rather remarkable thing to say about Hank's life.[21] But then, the story had little to do with Hank Williams. Exaggeration is a mild word for a script that had Hank dying in Rufus Payne's arms and no mention of any divorce. While Hank was shown freely swigging booze, never was there the inference that he was an alcoholic, just a guy looking for a good time with occasional fits of temper he quickly atoned for.

Even more remarkably, and as a testament to how little the world actually knew about Hank, the movie was given a rave by the *New York Times*, with Hamilton called "perfectly cast as the homespun hero."[22] But when it was released in November—THE IMMORTAL HANK WILLIAMS LIVES AGAIN, SINGS AGAIN, read the ads—its limited distribution kept it from making more than around $1 million in its first run, although it may have been a good thing that the run was so limited that Billie Jean didn't see it. Per Audrey's demand, she was disappeared from the picture, though one character, a prostitute, seemed loosely based on her. The Williams estate reeled in half of that $1 million. But when Billie Jean did get around to seeing the flick, there would be hell to pay.

· · ·

Billie had played the lead role in her own drama, that of the beleaguered wife of another country star dying too young. Johnny Horton, managed by Tillman Franks, rose on radio and the *Hayride*, and in the late '50s scored a No. 1 country song, "When It's Springtime in Alaska (It's Forty Below)," and then exploded with the crossover megahits "The Battle of New Orleans," winning a Grammy for Best

Country & Western recording, and two movie themes, "Sink the Bismarck" and "North to Alaska." While he had labored, she continued to sing, too, as Billie Jean Horton, given contracts by 20th Century Fox and Atlantic and recording songs with titles like "Ocean of Tears" (a Top 40 country hit), "Johnny Come Lately," and "Octopus." But she seemed cursed. In 1960, now the mother of Horton's three daughters, she became a widow for the second time in seven years. Horton—ironically, after a show at the Skyline Club in Houston, where Hank played his last club date—was driving back to Shreveport when his car, a Cadillac, collided with a truck driven by a drunk nineteen-year-old and was killed, at age twenty-eight.

Billie Jean had to put another young husband into the cold ground. Again she rebounded quickly, having a fling with Horton's best friend, Johnny Cash, who was married at the time. Older and tougher now, she also would become a force in the industry by virtue of her refusal to fade away quietly. Like Hank, Horton had a backlog of recordings that became posthumous hits, and when they ran out, she collected demos he had made and took them to Nashville under an arrangement she made with his label, Columbia Records, whereby she would hire musicians to sweeten the tapes and then split the royalties when released.

Those records would clear around a million dollars a year through the '60s. By the end of the decade, she had gotten remarried, to an insurance man, Kent Berlin, and opened her own production agency. She was a known figure, identifiable around Shreveport in her long silver Mark IV upholstered in burgundy velvet, her home a mansion. Having learned a lot about baring long claws in the business, when the CBS network ran *Your Cheatin' Heart* on TV in 1969 and she saw it on a local station, she bared her own claws, real long.

She first filed suit in federal court against MGM, CBS, and Storer Broadcasting, owner of the local station, asking $1.1 million in damages. A hail of depositions followed, reprising the old issue of the legality of her marriage to Hank. This had been supposedly adjudicated in 1953 when a judge ruled against her, but she fought hard, crowing later, "They just weren't ready for Billie Jean. . . . They portrayed me as a harlot, but there they were in court looking at my marriage certificate with mine and Hank's signature on it."[23] The judge would reverse that call, deciding in June 1971 that she was "the lawful wife of the deceased." Billie Jean came away gloating, with hardy exaggeration, "It grossed $44 million, but I shut 'em down. They had lawyers stacked on top of one another, but I whupped 'em all over town." She later guessed she'd received a million in damages. In reality, the movie grossed nothing like $44 million, and the judge cleared the studio of any malicious intent, awarding no damages. Worse, she had rejected a five-figure settlement offer.[24]

Still, the ruling about the marriage was worth far more in the long run. The defendants immediately filed an appeal, but as revenge-minded as Billie Jean was, she didn't wait to flex her new muscle. Her target: the most lucrative of all Hank Williams properties, the copyright renewals on his songs. This was something Hank had thought nothing about, letting Fred Rose handle all that. But it became a major issue because by copyright law such rights on each song expired after twenty-eight years, in this case the first ones in 1972, whereupon they could be renewed and reassigned at astronomical rates.

Acuff-Rose, naturally seeking to reacquire them, first raised the matter with Irene Smith as early as 1960, then began negotiating with her, though she may not have been aware of the value of these rights herself. She accepted an offer in 1968 for Acuff-Rose to renew the rights—six years early—for $30,000, of which $25,000 went to the estate and $5,000 to Irene as broker. Audrey, who estimated the value at around half a million dollars, was aghast, wanting them for Hank Jr. as the rightful heir of the estate, and sued Irene, with Hank Jr. as co-plaintiff. Audrey could call in a lot of big guns to back her up, including Mitch Miller and the great Broadway songwriter Frank Loesser, but it was to no avail. The court upheld Irene as the rights holder.

Enter Billie Jean. Even before suing over the movie and regaining her widow's rights, she had a businessman named Ernest Brookings shop the copyright renewals in her name, claiming she had never specifically signed them away in the $30,000 buyout from Lillie and that she owned 50 percent, with the estate owning the other 50 percent. It seemed a long-shot case, but she enlisted a powerful ally, the world's largest music publisher, Hill & Range, which owned all of Elvis Presley's copyrights and chose his music for records and movies. They agreed to fund a lawsuit by Billie Jean against Acuff-Rose, on condition that if she won they would administer her half-ownership of the copyrights. That suit was in the hopper when she beat MGM and CBS, which seemed small change compared to the outcome of the copyright case, and as she contested Audrey's appeal of the judge's ruling upholding her widow status. The reason was clear: if she won those cases, Audrey Williams would be vanquished.

• • •

Another problem among many for Audrey was that her own son was growing apart from her. Up until the '70s, she had ruled him, guiding his career and choosing the material he would record, which was almost exclusively Hank Sr.'s old tunes. She was rewarded when his cover of "Long Gone Lonesome Blues" from the movie was a gusher—indeed, his work on the soundtrack made the flick for many, one critic saying the movie was "better heard than seen." Hank Jr., who in his formative years was a clean-cut young man with short blond hair clad in conservative suits, sang the song on the *Ed Sullivan Show* in 1964, reaping his first country hit at fourteen. He then became the youngest singer to earn a gold country record, for the soundtrack of that awful movie, and lived a path similar to his father's during his teenage years.

However, running in that crowd, he became a booze and pill hound as a teenager. And he saw only skimpy allowance money from Audrey, not legally entitled to any pay for his work until he turned eighteen in 1967, even if he was already living beyond his years.

"When I was eight or ten," he recalled, "they'd say, 'Hey, have a drink, Little Hank.' It turned those old guys on to be giving a drink to Hank Williams's son. Of course I didn't mind. It was just a chance to get away from Mother."[25]

Hank Jr., too, became familiar with courtroom warfare, having to testify in various actions contesting his guardianship, though this became moot when he reached eighteen. He also became familiar with how fast and loose his mother had been with the family's finances.

Court papers showed that Audrey had managed to lose over $400,000 in three years and was virtually broke. She had sunk it into things like a company to self-publish Hank Jr.'s original songs (Ly-Rann Music, named after her two children), iffy investments, travel, clothes, a Jacuzzi, a car for Hank Jr. designed by Nudie Taylor—the "Silver Dollar Car," which had 574 silver dollars embedded in it—thirty-seven pistols, and horses, and she planned to build a ballroom and gym in a new wing of the Franklin Street house. Audrey's 50 percent royalty cut came from the Hank Williams estate. And a remarkably generous Irene had paid off Audrey and Hank Jr.'s debts, the upshot of which was that by 1969 the estate's net worth had dropped from $1.6 million to only $203,000.[26] Irene had had enough of having to bail out Audrey, and enough of the constant warfare. That year, she resigned as administrator and put Hank Jr. in charge. Only twenty, he would soon learn what kind of heartburn *that* job entailed.

As it happened, pretty much all of Hank's blood relatives had to survive some sort of travail, with Irene Smith's being perhaps the most harrowing one. That same year, forty-seven and divorced since 1961, she fell in love with a man named Jorge Garcia, who went by the alias Edgar Babe. He lived in Mexico and wanted her to join him there. She later explained that in one of her séances with Hank, he had told her through a medium that Garcia "was no good for me," but she went anyway, driving Garcia's car.

At the Laredo, Texas, border, she was stopped, and when the

car searched, it was discovered that she was attempting to smuggle $7 million worth of cocaine. In October, she was sentenced to eight years in federal prison—in, of all places, West Virginia. Pitifully, she defended herself by saying, "You have to be a 47-year-old woman so lonely you just don't know what to do and how gullible and lonely a woman of [that] age can be."[27]

By contrast, Audrey had a right to be proud of her son, and herself for nudging Irene out. But Hank Jr. had had enough of his mother. He may have been sitting atop his father's estate, but he was about penniless. Audrey, of course, was hoping for a windfall, if only she could win the copyright battle against Billie Jean, for whom she now had a maniacal hatred. But on the endless conveyor belt of lawsuits—which Ralph J. Gleason wrote back in the '60s "goes on . . . like some ghost walking the pine hills for eternity"—someone else would emerge as a highly relevant party, even if she didn't know it yet.[28]

This was the no-longer little girl who still didn't know her father was Hank Williams. In the depositions there had been an obscure mention of a nameless illegitimate child, whom Lillie had acknowledged during her adoption petition as the child of Hank Williams. There was also a rumor that when the Deuprees learned this, they considered filing a claim with the Williams estate but dropped it because under law an adopted child has no claim on inheritance—a law that would be amended, with enormous significance, to permit claims such as copyright inheritance. In any case, the revelation sat quietly, but it presaged something that Lillie and Irene had feared all along: that the little girl when grown up could make things very complicated.

On January 25, 1974, weeks after Cathy Louise Deupree, now a student at the University of Alabama, turned twenty-one, her mother received word that there was a check for Cathy at the Montgomery County Courthouse. It was from the estate of the late Lillian Stone: the $2,200 due her as an inheritance. Louise Deupree then told Cathy about the rumors about who her father was, but cautioned her that "there's nothing you can do about it, there's no proof."[29]

As it happened, only weeks later, on April 27, Bobbie Webb Jett Tippins died in obscurity in Norwalk, California, at fifty-one, never having broken silence about the child she left behind. That was a name that would have meant nothing to Cathy Deupree. But when Cathy set out on a mission to ascertain whether the rumors were true, it would be a small piece of a very big puzzle, one that would take another decade to fit together.

· · ·

Left out of all these skirmishes and subterfuges was the Williams family member lost in history, the broken-down patriarch of the Williams clan. Elonzo Williams had aged quietly, all but forgotten, a family man with fading memories of his son and deep regrets that he hadn't seen him just before his death. An author writing a book about country music found him in 1967 living "by the side of the road" in McWilliams, and Lon enjoyed spinning tales about Hank's youth. Asked why he had been reported as dead, Lon shrugged and said, "I don't know for sure. The boy's mother, Lillian, and I did not get along too well," or it might have been the doing of "Miss Audrey." He said the state wanted to erect a shrine to his son, and he was working on the project, even boasted a letter from the governor.

It never happened, and on October 23, 1970, Lon died at seventy-eight. He was buried at the Hopewell Methodist Church cemetery. Lon, who the author wrote was "one of the most respectable persons I have ever had the pleasure of meeting," had outlived all of his family except for Irene, who made it all the way to 1995.[30]

"Miss Audrey" didn't survive Lon by much. The steely mistress who had coldly plotted to ride Hank's fame into her own, Audrey by the 1970s was tired and old before her time as well, and as susceptible as Hank had been to the comfort of firewater. Although she was still steely in business matters, the rest of the time she was a worn-out alcoholic mess living off her concocted identity as Hank's "real" widow, judges' rulings notwithstanding; still making a buck or two off the legend, she toured as "Audrey Williams" backed by either the "Singing Cowgirls" or the "Cold, Cold Hearts." She often posed for pictures with the death-car Caddy, which she had sued to recover from Irene after Lillie's death and kept conspicuously on the driveway of the Franklin Street house. As she aged, she craved more and more attention, and was seen frequently at chic parties, posing with celebrities, glass of booze in her hand.

Her looks had been eroded by age and alcohol, and her mind was the next to go. A friend of hers would recall her as "not a pleasant drunk. Her thinking would become totally irrational, and she could be verbally and even violently abusive, like the time she got mad at [a friend] and shot the windows out of his car,"[31] a highly ironic turn, to be sure. This only fed the premise held by many that she was the villain who had driven Hank over the edge, or at the very least proven how much they were indeed soulmates.

In any case, her own son felt he had to put distance between them. Hank Jr. fled Nashville and moved to rural Cullman, Alabama. He fired the manager Audrey had hired for him years ago, Buddy Lee. "The only person I felt close to," he would say, "was Daddy, and he was dead. I understood him like I never understood him before."[32] Understood, yes. Learned from his old man's flaws? Not so much. Hank Jr., too, would be stuck in sanitariums and nearly crack up under the weight of a name that became a curse. At the same time, Audrey lurched toward her end, hastened by her humiliation by the person she hated most—the only legal "Mrs. Hank Williams."

That happened on October 22, 1975, when Billie Jean prevailed on all counts in the copyright war, based on her status as Hank Williams's "common law" wife. Her deal with Hill & Range on her half of the copyrights could now go through, sending Acuff-Rose into a tizzy, and Audrey into a bigger one. After being stripped of the mantle of being Mrs. Hank Williams, she would not make another penny from the royalties she had gained in the divorce, at the price of never marrying.

Hank Jr. was gone, as were her health and sanity. "That fall," Lycrecia recalled, "Mother was close to dying. I guess Mother couldn't see any reason to live, much less stay straight."[33]

Things had been going badly enough. Only three months before, divorced and hurting, Hank Jr. had been on a hunting trip near the Great Divide at Missoula, Montana, when he fell five hundred feet down a mountainside, peeling off most of his face. He was in critical condition for six days, and the lingering pain and disfigurement would keep him addicted to booze and painkillers for most of his adult life.

Audrey herself was constantly in ill health, and trouble. During the summer of 1972, she was arrested twice for drunk driving: in DeFuniak Springs, Florida, she was also charged with resisting arrest and destruction of county property when she broke windows in the county jail while waiting to be bailed out; in Brantley, Alabama, troopers simply escorted her to a friend's home. She had also attempted suicide with sleeping pills and when discovered motionless was taken to have her stomach pumped. The doctor told Lycrecia, "One day she'll destroy herself . . . and you won't be able to do anything about it." She had to undergo stomach surgery early in '75. Before that, for the past several years, she had tried to open a Hank Williams museum east of Nashville, coincidentally, or not, in a nearby town called Oak Hill, but the town refused her a permit because of the heavy traffic it would bring. All but broke, she once held a garage sale of items she had left of Hank's, sitting in the driveway, barely moving and inebriated, in front of a life-size cardboard cutout of him.

If all this wasn't bad enough, her mother, Artie Mae Sheppard, died of cancer that ominous fall of '75, and the IRS was after Audrey for $400,000 in unpaid back taxes and threatened to take her home, her *castle*, and a châlet she had bought in Gatlinburg. The IRS informed her they would be seizing the house on November 5. "They'll never take me out of this house alive. . . . I'll shoot anybody that tries to come in and take this house," she vowed to Lycrecia.

Unable to sleep, she would again pour sleeping pills down her throat, and two days before the IRS raid, she told a friend that during her drug-induced sleep she'd had a dream that Hank had come back and they had made love, and he had told her everything was going to be all right.[34] "God will get me out of this," she said. A day later, November 4, 1975, she was found dead in her bed, of heart failure, just like Hank.

Estranged as he was from her, Hank Jr. was devastated by her death. When he came to the funeral, one writer described him as looking "like death itself."[35] The IRS took no pity. They came on schedule and seized the house, selling it for $200,000, less than half of what Audrey owed. Neither did she go into the cold, cold earth next to Hank, not yet. She was buried in Oakwood Cemetery, where mourners included George Wallace and Wesley Rose, in a plain grave, dressed in a purple cowgirl outfit with pearl buttons and rhinestones. In 1983, after the second of the twin monuments at Hank's gravesite went up, as planned, Hank Jr. and Lycrecia moved her remains there. It was her only enduring victory, a posthumous slap at Billie Jean, the sole *living* Mrs. Hank Williams.

· · ·

Cathy Deupree's quest had sputtered. The '70s passed with no further light shed on the rumor she was Hank's daughter. Pushing thirty, she had been married and divorced, worked at a community center, and had been urged many times to forget the whole thing. But she had no doubt who her father was.

Watching an old video of him, she said, "when he turns to look at the camera, it felt like he was looking straight at me. When my eyes met his, I thought I was looking at myself."[36] On a visit to the Vital Statistics Bureau in Montgomery she saw her birth certificate, with Bobbie Jett listed as her mother and the father's name left blank. She learned of the contract signed by Bobbie Jett and Hank, which had been sealed by the courts in 1967. Then, in 1985, while snooping around Montgomery she ran into none other than Charles

Carr, who remembered her as a baby and said he'd known Bobbie Jett when she lived at the boardinghouse; he even made a cryptic reference, saying it was okay for him to talk to her because "the estate had been settled."

Carr also said she should talk to the now-elderly Marie Glenn Harvell, who was still living on Pickett Street. When she called on her, Marie recognized a scar on Cathy's arm from childhood and exclaimed, "My baby's come home!" Marie sat her down and went through the entire history with her, saying, not completely honestly, that "Hank's first cousin Bobbie Jett is your mother. But I raised you . . . you were my baby."[37]

After hiring attorney Keith Atkinson, whom she would later marry, she began inquiring about Hank's copyright renewals. That led Hank Jr. to slap a cease-and-desist suit on her. But now she was prepared to file her own action, against the estate for having pursued an "elaborate conspiracy of greed and silence" against her. Even before the case was filed in federal court in New York, she told her story to the press; cashing in on the publicity, she boldly changed her name to Jett Williams, to honor the mother and father she never knew, and formed a country band, even getting to sing and play with Don Helms and Jerry Rivers, as the Drifting Cowboys Band. But even though she won a separate trial in Alabama that declared her to be Hank's natural child, the federal case was thrown out on grounds that she had waited too long to file. She appealed, lost again, and in May 1989 took her appeal to the US Supreme Court.

Jett lost the appeal, too. However, she had other options. She had also sued in Alabama to be able to claim an inheritance from Hank's estate—i.e., the copyrights—and lost there as well, appealing that decision to the state supreme court. And then things took a new turn. First, the Alabama Supreme Court reversed the inheritance decision, saying she was in fact a victim of fraud and was entitled to a share of the estate. Now it was Hank Jr. who appealed to the highest court in the land. In September 1990, the Court refused to hear his appeal. That day, Jett said, "the neighbors came by in their boats, blowing their air horns and yelling congratulations. I think it makes people feel good to see someone win after having been done wrong."[38]

So now Hank's estate was a three-headed hydra, four with the copyrights still being administered by Acuff-Rose (which has been handed off from one publishing cartel to another in the age of corporate mergers and acquisitions and is now part of the massive global Sony Corporation). Somehow, all were expected to work smoothly, though the three people involved basically hated each other.

It became a two-headed creature in 2001 when Billie Jean, who had been reeling in around a quarter of a million dollars a year from the copyrights, sold her share of them back to Acuff-Rose. (By then Hill & Range had pawned off its holdings, selling their split of the Hank copyrights to Billie Jean.) And Hank Jr. and Jett together were fighting Polygram Records for joint ownership of the long-lost *Mother's Best Flour Show* recordings; after a lower court ruled they alone had the rights to sell the recordings, a Tennessee appeals court in 2006 upheld the ruling, leading to the prodigious collections of unreleased recordings by Time Life. They also apparently signed off on yet one more attempt at a Hank Williams movie, *I Saw the Light*, directed and produced by Marc Abraham, which after several snags finally hit the screen in March 2016, drawing reviews as stinging as those given the previous attempt and earning only $1.6 million as of midyear, far below its $13 million budget. When it comes to recreating Hank Williams on film, no one seems to be able to get it right. But while Hank Jr. may never accept the legitimacy of the half-sister sprung on him, when it comes to recreating him as a business commodity, they have gotten it very right. Hank Sr. might even be proud that in the end his blood united his children, at least in profit.

. . .

Blessedly removed from the infighting and avarice only members of the Williams family and their lawyers cared about, the legend of Hank Williams flourished. Through the years he seemed to pop up everywhere in pop culture. The soundtrack of Peter Bogdanovich's splendid 1971 adaptation of Larry McMurtry's 1966 novel *The Last Picture Show* unearthed a trove of Hank's songs, for many the first they'd heard of them. Willie Nelson's first break was when he was taken into Ray Price's post-Hank Cherokee Cowboys. Johnny Cash was so epoxied to Hank that Hank Jr. would present him with his father's old chrome-plated six-shooter, which Cash proudly brandished on the cover of his album *The Last Gunfighter Ballad* in 1977.

By the mid-'70s, whenever a movie dropped about a postmodern, existentialist Southern singer, the lead character was a thinly disguised Hank—e.g., Kris Kristofferson in the Barbra Streisand remake of *A Star Is Born*. Indeed, Kristofferson was said to have been one of the choices to play the lead in one of the many aborted movies about Hank, a 1978 project to have been directed by Paul Schrader, which was axed when either Hank Jr. or Acuff-Rose apparently thought the script "too dark."[39]

That lingering darkness, however, even in his brightest songs, keeps him uniquely *Hank*. His stamp on country is permanent, unyielding. It explains why his granddaughter Holly Williams has toured with a latter-day version of the Drifting Cowboys. Why Loretta Lynn once bought a bed Hank had slept in to keep in her house.[40] Why Tammy Wynette in 1992 bought the house where Audrey died—and where Tammy, herself plagued by ill health and addicted to painkillers, died in her sleep of a blood clot in her lung in 1998.[41] Why the house would remain in the country "family," bought next by Reba McEntire. And why "Little Joe" Pennington, at eighty-seven the last living Drifting Cowboy to have played with Hank, has kept old pictures and other keepsakes of Hank festooned around his Florida home to this day.

"People don't generally know that Hank only recorded two albums when he was alive," he says, "and I got one of 'em, right here, an original 78. I never played it, I just wanted to keep it. And now I'm thinkin' one day I'm gonna let it go and sell it for a big amount of money." A belly laugh. "It would be the only time Hank ever made me any money."[42]

It's also why, down Georgiana way, the curator of the Hank Williams Museum is busy on this hot May afternoon trying to tie up the details of the Hank Williams Festival hoedown to be held at the house in June. Today's visitors have included, he says, a group from Mobile's McGill-Toolen Catholic High School and "a young lady from Australia." A film crew from Japan is filming the house for a TV special about Hank for Nippon Hoso Kyokai, Japan's largest public network.

Up in "Capitol Cool," Montgomery's latest tourist slogan, meanwhile, foot traffic at Hank's gravesite is hectic, as always. Sometimes boneheads come looking for souvenirs. Years ago, two small statues of Hank's cowboy boots were so chipped that they were recast as urns. This sort of thing led Hank Jr. to erect a sign reading please don't desecrate this sacred site. Generally, though, people find their way here to find some peace while knocking back a tall one with a head. Just such a visit once led Waylon Jennings to ask himself, in song:

> *I stopped by today at Hank Williams' grave, my hero from the days*
> *of my youth*
> *Was that him or me that I used to be in the times when I searched*
> *for the truth?*

The answer would seem to be both. Perhaps like no other singer of sad, sad songs, when Hank Williams gets into the bloodstream through the ears, you don't hear him. You hear the sound of your own beating, cheating heart.

NOTES

✳ ✳ ✳ ✳ ✳ ✳ ✳

INTRODUCTION: JUST PLAIN HANK

1. Nick Kent, "The Allman Brothers: Brothers and Sisters," *New Musical Express*, August 18, 1973.
2. "Honky Tonk Women," http://www.timeisonourside.com/SOHonky.html.
3. Rev. A. S. Turnipseed, "Pulpit Echoes," *Montgomery Examiner*, December 11, 1947.
4. "Hank Williams Among 2010 Pulitzer Winners," *CNN.com*, April 13, 2010, http://www.cnn.com/2010/SHOWBIZ/Music/04/12/pulitzer.prize .winners/.
5. Paul Hemphill, *Lovesick Blues* (New York: Penguin Group, 2005), 5–6.
6. Loretta Lynn and George Vecsey, *Coal Miner's Daughter* (Washington, DC: Regnery, 1976), 101.
7. Ed Linn, "The Short Life of Hank Williams," *Saga*, January 1957, 10.
8. Chet Flippo, *Your Cheatin' Heart* (London: Plexus, 1981), 142.
9. Bob Dylan, *Chronicles: Volume One* (New York: Simon & Schuster, 2005), 97.
10. Christopher Lehman-Haupt, "Books of the Times: White Soul," *New York Times*, April 27, 1970, 31.
11. Patrick Huber, Steve Godson, and David M. Anderson, *The Hank Williams Reader* (New York: Oxford University Press, 2014), 5.
12. "Was Singer a Suicide?," *Oklahoma City Times*, March 18, 1943.
13. William E. Cleghorn, "Hank Williams Rides on down Trail of National Popularity on Air Records," *Montgomery Examiner*, August 21, 1947.
14. Griel Marcus, *Mystery Train: Images of America in Rock 'n' Roll Music*, 5th ed. (New York: Plume, 2008), 148.
15. Ralph J. Gleason, "Hank Williams, Roy Acuff and Then God!!" *Rolling Stone*, June 28, 1969.
16. Garrison Keillor, "'Lovesick Blues': Long Gone Daddy," *New York Times*, September 25, 2005.
17. Hugh Barker and Yuval Taylor, *Faking It: The Quest for Authenticity in Popular Music* (New York: W. W. Norton, 2007), 126.

18. Henry Pleasants, *The Great American Popular Singers* (New York: Simon & Schuster, 1974), 229.

19. Marcus, *Mystery Train*, 130.

20. Kim Makarechi, "Hank Williams Jr.: Obama Is 'a Muslim President Who Hates Farming, Hates the Military, Hates the U.S. and We Hate Him,'" *HuffingtonPost.com*, http://www.huffingtonpost.com/2012/08/18/hank -williams-jr-obama-is-muslim-hate_n_1804184.html.

21. Brian Tashman, "Kevin Swanson Speculates That Kacey Musgraves Would Have Been Killed for 'Promoting Homosexuality' in the 1960s," *Right Wing Watch*, April 22, 2014, http://www.rightwingwatch.org/content/kevin -swanson-speculates-kacey-musgraves-would-have-been-killed-promoting -homosexuality-1960.

22. Willie Nelson and Kinky Friedman, *Roll Me Up and Smoke Me When I Die: Musings from the Road* (William Morrow, 2012), x.

PROLOGUE: A WHEEL IN THE DITCH AND A WHEEL ON THE TRACK

1. Mills J. Thorton, "Selma to Montgomery March," *Encyclopedia of Alabama*, http://www.encyclopediaofalabama.org/article/h-1114.

2. Jay Reeves, "Alabama Still Collecting Tax for Confederate Vets," Associated Press, July 20, 2011; "Interracial Marriage Laws: A Short Timeline History," *About.com*, updated December 16, 2014, http://civilliberty.about .com/od/raceequalopportunity/tp/Interracial-Marriage-Laws-History -Timeline.htm.

CHAPTER 1: KING HIRAM

1. John L. Kilgore, *Hank's Alabama Heroes: A Civil War Family History* (CreateSpace/Amazon, 2013), 7–9.

2. US Census Bureau, "Selected Economic Characteristics, 2006–2010, American Community Survey 5-Year Estimates," http://factfinder.census .gov/faces/tableservices/jsf/pages/productview.xhtml?src=bkmk.

3. Brian Turpen, "Mary Ella 'Ada' Bolton Grace, Lillie's Mid-wife for Baby Hank," *Hank Williams Books*, http://hpcisp.com/~turp/adagrace.html.

4. Colin Escott and Kira Florita, *Hank Williams: Snapshots from the Lost Highway* (New York: Da Capo, 2001), 22.

5. Harper Lee, *To Kill a Mockingbird* (New York: Grand Central Publishing, Mass Market Paperback, 1988), 174.

6. Roger Williams, *Sing a Sad Song: The Life of Hank Williams* (Urbana: University of Illinois Press, 1970), 6, 7.

7. Chet Flippo, *Your Cheatin' Heart* (London: Plexus, 1981), 12.

8. Ibid., 13.

9. Ed Linn, "The Short Life of Hank Williams," *Saga*, January 1957, 88.

10. Williams, *Sing a Sad Song*, 11.

11. *Time*, April 15, 1935.

12. Bill C. Malone, *Don't Get Above Your Raisin'* (Urbana: University of Illinois Press, 2006), 17.

13. Rufus, Jarman, "Country Music Goes to Town," *Nation's Business*, February 1953, 51.

14. Williams, *Sing a Sad Song*, 8.

15. Ralph J. Gleason, "Hank Williams, Roy Acuff and Then God!!" *Rolling Stone*, June 28, 1969.

16. Williams, *Sing a Sad Song*, p, 11.

CHAPTER 2: AN AMERICAN TWANG

1. Charles Wolfe, *The Devil's Box: Masters of Southern Fiddling* (Nashville, TN: Vanderbilt University Press/Country Music Foundation Press, 1997).

2. Lynn Abbott and Doug Seroff, "America's Blue Yodel," *Musical Traditions* 11 (1999): 2.

3. Roger Williams, *Sing a Sad Song: The Life of Hank Williams* (Urbana: University of Illinois Press, 1970), 10.

4. Colin Escott, with George Merritt and William MacEwen, *Hank Williams: The Biography* (New York: Back Bay Books, 2004), 14.

5. Brian Turpin, "Hank's Georgiana, Alabama Homes," *Hank Williams Books*, http://hpcisp.com/~turp/georgianahomes.html.

6. Ibid.

7. Paul Hemphill, *Lovesick Blues* (New York: Penguin, 2005), 15.

8. Williams, *Sing a Sad Song*, 12.

9. Escott, *Hank Williams: The Biography*, 8.

10. Irene Williams Smith, "The Day Hank Williams Lived," *Washington Post*, January 1, 1993.

11. "Hank Williams: Honky Tonk Blues," documentary, BBC Four Arena, 2004.

12. Williams, *Sing a Sad Song*, 12.

13. Allen Rankin, "Rankin File: 'Cause Hank Is Moving In, Move It Over, Big Time," *Montgomery Advertiser*, April 4, 1948.

CHAPTER 3: "COUNTRY MUSIC AIN'T NOTHIN' BUT WHITE PEOPLE'S BLUES, ANYWAY"

1. Roger Williams, *Sing a Sad Song: The Life of Hank Williams* (Urbana: University of Illinois Press, 1970), 27.

2. Paul Hemphill, *Lovesick Blues* (New York: Penguin Group, 2005), 17.

3. Jay Caress, *Hank Williams: Country Music's Tragic King* (New York: Stein & Day, 1979), 11.

4. Mrs. W. W. Stone, with Allen Rankin, *Our Hank Williams, the Drifting Cowboy* (Montgomery, AL: Philbert Productions, 1953).

5. Williams, *Sing a Sad Song*, 21.

6. "Spina Bifida Association," http://spinabifidaassociation.org/what-is-sb/.

7. Colin Escott and Kira Florita, *Hank Williams: Snapshots from the Lost Highway* (New York: Da Capo, 2001), 202.

8. American Public Media, "New York Clashes with the Heartland," *American RadioWorks*, http://americanradioworks.publicradio.org/features/radio/b1.html.

9. Bill Koon, *Hank Williams: So Lonesome* (Jackson: University Press of Mississippi, 2001), 9.

10. Williams, *Sing a Sad Song*, 28.

11. Ken Morton Jr., "The Man Who Taught Hank Williams How to Play Guitar: The Story of Rufus Payne," *Engine145.com*, February 12, 2010, http://engine145.com/the-man-who-taught-hank-williams-how-to-play-guitar-the-story-of-rufus-payne.

12. Ralph J. Gleason, "Hank Williams, Roy Acuff and Then God!!" *Rolling Stone*, June 28, 1969.

13. "Hank Williams: Honky Tonk Blues," documentary, BBC Four Arena, 2004.

14. Ibid.

15. Irene Williams Smith, "The Day Hank Williams Lived," *Washington Post*, January 1, 1993.

16. Escott and Florita, *Hank Williams: Snapshots from the Lost Highway*, 27.

17. Maggie Martin, "Uncovering Secrets Buried at a Neglected Cemetery," *NPR.org*, August 9, 2012, http://www.npr.org/2012/08/09/158428314/uncovering-secrets-buried-at-a-neglected-cemetery.

CHAPTER 4: I GOT A HOME IN MONTGOMERY

1. "History Detectives: Radio in the 1930s," *PBS.org*, http://www.pbs.org/opb/historydetectives/feature/radio-in-the-1930s.

2. "Behind the Dial: Radio in the 1930's," *Radiostratosphere.com*, http://www.radiostratosphere.com/zsite/behind-the-dial/radio-in-1930.html.

3. Elizabeth Roe Schlappi, *Roy Acuff: The Smoky Mountain Boy* (Gretna, LA: Pelican, 1993), 37.

4. Mrs. W. W. Stone, with Allen Rankin, *Our Hank Williams, the Drifting Cowboy* (Montgomery, AL: Philbert Productions, 1953).

5. Andy Brown, "Schuffert Remembers Meeting Hank," *Greenville Advocate*, June 4, 2012.

6. "Hank Williams: Honky Tonk Blues," documentary, BBC Four Arena, 2004.

7. Chet Flippo, *Your Cheatin' Heart* (London: Plexus, 1981), 31.

8. Brown, "Schuffert Remembers Meeting Hank."

CHAPTER 5: "DON'T TELL MAMA"

1. Lon Willams, undated letter to *Progressive Era*, cited in Colin Escott and Kira Florita, *Hank Williams: Snapshots from the Lost Highway* (New York: Da Capo, 2001), 30.
2. Colin Escott, with George Merritt and William MacEwen, *Hank Williams: The Biography* (New York: Back Bay Books, 2004), 14.
3. Roger Williams, *Sing a Sad Song: The Life of Hank Williams* (Urbana: University of Illinois Press, 1970), 27.
4. Escott and Florita, *Hank Williams: Snapshots from the Lost Highway*, 35.
5. Ralph J. Gleason, "Hank Williams, Roy Acuff and Then God!!" *Rolling Stone*, June 28, 1969.
6. Ibid.
7. Bill Koon, *Hank Williams: So Lonesome.* (Jackson: University Press of Mississippi, 2001), 18, 19.
8. Escott, *Hank Williams: The Biography*, 24.
9. Ibid.
10. Escott and Florita, *Snapshots from the Lost Highway*, 39.
11. Escott, *Hank Williams: The Biography*, 23.
12. Ibid., 26.
13. Williams, *Sing a Sad Song*, 41.
14. Paul Hemphill, *Lovesick Blues* (New York: Penguin Group, 2005), 34.
15. Escott, *Hank Williams: The Biography*, 15.
16. Williams, *Sing a Sad Song*, 49.

CHAPTER 6: DRYDOCK

1. Mrs. W. W. Stone, with Allen Rankin, *Our Hank Williams, the Drifting Cowboy* (Montgomery, AL: Philbert Productions, 1953).
2. Roger Williams, *Sing a Sad Song: The Life of Hank Williams* (Urbana: University of Illinois Press, 1970), 42.
3. Ibid., 30.
4. Ibid., 40.
5. Ibid.
6. Jay Caress, *Hank Williams: Country Music's Tragic King* (New York: Stein & Day, 1979), 46.
7. Stone, *Our Hank Williams*.
8. Caress, *Country Music's Tragic King*, 47.
9. Lycrecia Williams and Dale Vinicur, *Still in Love with You: The Story of Hank and Audrey Williams* (Nashville, TN: Rutledge Hill Press, 1989), 12.
10. Ibid., 11, 12.
11. Stone, *Our Hank Williams*.

12. Colin Escott and Kira Florita, *Hank Williams: Snapshots from the Lost Highway* (New York: Da Capo, 2001), 47.
13. Escott, *Hank Williams: The Biography*, 32.
14. "Hank Williams: Honky Tonk Blues," documentary, BBC Four Arena, 2004.
15. Williams, *Sing a Sad Song*, 44.
16. Chet Flippo, *Your Cheatin' Heart* (London: Plexus, 1981), 38.
17. Author interview with Joe Pennington.
18. Stone, *Our Hank Williams*.

CHAPTER 7: "AUDREY, GET ME A BOTTLE"

1. Lycrecia Williams and Dale Vinicur, *Still in Love with You: The Story of Hank and Audrey Williams* (Nashville, TN: Rutledge Hill Press, 1989), 5.
2. Unpublished Audrey Williams manuscript, cited in ibid., 6.
3. Colin Escott, with George Merritt and William MacEwen, *Hank Williams: The Biography* (New York: Back Bay Books, 2004), 35.
4. Chet Flippo, *Your Cheatin' Heart* (London: Plexus, 1981), 41.
5. Escott, *Hank Williams: The Biography*, 37–38.
6. Roger Williams, *Sing a Sad Song: The Life of Hank Williams* (Urbana: University of Illinois Press, 1970), 43–44.
7. Escott, *Hank Williams: The Biography*, 36.
8. Jay Caress, *Hank Williams: Country Music's Tragic King* (New York: Stein & Day, 1979), 38.
9. Colin Escott and Kira Florita, *Hank Williams: Snapshots from the Lost Highway* (New York: Da Capo, 2001), 46.
10. Caress, *Country's Tragic King*, 38.
11. Williams and Vinicur, *Still in Love with You*, 14.
12. Bill Koon, *Hank Williams: So Lonesome* (Jackson: University Press of Mississippi, 2001), 23.
13. Caress, *Country Music's Tragic King*, 37.
14. "Hank Williams: Honky Tonk Blues," documentary, BBC Four Arena, 2004.
15. Ibid.

CHAPTER 8: "IT AIN'T A FUNNY SONG"

1. Colin Escott and Kira Florita, *Hank Williams: Snapshots from the Lost Highway* (New York: Da Capo, 2001), 51.
2. Lycrecia Williams and Dale Vinicur, *Still in Love with You: The Story of Hank and Audrey Williams* (Nashville, TN: Rutledge Hill Press, 1989), 18.
3. Jay Caress, *Hank Williams: Country Music's Tragic King* (New York: Stein & Day, 1979), 40.

4. Ibid., 42.
5. Colin Escott, with George Merritt and William MacEwen, *Hank Williams: The Biography* (New York: Back Bay Books, 2004), 43.
6. Ibid.
7. Chet Flippo, *Your Cheatin' Heart* (London: Plexus, 1981), 52.
8. Escott, *Hank Williams: The Biography*, 45.
9. Williams and Vinicur, *Still in Love with You*, 19.
10. Caress, *Country Music's Tragic King*, 50.
11. Escott, *Hank Williams: The Biography*, 46.
12. Caress, *Country Music's Tragic King*, 54.
13. "WSM Tower Gets 'Historic' Status," *Tennessean*, April 14, 2011.
14. Myron Tassin and Jerry Henderson, *Fifty Years at the Grand Ole Opry* (Gretna, LA: Pelican, 1975), 20.
15. Bill C. Malone, *Don't Get Above Your Raisin'* (Urbana: University of Illinois Press, 2006), 160.

CHAPTER 9: BOTTLE UP AND GO

1. Lycrecia Williams and Dale Vinicur, *Still in Love with You: The Story of Hank and Audrey Williams* (Nashville, TN: Rutledge Hill Press, 1989), 29.
2. Ibid., 23.
3. "Hank Williams: Honky Tonk Blues," documentary, BBC Four Arena, 2004.
4. Ibid.
5. Colin Escott and Kira Florita, *Hank Williams: Snapshots from the Lost Highway* (New York: Da Capo, 2001), 52.
6. Williams and Vinicur, *Still in Love with You*, 24.
7. Jay Caress, *Hank Williams: Country Music's Tragic King* (New York: Stein & Day, 1979), 54.
8. Roger Williams, *Sing a Sad Song: The Life of Hank Williams* (Urbana: University of Illinois Press, 1970), 58.
9. Colin Escott, with George Merritt and William MacEwen, *Hank Williams: The Biography* (New York: Back Bay Books, 2004), 54.
10. John Rockwell, "Molly O'Day, Singer of Country Music in Roughhewn Style," *New York Times*, December 8, 1987.
11. Escott, *Hank Williams: The Biography*, 56.
12. Williams, *Sing a Sad Song*, 59–60.
13. Mrs. W. W. Stone, with Allen Rankin, *Our Hank Williams, the Drifting Cowboy* (Montgomery, AL: Philbert Productions, 1953).
14. Bill Holdship, "The Wit & Wisdom of Prince Rogers Nelson," *Creem*, July 1985.
15. Williams and Vinicur, *Still in Love with You*, 31.
16. Ibid., 28.

17. Escott and Florita, *Hank Williams: Snapshots from the Lost Highway*, 54.
18. Paul Hemphill, *Lovesick Blues* (New York: Penguin Group, 2005), 63.
19. Caress, *Country Music's Tragic King*, 53.
20. Ibid., 55.
21. Ibid.
22. Hemphill, *Lovesick Blues*, 65.
23. Caress, *Country Music's Tragic King*, 67.
24. Hemphill, *Lovesick Blues*, 65.
25. Williams, *Sing a Sad Song*. 65.
26. Michael Streisgus, *Eddy Arnold: Pioneer of the Nashville Sound* (New York: Schirmer Trade Books, 1997), 106.
27. Escott, *Hank Williams: The Biography*, 60.

CHAPTER 10: FROM A MEAN BOTTLE

1. Rady Lewis, "Uncle Art Satherley, 96, Recording Industry Pioneer," *New York Times*, February 12, 1986.
2. Roger Williams, *Sing a Sad Song: The Life of Hank Williams* (Urbana: University of Illinois Press, 1970), 66–67.
3. Colin Escott, with George Merritt and William MacEwen, *Hank Williams: The Biography* (New York: Back Bay Books, 2004), 67.
4. Colin Escott and Kira Florita, *Hank Williams: Snapshots from the Lost Highway* (New York: Da Capo, 2001), 54.
5. Ibid., 57.
6. Allen Rankin, "Rankin File: 'Cause Hank is Moving In, Move It Over, Big Time," *Montgomery Advertiser*, April 4, 1948.
7. Chet Flippo, *Your Cheatin' Heart* (London: Plexus, 1981), 58.
8. "Hank Williams: Honky Tonk Blues," documentary, BBC Four Arena, 2004.
9. David Brackett, *Interpreting Popular Music* (Cambridge: Cambridge University Press, 1996), 106.
10. Ibid., 68.
11. Escott and Florita, *Snapshots from the Lost Highway*, 68.
12. Paul Hemphill, *Lovesick Blues* (New York: Penguin Group, 2005), 67.
13. Lycrecia Williams and Dale Vinicur, *Still in Love with You: The Story of Hank and Audrey Williams* (Nashville, TN: Rutledge Hill Press, 1989), 32.
14. Escott, *Hank Williams: The Biography*, 63.
15. Williams and Vinicur, *Still in Love with You*, 32.
16. Author interview with Joe Pennington.
17. Williams and Vinicur, *Still in Love with You*, 30.
18. Escott, *Hank Williams: The Biography*, 91.
19. "Chicago Stories: James C. Petrillo," *WTTW.com*, http://www.wttw.com/main.taf?p=1,7,1,1,38.

20. Escott, *Hank Williams: The Biography*, 75.
21. Nick Tosches, *Country: The Twisted Roots of Rock 'n' Roll* (New York: Da Capo Press, 1996), 230.
22. Escott, *Hank Williams: The Biography*, 65.
23. Escott and Florita, *Snapshots from the Lost Highway*, 69.
24. Williams and Vinicur, *Still in Love with You*, 31.
25. Allen Rankin, "Rankin File."

CHAPTER 11: "SYRUP SOPPER" OR "POPULIST POET"

1. Chet Flippo, *Your Cheatin' Heart* (London: Plexus, 1981), 65.
2. Colin Escot and Kira Florita, *Hank Williams: Snapshots from the Lost Highway* (New York: Da Capo, 2001), 66.
3. Ibid., 71.
4. Escott and Florita, *Snapshots from the Lost Highway*, 71.
5. Colin Escott, with George Merritt and William MacEwen, *Hank Williams: The Biography* (New York: Back Bay Books, 2004), 79.
6. Bill Koon, *Hank Williams: So Lonesome* (Jackson: University Press of Mississippi, 2001), 37.
7. Lycrecia Williams and Dale Vinicur, *Still in Love with You: The Story of Hank and Audrey Williams* (Nashville, TN: Rutledge Hill Press, 1989), 39.
8. "World War II and Alabama," *Encyclopedia of Alabama*, http://www .encyclopediaofalabama.org/article/h-1348.
9. "Hank Williams Rides On down Trail of National Popularity on Air Records," *Montgomery Examiner*, August 21, 1947.
10. A. S. Turnipseed, "Pulpit Echoes," *Montgomery Advertiser*, December 1, 1947.
11. Allen Rankin, "Rankin File: 'Cause Hank Is Moving In, Move It Over, Big Time," *Montgomery Advertiser*, April 4, 1948.
12. Roger Williams, *Sing a Sad Song: The Life of Hank Williams* (Urbana: University of Illinois Press, 1970), 70.
13. "Hank Williams: Honky Tonk Blues," documentary, BBC Four Arena, 2004.
14. All quotes from Joe Pennington in this chapter are from author interviews.
15. "The Mudcat Cafe: Leadbelly, King of the 12-String Guitar," http://www .mudcat.org/huddie.cfm.
16. Rachel Aviv, "Revenge Killing," *New Yorker*, July 6, 2015, http://www .newyorker.com/magazine/2015/07/06/revenge-killing.
17. Escott, *Hank Williams: The Biography*, 87.
18. Ibid., 87.
19. Lauren Bradshaw, ClotureClub.com, http://www.clotureclub.com/2016/03 /our-interview-with-tom-hiddleston-marc-abraham-for-i-saw-the-light/.
20. Escott, *Hank Williams: The Biography*, 94.

21. Williams and Vinicur, *Still in Love with You*, 40.
22. Flippo, *Your Cheatin' Heart*, 66.
23. Williams, *Sing a Sad Song*, 78–79.
24. Williams and Vinicur, *Still in Love with You*, 41.
25. Hours of Hank's $33^1/_3$ RPM transcription disks survived, though no one figured they'd be worth much in the future. And the journey of these disks would be circuitous; in the mid-'50s they would somehow become the property of Leonard Chess, the owner of the rock/R&B label Chess, who would sell them to MGM, and in the early '70s they were sold again when MGM was subsumed by Polydor; when Polydor, in turn, merged with the Universal Music Group in the '90s, the old MGM country catalog fell under the Universal Music Group Nashville imprint. Only then would the radio broadcasts be released on the Mercury label, which had also been bought by Polydor. Excerpts of the Johnnie Fair shows and Hank's later radio shows in Nashville went on Mercury's 1998 ten-CD avalanche of MGM's and Sterling's long-vaulted material, *The Complete Hank Williams*.

    However, only two of his *Hayride* shows seem to have been preserved, badly, though in one of them, from June 18, 1949, there is a faithful rendition of "Lovesick Blues," backed by Red Foley's band, the same unit that recorded Hank's record of it. The other is taken from a show in Germany on November 18, 1949, during a *Hayride* tour of military bases in Europe. These, too, would be among the material on the acetates sold by Leonard Chess to MGM and released decades later by Mercury.

    The surviving Johnnie Fair shows prove that Hank's range of material was broad, including Joe Pope's "Leave Me Alone with These Blues," Johnny Wright and Jim Anglin's "Little Paper Boy," and Pee Wee King's "My Main Trial Is Yet to Come" and "Sundown and Sorrow." Odell McLeod's "We Planted Flowers on My Darling's Grave," Fred Rose's "No One Will Ever Know," "Thank God" and "The Prodigal Son," Ralph Jones' "Please Don't Let Me Love You," Johnny Bond's "Rock My Cradle," Lonnie Glossom and Bill Carlisle's "Rockin' Chair Money," Eddie Hill and Jean Branch's "Someday You'll Call My Name," Pail Howard's "With Tears in My Eyes," Clyde Moody's "You Caused It All by Telling Lies," and Jimmie Work's "Tennessee Border." Notable by their absence in this argosy are his own compositions, which he would only sparingly perform; to Audrey's delight, among the exceptions was a duet she did on the air with Hank, "Lost on the River."
26. Colin Escott, *Hank Williams: The Biography*, 95.
27. Troy Washington, KSLA News, "Neighbors set sights on preserving Hank Williams' old home," March 19,2016, http://www.ksla.com/story/29827372 /neighbors-set-sights-on-preserving-hank-williams-old-home.

CHAPTER 12: "THE SORRIEST THING I EVER DID HEAR"

1. Garrison Keillor, "'Lovesick Blues': Long Gone Daddy," *New York Times*, September 25, 2005.
2. Lycrecia Williams and Dale Vinicur, *Still in Love with You: The Story of Hank and Audrey Williams* (Nashville, TN: Rutledge Hill Press, 1989), 48.
3. Colin Escott and Kira Florita, *Hank Williams: Snapshots from the Lost Highway* (New York: Da Capo, 2001), 104.
4. Jay Caress, *Hank Williams: Country Music's Tragic King* (New York: Stein & Day, 1979), 77.
5. Williams and Vinicur, *Still in Love with You*, 47.
6. Ibid.
7. Ibid., 45.
8. Ibid., 42.
9. Colin Escott, with George Merritt and William MacEwen, *Hank Williams: The Biography* (New York: Back Bay Books, 2004), 93.
10. Roger Williams, *Sing a Sad Song: The Life of Hank Williams* (Urbana: University of Illinois Press, 1970), 73.
11. Caress, *Country Music's Tragic King*, 81.
12. Paul Hemphill, *Lovesick Blues* (New York: Penguin Group, 2005), 78.
13. Sanford Mabrie, "The Strange Life and Death of Hank Williams," *Behind the Scene*, September 1955, 29.
14. Caress, *Country Music's Tragic King*, 91.
15. Escott, *Hank Williams: The Biography*, 98.
16. Hemphill, *Lovesick Blues*, 81.
17. Escott and Florita, *Snapshots from the Lost Highway*, 81.
18. Escott, *Hank Williams: The Biography*, 97.
19. Williams and Vinicur, *Still in Love with You*, 40.
20. Rick Bird, "Herzog Is Hallowed Ground," *CityBeat.com*, November 16, 2009, http://citybeat.com/cincinnati/article-19322-herzog-is-hallowed -ground.html.
21. "Lovesick Blues," http://www.revolvy.com/main/index.php?s=Lovesick %20Blues.
22. Escott, *Hank Williams: The Biography*, 99.
23. Williams and Vinicur, *Still in Love with You*, 44.
24. "Clyde Baum: He Picked Bluegrass Tunes with Hank Williams," *Shreveport Times*, July 10, 1980.

CHAPTER 13: "*NEVER* PUT ME ON AFTER HANK WILLIAMS!"

1. Lycrecia Williams and Dale Vinicur, *Still in Love with You: The Story of Hank and Audrey Williams* (Nashville, TN: Rutledge Hill Press, 1989), 42.

2. Ibid.

3. Kevin Richards, "Who Is Bocephus? Story Behind Hank Williams Jr.'s Nickname," *WGNA.com*, http://wgna.com/who-is-bocephus-story-behind -hank-williams-jr-s-nickname/?trackback=tsmclip.

4. "Hank Williams: Honky Tonk Blues," documentary, BBC Four Arena, 2004.

5. Williams and Vinicur, *Still in Love with You*, 49–50.

6. Colin Escott, with George Merritt and William MacEwen, *Hank Williams: The Biography* (New York: Back Bay Books, 2004), 101.

7. Ibid., 212–13.

8. Jay Caress, *Hank Williams: Country Music's Tragic King* (New York: Stein & Day, 1979), 100.

9. Chet Flippo, *Your Cheatin' Heart* (London: Plexus, 1981), 79-81.

10. Colin Escott and Kira Florita, *Hank Williams: Snapshots from the Lost Highway* (New York: Da Capo, 2001), 105.

11. Tracey E. W. Laird, *Louisiana Hayride: Radio and Roots Music Along the Red River* (Oxford and New York: Oxford University Press, 2004), 84.

12. Escott, *Hank Williams: The Biography*, 117.

13. Williams and Vinicur, *Still in Love with You*, 52.

14. Ibid.

15. Dorothy Horstman, *Sing Your Heart Out, Country Boy* (New York: E. P. Dutton, 1975), 170.

16. Roger Williams, *Sing a Sad Song: The Life of Hank Williams* (Urbana: University of Illinois Press, 1970), 130.

CHAPTER 14: PETTIN' PARTIES, CIGARETTES, AND GIN

1. Roger Williams, *Sing a Sad Song: The Life of Hank Williams* (Urbana: University of Illinois Press, 1970), 170.

2. Colin Escott and Kira Florita, *Hank Williams: Snapshots from the Lost Highway* (New York: Da Capo, 2001), 102.

3. Ann Anderson, *Snake Oil, Hustlers and Hambones: The American Medicine Show* (Jefferson, NC: McFarland, 2004), 152.

4. Two of these eight *Health and Happiness* shows, with seven songs, were packaged by MGM in 1962 in two 16-inch disks as *Hank Williams on Stage*; most of them went onto Mercury's 1993 *Health and Happiness Shows*, and all are on Time-Life's 2011 three-CD set *The Legend Begins*.

5. Lycrecia Williams and Dale Vinicur, *Still in Love with You: The Story of Hank and Audrey Williams* (Nashville, TN: Rutledge Hill Press, 1989), 56.

6. Escott and Florita, *Snapshots from the Lost Highway*, 100.

7. Paul Hemphill, *Lovesick Blues* (New York: Penguin Group, 2005), 106–7.

8. Williams and Vinicur, *Still in Love with You*, 57.

9. Ibid.

10. "Hank Williams: Honky Tonk Blues," documentary, BBC Four Arena, 2004.
11. Williams and Vinicur, *Still in Love with You*, 121.
12. Minnie Pearl with Joan Dew, *Minnie Pearl: An Autobiography* (Nashville, TN: Opryland & Richards, 1980), 211.
13. "Hank Williams: Fireball with a Guitar," *Pathfinder*, June 4, 1952.
14. Williams, *Sing a Sad Song*, 110.
15. Ibid, 113.
16. Hemphill, *Lovesick Blues*, 116.
17. Gert J. Almind, "Origin of the Term Jukebox," http://juke-box.dk/gert-origin.htm.
18. Williams, *Sing a Sad Song*, 104.
19. Pearl, *Minnie Pearl*, 216.

CHAPTER 15: "IT'S *NEVER* TOO COUNTRY"

1. Bruce Britt, "The 45-RPM Single Will Soon Be History," *Los Angeles Daily News*, August 10, 1989, C4.
2. Chet Flippo, *Your Cheatin' Heart* (London: Plexus, 1981), 108.
3. Lycrecia Williams and Dale Vinicur, *Still in Love with You: The Story of Hank and Audrey Williams* (Nashville, TN: Rutledge Hill Press, 1989), 62.
4. Colin Escott, with George Merritt and William MacEwen, *Hank Williams: The Biography* (New York: Back Bay Books, 2004), 143.
5. Ibid., 147.
6. Roger Williams, *Sing a Sad Song: The Life of Hank Williams* (Urbana: University of Illinois Press, 1970), 181.
7. Ibid., 181–82.
8. Williams and Vinicur, *Still in Love with You*, 66.
9. Williams, *Sing a Sad Song*, 164.
10. Ibid., 165.
11. Ibid.
12. Lycrecia Williams and Dale Vinicur, *Still in Love with You*, 67.
13. Flippo, *Your Cheatin' Heart*, 82.
14. Paul Hemphill, *Lovesick Blues* (New York: Penguin Group, 2005), 113.
15. Audrey Williams interview with Dorothy Horstman, 1973.
16. Flippo, *Your Cheatin' Heart*, 129.

CHAPTER 16: A BRAND-NEW RECIPE

1. John McWethy, "Hillbilly Tunes Boom," *Wall Street Journal*, October 2, 1951.
2. Joe Nick Patoski, *Willie Nelson: An Epic Life* (New York: Little, Brown, 2008), 150.

3. Chet Atkins and Bill Neely, *Chet Atkins: Country Gentleman* (Chicago: Regnery, 1975), 135.

4. Roger Williams, *Sing a Sad Song: The Life of Hank Williams* (Urbana: University of Illinois Press, 1970), 128.

5. Ibid., 127.

6. Chet Flippo, *Your Cheatin' Heart* (London: Plexus, 1981), 120.

7. Colin Escott and Kira Florita, *Hank Williams: Snapshots from the Lost Highway* (New York: Da Capo, 2001), 117.

8. Colin Escott, with George Merritt and William MacEwen, *Hank Williams: The Biography* (New York: Back Bay Books, 2004),156.

9. Lycrecia Williams and Dale Vinicur, *Still in Love with You: The Story of Hank and Audrey Williams* (Nashville, TN: Rutledge Hill Press, 1989), 82.

1. Ibid., 83.

11. Audrey Williams interview with Dorothy Horstman, 1973.

12. Jay Caress, *Hank Williams: Country Music's Tragic King* (New York: Stein & Day, 1979), 135.

CHAPTER 17: "DON'T HE KILL AN AUDIENCE?"

1. Roger Williams, *Sing a Sad Song: The Life of Hank Williams* (Urbana: University of Illinois Press, 1970), 117.

2. Colin Escott, with George Merritt and William MacEwen, *Hank Williams: The Biography* (New York: Back Bay Books, 2004), 157.

3. Tony Bennett on *Imus in the Morning*, MSNBC, 2006.

4. Tony Bennett, *The Good Life: The Autobiography of Tony Bennett* (New York: Simon & Schuster, 1998), 110–11.

5. Glenn O'Brien, "Tony Bennett: Rebirth of the Cool," *Spin*, February 1988.

6. "Gold in Them Hillbillies," unidentified Charleston, SC, newspaper, March 10, 1951.

7. Jay Caress, *Hank Williams: Country Music's Tragic King* (New York: Stein & Day, 1979), 119.

8. Ibid., 119, 120.

9. Charles Wolfe, Liner notes to *Life's Like Poetry* by Lefty Frizzell, Bear Family Records, 1992.

10. David Frizzell, *I Love You a Thousand Ways: The Lefty Frizzell Story* (Solana Beach, CA: Santa Monica Press, 2011).

11. Escott, *Hank Williams: The Biography*, 173.

12. Ibid., 174.

13. Lycrecia Williams and Dale Vinicur, *Still in Love with You: The Story of Hank and Audrey Williams* (Nashville, TN: Rutledge Hill Press, 1989), 75.

14. Chet Flippo, *Your Cheatin' Heart* (London: Plexus, 1981), 152–53.

15. Ibid., 153.

16. Escott, *Hank Williams: The Biography*, 170.
17. Promotional announcement, included on *The Complete Hank Williams* box set.
18. Williams and Vinicur, *Still in Love with You*, 70.
19. Colin Escott and Kira Florita, *Hank Williams: Snapshots from the Lost Highway* (New York: Da Capo, 2001), 110.
20. Williams and Vinicur, *Still in Love with You*, 71.
21. Toru Mitsui, "Jimmie Davis," in *The Encyclopedia of Country Music* (New York: Oxford University Press, 1998), 136.
22. Escott, *Hank Williams: The Biography*, 179.

CHAPTER 18: "THE GUN SHOT FOUR TIMES"

1. Colin Escott and Kira Florita, *Hank Williams: Snapshots from the Lost Highway* (New York: Da Capo, 2001), 131.
2. Minnie Pearl, with Joan Dew, *Minnie Pearl: An Autobiography* (Nashville, TN: Opryland & Richards, 1980), 212.
3. Colin Escott, with George Merritt and William MacEwen, *Hank Williams: The Biography* (New York: Back Bay Books, 2004), 188.
4. Ibid., 189.
5. "Hank Has a Method: Williams Tells How and Why His Disks Click," *Billboard*, November 24, 1951, 22.
6. Escott and Florita, *Snapshots from the Lost Highway*, 132.
7. Bill Koon, *Hank Williams: So Lonesome* (Jackson: University Press of Mississippi, 2001), 126.
8. Jerry Rivers, *From Life to Legend* (Denver: Heather Publications, 1967).
9. Escott, *Hank Williams: The Biography*, 189.
10. "Television Appearances," *Hank Williams: The Complete Website*, http://www.angelfire.com/country/hanksr/television.htm.
11. Escott, *Hank Williams: The Biography*, 192.
12. Mike Callahan, David Edwards, and Peter Preuss, "MGM Album Discography, Part 1, 10-inch LPs," http://www.bsnpubs.com/mgm/mgm10.html.
13. Susan Masino, *Family Tradition—Three Generations of Hank Williams* (New York: Backbeat Books, 2011), 81.
14. Recorded radio announcement, December 1951.
15. Chet Flippo, *Your Cheatin' Heart* (London: Plexus, 1981), 170.
16. Jay Caress, *Hank Williams: Country Music's Tragic King* (New York: Stein & Day, 1979), 139.
17. "Hank Williams: Honky Tonk Blues," documentary, BBC Four Arena, 2004.
18. Lycrecia Williams and Dale Vinicur, *Still in Love with You: The Story of Hank and Audrey Williams* (Nashville, TN: Rutledge Hill Press, 1989), 79.

19. Ibid., 78.
20. Mark Zwonitzer, with Charles Hirshberg, *Will You Miss Me When I'm Gone? The Carter Family and Their Legacy in American Music* (New York: Simon & Schuster, 2004), 295.
21. Williams and Vinicur, *Still in Love with You*, 71.
22. Ibid., 85.
23. Flippo, *Your Cheatin' Heart*, 171.
24. Williams and Vinicur, *Still in Love with You*, 73.
25. "Honky Tonk Blues," BBC.

CHAPTER 19: "ALMOST A CONTINUOUS NIGHTMARE"

1. *Audrey Mae Williams v. Hank Williams, et al.*, Office of Clerk and Master, Chancery Court of Davidson County, Nashville, Tennessee, Bill of Complaint of Audrey Mae Williams, filed January 10, 1952.
2. *Audrey Mae Williams v. Hank Williams, et al.*, Office of Clerk and Master, Chancery Court of Davidson County, Nashville, Tennessee, Answer and Cross-Bill of the Defendant and Cross-Complaint, Hank Williams, filed ca. March 5, 1952.
3. Edith Lindeman, "Hank Williams Hillbilly Show Is Different," *Richmond Times-Dispatch*, January 30, 1952.
4. Lycrecia Williams and Dale Vinicur, *Still in Love with You: The Story of Hank and Audrey Williams* (Nashville, TN: Rutledge Hill Press, 1989), 84.
5. Mark Zwonitzer, with Charles Hirshberg, *Will You Miss Me When I'm Gone? The Carter Family and Their Legacy in American Music* (New York: Simon & Schuster, 2004), 295.
6. Chet Flippo, *Your Cheatin' Heart* (London: Plexus, 1981), 173.
7. John Gilmore, *Laid Bare: A Memoir of Wrecked Lives and the Hollywood Death Trip* (Los Angeles: Amok Books, 1997), 27.
8. Ralph J. Gleason, "Hank Williams, Roy Acuff and Then God!!" *Rolling Stone*, June 28, 1969.
9. Colin Escott, with George Merritt and William MacEwen, *Hank Williams: The Biography* (New York: Back Bay Books, 2004), 191.
10. Esther Williams and Digby Diehl, *The Million Dollar Mermaid: An Autobiography* (Fort Washington, PA: Harvest Books, 2000), 203, 210.
11. Jay Caress, *Hank Williams: Country Music's Tragic King* (New York: Stein & Day, 1979), 149–50.
12. Gilmore, *Laid Bare*, 26–27.
13. Minnie Pearl, with Joan Dew, *Minnie Pearl: An Autobiography* (Nashville, TN: Opryland & Richards, 1980), 211–12.
14. Ibid., 213.
15. Bill Koon, *Hank Williams: So Lonesome* (Jackson: University Press of Mississippi, 2001), 127.

16. Paul Hemphill, *Lovesick Blues* (New York: Penguin Group, 2005), 155.
17. Zwonitzer, *Will You Miss Me When I'm Gone?*, 296.
18. Hemphill, *Lovesick Blues*, 156.

CHAPTER 20: HURTING FROM INSIDE

 1. Roger Williams, *Sing a Sad Song: The Life of Hank Williams* (Urbana: University of Illinois Press, 1970), 179–80.
 2. Ibid., 179.
 3. Lycrecia Williams and Dale Vinicur, *Still in Love with You: The Story of Hank and Audrey Williams* (Nashville, TN: Rutledge Hill Press, 1989), 100.
 4. Colin Escott and Kira Florita, *Hank Williams: Snapshots from the Lost Highway* (New York: Da Capo, 2001), 152.
 5. Ibid, 153.
 6. John Gilmore, *Laid Bare: A Memoir of Wrecked Lives and the Hollywood Death Trip* (Los Angeles: Amok Books, 1997), 27, 29.
 7. Williams, *Sing a Sad Song*, 194.
 8. "Hank Williams: Honky Tonk Blues," documentary, BBC Four Arena, 2004.
 9. Paul Hemphill, *Lovesick Blues* (New York: Penguin Group, 2005), 160.
10. "Honky Tonk Blues," BBC.
11. Jay Caress, *Hank Williams: Country Music's Tragic King* (New York: Stein & Day, 1979), 190.
12. Diane Diekman, *Live Fast, Love Hard: The Faron Young Story* (Urbana: University of Illinois Press, 2012), 23–24.
13. Williams and Vinicur, *Still in Love with You*, 77–78.
14. George Lipsitz, *Rainbow at Midnight: Labor and Culture in the 1940s* (Urbana: University of Illinois Press, 1994), 28.
15. David Brackett, *Interpreting Popular Music* (Cambridge: Cambridge University Press, 1996), 106.
16. Williams and Vinicur, *Still in Love with You*, 105.
17. Williams, *Sing a Sad Song*, 193.
18. H. B. Teeter, "Hank Williams Had Premonition of Death," *Nashville Tennessean*, January 2, 1953.
19. Colin Escott, with George Merritt and William MacEwen, *Hank Williams: The Biography* (New York: Back Bay Books, 2004), 215.
20. Ibid., 240.
21. Caress, *Country Music's Tragic King*, 183.
22. Williams, *Sing a Sad Song*, 185.

CHAPTER 21: SO FAR GONE

 1. Colin Escott, with George Merritt and William MacEwen, *Hank Williams: The Biography* (New York: Back Bay Books, 2004), 226.

2. Chet Flippo, *Your Cheatin' Heart* (London: Plexus, 1981), 184.

3. Ibid.

4. Billie Jean Williams Berlin deposition, *Billie Jean Williams Berlin vs. MGM Inc.*, *Civil Action No. 12,181*, filed December 13, 1968.

5. Roger Williams, *Sing a Sad Song: The Life of Hank Williams* (Urbana: University of Illinois Press, 1970), 197.

6. Ibid., 196.

7. Escott, *Hank Williams: The Biography*, 227.

8. Ibid., 228.

9. Ibid.

10. "Hank Williams: Honky Tonk Blues," documentary, BBC Four Arena, 2004.

11. Williams, *Sing a Sad Song*, 107.

12. Escott, *Hank Williams: The Biography*, 231.

13. "Trip to Cabin Paid for Hank Williams with Song, Daughter to Link Lineage," *Augusta Chronicle*, September 10, 2009.

14. Ibid.

15. Escott, *Hank Williams: The Biography*, 233.

16. Jay Caress, *Hank Williams: Country Music's Tragic King* (New York: Stein & Day, 1979), 194.

17. Oscar Davis interview, Country Music Foundation Oral History Project, September 24, 1974.

18. Colin Escott and Kira Florita, *Hank Williams: Snapshots from the Lost Highway* (New York: Da Capo, 2001), 165.

19. Escott, *Hank Williams: The Biography*, 235.

20. Ibid., 248.

21. Bill Koon, *Hank Williams: So Lonesome.* (Jackson: University Press of Mississippi, 2001), 74.

22. *Connie's Prescription Shop vs. McCann*, case number 37369, decided July 30, 1957, Supreme Court of Oklahoma, http://law.justia.com/cases/oklahoma/supreme-court/1957/26648.html.

23. Lycrecia Williams and Dale Vinicur, *Still in Love with You: The Story of Hank and Audrey Williams* (Nashville, TN: Rutledge Hill Press, 1989), 104.

24. Ibid., 103.

25. Williams, *Sing a Sad Song*, 207.

26. Ibid., 208.

27. "Honky Tonk Blues," BBC Four.

28. Rush Evans, "Separate Truth from Fiction in Country Icon Hank Williams' Final Days," *Goldmine*, April 21, 2010, http://www.goldminemag.com/article/feature-article-separate-truth-from-fiction-in-country-icon-hank-williams-final-days-2#sthash.33EMdIP6.dpuf.

29. Escott, *Hank Williams: The Biography*, 237.

30. *Billie Jean Williams Berlin vs. MGM Inc.*

31. Williams, *Sing a Sad Song*, 204.

32. "Honky Tonk Blues," BBC Four.

33. Audrey Williams interview with Dorothy Horstman, 1973.

34. *Billie Jean Williams Berlin vs. MGM Inc.*

35. Escott, *Hank Williams: The Biography*, 241.

36. Flippo, *Your Cheatin' Heart*, 192.

37. Oscar Davis interview, Country Music Foundation Oral History Project, 1974.

38. Williams and Vinicur, *Still in Love with You*, 106.

CHAPTER 22: "I SEE JESUS COMIN' DOWN THE ROAD"

1. Billie Jean Williams Berlin deposition, *Billie Jean Williams Berlin vs. MGM Inc.*, *Civil Action No. 12,181*, filed December 13, 1968.

2. Roger Williams, *Sing a Sad Song: The Life of Hank Williams* (Urbana: University of Illinois Press, 1970), 203.

3. Lycrecia Williams and Dale Vinicur, *Still in Love with You: The Story of Hank and Audrey Williams* (Nashville, TN: Rutledge Hill Press, 1989), 119.

4. Williams, *Sing a Sad Song*, 204.

5. Ibid.

6. *Billie Jean Williams Berlin vs. MGM Inc.*

7. Oscar Davis interview, Country Music Foundation Oral History Project, 1974.

8. "Country Boy Returns," *Montgomery Alabama Journal*, December 29, 1952.

9. Colin Escott, with George Merritt and WIlliam MacEwen, *Hank Williams: The Biography* (New York: Back BayBooks, 2004), 243.

10. Marriage certificate number 23624 on file at the Bossier City Parish courthouse, Benton, Louisiana.

11. Escott, *Hank Williams: The Biography*, 244.

12. Williams, *Sing a Sad Song*, 202.

13. Chet Flippo, *Your Cheatin' Heart* (London: Plexus, 1981), 197.

14. Ibid., 198.

15. Williams, *Sing a Sad Song*, 202.

16. Flippo, *Your Cheatin' Heart*, 196.

17. "Hank Williams: Honky Tonk Blues," documentary, BBC Four Arena, 2004.

18. Rush Evans, "Separate Truth from Fiction in Country Icon Hank Williams' Final Days," *Goldmine*, April 21, 2010, http://www.goldminemag.com/article/feature-article-separate-truth-from-fiction-in-country-icon-hank-williams-final-days-2#sthash.33EMdIP6.dpuf.

19. Escott, *Hank Williams: The Biography*, 249.

CHAPTER 23: "DON'T WORRY ABOUT OL' HANK"

1. Jay Caress, *Hank Williams: Country Music's Tragic King* (New York: Stein and Day, 1979), 195.

2. Colin Escott, with George Merritt and William MacEwen, *Hank Williams: The Biography* (New York: Back Bay Books, 2004), 246.

3. Escott, *Hank Williams: The Biography*, 250.

4. Colin Escott and Kira Florita, *Hank Williams: Snapshots from the Lost Highway* (New York: Da Capo, 2001), 167.

5. Roger Williams, *Sing a Sad Song: The Life of Hank Williams* (Urbana: University of Illinois Press, 1970), 208.

6. Chet Flippo ,*Your Cheatin' Heart* (London: Plexus, 1981), 198-199.

7. Paul Hemphill, *Lovesick Blues* (New York: Penguin Group, 2005), 174.

8. Flippo, *Your Cheatin' Heart*, 201.

9. Escott, *Hank Williams: The Biography*, 251.

10. Irene Williams Smith, "My Treasured Life with a Beloved Brother," in *Hank Williams: The Legend*, ed. Thurston Moore (Denver: Heather Enterprises, 1972), 5.

11. Rush Evans, "Separate Truth from Fiction in Country Icon Hank Williams' Final Days," *Goldmine*, April 21, 2010, http://www.goldminemag.com /article/feature-article-separate-truth-from-fiction-in-country-icon-hank -williams-final-days-2#sthash.33EMdIP6.dpuf.

12. Hemphill, *Lovesick Blues*, 175.

13. Escott, *Hank Williams: The Biography*, 253.

14. Rush, "Final Days."

15. Escott, *Hank Williams: The Biography*, 256.

16. Rush, "Final Days."

17. Williams, *Sing a Sad Song*, 211.

18. Ibid.

19. Ibid., 212.

20. Caress, *Country Music's Tragic King*, 204.

21. Escott, *Hank Williams: The Biography*, 258.

22. Escott and Florita, *Snapshots from the Lost Highway*, 169.

23. Escott, *Hank Williams: The Biography*, 261.

24. Caress, *Country Music's Tragic King*, 201.

25. Lycrecia Williams and Dale Vinicur, *Still in Love with You: The Story of Hank and Audrey Williams* (Nashville, TN: Rutledge Hill Press, 1989), 107.

26. Ibid., 109.

27. Escott, *Hank Williams: The Biography*, 255.

28. Escott and Florita, *Snapshots from the Lost Highway*, 170–71.

29. Ibid., 169.

30. Hank Williams Jr., with Michael Bane, *Living Proof: An Autobiography* (New York: G. P. Putnam's Sons, 1979), 61, 64.

31. Billie Jean Williams Berlin Deposition, *Billie Jean Williams Berlin vs. MGM Inc.*, *Civil Action No. 12,181*, filed December 13, 1968.

32. Ibid., 261.

33. *George Jones—Same Old Me*, documentary, DVD edition (West Long Branch, NJ: White Star, 2002).

CHAPTER 24: THEN CAME THAT FATEFUL DAY

1. Colin Escott, with George Merritt and William MacEwen, *Hank Williams: The Biography* (New York: Back Bay Books, 2004), 265.
2. "Hank Williams: Honky Tonk Blues," documentary, BBC Four Arena, 2004.
3. Ibid.
4. Ibid.
5. Alan Williams, "Former Knoxville Bellhop Sheds Light on Hank Williams Sr's Final Hours," WVLT, Knoxville, April 2, 2009, http://www.local8now.com/news/headlines/42307217.html; Wayne Bledsoe, "The Night Hank Died: Mystery Still Shrouds Country Legend's Death 50 Years Ago," Scripps Howard News Service, *Topeka Capital Journal*, January 3, 2003.
6. "Charles Carr Dies at 79; Driver on Hank Williams Sr.'s Final Trip," *Los Angeles Times*, July 7, 2013.
7. Ibid.
8. Jim Thorpe, "Hank Williams' Last Ride: Driver Recalls Lonesome End," *Atlanta Journal-Constitution*, December 30, 2002.
9. Bledsoe, "The Night Hank Died."
10. Thorpe, "Hank Williams' Last Ride."
11. Colin Escott and Kira Florita, *Hank Williams: Snapshots from the Lost Highway* (New York: Da Capo, 2001), 172.
12. Roger Williams, *Sing a Sad Song: The Life of Hank Williams* (Urbana: University of Illinois Press, 1970), 215.
13. Thorpe, "Hank Williams' Last Ride."
14. Billie Jean Williams Berlin deposition, *Billie Jean Williams Berlin vs. MGM Inc., Civil Action No. 12,181*, filed December 13, 1968.
15. Lycrecia Williams and Dale Vinicur, *Still in Love with You: The Story of Hank and Audrey Williams* (Nashville, TN: Rutledge Hill Press, 1989), 113.
16. Ibid.
17. Williams, *Sing a Sad Song*, 216.
18. Ibid.
19. Escott, *Hank Williams: The Biography*, 275.
20. Ibid.
21. "Honky Tonk Blues," BBC Four.
22. George Jones, *I Lived to Tell It All* (New York: Villard, 1996), 39.
23. *Billie Jean Williams Berlin vs. MGM Inc.*
24. Billie Jean Horton, "Fear and Loathing at Hank's Funeral," *Texas Music*, June 1976, 45, 46.

25. Escott, *Hank Williams: The Biography*, 274.
26. Maura Kistler, "I Won't Be Home No More: The Death of Hank Williams," *Goldenseal* 28 (Winter 2002): 291; Thorpe, "Hank Williams' Last Ride."
27. Irene Williams, letter to Robert B. Stewart, January 28, 1972.
28. Horton, "Fear and Loathing at Hank's Funeral."
29. Williams, *Sing a Sad Song*, 227.
30. Williams and Vinicur, *Still in Love with You*, 114.
31. Irene Williams, letter to Robert B. Stewart, January 28, 1972.
32. Escott and Florita, *Snapshots from the Lost Highway*, 180.
33. Escott, *Hank Williams: The Biography*, 279.
34. Eli Waldron, "Country Music: The Death of Hank Williams," *Reporter*, May 19, 1955, 35.
35. Escott, *Hank Williams: The Biography*, 279.
36. Kistler, "I Won't Be Home No More."
37. Ibid.
38. Norbert F. Voeklel et al, "Right Ventricular Function and Failure," *American Heart Association Journal* 114 (2006): 1883–91, http://circ.ahajournals.org/content/114/17/1883.full.
39. Flippo, *Your Cheatin' Heart*, 208.
40. Williams, *Sing a Sad Song*, 218.
41. Bill Koon, *Hank Williams: So Lonesome* (Jackson: University Press of Mississippi, 2001), 79.
42. *Nashville Banner*, January 2, 1953; *Nashville Tennessean*, January 3, 1953.
43. *Spokane Daily Chronicle*, January 8, 1953.
44. "A New Category of National Hero," *Hartford Courant*, January 12, 1953.
45. Horton, "Fear and Loathing at Hank's Funeral."

EPILOGUE: OF MYTH AND MEN

1 Christie's auction results, Sale 2276, Lot 40, December 3, 2009, http://www.christies.com/lotfinder/musical-instruments/hank-williams-cf-martin-and-company-a-5273014-details.aspx.
2. Colin Escott and Kira Florita, *Hank Williams: Snapshots from the Lost Highway* (New York: Da Capo, 2001), 189.
3. Roger Williams, *Sing a Sad Song: The Life of Hank Williams* (Urbana: University of Illinois Press, 1970), 234.
4. Jay Caress, *Hank Williams: Country Music's Tragic King* (New York: Stein & Day, 1979), 217.
5. Ibid.
6. Chet Flippo, *Your Cheatin' Heart* (London: Plexus, 1981), 228.
7. Colin Escott, with George Merritt and William MacEwen, *Hank Williams: The Biography* (New York: Back Bay Books, 2004), 284.

8. "No Connection of Pills and Death," *Ada* (Oklahoma) *Weekly News,* March 31, 1953.

9. Mrs. W. W. Stone, with Allen Rankin, *Our Hank Williams: The Drifting Cowboy* (Montgomery, AL: Philbert Publications, 1953).

10. Audrey Williams, "Hank's First Wife Tells Up and Downs of Marriage," *Montgomery Advertiser,* January 13, 1953.

11. Lisa L. Rollins, "Hank Williams Sr. Daughter Gives Rare Interview," *Suite. io,* November 12, 2008, https://suite.io/lisa-l-rollins/15m92k2.

12. Escott, *Hank Williams: The Biography,* 289.

13. Hank Williams Jr., with Michael Bane, *Living Proof: An Autobiography* (New York: G. P. Putnam's Sons, 1979), 63.

14. Escott, *Hank Williams: The Biography,* 283.

15. Irene Williams Smith, "Hank's Corner," *Country Song Roundup,* February 1957, 8.

16. Ibid., June 1957, 8.

17. Sanford Mabrie, "The Strange Life and Death of Hank Williams," *Behind the Scene,* September 1955, 29.

18. Jack Isenhour, *He Stopped Loving Her Today: George Jones, Billy Sherrill, and the Pretty-Much Totally True Story of the Making of the Greatest Country Record of All Time* (Jackson: University Press of Mississippi, 2011), 155.

19. "20 Questions With Hank Williams Jr.," *CMT.com,* June 14, 2006, http://www.cmt.com/news/1534326/20-questions-with-hank-williams-jr/.

20. George Hamilton and William Stadiem, *George Hamilton: Don't Mind If I Do* (New York: Touchstone, 2008), 180.

21. Ibid.

22. Escott, *Hank Williams: The Biography,* 305.

23. Associated Press, "She's Living Off Two Country Music Legends," October 1, 1975.

24. United Press International, "Late Star's Widow Wins Court Battle," June 11, 1971.

25. Peter Guralnick, *Lost Highway: Journeys and Arrivals of American Musicians* (Jaffrey, NH: David R. Godine, 1979), 221.

26. Escott, *Hank Williams: The Biography,* 294.

27. Irene Williams Smith, "My Treasured Life with a Beloved Brother," in *Hank Williams: The Legend,* ed. Thurston Moore (Denver: Heather Enterprises, 1972), 7.

28. Ralph J. Gleason, "Hank Williams, Roy Acuff and Then God!!" *Rolling Stone,* June 28, 1969, 32.

29. Michelle Green, "Vindicated in Court, Hank Williams's Daughter, Jett, Can Claim a Share of Her Father's Estate—and His Heritage," *People,* September 17, 1990.

30. Harry E. Rockwell, *Beneath the Applause: A Story About Country & Western Music and Its Stars—Written by a Fan* (Chambersburg, PA: privately published, 1973), 13–15.

31. Lycrecia Williams and Dale Vinicur, *Still in Love with You: The Story of Hank and Audrey Williams* (Nashville, TN: Rutledge Hill Press, 1989), 159.

32. Ibid., 180.

33. Ibid., 171, 184.

34. Ibid., 185.

35. John Morthland, "Hank Williams Jr. and Friends," *Rolling Stone*, April 8, 1976.

36. Green, "Vindicated in Court."

37. Jett Williams, with Pamela Thomas, *Ain't Nothin' as Sweet as My Baby* (Hartsville, TN: AdJett Productions, 1997), 69–72.

38. Green, "Vindicated in Court."

39. Escott, *Hank Williams: The Biography*, 306.

40. Loretta Lynn and George Vecsey. *Coal Miner's Daughter* (Washington, DC: Regnery, 1976), 128.

41. Jimmy McDonough, *Tammy Wynette: Tragic Country Queen* (New York: Viking, 2010), 314.

42. Author interview with Joe Pennington.

INDEX

✳ ✳ ✳ ✳ ✳ ✳ ✳